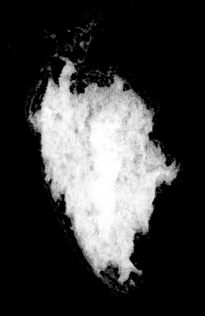

LEWIS CARROLL & HIS ILLUSTRATORS

EGJ.

"Lewis Carroll."

Lewis Carroll &
His Illustrators

COLLABORATIONS
& CORRESPONDENCE,
1865-1898

edited by
Morton N. Cohen &
Edward Wakeling

MACMILLAN

First published 2003 by Cornell University Press, USA

First published in Great Britain 2003 by Macmillan
an imprint of Pan Macmillan Ltd
Pan Macmillan, 20 New Wharf Road, London N1 9RR
Basingstoke and Oxford
Associated companies throughout the world
www.panmacmillan.com

ISBN 0 333 78307 7

9 8 7 6 5 4 3 2 1

A CIP catalogue record for this book is available from
the British Library.

Printed and Bound in the United States of America

In memory of Philip Dodgson Jaques
with gratitude for his friendship
and help through the years

Contents

Illustrations

Acknowledgments

WE OWE A DEBT to the people who have helped in the preparation of this volume. Our thanks go to Janet McMullin (Christ Church Library), James Kilvington and Terence Pepper (National Portrait Gallery), Brion Purdey (Hastings Library), Jannie Rathbun and Melanie Wisner (Houghton Library, Harvard University), Victoria Williams (Hastings Museum and Art Gallery), Leonee Ormond, and the staffs at other institutions who supplied the photocopies of letters and additional material. We are grateful to Matthew Demakos, Jonathan Dixon, Lewis Falb, Hugues Lebailly, Jon Lindseth, Frankie Morris, Gerald Pinciss, John D. Rosenberg, Bea Sidaway, Maynard Soloman, Sarah Stanfield, and Richard N. Swift, who have assisted in various ways. We wish to thank Philip Dodgson Jaques, Beth Mead, and Caroline Luke, the Dodgson family representatives, for making this publication possible. We are indebted to Tenniel Evans, descendant of Sir John Tenniel, for his support and encouragement in this project. Every effort has been made to contact descendants of the other illustrators, but without success. We will be pleased to acknowledge the source and location of original material in any future edition of this book, and we will be happy to give due acknowledgment to any family representatives of illustrators mentioned.

MORTON N. COHEN
EDWARD WAKELING

Introduction

Alice . . . had peeped into the book her sister was reading, but it had no pictures or conversations in it, "and what is the use of a book," thought Alice, "without pictures or conversations?"

THUS BEGINS *Alice's Adventures in Wonderland*, that remarkable children's book by Lewis Carroll that for over 135 years has charmed not only children but also their parents and a host of specialists in science as well as literature all over the world. Its author, never dreaming that he had created one of the great classics of all time, nevertheless saw to it that his book would contain plenty of conversations—and a good supply of pictures. Even more than that: a perfectionist in all he did, he wanted the best illustrations he could obtain for his readers, at any cost. The *Alice* books, *Alice's Adventures* and *Through the Looking-Glass, and What Alice Found There*, are, as a result, remarkable examples of the finest Victorian printing, bookbinding, and—perhaps most important—illustration.

Pictures played a large part in the life of Charles Dodgson, the real name of Lewis Carroll, and it is those pictures, or a good many of them, that concern us here. We cannot tell when Dodgson himself started to draw pictures, but we do know that by 1845, when he was thirteen, he had filled a scrapbook he titled *Useful and Instructive Poetry* with sixteen compositions of his own poetry and prose, and on pages facing them he drew a variety of pictures as illustrations, some of them colored by hand.

These earliest drawings are childlike and crude, to be sure, but not without interest and even a touch of humor. The contents of the volume, words and pictures—and the handwriting—reveal a precocious youngster at work and play, and that precocious youngster would soon go on to spin much more elaborate tales and produce substantially better drawings. Even before we get to the *Alice* books in the 1860s, when Dodgson was in his early thirties, he produced eight more scrapbooks, or family magazines as they are conventionally called (four of them, alas, lost). Most of the domestic magazines that survive contain a good amount of Dodgson's youthful prose, poetic inventions, and drawings.

The author of the *Alice* books was born on January 27, 1832, at Daresbury in Cheshire, where his father was Perpetual Curate. In 1843 the senior Dodgson was made rector of Croft, Yorkshire. Charles, third of eleven children and the eldest son, enjoyed a happy and lively, if serious and disciplined, upbringing. His father provided him with a solid grounding in mathematics and Latin as well as religion even before he entered Richmond School at the age of twelve. From Richmond he went to Rugby, where the rough-and-tumble life of the public school caused him some anguish. From Rugby he went to Christ Church, Oxford, where he would live and work until his death forty-seven years later. Unlike many of his fellow students, he took his studies seriously, working, by his own account, twenty-five hours a day; he earned first-class honors in mathematics. From 1852 he had the title of Student (the equivalent of Fellow at other colleges), and from 1855 Mathematical Lecturer. In 1861 he was ordained deacon, but he chose not to take a priesthood or a curacy; he suffered from deafness in his right ear and a stammer, handicaps not conducive to parish work. Besides, he was a trained mathematician and logician, hoping to teach Oxford undergraduates and to push logical thinking beyond the boundaries recognized in his time. He was pleased when the bishop of Oxford assured him that his clerical status and professional avocation were compatible. He remained a Christ Church mathematics lecturer for a quarter of a century, until shortly before his fiftieth birthday, and wrote a variety of texts to help students meet the university's mathematics requirements as well as other far more arcane studies, many grounded on the works of his idol Euclid. As a volunteer, for the sheer pleasure of introducing young people to mathematics and logic, he taught these subjects at several Oxford and Eastbourne colleges and schools.

His interests were eclectic. He was drawn to gadgets and invented a few himself. All matters mechanical, technological, medical, and scientific fascinated him. He would have embraced enthusiastically the fax machine and the computer with all its ramifications: E-mail, CD-ROMs, the Internet, the World Wide Web. He would, in fact, have made a superb Webmaster at Christ Church if such a position had existed. He was actually acquainted with Charles Babbage, generally regarded as the founding father of the computer.

Dodgson was an early art photographer, and an array of celebrities sat before his lens, including Crown Prince Frederick of Denmark; Queen Victoria's youngest son, Prince Leopold; John Everett Millais; the Rossettis; Ruskin; Lord Salisbury, the prime minister; Tennyson; Charlotte M. Yonge; George MacDonald; F. D. Maurice; and Ellen Terry and her famous actor siblings.

His ties to the stage ran deep. He had written plays for, and acted in, amateur theatricals, and he spoke out courageously for the professional theater as a source of wholesome entertainment and education in an age when the church opposed it.

When his father died in 1868, Dodgson leased "The Chestnuts" at Guildford in Surrey for his unmarried sisters and younger brothers, and, solicitous of their welfare, went there regularly. In the summer he took lodgings by the sea, usually at Eastbourne, for working holidays.

All his life Dodgson was genuinely religious, but he stood apart from the theological storms that raged around him. He never married, though he probably wished to and would have made a loving husband and doting father. He claimed generally to be happy, but at least one observer guessed that he was a "lonely spirit and prone to sadness."[1] He lived an orderly, careful life, ate little, and chose hard work as his road to salvation. He was a compulsive record keeper: his letter register showed that in the last thirty-five years of his life, he sent and received no fewer than 98,721 letters.

Contrary to myth, Dodgson was anything but a shy recluse sequestered behind college walls. He traveled frequently in Britain, sometimes with his cumbersome camera in tow; he was often to be seen in London theaters and art galleries, even in corridors of power, and he hobnobbed with artists, writers, and actors. He left England only once, accompanying his friend the theologian Henry Parry Liddon across Europe on a mission to Russia, where Liddon explored the possibilities of rapprochement between the Eastern and Western churches.

He was about six feet tall, slender, had either gray or blue eyes—observers disagree—wore his hair long, and "carried himself upright, almost more than upright, as if he had swallowed a poker." He dressed customarily in clerical black and wore a tall silk hat, but when he took Alice and her sisters, the daughters of his college dean, H. G. Liddell, out on the river, he wore white flannel trousers and a stiff white straw hat.[2] He never cultivated a beard or mustache. He wore no spectacles, although he frequently used a magnifying glass. He enjoyed a glass of wine. He had a pleasant speaking voice. Unfortunately we have no recording of it, although wax cylinders made at the time of Tennyson and others can be heard today. He had a tolerably good singing voice which he did not mind using. He sometimes talked to himself. Instead of birthday presents, he preferred to give un-birthday presents because he could give them so many more times in the year. Tuesdays, he said, were his lucky days.

He was interested in many branches of science, particularly medicine, and was a member of the Society for Psychical Research. Art and music were two of his delights, and he was fond of quotations. He disliked physical sports but was known to play croquet. He went on long walks, sometimes covering twenty-three miles in a day. He was orderly in all things. While many attest to his kind, considerate, courteous nature, he could be rude to those who offended his high standards of propriety. Certainly he stomped out of theaters when he found anything on the stage irreligious or otherwise offensive. He once reprimanded the bishop of Ripon for including in a Bampton lecture an anecdote that elicited laughter from the audience.

He planned but never completed a volume of Shakespeare plays especially for girls which would have out-Bowdlerized Bowdler. He so resented Shakespeare's lines at the end of *The Merchant of Venice* requiring Shylock to abandon his faith and become a Christian that he wrote to Ellen Terry, after seeing her and Henry Irving perform the play, asking her to delete them from future performances, saying, "It is . . . entirely horrible and revolting to . . . all who believe in the Gospel of Love."[3]

He was an anti-vivisectionist and denounced blood sports. He valued his privacy and hated the limelight, jealously concealing the true identity of Lewis Carroll from strangers, and was known to leave tea parties when his hostess revealed his pseudonym or when he was unduly fussed over or lionized. He was by many accounts unselfish and generous. He helped support his sisters and brothers, other relatives, friends, and even strangers. He was always willing to take on new students, and he was ready, though in all modesty, to try to help young and old with spiritual problems.

Dodgson was constantly involved in extramural (if not worldly) affairs. Essentially conservative, he nonetheless fought for reforms that won for him and his fellow Christ Church dons a voice in college matters. He frequently showered members of his college and university with broadsheets and pamphlets, in prose and verse, which he had privately printed, on a multiplicity of subjects that range from opposing cricket pitches in University Parks to a spoof, dripping in irony, of the wooden cube that Dean Liddell had erected atop Tom Quad's Great Hall staircase to house bells removed from the cathedral. He also dispatched, from his Christ Church aerie, letters and articles to a number of periodicals, including *The Times*, the *Pall Mall Gazette*, *Aunt Judy's Magazine*, the *Fortnightly Review*, the *St. James's Gazette*, the *Observer*, and *Mind*. The subjects varied widely and include Gladstone and parliamentary cloture, vivisection, hydrophobia, education for child actors, and logical paradoxes.

Throughout his entire mature life, Dodgson sought close friendships with a coterie of female children. In spite of some gossip and suspicions about his motives, these were uncomplicated and superficially innocent affairs, grounded in an aesthetic that Dodgson inherited from William Blake and the romantics. He convinced himself and others that the objects of his worship were his child friends' beauty and purity. He loved the child's unspoiled, untutored naturalness and what he saw as a closeness to God. By some magical combination of memory and intuition, he knew what it was like to be a child in a grown-up society. He could instinctively speak a child's language, capture his young friends' interest, engage them in conversation, move them, and, best of all, make them happy and evoke peals of laughter from them. He treated children, both in his books and in real life, as equals. For his part, he lost his awkwardness — and, some say, his stammer — in their presence.

These fairy creatures sparked his creative energies, and for them he composed his masterpieces: *Alice's Adventures in Wonderland* (1865), *Through the Looking-Glass, and What Alice Found There* (1872), *The Hunting of the Snark* (1876), *Sylvie and Bruno* (1889), and *Sylvie and Bruno Concluded* (1893). He doted on children and devoted more of his time, energy, and money to doing things for them than to any other single end. In a letter to the father of one of his child friends, he wrote in 1877, "The pleasantest thought I have, connected with Alice, is that she has given real and innocent pleasure to children."[4] And when some children from the United States wrote asking him to explain the meaning of *The Hunting of the Snark*, he answered, "I'm very much afraid I didn't mean anything but nonsense," but added: "The best explanation that I've seen is by a lady . . . that the whole book is an allegory on the search for happiness. I think this fits beautifully in many ways — particularly, about the bathing-machines: when the people get weary of life, and can't find happiness in town or in books, when they rush off to the seaside, to see what bathing-machines will do for them."[5]

He also invented a myriad of games and puzzles for his child friends and published many of these in newspapers and in books to edify and amuse an army of children he did not personally know. Among these works are *Word-Links* (1878), *Doublets* (1879), *Mischmasch* (1882), *A Tangled Tale* (1885), *The Game of Logic* (1886), and *Syzygies and Lanrick* (1893).

Two of his three volumes of poetry, *Phantasmagoria and Other Poems* (1869) and *Rhyme? and Reason?* (1883), contain witty narratives, including a long poem about a ghost who hates haunting drafty houses because he always catches cold in them. These volumes also contain nonsense lyrics similar to those in the *Alice* books, the *Snark*, and in the *Sylvie and Bruno* volumes, but they are encumbered by more than a sampling of tedious and uninspired serious verse. His last volume of verse, *Three Sunsets and Other Poems*, published posthumously, contains only serious verse.

Many of Dodgson's publications were the work of a professional mathematician-logician. These include *A Syllabus of Plane Geometry*, published in 1860; *An Elementary Treatise on Determinants with Their Application to Simultaneous Linear Equations and Algebraical Geometry* (1867); *Euclid and His Modern Rivals* (1879); *Curiosa Mathematica* (1888, 1893); and *Symbolic Logic, Part I* (1896).

These works established a modest reputation for him, though his standing as an original mathematical thinker has risen in recent years, a reappraisal owed in large part to two works: the publication of *Symbolic Logic, Part II*, the book that Dodgson had virtually completed before he died in 1898 but that remained unpublished until 1977, and the collection of the mathematical pamphlets he had published over his entire mature life.[6] But he did more. In a sense he turned mathematics and logic on their heads, adding humor to studies that are ordinarily deadly serious. Specialists take warmly to the added spice and whimsy in almost all of Dodgson's mathematical writings, however serious the purpose. The exercises he invented, the paradoxes he posed, the examples he supplied are all couched in drama and suspense and are infused with an intrinsic sense of fun, a quality of real life. No wonder, then, that professional mathematicians the world over smile irrepressibly when they refer to Dodgson's "Barber-Shop Paradox" or to his "Paradox of Achilles and the Tortoise." Even his syllogisms are amusing. Here is one of them:

> All lions are fierce;
> Some lions do not drink coffee.
> Conclusion: Some creatures that drink coffee are fierce.

Here is another:

> No Professors are ignorant;
> All ignorant people are vain.
> Conclusion: No Professors are vain.

Or this:

> All uneducated people are shallow;
> Students are all educated.
> Conclusion: No students are shallow.

These inventions bear the humor and the genius characteristic of the Alice books and, like those books, are ingrained in our culture.

But even this description of Dodgson's labors does not do him justice. A stern disciplinarian, he pushed himself to work steadily in areas that ranged far and wide. He contributed significantly to the history of voting theory[7] and even concocted new rules for making lawn tennis competitions fairer.[8]

But Dodgson did much more than write and teach. Though he never held a curacy, he would, from time to time, take Sunday service for others. On a number of occasions, in fact, a university congregation filled St. Mary's, Oxford, to capacity to hear him preach. He also did a good amount of parochial work, helping those in need, consoling those who were ill. For more than nine years he was curator of Christ Church Senior Common Room, an arduous job requiring close attention to detail and keen business acumen.

Dodgson allowed himself only modest pleasures. On February 17, 1880, a most remarkable entry appears in his diaries: "Sent to the Dean the paper in which I propose to the 'Staff-Salaries Board' that, as my work is lighter than it used to be, I should have £200 instead of £300 a year." Then he adds, "Offer was accepted March 11." What university teacher today would ask to have his salary reduced?

He could be witty and engaging in person as well as in print, but he could also be censorious, snobbish, even prickly. Perhaps the most important quality of the man is his forthright faith. For he was a true Christian who knew his Bible, thought carefully about moral questions, and lived a righteous if somewhat guilt-ridden life troubled by small transgressions and forces he saw within himself which he could not reconcile with his faith. He was at heart a generous man, a romantic who believed that love is what makes the world go round. Here is how he put it to one of his child friends:

> Photographs are very pleasant things to have, but *love* is the best thing in the world. . . . Of course I don't mean it in the sense meant when people talk about "falling in love": that's only *one* meaning of the word, and only applied to a few people. I mean in the sense in which we say that everybody in the world ought to "love everybody else." But we don't always do what we ought. I think you children do it more than we grown-up people do.[9]

All his life Dodgson strove to cure his stammer and to become a fine artist—but he did not succeed. He went to speech therapists and learned how to avoid the pitfalls that caused him to stammer, particularly when delivering sermons. To improve his drawing, he studied art techniques, attended art classes, mixed with artists, and regularly went to exhibitions in Oxford and London. But eventually he had to face the facts, and at one point, perhaps even before John Ruskin told him that he had not enough talent to make it worthwhile to devote much time to sketching,[10] he himself decided that his meager skill would not be enough to illustrate the books he wanted to publish. Failing as an artist was one of the real disappointments of his life and may have been one of the strong motives for his taking up photography. His results in the new medium were so successful that he felt justified in inscribing some of the photographs he gave to friends as "from the Artist."

He did actually provide his own illustrations to the first *Alice* book, the one he wrote out in a green leatherbound notebook for the real Alice Liddell as a Christmas gift in 1864, after she had pestered him time and again to write down the story he had first told her and her two sisters, Lorina and Edith, on their river picnics. The drawings are not fine or subtle, and professional artists tend to dismiss them, but they bear a charm all their own. In a sense, Dodgson was his own worst critic: had he not himself damned his drawing in advance and allowed the public to judge it *ab initio*, he might have been pleasantly surprised. But when it came to publishing *Alice's Adventures in Wonderland*, he was keen enough to know that he would have at least to double the length of the original text he had written in the notebook he had given Alice Liddell—and he convinced himself that he needed a professional artist to supply the illustrations.

Soon after Alexander Macmillan agreed to publish *Alice's Adventures in Wonderland*, Dodgson set out to find a suitable illustrator. Nothing but the best would do for him, by then a seasoned man in his early thirties with highly refined and extremely sensitive taste.

Dodgson would, in fact, spend the rest of his life not only writing books but also searching for appropriate artists to create illustrations for them and then negotiating with them over minor, sometimes pernickety details. Artists are not, on the whole, the most patient breed, and at least three of Dodgson's collaborators caused him a good deal of grief. John Tenniel always took his time—usually a very long time—to produce the pictures for the *Alice* books; Dodgson relentlessly pursued Arthur Burdett Frost, who illustrated *Rhyme? and Reason?*, before the artist completed his commitment; and Harry Furniss, who illustrated the *Sylvie and Bruno* books, might have caused a weaker writer a nervous breakdown. The two artists with whom Dodgson seems to have had no great difficulty were Henry Holiday, over the illustrations for *The Hunting of the Snark*, and the ever-conciliatory Emily Gertrude Thomson, who supplied the fairy drawings for Dodgson's last book, *Three Sunsets and Other Poems*.

Dodgson knew a great deal about book production; he taught himself all the mechanics of typesetting, carving woodblocks, bookbinding, and even bookselling.[11] When electroplating and other advances came into easy reach, he immediately took advantage of them. In all the processes and negotiations involved, he set high standards, for himself to be sure, but for others as well, certainly for his publisher, his printers, his engravers—and indeed his illustrators. Normally polite and gentlemanly, he nonetheless filled his letters to his artists with a myriad of details, requests, even complaints when they did not follow his instructions. He often provided his own crude sketches in his letters to them as examples of the illustrations he wanted. Dickens and a few other writers had sought to have the illustrations for some of their books placed so that they were integrated with the text. But Dodgson absolutely insisted on precise placement in every case, even if it meant rearranging or rewording the text or redrawing the picture entirely to achieve his goal. One can hardly blame him for wanting the drawings to comply with the details in the story, and when his artists, either not having bothered to read Dodgson's text carefully or forgetting the details, drew pictures that violated the description in the text, Dodgson resolutely appealed to them to alter the drawings. He was not, however, unreasonable, and as we shall see, sometimes when his efforts with an artist seemed to have reached an impasse, he himself altered the text of his story to comply with the details in the artist's drawing. In the end, he usually gave way.

Dodgson's role in book publishing history is extremely different from what an author in later years would assume. Although the London firm of Macmillan & Company were his "publishers," they in reality served only as his distributors and advisers. Dodgson was in control, making all the decisions and footing all the bills. Indeed, he took on all the expenses connected with publishing his books—for the paper and the bindings, for printing, engraving, illustrating, even for advertising. And he paid Macmillan 10 percent of sales for their services. The arrangement seems inconceivable to us today, but if not altogether commonplace in Victorian times, it was not entirely out of the ordinary. It certainly gave Dodgson some extraordinary powers and led him to make some incredible, some might say diabolical, decisions. It enabled him, in 1865, to suppress the first edition of *Alice's Adventures* because the temperamental Tenniel deemed the printing of the illustrations unsatisfactory. In 1886 Dodgson instructed his publisher to discard the first edition of *The Game of Logic*, also meant for children, because, as he wrote to Alexander Macmillan, the "appearance of the book is not up to the standard I have set myself." In 1889 he rejected the entire first run of ten thousand copies of *The Nursery "Alice"* because he found the pictures "*far* too bright and gaudy." And in 1893 he ordered Macmillan to scuttle a full printing of the *Alice* sequel, *Through the Looking-Glass*, because he found that most of the pictures were "over-printed."[12] It is hard to blame Dodgson, given the arrangements he had forged with Macmillan, for wanting to get value for his money, and to him value for money meant the highest standard of technical and aesthetic production.

Dodgson's life was reasonably healthy and, if not entirely fulfilled in personal terms, certainly rewarding for him as a writer and professional mathematician. One detects no decline in either physical or mental agility as he grows older. Twice when he was sixty-five he walked from Eastbourne to Hastings, some twenty miles, in five hours and twenty-two minutes: "I was hardly at all tired and not at all footsore," he wrote in his diaries on July 29,

1897.[13] A quiet contentment overtakes him in these years as he works away at his writing. He explains it best himself in a letter to one of his sisters:

> News [of other people's deaths] comes less and less of a shock: and more and more one realises that it is an experience each of *us* must face, before long. That fact is getting *less* dreamlike to me, now: and I sometimes think what a grand thing it will be to be able to say to oneself "Death is *over*, now: there is not *that* experience to be faced, again!" . . . I am beginning to realise that, if the *books* I am still hoping to write, are to be done *at all*, they must be done *now*, and that I am *meant* thus to utilise the splendid health that I have had, unbroken, for the last year and a half, and the working-powers, that are fully as great as, if not greater than, what I have ever had.[14]

In early January 1898, while with his family in Guildford, Dodgson came down with a fever and chest cold. Today his symptoms would have been dealt with routinely with antibiotics. But in 1898 bronchial infections were much more serious than they are now. His condition worsened, and on January 14, thirteen days before he would have turned sixty-six, he died of pneumonia. He was buried where he died, in Guildford, the only home he then had away from Oxford.

He had lived in an age that followed hard on the Industrial Revolution, and he enjoyed the fruits of another revolution, one that would alter the face of culture, education, the way people thought and lived.

This revolution was caused by advances in technology and the adaptation of technology to daily life. More inventions occurred in the nineteenth century than in any previous century. As part of this technological revolution, book production and book illustration changed dramatically. Books were still largely handcrafted at the beginning of the century. Paper was made by hand, print was set by hand, and what machines were available were mostly operated by hand. Books were heavy and expensive, and very few, rather special volumes were illustrated, usually by wood engravings. Novels came in the form of "three-deckers," that is, three volumes. Then, in the late 1830s the mechanical typecaster was invented in America, and by the mid-1850s, it was in common use in England as well as the United States, producing in a single day five times as much type as the old hand-setting method. By the 1860s, mechanized book production began to make an impact, and by the 1880s, the combined casting and composing machine became a reality.[15] By the end of the century, the craftsman had almost vanished. Along the way, photography was invented, electrotype and monotype succeeded the stereotype for reproducing text and pictures, and the lithographic power press and many other new machines driven by electricity came into standard use. Gradually books became increasingly beautiful; John Ruskin's and William Morris's handsomely crafted and illustrated volumes led many authors and publishers to aspire to astonishingly grand heights of production.[16]

More books were published on religion than on any other subject in the first half of the nineteenth century, and religious fervor helped bring about the explosion of popular publishing in mid-century.[17] Clerics and other church leaders, determined to teach literacy to the working poor, were responsible for establishing Sunday schools, for printing and distributing religious tracts, and for the wide distribution of Bibles. By 1861, the year before *Alice's Adventures* was conceived, the Religious Tract Society was distributing millions of pamphlets and copies of periodicals annually. The Mechanics' Institutes Village Reading Rooms opened their doors to the poor and provided educational, uplifting material. Dodgson later sent copies of his books to these Reading Rooms.

The Education Acts of 1870, 1876, and 1880 and the advent of compulsory education created a whole new reading public. The improvement in transportation, particularly the invention and growth of the railroad, and a more efficient postal system which made book distribution so much easier than it had been, created a boom in the book industry. Increased longevity and leisure as a result of scientific advances and medical innovations all contributed to the demand for more books, more titles. The new machinery produced ever larger runs of volumes more efficiently and at lower cost. The printing industry, and all the other industries that both fed it and depended on it, vastly expanded as the population of England and Wales grew in the course of the century from 14 to 33 million. From mid-century onward, the reading public, like Rip Van Winkle, awoke, gradually became literate, and turned to the printed paper and book for edification and amusement.

The 1850s were, as one historian puts it, "the great turning-point in the history of the English book trade's relations with the mass public." The average price of a book declined by 40 percent between 1828 and 1853; Mudie expanded his circulating library, book clubs flourished, and cheap reprints multiplied. By the end of the 1860s, W. H. Smith had over five hundred railway station bookstalls throughout the nation. John Cassell made a great success with inexpensive periodicals such as *Working Man's Friend* (in its second year its circulation reached fifty thousand), *Cassell's Popular Educator* (Thomas Hardy learned German with its aid), *The Illustrated Bible*, and *The Illustrated History of England*.[18] In 1852 there were 367 established printers in London; in 1900, 1,511; in 1852, 123 lithographers, and in 1900, 429; in 1876, London could boast a single photographic and automatic engraver; in 1900 there were 94 photo- and process-engravers at work in the capital.[19]

In 1852 a band of major publishers, booksellers, and authors who sought wide circulation of their books challenged the prohibition on discount selling and won the day for a free market, in which prices fell dramatically.[20] In 1855 the newspaper stamp duty was abolished, in 1861 the duty was lifted from paper, and at about the same time esparto, a cheap grass from North Africa, replaced the use of rags in the production of paper; all reduced the cost of book and periodical production and brought printed works within reach of an ever-widening audience.

Publishers and authors soon realized that another way of stimulating a broad interest in the printed word was through images, and the illustrated newspaper, journal, magazine, and book captured the interest of the new and growing reading public. Printed papers "were probably bought quite as much for their pictures as for their text," writes Richard D. Altick; the "horrifying illustrations in [John Foxe's] *Book of Martyrs* cost many an impressionable English child his sleep"; and even "the illiterate found a good pennyworth of enjoyment in the illustrations each issue of the *Penny Magazine* contained."[21] *Punch* "shifted its emphasis from writing to cartoons."[22]

Wood engraving was the standard method for printing illustrations in mid-Victorian England, and punctilious as ever, Dodgson required the best engravers, the Dalziel brothers and Joseph Swain, to cut the blocks for his books, as well as the best printers, the University Press at Oxford and Richard Clay in London. Tenniel's blocks for *Alice's Adventures* and Henry Holiday's for *The Hunting of the Snark* survive and are available for examination and study.[23] Tenniel was a master at working with woodblocks, and we have his precise account of how he worked against deadlines—alas, not for Charles Dodgson—but for successive editions of *Punch*:

> I get my subject on Wednesday night; I think it out carefully on
> Thursday, and make my rough sketch. On Friday morning I begin,

and I stick to it all day, with my nose well down on the block. By means of tracing paper—on which I make such alterations of composition and action I may consider necessary—I transfer my design to the wood and draw on that. The first sketch I may, and often do, complete later on a commission. . . . Well, the block being finished, it is handed over to Swain's boy at about 6.30 to 7 o'clock, who has been waiting for it for an hour or so, and at 7.30 it is put in hand for engraving. That is completed on the following night, and on Monday night I receive by post the copy of next Wednesday's paper.[24]

Alice's remark about books without pictures speaks for Charles Dodgson's own attitude and his eagerness to excite and delight readers, not only with words but with images too. His high standards and the superb quality of his illustrators' work together help explain why his books have become classics. Dodgson knew all too well how to appeal to readers, especially the children for whom he told the *Alice* story in the first place and, later, when he wrote it down for a wider audience. Perfectionist that he was, he sought out the best illustrators, the best engravers, printers, and publisher. The same is true of the quality of the paper and binding for his books. His illustrators, though of varying renown, were all thoroughly accomplished professionals; he would not have been content with less. This volume of the letters that he exchanged with those artists charts Dodgson's high aspirations, his knowledge, and his attitudes, as it reflects his artists' responses, and intimates that crucial ethos in which authors and artists came together to produce a relatively new form of British art: the illustrated book for the masses. To be sure, these developments had a direct effect upon both authors and their illustrators.

1. Ethel M. Rowell, "To Me He Was Mr. Dodgson," *Harper's Magazine* (February 1943): 319–23.
2. "Alice's Recollections of Carrollian Days, as Told to Her Son," *Cornhill Magazine* 73 (July 1932): 1–12.
3. *Letters*, p. 365.
4. Ibid., p. 267.
5. Ibid., p. 548.
6. See *Lewis Carroll's Symbolic Logic*, parts 1 and 2, ed. W. W. Bartley III, 1977; and *The Mathematical Pamphlets of Charles Lutwidge Dodgson and Related Pieces*, ed. Francine Abeles, 1994.
7. See particularly Iain McLean and Arnold B. Urken, eds., *Classics of Social Choice*, 1995.
8. See G. C. Heathcote, *Lawn Tennis*, 1890.

9. *Letters*, p. 869.

10. Collingwood, p. 102.

11. For a running display of his knowledge of these specialities, see *Macmillan Letters*.

12. Ibid., pp. 216–17, 256–57, 292–93.

13. *Diaries*, p. 537.

14. Letters, p. 1100.

15. S. H. Steinberg, *Five Hundred Years of Printing*, 1974, p. 275.

16. Allan C. Dooley, *Author and Printer in Victorian England*, 1992, passim, esp. pp. 21–22, 68–71, 78–79.

17. See Simon Eliot, *Some Patterns and Trends in British Book Production, 1800–1919*, 1944; John O. Joradan and Robert L. Patten, eds., *Literature in the Marketplace*, 1996.

18. John Gross, *The Rise and Fall of the Man of Letters*, 1960, pp. 193, 294, 303; Royal A. Gettmann, "Colburn-Bentley and the March of Intellect," *Studies in Bibliography*, ed. Fredson Bowers, 1957, pp. 197–213; Richard D. Altick, *The English Common Reader*, 1957, passim, esp. pp. 81, 208, 270–71, 305; Paul Goodman, *Victorian Illustrated Books, 1850–1870*, 1994, pp. 33–44; and Morna Daniels, *Victorian Book Illustration*, 1988, p. 5.

19. *Post Office London Trades Directory*, 1852; *Kelly's Post Office Directory of Stationers, Printers, etc.*, 1876, 1900, as cited in Geoffrey Wakeman, *Victorian Book Illustration*, 1973, p. 15.

20. Later in the century both John Ruskin and Charles Dodgson would rebel against discounting of their books and spearheaded the move that would eventually lead to the Net Book Agreement. See *Macmillan Letters*, passim, esp. pp. 26, 115, 175–84, 227, 280–84, 365–69.

21. Altick, *Common Reader*, pp. 56, 335.

22. Alvin Sullivan, ed., *British Literary Magazines*, 1984, p. 327.

23. The *Alice* blocks are in the British Library, the *Snark* blocks in the Osborne Collection of Early Children's Books at the Toronto Public Library.

24. M. H. Spielmann, *The History of "Punch,"* 1895, pp. 463–64.

Editorial Principles

THIS VOLUME CONTAINS all the letters to Lewis Carroll's illustrators that we have been able to locate (more than two hundred) and a few of the pertinent letters that his artists wrote to him. Of these only about forty have previously appeared in print, mainly in Stuart Dodgson Collingwood's *Life and Letters of Lewis Carroll* (1898) and *The Letters of Lewis Carroll*, ed. Morton N. Cohen with the assistance of Roger Lancelyn Green (2 vols., 1979). Details about where letters were previously published have such limited value that we have deliberately excluded them.

Whenever possible, the text of a letter comes from a photocopy of the original or from the editors' own transcripts; otherwise, the best available source is used, usually a previously printed version. Above all, our goal has been to be as faithful as possible to Dodgson, himself a painstaking letter writer, and to his orthographic gems and oddities. To this end, the texts retain almost all his own punctuation (including the omnipresent colon), altered only when ambiguity required a change. The horizontal linear strokes that Victorians used to indicate a pause or a stop are everywhere in Dodgson's writing, and they appear here as commas or periods, whichever seemed best. These strokes usually differ from his dashes, which are transcribed as they appear, only sometimes shortened.

Although we have retained a fair number of Dodgson's inconsistencies, some standardizing seemed desirable, especially in citing the titles of works: titles of poems, articles, stories, and other entities not published separately appear in Roman type within quotation marks; titles of books, periodicals, plays, and other separately published works appear in italics. Foreign words and phrases are in italics, and, in deference to a decline in classical skills that would have appalled Dodgson, we have translated some less common Latin phrases. We have glossed words and phrases only when they are not found in the *Oxford English Dictionary* or its supplements. Occasional misspellings and a few other unintended lapses have been silently corrected.

To produce a readable text, we have expanded some of Dodgson's abbreviations and modernized some of his contractions. We have, for instance, expanded ampersands (except when intrinsic to titles and company names), the names of months, and much of his shorthand ("wd," "cd," "shd," "wh," "thro," "yr," "yrs," "affte," "afftely"); we have expanded "Ch. Ch." to "Christ Church"; standardized his expressions of weight, measure, time, distance, and sums of money; and modernized his spelling of "to-day," "to-morrow," and the names of a few places.

We have normalized all return addresses and dates and placed them in fixed positions at the top of his letters and standardized the punctuation after superscriptions and subscriptions. Where Dodgson ends a letter with "Believe me," "I am," "I remain," "Haste," or "In haste," we have run these phrases in to the previous paragraph to save space. Dodgson's signatures vary enormously, ranging from his famous three-initial monogram through "Lewis Carroll," "C. L. Dodgson," and "Charles L. Dodgson." We have approximated these signatures as closely as we could.

Wherever possible, all letters appear in their entirety. Where only fragments survive, we have reproduced these faithfully. The only ellipses that we have supplied appear at the beginning or close of a fragment; internal ellipses are Dodgson's own. In footnotes, however, where salient passages are quoted from other letters, ellipses are used.

We have not tried to give the size of writing paper; Dodgson used many different sizes, always trying to anticipate exactly how large or small a sheet he would need to convey his thoughts.

Dodgson's surviving diaries cover all the years of his collaboration with his illustrators, and we have used them liberally in annotating the text. Not all the diary entries are yet in print, however. We have explained in the list of abbreviated short titles our method of indicating whence come our supporting entries.

Owners of Letters &
Other Sources

Berol The Alfred C. Berol Collection, Fales Library, New York University

Bodleian Bodleian Library, Oxford

Brabant The late Mr. Joseph A. Brabant (collection in Fisher Rare Books Library, University of Toronto)

Christ Church The Library, Christ Church, Oxford

Cohen Morton N. Cohen

Dodgson Family Dodgson Family Archive and Papers (Surrey History Centre, Woking)

Harkness Harkness Collection, New York Public Library

Harvard Houghton Library, Harvard University

Huntington Henry E. Huntington Library, San Marino, California

Lilly Lilly Library, Indiana University, Bloomington

Morgan Pierpont Morgan Library, New York

Princeton Morris L. Parrish Collection, Princeton University

Punch The Punch Library, London

Rosenbach Philip H. and A. S. Rosenbach Foundation, Philadelphia

Sambourne The Edwin Linley Sambourne Archive, Kensington, London

Stern Jeffrey Stern, York

Texas The Harry Ransom Humanities Center, University of Texas, Austin

Short Titles

LEWIS CARROLL & HIS ILLUSTRATORS

1. John Tenniel (1820-1914)

"TENNIEL HAS MUCH of the largeness and symbolic mystery of the imagination which belong to the great leaders of classic art," John Ruskin proclaimed in 1884; "in the shadowy masses and sweeping lines of his great compositions, there are tendencies which might have won his adoption into the school of Tintoret; and his scorn for whatever seems to him dishonest or contemptible in religion, would have translated itself into awe in the presence of its vital power."[1]

That is great praise for any artist from one of the greatest art critics of all time, but there is a dimension to Ruskin's view that is particularly apt to this study—Ruskin's insistence on the indissoluble tie between art and morality, a belief that both John Tenniel and Charles Dodgson embraced.

Although some have come to think of the collaboration of John Tenniel and Charles Dodgson as a troubled one, that the artist and the author, at best, struggled to get along with each other, the simple fact is that they had a great deal in common, so much so that in describing either of the two, what one says of one can often apply to the other. They were both proper Victorian gentlemen of the old school—formal, obsessively private, conservative, uncompromising, correct in their behavior and in their dealings with others, restrained in manner—and both refrained from personal intimacies. As artists, they were temperamental, even testy, disputing with each other repeatedly. Both suffered physical disabilities throughout their mature lives, Tenniel

The essential works on Tenniel other than those that appear in the citations below are: Frances Sarzano, *Sir John Tenniel, Art and Technics*, 1948; Eleanor M. Garvey and W. H. Bond, *Tenniel's Alice*, 1978; Michael Hancher, *The Tenniel Illustrations to the "Alice" Books*, 1985; Leo John De Freitas, *A Study of Sir John Tenniel's Wood-Engraved Illustrations to "Alice's Adventures in Wonderland" and "Through the Looking-Glass,"* 1988; Justin G. Schiller and Selwyn Goodacre, *Alice's Adventures in Wonderland: An 1865 Printing Re-discovered*, 1990; Roger Simpson, *Sir John Tenniel: Aspects of His Work*, 1994; Mark Arman, *The Story of the Electrotypes Used to Illustrate Sir John Tenniel's Drawings for "Alice's Adventures in Wonderland" and "Through the Looking-Glass,"* 1996.

1. John Ruskin, *The Art of England*, 2d ed., 1887, p. 195.

accidentally blinded in one eye in a fencing match with his father when he was twenty, Dodgson deaf in his right ear and hampered by a stammer from childhood. Both were touched by genius.

John Tenniel was born in Kensington on February 28, 1820, twelve years before Charles Dodgson. He was the youngest son of a Huguenot dancing master and instructor in arms. He showed artistic skill early and became a student at the Academy Schools. He was unhappy there, however, and enrolled instead in the Clipstone Street Life Academy, where he met Charles Keene, who became a friend for life. Together they worked on a series of humorous sketches, the "Book of Beauty," which were exhibited and sold. At sixteen, Tenniel exhibited and sold an oil painting at the Society of British Artists, and for five years, from age seventeen, works of his appeared at the Royal Academy. Tenniel entered the competition for decorating the new Houses of Parliament and was chosen to paint a fresco for the House of Lords. To school himself properly for the task, he went to Munich to study the art of fresco. Ultimately he produced a successful illustration of Dryden's "Saint Cecilia."

Although he sought fame through serious oil painting, he came to realize that he was getting nowhere along that road, and he turned to book illustration as an alternative. His first drawings appeared with other English artists' work in Samuel Carter Hall's verse anthology *The Book of British Ballads* (1842–44). In 1848 his illustrations for Thomas James's version of *Aesop's Fables* were widely acclaimed, and in 1850 Mark Lemon, the editor of *Punch*, brought Tenniel onto his staff to replace Richard Doyle, who had left. It took time for Tenniel to find his métier, but slowly his talent for political cartoons sharpened, his work achieved critical attention, and his reputation grew. A natural gift for bold political parody and a humorous flair attracted wide interest and gained him approval. He achieved an important feather in his cap when he was commissioned to provide the cover illustration for the 1851 *Official Descriptive and Illustrative Catalogue of the Great Exhibition*. In 1857 his *Punch* cartoon "The British Lion's Vengeance on the Bengal Tiger" was a milestone. When in 1864 John Leech, the top *Punch* artist, died, Tenniel, who had been sub-cartoonist on the paper, filled Leech's shoes. He was to hold that post for thirty years, for a total of half a century's service on the *Punch* staff.

Within a year of Tenniel's elevation as *Punch's* top artist, Charles Dodgson, an unknown, sought to approach the famous cartoonist and ask him to illustrate a children's book he was soon to publish. Tenniel's style had impressed Dodgson early. On December 20, 1863, Dodgson wrote his playwright friend Tom Taylor, asking him if he knew Tenniel well enough "to say whether he could undertake such a thing as drawing a dozen wood-cuts to illustrate a child's book" and if so whether Taylor would be willing to put him in touch with Tenniel. "The reasons for which I ask," Dodgson wrote Taylor, "are that I have written such a tale for a young friend, and illustrated it in pen and ink. It has been read and liked by so many children, and I have been so often asked to publish it, that I have decided on so doing. . . . If [Mr. Tenniel] . . . should be willing to undertake [the illustrations] . . . , I would send him the book to look over, not that he should at all follow my pictures, but simply to give him an idea of the sort of thing I want."[2]

A month later, on January 25, 1864, Dodgson called on Tenniel in London, carrying a letter of introduction from Taylor. He "was very friendly," Dodgson wrote in his diaries, "and seemed to think favourably of undertaking the pictures."[3] On April 5, Dodgson noted, "Heard from Tenniell [sic] that he consents to draw the pictures."[4] Tenniel first saw the early text that Dodgson had written out for Alice Liddell, the middle of three daughters of his college dean, and later the expanded tale, more than twice the length of the original. Once he had decided to publish the story, Dodgson labored hard at it. He reworked the Mouse's Tale considerably; the Mad Tea-Party appeared for the first time; and the trial scene at the end, occupying two pages in the early version, grew to two chapters amounting to twenty-six pages. He also changed the title. He called the booklet he had given Alice Liddell, in which he wrote out the original version in his own script and supplied his own illustrations, *Alice's Adventures Under Ground*. But he was unhappy with that title and, after casting about for a new one, settled on *Alice's Adventures in Wonderland*.

A good many letters must have passed between Dodgson and Tenniel from then onward, but only few survive. Tenniel probably destroyed letters once he had dealt with their contents. Nonetheless, we have a record of how the collaboration progressed from Dodgson's diaries and from his correspondence with his publisher, Alexander Macmillan. Dodgson must surely have

---

2. *Letters*, p. 62.
3. DIARIES, 4:272.
4. Ibid., p. 284.

barraged Tenniel with letters containing his ideas for the illustrations, and from time to time he visited the artist in London. On May 30, 1864, for instance, he went to London and called on Tenniel "and had a talk."[5] He did the same on June 20 and records his disappointment: Tenniel "has not begun the pictures yet."[6] On July 17, Dodgson was again on Tenniel's doorstep, but the artist was out. The remainder of the summer draws a blank—Dodgson spent the summer mostly on the Isle of Wight and at home in Yorkshire—but on October 13, when he was back at his college duties, he went up to London to see his publisher and then his artist. Tenniel "showed me one drawing on wood, the only thing he had, of Alice sitting by the pool of tears, and the rabbit hurrying away. We discussed the book," Dodgson adds, "and agreed on about 34 pictures."[7]

The collaboration showed promise at this point, six months after Tenniel had agreed to do the pictures. Dodgson did not despair. Interestingly enough, Tenniel must have been thinking about the *Alice* illustrations, for when the January–June bound volume of *Punch* appeared, Tenniel's prototype of the Alice figure appeared on the title page along with a garlanded British lion—the first published image of a Tenniel Alice.

On October 28, Dodgson called again on Tenniel, and again the artist was not at home. He went on to the Dalziel brothers' workshop and indeed did see "proofs of several of the pictures, including the four for 'Father William,' "[8] assurance that Tenniel was now producing the illustrations. During the visit, George Dalziel advised Dodgson to print from the woodblocks, but aware of how easy it would be to damage the artwork on wood, he decided to have electrotypes made for printing.

Still, progress was slow, sometimes nonexistent. On November 20, Dodgson reports to Alexander Macmillan: "I fear my little book . . . cannot appear this year. Mr. Tenniel writes that he is hopeless of completing the pictures by Christmas. The cause I do not know, but he writes in great trouble, having just lost his mother, and I have begged him to put the thing aside for the present. Under these circumstances what time should you advise our aiming at for

5. Ibid., p. 304.
6. Ibid., p. 310.
7. DIARIES, 5:16.
8. Ibid., p. 22.

bringing out the book? Would Easter be a good time, or would it be better to get it out before then?"[9]

On December 15, Dodgson sent Macmillan the entire text of the book in proof, and on the following day he received the first twelve illustration proofs from Tenniel.[10] When Dodgson went to see his publisher four days before Christmas, they agreed that binding should begin about the middle of March and that the book should appear on April 1, 1865.

But that was not to be. Tenniel did not supply the illustrations in time. Dodgson called on his artist again on January 26, 1865, but we have no account of their discussion. It may have been then, or earlier, that they decided to increase to forty-two the number of illustrations that Tenniel would do for the book. But progress was slow: when, on April 8, Dodgson again met Tenniel in London, he noted that the artist was working on the thirtieth picture.[11] On June 18, Dodgson finally received proofs of the last three illustrations from Tenniel,[12] and when, on June 27, he learned that the Clarendon Press had sent copies of the completed book to his publisher in London, he immediately wrote to Macmillan asking them to send a copy bound in white vellum to Alice Liddell "so as to be received on July 4,"[13] the third anniversary of the river expedition on which he had created the tale.

On July 7, Dodgson called on Macmillan in London to talk about the book, and on the fifteenth, again in London, he went to the Macmillan offices and "wrote in twenty or more copies of *Alice* to go as presents to various friends." He then visited the Terrys, spent most of the afternoon photographing, had tea with them, and went off to the theater. He spent much of the next week in London, visiting friends, photographing, seeing other theatrical pieces, and the like.[14]

Dodgson was evidently satisfied with the final result of *Alice*. Had he detected any flaw or fault, he certainly would have made his views known to printer and publisher.

Then, on Wednesday the nineteenth, the sharp blade of the guillotine

9. *Macmillan Letters*, p. 35.
10. DIARIES, 5:9.
11. Ibid., p. 64.
12. Ibid., p. 9.
13. Ibid., p. 10.
14. Ibid., pp. 89, 93.

struck and the book was doomed. With extraordinary restraint, Dodgson records, "Heard from Tenniel, who is dissatisfied with the printing of the pictures." And on the following day, "Called on Macmillan, and showed him Tenniel's letter about the fairy-tale—he is entirely dissatisfied with the printing of the pictures, and I suppose we shall have to do it all again." Less than a fortnight later (on August 2), Dodgson writes: "Finally decided on the re-print of *Alice*, and that the first 2000 shall be sold as waste paper. Wrote about it to Macmillan, [Thomas] Combe [director of the Clarendon Press] and Tenniel." He goes on to calculate the cost of the disaster at £600, a monumental sum for an Oxford don earning less than that amount in a year.[15] These fantastic, almost fairy-tale details chronicle perhaps the greatest instance of Dodgson's willingness to reconcile himself with the temperamental demands of an illustrator.

Was Tenniel justified? That question is disputed to this day. Certainly some copies are flawed. But other copies, when placed next to the later, second edition, which Tenniel sanctioned, prove to be just as good and indistinguishable from the second printing. Perhaps bad luck played a part in the drama. Could Tenniel have been sent one of the flawed copies?

Dodgson immediately set about recalling all the copies he had inscribed and sent to friends, promising them replacements as soon as the new printing was available. He engaged a different printer for the job, Richard Clay of London, and he received his first copy of the new impression on November 9, 1865. On November 28 he "heard from Tenniel, approving the new impression."[16]

For a long time, literary historians jumped to the conclusion that it was Dodgson who wanted Macmillan to scrap the first edition of *Alice*, but we now know otherwise. Could it, one wonders, have been simply a matter of the *Punch* artist's temperament having its way? Certainly in a letter he wrote at the time to one of the Dalziel brothers he boasted, "I protested so strongly against the disgraceful printing that . . . [Dodgson] *cancelled the edition*."[17] But even Tenniel's biographer, Rodney Engen, believes that the artist was not justified in damning the edition and suggests that Tenniel might have been acting out of pique—"repressed anger," he calls it—at Dodgson's earlier requests for changes

15. Ibid., pp. 97, 100–101.
16. Ibid., p. 10.
17. MS: Huntington.

in Tenniel's work. Tenniel "rarely gave his *Punch* engravings a second glance," he writes, "never proofed them, and even accepted the poorly printed overall greyness of his early anthology drawings as part of commercial publishing. Could he have decided at the final hour to reassert himself over Dodgson after submitting to the author's demands for so long?" he asks.[18]

Both Dodgson and Tenniel would be stunned to know that a single copy of that "inferior" first edition brings many thousands of pounds when it comes up for sale these days. It does not come up for sale very often, either, for only twenty-three copies have been located. So choice a book has it become that collectors would trade whole portions of their libraries for a single copy of the "first" *Alice*, bibliographers dream of uncovering an unrecorded copy, and literary chroniclers are at a loss to explain how, even in the heyday of Victorian publishing, such extravagant decisions could be taken over a single children's book.

Alice's Adventures in Wonderland, when finally available for the Christmas season of 1865, was not an instant best-seller by any means. It was widely reviewed and earned considerable praise. The *Reader* (November 12) called it "a glorious artistic treasure"; the *Press* (November 25) judged it "amusingly written" and the illustrations "beautiful"; the *Publisher's Circular* (December 8) deemed it "the most original and most charming" of the two hundred books for children it had received that year and added that "Mr. Tenniel has helped little Alice with his best pictures which we have seen for many a day." The *Guardian* (December 13) also approved and thought the illustrations "still better than the story."

Letters praising the book arrived from friends. Christina Rossetti sent Dodgson a "thousand and one thanks . . . for the funny pretty book" and added that she thought the "woodcuts . . . charming." Her brother Dante Gabriel Rossetti wrote to say that some of "Alice's perverted snatches of school poetry are among the funniest things I have seen for a long time." Henry Kingsley declared that he could not stop reading it till he had finished it: "The whole thing is delicious."[19]

The difficulty over the first edition having been surmounted, leaving no rancor in its wake, and the book showing signs of increasing success,

18. Rodney Engen, *Sir John Tenniel, Alice's White Knight*, 1991, p. 82.
19. *Letters*, p. 81.

Dodgson and Tenniel went their separate ways. For a long while, no meetings or exchange of letters appear to have taken place between them.

With every increase in the sales of *Alice*, Dodgson, a practical man as well as an artist, must have realized that the vein he had struck so successfully with his first children's book should perhaps be mined further, especially as he did not use in the published book all the episodes of the story that he had told the Liddell sisters. In fact, a mere nine months after the publication of the second impression of *Alice*, we find him confiding to Macmillan: "It will probably be some time before I again indulge in paper and print. I have, however, a floating idea of writing a sort of sequel to *Alice*, and if it ever comes to anything, I intend to consult you at the very outset, so as to have the thing properly managed from the beginning."[20]

But nothing happened for quite a while. Then, a year and a half later (December 15, 1867), he broke the silence about a second *Alice* in a letter to a friend, though even at that time he merely writes that "Alice's visit to Looking-Glass House is getting on pretty well."[21] A month after that (January 16, 1865), he wrote in his diary that over the Christmas vacation "I have . . . added a few pages to the second volume of *Alice*,"[22] and on February 6, 1867, he made a flat statement about it when he wrote to his publisher: "I am hoping before long to complete another book about 'Alice.' . . . You would not, I presume, object to publish the book, if it should ever reach completion."[23]

A major hurdle still stood in Dodgson's way, however. Once again, he needed an illustrator. Tenniel was an obvious choice, particularly because his illustrations for *Alice* had been so highly praised, and Dodgson knew that it would be difficult to find anyone else as good. He made the approach, but the answer was an immediate and unconditional no: Tenniel was too busy.

Dodgson turned elsewhere. He tried Richard Doyle, Sir Joseph Noël Paton, and even W. S. Gilbert, whose "Bab Ballads" were then appearing with his illustrations in the humor magazine *Fun*. But for one reason or another, none of them could come to the rescue. In fact, two and a half years would pass, and Dodgson was still without an illustrator. On May 19, 1868, Dodgson "wrote to Tenniel again, suggesting that I should pay his publishers for his

20. *Macmillan Letters*, p. 44.
21. *Letters*, p. 94.
22. DIARIES, 5:379.
23. *Macmillan Letters*, p. 48.

time for the next five months. Unless he will undertake it, I am quite at a loss."[24] Tenniel finally capitulated and agreed to illustrate *Through the Looking-Glass, and What Alice Found There*, but even then, he consented to provide the pictures only "at such time as he can find."[25]

And so it came to be. Tenniel supplied illustrations at a snail's pace when he supplied them at all. In March 1869, almost a year after Tenniel had agreed to provide the illustrations, Dodgson called on him in London to discover that he "has not yet begun drawing" the pictures.[26] Ten months later (January 20, 1870), calling again on his artist, Dodgson "saw the rough sketches of about ten of the pictures."[27] On March 12, Dodgson had "about two hours' talk" with Tenniel, and arranged for about thirty pictures: three have gone already to be cut," Dodgson adds.[28] On January 13, 1871, Dodgson received the final proof sheets for the book, and two days later he sent them off to Tenniel. "It all now depends upon him," Dodgson wrote in his diary, "whether we get the book out by Easter or not."[29] But that was simply wishful thinking on Dodgson's part: "*Through the Looking-Glass* yet lingers on," Dodgson wrote on April 25, 1871, "though the text is ready, but I have only received twenty-seven pictures as yet."[30] On August 29 he wrote to Tenniel "accepting the melancholy, but unalterable fact, that we cannot get *Through the Looking-Glass* out by Michaelmas. After all, it must come out as a Christmas book."[31]

Finally, in November 1871, three and a half years after Tenniel agreed to illustrate the book, Dodgson was relieved to record in his diary that "'Alice Through the Looking Glass' is now printing off rapidly."[32] *Through the Looking-Glass* appeared for Christmas 1871 (although the title page bore the date 1872), six years after the appearance of the second impression of *Alice's Adventures in Wonderland*.

Certainly Dodgson breathed a sigh of relief when he finally held a published copy of *Looking-Glass* in his hand and heard that Tenniel approved.

24. *DIARIES*, 6:30–31.
25. Ibid., p. 37.
26. Ibid., p. 79.
27. Ibid., p. 112.
28. Ibid., p. 113.
29. Ibid., p. 140.
30. Ibid., pp. 145–46.
31. Ibid., pp. 178–79.
32. Ibid., p. 187.

Dodgson had endured a good amount of anxiety over the publication delays that Tenniel caused and, of course, over Tenniel's dismissal of the first edition of *Alice*. But Tenniel must have felt his share of irritation over the collaboration. Though almost all of Dodgson's letters to Tenniel are missing, we may be sure that they contained intricate and lengthy instructions about the drawings he wished to have, and then, when the illustrations arrived, he surely must have found fault with some or required emendations in others. So particular was his way, such a perfectionist was he by nature, that Tenniel must have wearied of some of Dodgson's requirements.

The relationship never came to grief, however, and after the publication of the second *Alice*, although they did not meet the way they had when they were working on the books, relations remained cordial. Dodgson published a good many other books, for some of which he engaged other illustrators, and he sent Tenniel copies with friendly inscriptions.

For his part, Tenniel grew busier and busier with his work at *Punch*, and his fame increased accordingly. And yet, when, somewhat over three years after *Looking-Glass* appeared, Dodgson proposed (March 1, 1875) that Tenniel draw a frontispiece for a book that Dodgson intended to write and call "Alice's Puzzle Book," Tenniel "consented."[33] Alas, the book never materialized.

In the early 1880s, Tenniel also agreed to supply twenty large renderings of the *Alice* illustrations, in color, for *A Nursery "Alice,"* which Dodgson wrote for the very young. Although some of Tenniel's original drawings could be enlarged, the artist actually redrew some of the pictures for the new book. Dodgson himself objected to the first printing of the pictures as "too bright and gaudy," and apparently had the printer redo them before Tenniel saw them. Both he and Tenniel were fully satisfied with the second attempt. The book was published in 1890.[34]

The Nursery "Alice" was the last of their collaborative efforts. Tenniel remained the artist supreme on *Punch*'s staff. In 1893 he was knighted. Any animus that existed between the two men must have evaporated, for when Dodgson died, Tenniel wrote to a friend: "Poor Lewis Carroll is in his grave, and we are trying to collect £1,000 to endow a 'Cot' in the Children's Hospital, in his name, as the most fitting Memorial of him, and his work." The "Cot"

33. Ibid., pp. 381–82.
34. *Macmillan Letters*, p. 257; Tenniel to the printer Edmund Evans, December 18, 1889 (MS: Rosenbach).

was indeed established. Tenniel retired from *Punch* in 1901; he grew increasingly blind, and died on February 25, 1914.

Toward the end of his life, Tenniel took up brush, oils, and canvas again in the hope of making a name for himself in the world of high art, but, sadly, he did not succeed. His fame rested, in his time, with his political cartoons. Today, some readers are aware that he was an important *Punch* cartoonist, but the general public knows him only for his illustrations in the *Alice* books, an irony not lost on historians. For when as an established artist he undertook to illustrate the first *Alice* book by an unknown author and lent his established reputation to the venture, he knew, of course, that his name would demand critical attention for the book and would in great measure be responsible for any success it might meet with. Tenniel's attitude toward Dodgson throughout must have been at least slightly patronizing: his biographer writes that he "kept himself aloof from those things (or people) that he did not find worthy of his attention."[35] Nor did he hesitate to refuse to do work that displeased him: he would not, as a rule, work with models ("children were not his favourite subjects"),[36] and he often refused to illustrate ideas that he did not find congenial, for instance, Dodgson's wasp in a wig, which forced the author to omit a whole section from *Looking-Glass*. Surely, under the circumstances, Tenniel would not have put the work for Dodgson's book ahead of his other commitments. One ponders, moreover, the possibility that Tenniel began to consider book illustration something he had put behind him in his desire to get on with bigger and better projects.

But history is merciless, often turning the tables on the very best of intentions, and today Tenniel, having "raised the political cartoon to a new level of dignity and importance," as Edward Hodnett notes, is "one of the best known of all English book illustrators solely because his drawings are inseparable from Lewis Carroll's immortal *Alice's Adventures in Wonderland* and *Through the Looking-Glass*."[37] One may even surmise that Dodgson's relentless insistence on perfect results compelled Tenniel to achieve a quality of art that transcends the ephemeral and makes his illustrations for the *Alice* books his greatest achievement.

35. Engen, *Sir John Tenniel*, p. 32.
36. Ibid., p. 76.
37. Edward Hodnett, *Image and Text*, 1982, p. 167.

MS: *Bodleian*

10 Portsdown Road, London
March 8, 1865

Dear Mr. Dodgson,

I cannot see your objection to the page as at present arranged, but if you think it would be better to place the picture further on in the text, do it by all means. The "two Footmen" picture is certainly too large to head a chapter.[1] Could you manage to let me have the text of "A Mad Tea-party" for a day or two? There is much more in it than my copy contains. The subjects I have selected from it are—The Hatter asking the riddle; which will do equally well for any other question that he may ask, and can go anywhere;

FIG. 2
"The Two Footmen" from
Alice's Adventures in Wonderland

FIG. 3

Three illustrations from Alice's Adventures in Wonder-land: "A Mad Tea-Party," "The Hatter asking the Riddle," and "Putting the Dormouse into the Tea-pot."

and—The March Hare and the Hatter, putting the Dormouse into the tea-pot.

We now want an intermediate one, but I don't think "Twinkle twinkle" will do, as it comes close upon the first subject, i.e. in *my copy*.[2] In great haste

Yours very sincerely,
J. Tenniel

P.S. I am very glad you like the new pictures.

1. The illustration in *Alice* of the "two Footmen" does not appear as a chapter head; it appears instead on the second page of the chapter, "Pig and Pepper," at p. 77.

2. "A Mad Tea-party" was a chapter in *Alice's Adventures in Wonderland*, a new episode, not in *Alice's Adventures Under Ground*. Tenniel apparently received the text of *Under Ground* set in type, with corrections by Dodgson, a fact confirmed by a galley sheet that survives at the Library, Christ Church. Obviously, Dodgson sent later chapters to Tenniel as he completed them. The illustration of the Hatter asking the riddle appears in *Alice* at p. 97, and the Dormouse being put in the tea-pot at p. 110. Tenniel evidently drew the intermediate picture of the Hatter singing "Twinkle, twinkle," and it appears at p. 103.

MS: *Berol*

10 Portsdown Road, London
April 4 [?1870][1]

My dear Dodgson,

I should have written sooner but I have been a good deal worried in various ways.

I would infinitely rather give no opinion as to what would be best left out in the book, but since you put the question point-blank, I am bound to say, supposing excision somewhere to be absolutely necessary, that the Railway scene never *did* strike me as being *very* strong, and that I think it might be sacrificed without much repining; besides, there is no subject down in illustration of it in the condensed list.

Please let me know to what extent you have used, or intend using, the *pruning-knife*; my great fear is that all this indecision and revision will interfere fatally with the progress of the book.[2] In haste to claim post.

Yours sincerely,
J. Tenniel

You shall have some more sizes in a few days.

1. The date is a guess. The notepaper is watermarked 1868, but Tenniel more likely wrote this letter in 1870, when Dodgson was looking for ways to shorten *Looking-Glass*. A subsequent letter, dated June 1, 1870, takes up the same theme, but centers on pruning the "Wasp" episode, which was eventually excised. Dodgson records a meeting with Tenniel on January 20, 1870, to discuss the progress of the illustrations: "Called on Tenniel, and saw the rough sketches of about ten of the pictures for *Behind the Looking-Glass*." On March 12 he made "a call on Tenniel, with whom I had about two hours' talk, and arranged about thirty pictures: three have gone already to be cut" (DIARIES, 6:112–13). *Looking-Glass* evidently began to take shape in 1870, and at this time Dodgson was probably considering ways of reducing the text of the book.

2. Progress with *Looking-Glass* was slow, but owing, in the main, to Tenniel's delays in supplying the illustrations. On June 25, 1870, "Lady Salisbury and the children came again, first to my rooms, where I showed them pictures, etc., including the seven first pictures for *Through the Looking-Glass*" (DIARIES, 6:120–21). Dodgson completed the manuscript of *Looking-Glass* in January 1871, and he "sent the slips off to Tenniel: it all now depends upon him, whether we get the book out by Easter or not" (ibid., p. 140). The book appeared in December 1871 with "1872" printed on the title page.

Facsimile: Collingwood, pp. 147-49

10 Portsdown Road, London
June 1, 1870

My dear Dodgson,

I think that where the *jump* occurs in the Railway scene[1] you might very well make Alice lay hold of the Goat's *beard* as being the object nearest to her hand, instead of the old lady's hair. The jerk would naturally throw them together.

Don't think me brutal, but I am bound to say that the "*wasp*" chapter doesn't interest me in the least, and I can't see my way to a picture. If you want to shorten the book, I can't help thinking, with all submission, that *there* is your opportunity.[2] In an agony of haste.

Yours sincerely,
J. Tenniel

1. See *Looking-Glass*, p. 50. Tenniel perhaps modeled the gentleman, dressed in "parliamentary" white papers, on Disraeli.

2. Dodgson suppressed the "Wasp" episode. In another letter Tenniel insists that "a wasp in a *wig* is beyond the appliances of art" (Collingwood, p. 146). Far from shortening the book, Dodgson replaced the "Wasp" with an expanded "White Knight" episode and added another eight illustrations. The corrected galley proofs of the "Wasp" episode were sold at Sotheby's as lot 76 on June 3, 1974, and published in 1977 as a limited edition in facsimile by the Lewis Carroll Society

FIG. 4

Tenniel's Sketch: "Interior of Railway Carriage" from Through the Looking-Glass. *Railway compartment (first class). Alice on seat by herself. Man in white papers reading, and Goat, very shadowy and indistinct, sitting opposite Alice. Guard (with opera-glass) looking in at window.*

of North America, with an introduction by Martin Gardner. The episode was first published in Great Britain in the *Telegraph Sunday Magazine*, no. 51, September 4, 1977, pp. 12–21, with an accompanying article by Morton N. Cohen, and in book form later that year by Macmillan.

———

MS: *Morgan*

10 Portsdown Road, London
Sunday, July 24 [1870][1]

My dear Dodgson,

Of course I am *always* happy to see you. At the same time, I know of no special need for you to undergo a broiling, in this *briling*, I might say "brillig," weather.[2]

I am always at home till 4 *o'clock*.

Yours sincerely,
J. Tenniel

1. July 24 was a Sunday in 1870. Dodgson reports no visit to Tenniel in his diaries after July

24, 1870, although he may have visited the artist to discuss the progress of *Looking-Glass* and failed to record it.

2. A reference to Dodgson's poem "Jabberwocky" in *Looking-Glass*, which begins " 'Twas brillig . . .'" (p. 21), later explained by Humpty Dumpty as meaning "four o'clock in the afternoon— the time when you begin *broiling* things for dinner" (p. 126).

MS: *Harkness*

[Christ Church, Oxford]
April 18, 1872

My dear Tenniel,[1]

Please get the writer of *"Punch*'s Essence of Parliament" to make no further allusions to the *name* of the writer of *Alice*.[2]

Sincerely yours,
C. L. Dodgson

1. This is the only letter from Dodgson to Tenniel that has come to light. Perhaps Tenniel discarded his incoming letters. Dodgson must have sent Tenniel dozens if not hundreds of letters in connection with the *Alice* books.

2. "The Waggawock," parodying "Jabberwocky," appeared in *Punch* on March 16, 1872, with due acknowledgments to Lewis Carroll. About a month later, in the issue dated April 20, 1872, the following reference appeared in *"Punch*'s Essence of Parliament": "Mr. Dodson, Chairman of Committees, announced his retirement, and he was duly complimented by the two Leaders of party. When Mr. Dodson publishes a third volume of the enchanting adventures of Miss Alice, of Wonderland and Looking-glassland, he shall be duly complimented by the Great Leader of all, *Mr. Punch*. The latter cannot as yet recover from his admiration of the marvellous poem, 'Jabberwocky,' and of his own miraculous adaption thereof. His only regret is that his amber embalms a bloated blow-fly." The *Punch* article, by Shirley Brooks, refers to Mr. J. G. Dodson, M.P., later Lord Monkbretton. Brooks writes (G. S. Layland's *Shirley Brooks of Punch*, 1907, p. 515): "I laid a trap in last week's 'Essence' about Dodson and 'Alice in Wonderland.' The author has walked into it, and writes to Tenniel to say that he should be glad if the *error* were not corrected, as he does not wish his name known! 'How blest are we that are not simple men.'" The "error" also spawned a reply from the parliamentarian Mr. Dodson (MS: Harkness): "In the 'Essence of Parliament' in the last number of *Punch* you appear to give me credit for being the author of *Alice in Wonderland*, etc. I have no claim to that honour. I wish I had."

MS: *Berol*

10 Portsdown Road, London
July 22, 1890

My dear Dodgson,

Very many thanks for the little *Wonderland Postage Stamp-Case*. It is very "dainty!" and ought, I think, to be immensely popular, especially with young, very young, ladies; at any rate I hope it will.

The nine *Wise Words* are full of *wisdom*, besides being decidedly *funny*.[1] Haste.

Sincerely yours,
John Tenniel

1. Dodgson invented the *"Wonderland" Postage Stamp-Case* in October 1888 and published it in 1890. To accompany the *Stamp-Case*, he published a little booklet called *Eight or Nine Wise Words about Letter-Writing*. The title is a quote from Shakespeare's *Much Ado About Nothing* 3.2, where Benedick says: "Yet is this no charm for the toothache. Old Signior, walk aside with me: I have studied eight or nine wise words to speak to you, which these hobby-horses must not hear." For details of the various editions of the *Stamp-Case* and booklet, see *Handbook*, pp. 170–73.

MS: *Berol*

10 Portsdown Road, London
July 4, 1893

My dear Dodgson,

Very many thanks for your kind recognition of my new "dignity"(!). It is always delightful to receive the congratulations of old friends, and I have had *heaps* of them!!

How true it is that "some have *greatness thrust* upon them!"[1] — and you may be quite sure that it was none of *my* seeking.[2] Haste.

Yours always sincerely,
John Tenniel

1. *Twelfth Night* 2.5.
2. Tenniel had just received his knighthood from the Gladstone government. "It surprised no one else and pleased a great many people: telegrams and letters piled up in his house at 10 Portsdown Road. The *Punch* staff celebrated tumultuously with a banquet at the *Mitre*,

Hampton Court, and, at the Arts Club, Val Prinsep rose to propose a toast to Sir John Tenniel"
(Frances Sarzano, *Sir John Tenniel*, 1948, p. 36).

MS: *Harvard*

10 Portsdown Road, London
January 29, 1894

My dear Dodgson,

Pray accept my best thanks for the copy of the new *Sylvie and Bruno*, duly received.[1] I am quite ashamed that your kindness should have remained so long un-acknowledged, but I have been "worried out of my life," lately, in having to attend to other people's business, so you must forgive me.

With all good wishes for the success of the book. I remain

Always sincerely yours,
John Tenniel

1. *Sylvie and Bruno Concluded*, published on December 29, 1893.

MS: *Berol*

10 Portsdown Road, London
September 5, 1896

My dear Dodgson,

Certainly! and I will do what you wish in regard to supervising the pictures with much pleasure; of course everything will depend on the *printing*.[1]

With the best of all good wishes for the success of the new venture, believe me, as always,

Sincerely yours,
John Tenniel

1. Dodgson was preparing new editions of *Alice's Adventures in Wonderland* and *Through the Looking-Glass*, which were to be completely reset in new type, with new electrotypes for the illustrations from the original woodblocks. In a letter to Macmillan dated September 6 he writes, "I have asked Sir John Tenniel whether the sheets of the 2 *Alice* books may be sent, as fast as they are made up for working off, to *him* instead of to me." Dodgson quotes the first paragraph of this

letter from Tenniel. He suggests a course of action that would involve Tenniel in checking the illustrations as they are prepared for press (*Macmillan Letters*, p. 341).

MS: *Berol*

10 Portsdown Road, London
September 9, 1896

My dear Dodgson,

I think Macmillan's suggestion a very good one, and beyond this I can really offer no opinion; indeed, I am sorry in having to tell you that I find I was over-hasty in consenting to revise the *Alice* pictures. It was done on the spur of the moment, and simply with the view to helping you, but in thinking the matter over since I find that the responsibility is too great, and more than I can manage.[1]

I have a deal of work, quite outside my ordinary work, on hand, and it *must* be done between now and Christmas. It will take up all my time (and thought) and therefore I cannot face the risk of the inevitable interruptions which the frequent visits of the "Printer's Boy" would entail, and which, I foresee, would become intolerable, absolutely!

As to making it a "matter of business," that (with much thanks) is equally impossible. The idea of remuneration never entered my head for a moment, and, in the circumstances, I certainly should not think of accepting it.

That being so, and putting this and that together, I can only beseech you to forgive my stupidity and kindly hold me excused in breaking the engagement, at the same time reminding you that I am now in my *76th* year and *that*, I take it, at any rate from my own point of view, covers a multitude of—shortcomings!

With many thanks for the *Symbolic Logic*,[2] I remain

Sincerely yours,
John Tenniel

1. Macmillan replied to Dodgson's letter of September 6 saying that his proposal of sending single sheets to Tenniel, to get his approval before the rest of the sheets were worked off, was totally impractical because it kept the printing machines idle. Macmillan offered an alternative in which Clay, the printer, would send careful impressions from all the woodcuts for Tenniel's approval, and then Clay would take the responsibility for seeing that the impressions of the printed sheets matched the prints approved by Tenniel (*Macmillan Letters*, pp. 341–42). Dodgson wrote

to Macmillan on September 10, "I am consulting Sir John Tenniel as to your new suggestion" (ibid., p. 342). We do not have Tenniel's reply, but Dodgson wrote on September 13 (*Diaries*, p. 528), "Yesterday I heard from Tenniel, agreeing to examine proofs of the pictures for the new issue of *Alice* and *Looking-Glass*." The new editions of both books appeared in 1897, with new prefaces dated Christmas 1896.

2. *Symbolic Logic: Part 1, Elementary* appeared in February 1896.

2. Henry Holiday (1839-1927)

"IT WAS AN agreeable surprise when one morning Lewis Carroll . . . came to see me and my work," the painter and stained-glass artist Henry Holiday wrote in his autobiography. "We became friends on the spot and continued so till his death."[1]

Dodgson admired Holiday's work, but the surviving diaries and letters do not reveal what led to Dodgson and Holiday's first meeting. By July 1870, however, they were well enough acquainted for Dodgson to set up his camera and darkroom at the Holiday home in London and to do a good amount of photography there.[2] Dodgson had already photographed female children "*sans habilement*," as he put it,[3] and he sought to have on hand samples of beautiful children beautifully drawn without clothing to show to parents in the hope of achieving their consent to photograph their children in a similar state. He evidently engaged Holiday in his enterprise. "Up to London in the morning," Dodgson writes in his diaries on January 15, 1874, "and . . . called on the Holidays. . . . He showed me the drawings he is doing for me (suggestions for groups of two children—nude studies—for me to try to reproduce in photographs from life), which are quite exquisite."[4] Dodgson must have treasured Holiday's drawings and, indeed, used them to interest parents. Three years after he acquired them, he wrote to a mother whose daughters he hoped to photograph: "Did I ever show you those drawings Mr. Holiday did for me, in order to supply me with some graceful and nonobjectionable groupings of children without drapery? He drew them from life, from 2 children of 12 and 6—but I thought sadly, 'I shall never get 2 children of those ages who will

---

1. Henry Holiday, *Reminiscences of My Life*, 1914, pp. 165, 244–46. For more on Holiday, see his *Reminiscences* and his essay "The Snark's Significance," *Academy*, January 29, 1898, reprinted later in this chapter.

2. DIARIES, 6:124–26.

3. Ibid., 5:244.

4. Ibid., 6:313–14.

consent to be subjects!' and now I seem to have a *chance* of it. . . . So my humble petition is, that you will bring the 3 girls, and that you will allow me to try some groupings of Ethel and Janet . . . without any drapery or suggestion of it."[5]

A collaboration between Dodgson and Holiday was born the day after Dodgson saw the drawings that Holiday had prepared for him. "Told Holiday of an idea his drawings suggested to me, that he might illustrate a child's book for me," Dodgson wrote in his diaries. "If *only* he can draw grotesques, it would be all I should desire—the grace and beauty of the pictures would quite rival Tenniel, I think."[6]

The collaboration did not take root immediately, but on February 4 of that year, Dodgson received "from Holiday the five drawings of children he has done for me, as well as a very lovely drawing for *Sylvie and Bruno*."[7]

On the following July 18, while on a walk from his family home in Guildford, Dodgson conceived the notion of writing a long nonsense poem that would become *The Hunting of the Snark*, and by November 23, Holiday had, in fact, submitted drawings for illustrating the poem: "Ruskin came, by my request," Dodgson writes in his diaries, "for a talk about the pictures Holiday is doing for the 'Boojum'—one (the scene on board) has been cut on wood. He much disheartened me by holding out no hopes that Holiday would be able to illustrate a book satisfactorily."[8]

Dodgson nevertheless retained Holiday to illustrate the *Snark* and kept the artist as a friend as well. In July 1875 we find Dodgson again using Holiday's home as a base for his photography.[9] Soon after this photographic visit, Dodgson gave Holiday an album of photographs inscribed: "To Henry Holiday, in memory of a pleasant week spent with him in the summer of 1875, this collection of amateur photographs, taken during that visit, is presented by his sincere friend, C. L. Dodgson."[10] Holiday may also have had a hand in

5. *Letters*, p. 338. Although, in the end, Dodgson did not succeed with the Mayhew children, he did with others. See Morton N. Cohen, *Lewis Carroll, Photographer of Children: Four Nude Studies*, 1979.

6. DIARIES, 6:314–15.

7. Ibid., p. 321; the *Sylvie and Bruno* drawing is reproduced in Collingwood, p. 264.

8. DIARIES, 6:368.

9. Ibid., pp. 401–6.

10. Princeton.

designing Dodgson's *An Easter Greeting to Every Child Who Loves "Alice."*[11] On April 1, 1876, *The Hunting of the Snark* was published, with nine illustrations by Holiday, and, naturally, Dodgson sent the artist a copy of the book: "Presented to Henry Holiday, most patient of Artists, by Charles L. Dodgson, most exacting, but not most ungrateful of Authors. March 29, 1876."[12]

The Hunting of the Snark, like the *Alice* books, is a tale of adventure. But unlike the *Alices*, it is all verse, 141 rhymed four-line stanzas. It tells the story of a handful of eccentrics—a Baker, a Butcher, a Beaver, a Barrister, a Bonnet-maker, a Banker, a Boots, a Broker, a Billiard-marker—all of whom set off in an ailing ship that sometimes sails backward and is captained by a wise Bellman. The purpose of the journey is to find, lure, and capture the mythical Snark.

Although we never learn where the strange crew set out from or where they sail to, we know that they sail for many months. As they approach their destination, the Bellman reminds them of the five unmistakable traits by which they may recognize the Snark: first, the way it tastes (meager and hollow, but crisp); second, its habit of getting up late (it frequently breakfasts at five o'clock tea and dines on the following day); third, its slowness in taking a jest (it always looks grave at a pun); fourth, its fondness for bathing machines (which it constantly carries about); and fifth, its ambition.

No one has any idea what the Snark looks like—Dodgson wanted to leave the beast to the reader's imagination—but the poem's refrain describes how the crew, having arrived in Snarkland, conduct their hunt:

> They sought it with thimbles, they sought it with care,
>   They pursued it with forks and hope;
> They threatened its life with a railway-share;
>   They charmed it with smiles and soap.

Snark hunting is a treacherous occupation, for our heroes encounter frightful animals along the way: the Jubjub, for instance, a dangerous bird with a high, shrill screech; and the Bandersnatch, with its savagely snapping, frumious jaws. The Bandersnatch attacks the Banker, but the rest of the party drive it off. Finally, as evening comes on, the Baker, out ahead of the pack,

---

11. See *Macmillan Letters*, pp. 110, 128.
12. *Letters*, p. 228.

encounters the Snark from the top of a crag. He pursues it, plunging courageously into the chasm, shouting, "It's a Snark. . . . It's a Boo—" and then, nothing but silence.

> They hunted till darkness came on, but they found
>   Not a button, or feather, or mark,
> By which they could tell that they stood on the ground
>   Where the Baker had met with the Snark.

> In the midst of the word he was trying to say,
>   In the midst of his laughter and glee,
> He had softly and suddenly vanished away—
>   For the Snark *was* a Boojum, you see.

The *Snark* got a bad press, both for its nonsense verse tale and for its illustrations. The *Standard* minced no words and called it a failure.[13] The *Saturday Review* liked the poem but added that "the illustrations display that strange want of any sense of fun which distinguishes most comic draughtsmen."[14] The *Courier* missed "the delicate grace of Tenniel . . . ; by the side of . . . *Alice*, these [illustrations] . . . look poor and coarse."[15] Andrew Lang, in a long notice in the *Academy*, did not at all approve;[16] and the *Athenaeum* also disapproved, speculating that Lewis Carroll "may . . . merely [have] been inspired by a wild desire to reduce to idiocy as many readers, and more especially reviewers, as possible."[17] Indeed, Martin Gardner suggests that *"The Hunting of the Snark* is a poem over which an unstable, sensitive soul might very well go mad."[18]

And yet, whether a poem to drive people mad or a work of genius, the *Snark* has proved itself a stout warrior and has grown in stature as the years pass by; time has dignified it and brought it the respect of generations of Snarkists. Serious critics, philosophers, psychologists, and psychoanalysts have built a mountain of commentaries about the poem. Specialists in wit, nonsense, and comic theory have addressed themselves to this landmark, and

---

13. April 24, 1876.
14. April 15, 1876.
15. May 11, 1876.
16. April 8, 1876.
17. April 8, 1876.
18. Introduction to Tanis and Dooley, p. 3.

their critiques sometimes illuminate, but often obfuscate, offering a brand of madness all their own.

We have had musical versions; radio recitals, one by Alec Guinness; and recordings, one by Boris Karloff, of the *Snark*. The poem has been performed on the stage, and at least one opera recounts the journey. *Snark* clubs flourish on both sides of the Atlantic.[19]

19. Tanis and Dooley contains the most nearly comprehensive collection of works on the *Snark*, including Martin Gardner's update of *The Annotated Snark*, followed by a bibliography of writings about the poem; Charles Mitchell's essay "The Designs for the Snark"; and Selwyn Goodacre's update of the list of editions of the *Snark*.

Henry Holiday, "The Snark's Significance,"
Academy, January 29, 1898, pp. 128 – 29

The Chestnuts, Guildford
January 15, 1876

My dear Holiday,

I finished off my letter at Brighton yesterday in a hurry, and omitted to say how pleased I am with the proofs you sent me. They seem to me *most* successfully cut, and I agree with you in thinking the head of "Hope" a great success; it is quite lovely.

On my return here last night, I found the charming chess-boards, for which accept my best thanks. My sister and I have played several games of "Go-bang" on them already.[1] (I need hardly remark that they serve just as well for that, or for draughts, as they do for chess.)

Now for another bit of designing, if you don't mind undertaking it. Macmillan writes me word that the gorgeous cover will cost 1s. 4d. a copy! Whereas we can't really afford more than 5d. or 6d., as we must not charge more than 3s. for the book. My idea is this, to have a simpler cover for the 3s. copies, which will, no doubt, be the ones usually sold, but to offer the gorgeous covers also at 4s., which will be bought by the rich and those who wish to give them as presents. What I want you to do is to take *Alice* as a guide, and design covers requiring about the same amount of gold, or, better, a little less. As *Alice* and the *Looking-Glass* have both got grotesque faces outside, I should like *these* to be pretty, as a contrast, and I don't think we can do better than to take the head of "Hope" for the first side, and "Care" for the second, and, as these are associated with "forks" and "thimbles" in the poem, what do you think of surrounding them, one with a border of interlaced forks, the other with a shower of thimbles? And what do you think of putting a bell at each corner of the cover, instead of a single line? The only thing to secure is that the total amount of gold required shall be rather less than on the cover of *Alice.*

All these are merely suggestions: *you* will be a far better judge of the matter than I can be, and perhaps may think of some quite different, and better, design.[2]

Yours very truly,
C. L. Dodgson

1. The board game "Go-bang" (adapted from a Japanese game played on a board with four hundred squares), is played on a chessboard using twelve pieces (draughts) for each of two players. The object, placing or moving pieces alternately, is for one player to get five in a row, thus enabling one of the opponent's pieces to be removed, and ultimately for these to be swept away completely (*Dictionary of Games*, ed. J. B. Pick, 1952).

2. Dodgson's strange band of hunters set out in the fourth fit of the *Snark*:

To seek it with thimbles, to seek it with care;
    To pursue it with forks and hope;
To threaten its life with a railway-share;
    To charm it with smiles and soap!

The drawing that faces the verse (p. 41) shows the hunters marching forth with "Care" and "Hope" in their midst. Dodgson's suggestions for the covers did not prevail. The front cover shows the Bellman atop his ship's mast; the back cover shows a buoy inscribed with part of the last line of the poem: "It was a Boojum." On January 17, Dodgson wrote to Macmillan (*Macmillan Letters*, pp. 117–18): "When Mr. Holiday has designed the simpler covers which I have asked

(a)   (b)

FIG. 6

Holiday's illustrations for "Hope" from The Hunting of the Snark: *(a) roundel, (b) proof drawing.*

him to do, I suppose they had better begin printing covers at once. . . . The 'richly emblazoned' copies I should like done in that dark blue cloth which Mr. Holiday recommended." For variant bindings and pricing, see *Handbook*, pp. 84–87; and Selwyn H. Goodacre, *The Listing of the Snark* (1974).

Transcript: Cohen

Christ Church, Oxford
July 15, 1883

My dear Holiday,

Do not, oh do not indulge such a wild idea as that a newspaper might err! If so, what *have* we to trust in this age of sham? Bid me distrust my bosom-friend, but when once a thing has appeared *in print in a newspaper*—. However, in this case the paper is, if possible, more infallible than usual. There is a *third* hypothesis, which does not seem to have occurred to you. *Rhyme? and Reason?* is (nearly all of it) a *réchauffé*. It will embody most of the comic pieces in *Phantasmagoria*, etc., as well as *The Hunting of the Snark*. I hope to get it out during August, but seeing a book through the press is weary work![1] With kind regards

Yours sincerely,
C. L. Dodgson

1. Holiday had written to Dodgson to ask if a newspaper report of a new book by Lewis Carroll, illustrated by Henry Holiday, was based on fact or was instead a joke or error on the newspaper's part (Sotheby Parke Bernet catalogue 4057, December 6, 1977, lot 69). Dodgson's first copies of *Rhyme? and Reason?* arrived later that year, on December 6.

Much fruitless speculation has been spent over supposed hidden meanings in Lewis Carroll's *Hunting of the Snark*. The inclination to search for these was strictly natural, though the search was destined to fail.

It is possible that the author was half-consciously laying a trap, so readily did he take to the inventing of puzzles and things enigmatic; but to those who knew the man, or who have divined him correctly through his writings, the explanation is fairly simple.

Mr. Dodgson had a mathematical, a logical, and a philosophical mind; and when these qualities are united to a love of the grotesque, the resultant fancies are sure to have a quite peculiar charm, a charm so much the greater because its source is subtle and eludes all attempts to grasp it. Sometimes he seems to revel in ideas which are not merely illogical but anti-logical, as where the Bellman supplies his crew with charts of the ocean in which the land is omitted for the sake of simplicity, and "north poles and equators, tropics, zones and meridian lines" are rejected because "they are merely conventional signs." Or, as in the Barrister's dream, where the Pig, being charged with deserting his sty, the Snark pleads an *alibi* in mitigation. At other times, when the nonsense seems most exuberant, we find an underlying order, a method in the madness, which makes us feel that even when he gives Fancy the rein the jade knows that the firm hand is there and there is no risk of a spill, such as seems to be the fate of so many nonsense writers, if we may judge by the average burlesques of the day. Take "Jabberwocky," for instance. The very words are unknown to any language, ancient or modern; but they are so valuable that we have adopted them and translated them into languages, ancient and modern. What should we do without "chortle," "uffish," "beamish," "galumphing," and the rest? The page looks, when we open it, like the wanderings of one insane; but as we read we find we have a work of creative genius, and that our language is enriched as to its vocabulary.

Whether the humour consists chiefly in the conscious defiance of logic by a logical mind, or in the half-unconscious control by that logical mind of its lively and grotesque fancies, in either case the charm arises from the author's well-ordered mind; and we need not be surprised if the feeling that this is so leads many to look for some hidden purpose in his writings.

The real origin of *The Hunting of the Snark* is very singular. Mr. Dodgson was walking alone one evening, when the words, "For the Snark was a Boojum, you see," came spontaneously into his head, and the poem was written up to them. I have heard it said that Wagner began "The Ring of the Nibelungs" by writing Siegfried's "Funeral March," which certainly contains the most important motives in the work, and that the rest of the trilogy, or tetralogy, was developed out of it; but as this great work, though finished after the publication of *The Hunting of the Snark* (1876), was certainly begun before it, it is scarcely open to me to maintain that the great German master of musical drama plagiarised in his methods from our distinguished humorist.

Starting in this way, our author wrote three stanzas of his poem (or "fits" of his "agony," as he called them), and asked if I would design three illustrations to them, explaining that the composition would some day be introduced in a book he was contemplating; but as this latter would certainly not be ready for a considerable time, he thought of printing the poem for private circulation in the first instance. While I was making sketches for these illustrations, he sent me a fourth "fit," asking for another drawing; shortly after came a fifth "fit," with a similar request, and this was followed by a sixth, seventh, and eighth. His mind not being occupied with any other book at the time, this theme seemed continually to be suggesting new developments; and having extended the "agony" thus far beyond his original intentions, Mr. Dodgson decided to publish it at once as an independent work, without waiting for *Sylvie and Bruno*, of which it was to have formed a feature.

I rather regretted the extension, as it seemed to me to involve a disproportion between the scale of the work and its substance; and I doubted if the expansion were not greater than so slight a structure would bear. The "Walrus and Carpenter" appeared to be happier in its proportion, and it mattered little whether or not it could establish a claim to be classified among literary vertebrata. However, on re-reading the *Snark* now I feel it to be unquestionably funny throughout, and I cannot wish any part cut out; so I suppose my fears were unfounded.

I remember a clever undergraduate at Oxford, who knew the *Snark* by heart, telling me that, on all sorts of occasions, in all the daily incidents of life, some line from the poem was sure to occur to him that exactly fitted. Most people will have noticed this peculiarity of Lewis Carroll's writings. In the thick of the great miners' strike of 1893 I sent to the *Westminster Gazette* a quotation from *Alice in Wonderland* about a mine; not a coal-mine, it is true, but a mustard-mine. Alice having hazarded the suggestion that mustard is a mineral, the Duchess tells her that she has a large mustard-mine on her estate, and adds, "The moral of that is—the more there is of mine the less there is of yours"; which goes to the root of the whole system of commercial competition, and was marvellously apt when landowners were struggling for their royalties, mine-owners for their profits, railway companies for cheap fuel, and miners for wages; each for *meum* against *tuum*.

In our correspondence about the illustrations, the coherence and consistency of the nonsense on its own nonsensical understanding often became prominent. One of the first three I had to do was the disappearance of the Baker, and I not unnaturally invented a Boojum. Mr. Dodgson wrote that it was a delightful monster, but that it was inadmissible. All his descriptions of the Boojum were quite unimaginable, and he wanted the creature to remain so. I assented, of course, though reluctant to dismiss what I am still confident is an accurate representation. I hope that some future Darwin, in a new *Beagle*, will find the beast, or its remains; if he does, I know he will confirm my drawing.

When I sent Mr. Dodgson the sketch of the hunting, in which I had personified Hope and Care:

"They sought it with thimbles, they sought it with care;
    They pursued it with forks and hope"

he wrote that he admired the figures, but that they interfered with the point, which consisted in the mixing up of two meanings of the word "with." I replied, "Precisely, and I intended to add a third—'in company with'—and so develop the point." This view he cordially accepted, and the ladies were admitted.

In the copy bound in vellum which he gave me the dedication runs: "Presented to Henry Holiday, most patient of artists, by Charles L. Dodgson, most exacting but not most ungrateful of authors, March 29, 1876."

The above instance will show that though he justly desired to see his meanings preserved, he was not exacting in any unreasonable spirit. The accompanying letter, written after the work was complete, will sufficiently show the friendly tone which had characterised our correspondence.

Henry Holiday notes in his autobiography, *Reminiscences of My Life* (1914), his first meeting with Dodgson in 1869:

It was an agreeable surprise when one morning Lewis Carroll (the Rev. C. L. Dodgson) came to see me and my work, in company with a friend of his and mine. We became friends on the spot and continued so till his death. He was intimate with Dr. Kitchin and his family, and shared my admiration for the beautiful little daughter, of whom he took photographs at frequent intervals from then till she was grown up. He made a highly characteristic conundrum about these portraits. The girl was called Alexandra, after her godmother, Queen Alexandra, but as this name was long she was called in her family X, or rather Xie. She was a perfect sitter, and Dodgson asked me if I knew how to obtain excellence in a photograph. I gave it up. "Take a lens and put Xie before it." I have a collection of these portraits, all good. (p. 165)

Holiday goes on to describe Dodgson's many visits, and the events that led to the commission to illustrate *The Hunting of the Snark*:

We saw a good deal of Mr. Dodgson (Lewis Carroll) at this time. He stayed with us a week or more in 1875 when he spent most of his time photographing. He had been a week with us at Marlborough Road pursuing the same hobby. On that occasion some of the young Cecils came, the children of the Marquis of Salisbury, Lady Gwendolen, and two of the sons, I think the present Marquis and Lord Robert Cecil.

This time at Oak-Tree House, he took many of his friends, and gave me a complete set of prints mounted in a beautifully bound book, with his dedication, "In memory of a pleasant week." Among others he photographed Miss Marion Terry in my chain-mail, and I drew her lying on the lawn in the same.

Shortly after this he wrote to me asking if I would design three illustrations to *The Hunting of the Snark*, in three cantos, of which he sent me the ms. It was a new kind of work and interested me. I began them at once, and sent him the first sketches, but he had in the meantime written another canto, and asked for a drawing for it; I sent this, but meantime he had written a new canto and wanted another illustration; and this went on till he pulled up at the eighth canto, making, with the frontispiece, nine illustrations.

We had much correspondence of a friendly character over the drawings. I remember that Dodgson criticised my introduction of the figures of Hope and Care in the scene of "The Hunting," on the ground that he had intentionally confounded two meanings of the word "with" in the lines:

"They sought it with thimbles, they sought it with care;
   They pursued it with forks and hope,"

where "with" is used in the mixed senses of indicating the instrument and the mental attitude, and he thought I had missed this point by personifying Hope and Care. I answered that, on the contrary, I had particularly noted that confusion, and had endeavoured to make confusion worse confounded by laying yet another meaning on the back of poor "with,"—to wit "in company with." Dodgson wrote cordially accepting this view, so the ladies were allowed to join the hunt.

I have often found an unexpected use for a casual sketch taken without special purpose, and the cover of the "Snark" is a case in point. A year or more after my return from India I had to go to Liverpool on business, and, having become enamoured of the sea on that trip, I decided to go by boat instead of by rail, and I invited Almquist to go with me. I do not recommend this as an economical way of reaching Liverpool, as it took us four days and nights, instead of four hours, with travelling and board for two all the time; but it was very interesting. We went down the Thames, round the Forelands, coasted round the Isle of Wight (where I could recognise all my old haunts of 1852 and 1858) into Plymouth Harbour, round Land's End, along the Welsh coast and all round Holyhead and Llandudno to Liverpool.

At the Land's End I made a sketch which included a bell-buoy, picturesque to eye and ear, with the weird irregular tolling of the bell, and when Dodgson wanted a motive for the back-cover, something that would bear the words, "It was a Boojum," I bethought me of my bell-buoy, which exactly met his want.

He gave me a presentation-copy, bound in vellum, with the following dedication: "Presented to Henry Holiday, most patient of Artists, by Charles L. Dodgson, most exacting, but not most ungrateful of Authors. March 29th, 1876. (pp. 244–46)

FIG. 7
*Arthur Burdett Frost.
Courtesy of the Collec-
tion of Henry M. Reed.*

3. *Arthur Burdett Frost (1851–1928)*

"Pure American homespun" with "a deft comic touch" is how Percy Muir characterized Arthur Burdett Frost. He represents the "heyday of the American illustrated magazine and much of his best work will be found in *Harper's, Scribner's* and *St. Nicholas*."[1] After Frost illustrated Max Adeler's popular *Out of the Hurly-Burly* in 1874, Harper and Brothers gave him his first big chance, and he made his early mark there.[2] Frost was one of the first American artists to succeed in England, where he appeared as the illustrator of Mark Twain and Charles Dickens.

Ever on the lookout for good illustrators, Dodgson cast an eye over the field when he contemplated reissuing an expanded version of *Phantasmagoria and Other Poems* (1869), which had appeared without any illustrations. He lit upon Frost as a possible illustrator and sent the artist the first of the letters that follow without any formality or need for an introduction, now that he could refer to the *Alice* books.

Dodgson published sixty-five illustrations by Frost in *Rhyme? and Reason?* (1883), which also contained a reprint of *The Hunting of the Snark* with Holiday's illustrations. In fact, apart from Frost's illustrations, the book contains little new material. Dodgson made some textual changes to the earlier verse and added four new poems.

Phantasmagoria and Other Poems was Dodgson's first collection of verse, containing over two dozen poems in all and covering over two hundred printed pages. The contents are a potpourri—some hilariously humorous verse, some nonsense, and one group that deserves more attention than it has received through the years: narrative verse. The eponymous poem, "Phantasmagoria," is the best; it is a long, deftly wrought narrative, inspired by

1. Percy Muir, *Victorian Illustrated Books*, 1971, pp. 259–60.
2. In 1986, Gene E. Harris provided biographical detail about Frost in the catalogue for an exhibition of Frost's work, *Arthur Burdett Frost, Artist and Humorist*, published by Brandywine River Museum, Chadds Ford, Pennsylvania.

Victorian darkness and the ghosts that inhabit it. Dodgson forges a tight story with numerous original twists, a down-to-earth account of how ghosts live and go about their nocturnal business. One of the original turns of the 150-stanza poem is that it is not about people dealing with and fearing the idea of ghosts—quite the opposite: it is about ghosts themselves and the troubles they encounter in trying to do their proper jobs of haunting houses. We get, for example, an apologia of a terribly overburdened, put-upon little ghost who dilates on the onerous conditions under which he lives and works, often out of doors, cold, windblown, rain-soaked, sitting atop castle gates with no protection against the storm.

The volume contains other bravura pieces, not least of all parodies of Wordsworth, Swinburne, Tennyson, and a magnificent one of Longfellow titled "Hiawatha's Photographing," a riotous piece satirizing the Victorian craze for being photographed.

Frost also supplied six illustrations for *A Tangled Tale* (1885), Dodgson's book of ten prose puzzles which first appeared in the *Monthly Packet* as a challenge to young ladies with mathematical acumen.

MS: Rosenbach

The Chestnuts, Guildford
January 7, 1878

Dear Sir,

Excuse the liberty I am taking in addressing you, though a stranger. My motive for doing so is that I saw a page of pictures, drawn by you in *Judy* last month, on "The Eastern Question" as discussed by 2 barbers, which seemed to me to have more comic power in them than anything I have met with for a long time, as well as an amount of good drawing in them that made me feel tolerably confident that you could draw on wood for book illustrations with almost any required amount of finish.[1]

Let me introduce myself as the writer of a little book (*Alice's Adventures in Wonderland*) which was illustrated by Tenniel, who (I am sorry to say) will not now undertake woodcuts, in order to explain my enquiry whether you would be willing to draw me a few pictures for one or two short poems (comic), and on what sort of terms, supposing the pictures to range from 5 x 3 1/2 downwards to about half that size, and to have about the same amount of finish as Tenniel's drawings usually have. Believe me

Faithfully yours,
C. L. Dodgson

1. *Judy, or the London Serio-Comic Journal,* a magazine along the lines of *Punch,* not to be confused with *Aunt Judy's Magazine.* Dodgson refers to a set of six Frost drawings occupying a full page, titled "Discussions of the Eastern Question at a Certain Barber's," which appeared on December 5, 1877 (p. 80).

MS: *Rosenbach*

The Chestnuts, Guildford
January 19, 1878

Dear Sir,

I am sending a copy of my verses, *viz.*, *Phantasmagoria*;[1] please take the greatest care of it: it belongs to one of my sisters.

Would you look at "The Three Voices," and tell me if you think you could make anything of it? Or, if it is *not suggestive*, look at any other, except "Phantasmagoria" itself and "The Lang Coortin'." In haste

Truly yours,
C. L. Dodgson

1. Although Dodgson had approached George du Maurier to supply drawings for this book, ill health prevented the artist from accepting the commission. E. L. Sambourne had agreed to illustrate "The Lang Coortin'," and although he did a drawing for it, nothing apparently came of the venture. Eventually Frost supplied all the illustrations for the book.

––––––––––

MS: *Rosenbach*

Christ Church, Oxford
January 25, 1878

Dear Sir,

Would you kindly give me the names (and publishers' names) of the books you have illustrated,[1] and say also which you think is your best work.

I doubt if "Size and Tears"[2] is worth a picture: and it would be almost impossible to do one on it which would be other than vulgar and commonplace. I should prefer avoiding any pictures involving the costumes of everyday life. I should like much to know your ideas about "The Three Voices," what costumes you would choose, and how many pictures it would allow of, of various sizes and shapes, taking 5 1/4 x 3 1/2 as your outside limit.

The *Alice* pictures would be a good guide as to the amount of finish and fineness of drawings which I desire, and will I hope enable you to give me some idea of your terms.

Perhaps your editor may think the enclosed worth a corner in *Judy*.[3]

Truly yours,
C. L. Dodgson

1. By this time Frost had illustrated *Out of the Hurly-Burly* (1874) by Max Adeler (pseudonym of Charles H. Clarke) with nearly four hundred line drawings. The success of the book, which sold over a million copies across the United States and Europe, brought the young artist to public notice. Frost also illustrated the 1878 Household edition of Charles Dickens's *American Notes* (first published in 1842).

2. This poem was originally titled "Bloggs' Woe" when Dodgson wrote it into *Mischmasch*, one of the Dodgson family domestic magazines, in November 1862. In June 1863 it was published in *College Rhymes*. Bloggs, whose name was changed to Brown when the poem was reprinted in *Rhyme? and Reason?*, is an obese young man who bemoans the fact that he does not attract the ladies, unlike the slim Jones. Frost drew three illustrations for the poem that appeared in *Rhyme? and Reason?*, the characters dressed in everyday costumes.

3. We do not know what Dodgson submitted to the editor of *Judy*.

MS: *Rosenbach*

Christ Church, Oxford
February 7, 1878

Dear Sir,

By all means draw a picture, as you propose, for "The Three Voices." Your terms will suit me very well.

I have so bad a memory for names that I had quite forgotten your name in connection with *Out of the Hurly-Burly*. You will be surprised to hear that I know the book well, and examined the pictures carefully, more than a year ago, to see if the Artist would be likely to suit me. The conclusion I came to at the time was *not* in favour of applying to him: and since then the name has passed out of my memory. But I sent the book, at the time, to my friend Mr. Tenniel for an opinion: and I think I may, without breach of confidence, copy what he said. I would not do it if it had been written in a harsh tone, but I think it will not wound your feelings, and possibly, now that you have reached a higher level, you will agree with some of his criticism. He says: "The designs of Mr. A. B. Frost appear to me to possess a certain amount of quaint and grotesque humour, together with an *uncertain* amount of dextrous drawing, which might no doubt be developed into something very much better, but which is at present, as it seems to me, judging by the book, somewhat crude and commonplace in execution; but the pictures are obviously very slight, and perhaps it is hardly fair to give an opinion."

I must conclude. Believe me

Very truly yours,
C. L. Dodgson

Have you a preference for any particular woodcutter or will Messrs. Dalziel do?[1]

1. Frost accepted Messrs. Dalziel as the woodcutters for Dodgson's illustrations.

MS: *Rosenbach*

Christ Church, Oxford
March 14, 1878[1]

Dear Sir,

No man should be hurried in his work, and an artist least of all. Pray do not put yourself out on my account. I am in no hurry, and will wait till you have convenient leisure to draw for me.

Yours very truly,
C. L. Dodgson

1. The date is given as 1877, which is almost certainly a mistake. Although the recipient is unclear, the letter is deposited with other Frost letters at the Rosenbach Foundation, Philadelphia.

MS: *Rosenbach*

Christ Church, Oxford
March 29, 1878

Dear Sir,

Do not suppose, by my writing, that I wish to hurry you in the least: only it occurs to me to write a line, just to ask if you yet see your way to finding time for an attempt at "The Three Voices," and to express my admiration of your picture of the "Master of the Rolls."[1] It seems to me just what grotesque drawing *should* be.

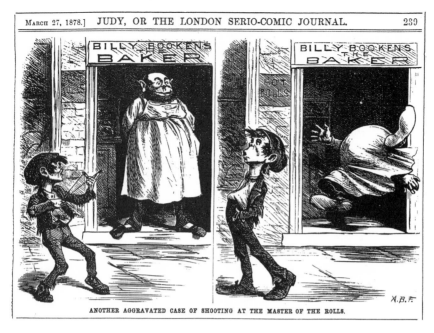

ANOTHER AGGRAVATED CASE OF SHOOTING AT THE MASTER OF THE ROLLS.

FIG. 8

Frost's illustration of "Another Aggravated Case of Shooting at the Master of the Rolls" in Judy *for March 27, 1878.*

I only hope you may have the same amount of *vis comica*[2] at hand when you draw for me! Believe me

Truly yours,
C. L. Dodgson

1. Frost's illustration titled "Another Aggravated Case of Shooting at the Master of the Rolls" appeared in *Judy* for March 27, 1878 (p. 239). The two-part picture shows a scruffy boy about to shoot a catapult at a rotund baker standing in the doorway of his bakery, and then the outcome with the baker falling backwards and the boy walking away, whistling, with hands in pockets pretending innocence.

2. Comic power or talent.

MS: *Rosenbach*

Christ Church, Oxford
April 12, 1878

Dear Mr. Frost,

I am glad to hear you are at work on "The Three Voices," and glad also that you are not hurrying the work. It would be a needless risk to send me the blocks themselves: rough sketches would do very well to give me an idea of your treatment, and to enable me to suggest any necessary changes before cutting them. But you need not even send sketches at present: I leave here tomorrow for "The Chestnuts, Guildford," where I stay till Easter Tuesday, and during that time I expect to have a day or two in town, and will try to find an opportunity of calling, which will also give me the pleasure of making your acquaintance in person.[1]

I notice that you have not guessed (and no wonder) that my address is "Rev. C. L. Dodgson." If you won't mind my mentioning it, the English form of address, where one is not "Rev.," is "So-and-so, Esq.," *not* "Mr. So-and-so." The usage is really a curious anomaly: my friend leaves his card on me as "Mr. J. Smith," and I begin my letter to him "Dear Mr. Smith," but I *direct* it "J. Smith, Esq." I should only write "Mr. J. Smith" if he were a tradesman. I am almost afraid of mentioning these trifles, for fear you should think I had taken offence at being directed to as "Mr." Nothing could be further from my thoughts.

Do you think the enclosed would suit any of the *Judy* artists? (With marginal illustrations, winding in and out, I think it would be a good pageful). If so, *Judy* is welcome to print it, provided she does not object to my republishing it at some future time.[2] Believe me

Very truly yours,
C. L. Dodgson

1. Ill health forced Dodgson to delay his visit to Frost until April 24.
2. Dodgson enclosed an early manuscript version of his poem "A Game of Fives" (MS: Rosenbach) which he published for the first time, with alterations, in *Rhyme? and Reason?*, accompanied by two Frost drawings (pp. 120–22).

MS: *Rosenbach*

The Chestnuts, Guildford
April 16, 1878

Dear Mr. Frost,

I may be in town tomorrow (Wednesday) and if so I hope to be able to call on you about 1. If you have to go out, could you leave orders that I may see the blocks?

Yours very truly,
C. L. Dodgson

MS: *Rosenbach*

The Chestnuts, Guildford
April 19, 1878

Dear Mr. Frost,

I have had such a cold all this week that I have not ventured to come up to town.[1] But I am engaged to come on Tuesday, and am going on to Oxford on Wednesday: so one of those 2 days I hope to have the pleasure of calling upon you.

Very truly yours,
C. L. Dodgson

1. Dodgson wrote: "Two days of homeopathy (aconite and arsenic) seem to have cured the cold which had kept me in for several days" (Diaries, April 20).

MS: *Rosenbach*

Christ Church, Oxford
April 24, 1878

Dear Mr. Frost,

I have changed my mind about "A Game of Fives," and I think I *won't* ask you to offer them to *Judy*. If you will not mention my name, you are quite welcome to take them to America, and offer them, with your own drawings, to the magazine you mentioned: you need not, I should think, say anything about the writer at all: but at any rate don't say more than that they are "by a friend." I give them you to do as you like with, only bargaining that I am free to re-publish: if I ever [wish] to do so, I shall probably wish, if possible, to buy the blocks of your illustrations.

I had not time to look through that ingenious photograph catalogue: would you mind lending it me (both the series), and I will then send you a few numbers I should like to have, if you could buy them for me. Perhaps you could let me see at the same time the "cabinets" you possess of the series: I will return the packet in a day or two. I should be glad if you could find out whether the man also keeps *Les Beaux Arts* published by Marconi, 11 Rue de Buci, Paris.[1] I can't find any London dealer: I suppose they are all afraid of being thought to be connected with some (who are a disgrace not only to all true Art, but to all decent society) dealers in immoral photographs.

Yours very truly,
C. L. Dodgson

Please do the "Cupid" in pencil or ink, whichever you think will look best: I fancy pencil admits of more delicate treatment but perhaps ink would look best framed.[2]

1. "Paid a long visit to Mr. Frost, whom I had not seen before," Dodgson wrote on April 24. "He showed me two blocks done for 'The Three Voices,' which are deliciously funny and extremely well drawn. A Miss Barnard came to sit (head only), and while he drew I looked through two very interesting portfolios of studies, etc. He is regularly working at Art now, and can evidently do anything he likes" (*Diaries*, pp. 370–71). The portfolios were produced by Gaudenzio Marconi (b. 1842), painter and photographer, who had studios in Paris, first at 16 rue de Buci and then at 13 rue des Beaux-Arts. He photographed nudes, children and adults, and nude sculptures, including some by his friend Auguste Rodin, and used the same wet collodion process that Dodgson did. See *Photographie* 7 (1985): 110–12.

2. "The idea occurred to me to get him to make me a drawing of 'Sallie' [Sinclair] as 'Cupid,' and he readily undertook it," Dodgson wrote on April 24 (*Diaries*, p. 371). The same day, he wrote to Mrs. Sinclair: "I have thought of a plan by which I can at once do you a photograph of Sallie, if you don't mind the trouble of taking her to Haverstock Hill. I was talking to an artist-friend there, and the idea occurred to me of asking whether he would make me a drawing of 'Cupid,' if I could get you to bring her: he undertook it readily, and as he is a very clever artist, I think he would make a very pretty thing of it: and I will photograph the drawing for you: drawings generally photograph extremely well. If you consent to this, could you take her (and the 'Cupid' dress) on Saturday, as soon after 10 as you like?" (*Letters*, p. 307). Maria Sinclair (d. 1879) was married to Joseph Henry Scrivener (1829–79), an actor who took the stage name Sinclair.

They had four children: Sarah Caroline "Sallie" (1868–1956); Jessie Josephine (1865–1952); Kate Jemima (b. 1869); and Harry Sinclair (1872–1940). See *Letters*, pp. 294–95, n. 3.

MS: *Rosenbach*

Christ Church, Oxford
April 25, 1878

Dear Mr. Frost,

You will think me very fickle, but after all I would rather "A Game of Fives" were kept to come out new in the volume. There seems to be no sufficient reason for sending it to that magazine.

And now as to the volume itself, I have been thinking the matter well over, and you shall illustrate the whole of it, if you like; i.e. the comic poems, all but "The Lang Coortin'," which Sambourne is doing. And I sincerely hope it may prove, as you seemed to think likely, a means of advancing your own reputation.[1]

It will be as well to have the £. *s. d.* arrangements in black and white, and then no difficulty would arise, even in case of my death: but we can talk over all that when I have the pleasure of seeing you over here.

When I said "avoid Monday, Wednesday and Friday," it was only that there is a lecture from 11 to 12 these days which I could not alter: but you could easily be independent of me for an hour or two. Would you come in the middle of the day, any day you like to fix, and stay the night? That would give you an afternoon, and the following day, to see Oxford, and an evening for business.

I enclose a scrawl of an idea I have for a half-page picture, to go at the foot of the page, for the last verse of "The Three Voices." A shadowy figure, winding round and round him and running him through with her umbrella. Don't adopt any of it if you don't like it.[2]

Would you bring that volume of *Phantasmagoria* back with you, and I will give you a copy for your own.

Very truly yours,
C. L. Dodgson

I may as well mention that we *don't* assume evening dress for Hall dinner this term. I have written to Mrs. Sinclair about "Cupid."

FIG. 9
*Dodgson's sketch for "The Three Voices" in
letter dated April 25, 1878.*

1. We have not located the Sambourne drawings.
2. Dodgson's two other drawings for this poem appear in *Mischmasch*. Frost did fourteen drawings for "The Three Voices."

MS: *Huntington*

Christ Church, Oxford
April 26, 1878

Dear Mr. Frost,

Mrs. Sinclair has not been very well lately, but if she is well enough on Saturday she will bring her little "Sallie" to you, and the "Cupid" dress. She says they will set out about 10, and so will be with you, I suppose, about 11. I don't think I ever gave you her address. It is "The Hollies, 142 South Lambeth Road." Believe me

Very truly yours,
C. L. Dodgson

MS: Rosenbach

Christ Church, Oxford
April 30, 1878

Dear Mr. Frost,

You will be very welcome on Thursday, if that is the only day you can manage: but could you not, by waiting till next week, find a day when you could stay the night also? That would give us more leisure to talk matters over. If you come on Thursday, you can at any rate stay dinner, as we dine at 7, and the last train goes at 9.15.[1]

I shall probably be engaged from 12 to 2, but you had better come here directly you arrive, and I will start you on your rambles. It is only about 10 minutes walk from the railway (if you prefer a cab, the legal fare is 1s.). You had better ask your way to "Tom Gate, Christ Church," and the porter at the gate will direct you to my rooms. Don't forget to bring my sister's copy of *Phantasmagoria* with you.

Yours very truly,
C. L. Dodgson

1. "Mr. Frost came over for the day," Dodgson noted on Thursday, May 2 (Diaries). "We talked over *Phantasmagoria*, looked at photographs, and went to Magdalen Chapel, St. John's gardens, etc. He dined with me and slept at the Clarendon (having missed his train through my stupidity in misreading *Bradshaw*)."

MS: Rosenbach

Christ Church, Oxford
May 3, 1878

Dear Mr. Frost,

One thing I forgot to ask you when I gave you my photograph, which was never to let it out of your own possession. If a photographer got hold of it, and copied it, it would be a great annoyance to me: I specially wish my *face* to remain unknown to the public. I like my *books* to be known, of course: but *personally* I hope to remain in obscurity. Please don't show it (except to your own friends): I mean, don't put it where casual strangers can see it.

What does the "A" mean in "Philadelphia P. A." or ought it to be "Pa" (as an abbreviation for "Pennsylvania")?

Yours very truly,
C. L. Dodgson

MS: Rosenbach

Christ Church, Oxford
May 7, 1878

Dear Mr. Frost,

Many thanks for the silhouette: I like it very much, but you are bold to take a style which so directly challenges comparison with Konewka![1] I quite think you may be his *equal* some day, but you will find it hard to *beat* him! To me, at least, his designs seem faultless. You talk of sending me the "little Cupid" at once, now. If you mean the design for the enclosed verses,[2] there is no sort of hurry: in fact I would rather you delayed it till you are quite at leisure again, as the fairies ought to be done in happy moments of inspiration. But if you mean the study which you have kindly purposed to draw for me, *then* I don't know why you call it "Cupid." I doubt if we quite understand each other: I don't want *two* Cupids. Let me try to put it clearly.

(1) I want a design on wood, for the book, to illustrate these verses. It should represent Cupid sleeping, fairies watching, and lots of roses. As this is for publication, I should like a draped Cupid—a tunic will do very well—but the critics would be "down on me" directly, if he were not enough dressed. His *face* should be, if possible, a portrait of little Sallie Sinclair.

(2) The figure you kindly proposed to draw for me: If you mean the silhouette for it, I will accept it gratefully as such, but if you intend yet to do another, then, if I might suggest what I should like, it would be a shaded pencil drawing, a study from life (but *not* a Cupid) that I may keep it as a specimen of your power in drawing a beautiful figure. As it is *not* for publication, you need not put an atom of drapery on it, and I can quite trust you, even if you made it a full-front view, to have a simple classical figure. I had rather not have an adult figure (which always looks to me rather in need of drapery): a girl of about 12 is *my* ideal of beauty of form. A pretty *face* would

be a pleasant addition, but by no means essential: a beautiful *form* is what I should specially like to have as a specimen of your skill.

I write in haste to catch post.

Would you not like to have something paid "on account" for "Phantas-magoria"? Cash is apt to run short when one is winding up affairs, and paying bills. Shall I send you £50?

Yours very truly,
C. L. Dodgson

P.S. If you know any child-model (about 10) that is *not* forward and vulgar, you might just ask the question of the mother if she would be willing to have the child photographed (the photograph to be for me and for her *only*, unless she gave further leave, but certainly not for sale.)

1. Paul Konewka (1840–71), German artist, who worked mainly in silhouettes, occasionally illustrated English books.

2. Dodgson enclosed a manuscript copy of the acrostic poem "Love Among the Roses." The first letter in each line, read down, spells "Sarah Sinclair" (MS: Rosenbach):

"Seek ye Love, ye fairy-sprites?
Ask where reddest roses blow:
Rosy fancies he invites,
And in roses he delights—
Have ye found him?" "No."

"Seek again, and find the boy
In Childhood's heart, so pure and clear."
Now the fairies leap for joy,
Crying "Love is here!"

"Love has found his proper nest,
And we guard him while he dozes
In a dream of peace and rest
Rosier than roses!"

The poem first appeared in *The Lewis Carroll Picture Book*, 1899, p. 204. We do not know whether Frost drew Sallie Sinclair as Cupid or at all; if he did, the drawing(s) have not come to light.

MS: *Rosenbach*

Christ Church, Oxford
May 8, 1878

Dear Mr. Frost,

If business should ever take you down Tottenham Court Road (not otherwise), could you ask a question for me of Mr. Mansell (Art Publisher), 2 Percy Street. (It is on the West side, a little North of Oxford Street.) He undertook to enquire, for me, about the *Beaux Arts* photographs, published by Marconi, 11 Rue de Buci, Paris. But he has never written again. I want to know whether I can see the collection anywhere in London, to make selections from.

Yours very truly,
C. L. Dodgson

I am hoping to hear that you can come over again.

———————

MS: *Rosenbach*

Christ Church, Oxford
May 9, 1878

Dear Mr. Frost,

I have written to my friend Mr. Tolhurst[1] asking him to pay you the sum you named, on your presenting the enclosed note, with the amount filled in. I send it with blanks for *you* to fill in, as a precaution, lest this letter should fall into wrong hands. I think the chances are about 10,000 to 1 against the thief being able to guess *what* sum ought to be filled in!

Wishing you a pleasant journey to America,[2] and that you may find your brother on the high road to recovery, I remain

Yours very truly,
C. L. Dodgson

1. Charles Edmeades Tolhurst (1828?–91) is described in official records as a "fundholder" and a "diamond merchant." Clearly, Dodgson relied on Tolhurst to assist in financial transactions. Dodgson met the Tolhurst family in June 1869 and invited them to visit him at Oxford. He took several photographs of their daughter, Mary Beatrix (1863–1915). See *Letters*, p. 299, n. 1.

2. On May 12, Dodgson "called on Mr. Frost (he leaves for America this week)" (*Diaries*, p. 371). All future letters between the two had to cross the Atlantic.

MS: Rosenbach

Christ Church, Oxford
November 25, 1878

Dear Mr. Frost,

I have been meaning to write to you for a long time, in fact ever since July 22, when I received your letter dated July 7, but it seems so greater an undertaking to write a letter that is to be a fortnight on its way than a note that will be delivered next day, that one keeps putting off the former, in favour of what seem the more pressing claims of the latter.

I am very glad indeed to hear of your brother being so much better, and sincerely hope that he is now quite recovered. I hope also that you have got through all preliminary difficulties of settling and hunting for models, and are comfortably at work in your new studio.

As to the pictures for my book, I do not remember now how much we settled with regard to what passages were to be illustrated, and how. Whatever we settled you can of course carry out, even to the finishing the drawings on the wood. In all other cases I think it would be much more satisfactory to let me see, by rough sketches and descriptions, what your ideas are, before going to much expense of time and trouble in elaborating them. For instance, in "Phantasmagoria" itself, it would be a grievous annoyance if you were to finish off several pictures including the "little ghost" and then find after all that our ideas were entirely at variance as to what that "little ghost" should look like! It is of course a tremendous drawback to the work that every question and answer that passes should cost us a month, but it can't be helped with an ocean between us. I shall be truly rejoiced when I hear that you find you can pay England another visit.

Your little black fairy is often admired by my friends here: it certainly is as graceful as a fairy well can be.[1] I wish I could draw 1/10 as well! My "figure-drawing" is just where it was. I bought a lovely cast of a hand at that shop near Drury Lane Theatre, but I have had no time to draw, as my mathematical book is still on hand.[2] When you are in London again, I shall hope to have more time, and that you will be willing to give me a lesson or two.

Hoping to have before long good news of you and yours, and of the pictures, I am

Very truly yours,
C. L. Dodgson

1. We find no trace of Frost's black fairy anywhere.

2. Dodgson spent much of the time between 1876 and 1878 working on his mathematical drama *Euclid and His Modern Rivals*, an attack on the new geometers who had abandoned the logical sequence of Euclid's *Elements*. On October 25, 1878, he wrote, "At last sent to press some slips of *Euclid and His Modern Rivals* to be made up in pages," and on December 21, "Have been working at *Euclid*, etc., and today took the whole thing back to the Press" (*Diaries*, p. 375). The book was published in March 1879.

———————————

MS: *Harvard*

1338 Chestnut Street,
Philadelphia
December 12, 1878

Dear Mr. Dodgson,

I sent you by Express today the drawings for "The Three Voices" and a letter enclosed in the parcel. In the letter I said I had enclosed the account. But on coming back to my studio I find I have left it out.

I enclose it in this.[1]

Very truly yours, dear Sir
Arthur Burdett Frost

1. This is just one of a handful of letters from Frost to Dodgson which have survived. The account enclosed with this letter is missing.

———————————

MS: *Rosenbach*

[The Chestnuts] Guildford
December 28, 1878

Dear Mr. Frost,

Your letter and account have followed me here: the parcel I shall no doubt find when I return to Oxford, which will be in about 3 weeks, but it will not do to wait till then before writing to tell you, what I fear you will be disappointed to hear, that the number of pictures you have drawn for that one poem is far in excess of what I can possibly undertake to make use of. It is no doubt very awkward for us to have the Atlantic between us, as it makes all consultation so tedious and difficult: but it is a great pity you ran the risk of drawing so many blocks without a previous agreement. Forty or fifty pictures for the whole book (consisting of "Phantasmagoria," "A Sea Dirge," "Ye Carpette Knyghte," "Hiawatha," "The Lang Coortin'," "Melancholetta," "The Three Voices," "Size and Tears," "Poeta Fit," "Atalanta" and the two new ones which you have in MS) is the outside that I could venture on. "The Three Voices" is about 1/7 of the whole, and therefore must not have more than 7 or 8 pictures. To give it more would simply kill the rest of the book, unless the whole thing were done in the same lavish way, and *that* I need hardly say is entirely out of the question, as it would be about 105 pictures, costing for drawing (say) £350, for cutting between £400 and £500, making about £800 for pictures alone: I could not afford to bring out the book at such a heavy loss as that would entail.[1] How *you* are to be compensated for the time and trouble lost on the extra pictures is a question we can settle at a future time. What I want to secure *now* is that we should settle exactly, before you draw the other pictures for the book, how many they are to be, what sizes, and which passages they are to illustrate: and we ought also, by means of rough sketches, to make sure that we agree as to treatment. Especially will this be necessary as to "Phantasmagoria" itself and "Hiawatha": it will be a most difficult point to settle, what sort of ghosts to have, and the costume of Hiawatha and his friends.

I will write again when I have seen the parcel. Believe me

Very truly yours,
C. L. Dodgson

1. Dodgson used sixty-five drawings by Frost in *Rhyme? and Reason?*; fourteen illustrate "The Three Voices," nine of them full-page drawings.

Christ Church, Oxford
January 30, 1879

Dear Mr. Frost,

Now that I have returned to Oxford, and have opened your parcel of blocks, and read the letter accompanying them, I see how entirely mistaken I was in my last letter. I hope you will forgive my hastiness in writing it: but I was away from Oxford, and it seemed to me that no time was to be lost in stopping what I thought a far too great profuseness in drawing the pictures. I fancied the "15" were all large pictures, and had quite forgotten about head-pieces and tail-pieces. No doubt you are quite right as to the number we agreed on: I had forgotten it.

Now let me say how *intensely* I admire what you have done. The drawing is perfect, and exquisite to a degree which one *very* rarely finds in wood-cuts. I have told Messrs. Dalziel that they will require the very best available skill in cutting them, and that I am willing to pay for the best workmanship. Of course I shall use all the pictures—I revoke entirely all I said about keeping back some of them. I only wish the poem had a little more back-bone in it: it is almost too weak and flimsy a thing to be so splendidly illustrated![1]

The last tail-piece (of the prostrate hero with something hovering over him) I have not yet sent to Dalziel. I think I must ask you to let me send it you again to have that "something" re-touched. *I* failed in making out what you meant it for: I could make nothing of it but either a ballet-dancer (which would have been unmeaning) or the "she" of the poem, in the condition of the "little old woman" of the nursery-song, when the pedlar had "cut short her petticoats round about," and neither idea pleased me. A friend has been looking at it, and thinks it means "the umbrella, hat, and tippet, without any living form at all," but even if it is so, I don't think the ordinary reader will guess it. Couldn't you make it a ghostly "she," standing in front of him and brooding over him, and transparent, so that she does not conceal the prostrate figure?[2]

Now to answer your questions as to *numbers* of pictures. I think we should aim at about 50 for the volume, and as Mr. Sambourne is doing 5 for "The Lang Coortin'," and we have 9 (I am not counting head- and tail-pieces) done by you, it leaves from 30 to 40 still to be done. "Phantasmago-ria" would not be overdone, I think, with 20, or even 25.³ Some of the poems (e.g. "Poeta Fit") will need very few. Some I think not worth illustrating or reprinting: these are "A Valentine" and "A Double Acrostic," and (of course, as it had a temporary interest only) "Elections to Council."⁴

Then there is the poem you have in MS about 5 little daughters.⁵

But I think you had better send a list of subjects with rough sketches, for one or more of the poems, as you prefer. As to the "little ghost," I find it very hard to make suggestions: I should like to see a few rough sketches to select from. My idea of him is of a little old man, dressed in long frock-coat, long flowered-waistcoat, silk stockings, buckles — in fact a sort of Charles I style: with an anxious frightened look (except in the latter part of the poem, when he has recovered his confidence, where he should wear an impudent grin). But I think your sketches will be the best guide. I hope you will suc-ceed in inventing some startling varieties of ghosts for all the different species I have named!

Messrs. Coutts and Co. of London have instructed Messrs. Morris, Walrond and Co. of Philadelphia to pay you the sum due.

I end in haste to catch a post: the letter has been far too long delayed as it is now February 5.

I hope to send you the photos (or at least some of them) very soon.⁶

Yours very sincerely,
C. L. Dodgson

I send a scrawl of a "little ghost."

It is dreadfully inconvenient, having the Atlantic between us. I *hope* you'll be able to manage a visit to England this summer.

I am very glad your brother is well again, and wish him all happiness in his new state of life.

P.S. In my Medical studies I have met with 2 excellent books by Dr. Meigs, published by Lea and Blanchard, Philadelphia, and wish to possess his other books, but can't meet with them here. If you ever are near their shop (or is it "store"?), I should be much indebted if you would ascertain which of his books they can supply: and if they are good clean copies, and not exorbitantly dear, you might order them to be sent to me. I leave it to your discretion. The two I do *not* want are called *Females and their Diseases*

FIG. 10
Dodgson's sketch for "Phantasmagoria" in letter dated January 30, 1879, with Frost's final drawing.

and *Obstetrics*. The others (any or all of which I should like to have) are some such titles as these:

> *Philosophy of Marriage*
> *Prostitution*
> *Medical Jurisprudence*

and there may be others. He is a most genial, and a thoroughly *healthy*, writer.[7]

1. Dodgson made many changes to "The Three Voices"; the original appeared in *Mischmasch* (July 1856), and he revised it in *The Train* (November 1856), *Phantasmagoria* (1869), and again in *Rhyme? and Reason?* (1883). From the *Mischmasch* version to the final version in *Rhyme? and Reason?* he omitted four verses and added twenty-three new verses. He also made over forty changes to the text and punctuation, adding, no doubt, to the "backbone."

2. Dodgson eventually rejected this illustration.

3. Twenty-three Frost drawings accompany "Phantasmagoria."

4. "Poeta Fit" has three illustrations; "A Valentine" has none; "A Double Acrostic" and "The Elections to the Hebdomadal Council" do not appear in *Rhyme? and Reason?*

5. "A Game of Fives," which accompanied Dodgson's letter of May 7, 1878.

6. We do not know which photographs Dodgson had in mind here.

7. Dodgson has mistaken the author of the books he wants. They were not by Dr. Charles Delucena Meigs (1792–1869), author of books on midwifery, but by Dr. Michael Ryan (1800–1841), author of *The Philosophy of Marriage* (1837), *Prostitution in London* (1839), and *A Manual of Medical Jurisprudence* (1831).

MS: *Rosenbach*

Christ Church, Oxford
February 26, 1880

Dear Mr. Frost,

I have been putting off writing to you, from week to week, and month to month. However, a letter shall go, however short, by *this* post. There is no use waiting for leisure to write a long letter. The last letter I have from you is dated February 26, 1879! How time flies!

I hope you are alive and well, and that you are making some progress in the sketches for "Phantasmagoria." It will not do to make the finished drawings on wood till we have come to some agreement as to the general character of the designs.

Your pictures for "The Three Voices" have been cut, and the results are beyond all praise. I don't think I have *ever* seen better woodcuts, of that class, anywhere. With both drawing, and cutting, I am more than satisfied—I am delighted.

The last little vignette, which you said you would alter, has been sent by mistake to Dalziel, and has been cut with the others (I retained, instead of it, the head at the end of Voice I). But I don't like the result. Every one takes it for a sort of ballet-dancer, so I shall not put it in, but of course shall pay for it, as it is *my* fault it was not sent back to you to be altered. Would you draw another tail-piece to take its place. I *think* we should find a full-length of the female, transparent, in front of the prostrate man, more effective than an umbrella and cloak only.[1]

I have not forgotten my promise of photographs, but must send some another day. I have done some lovely nude studies of children, and I think I have leave to send you some.

If *you* ever meet with a pretty child-figure to draw from, even if you don't find time to make the finished drawing which you kindly said you would some day give me, at least send me a few rough sketches of her. I have an intense appreciation of artists' rough sketches of the human form: they leave more to the imagination, and so are more poetical (if one may use the word of pictures) than more finished studies.

Yours very truly,
C. L. Dodgson

I hope Dalziel has sent *you* a set of proofs. I'll ask him.

1. Although Dodgson sent a sketch to help Frost draw his picture, he later decided to do without a tail-piece to "The Three Voices" (see December 9, 1880).

MS: *Rosenbach*

Christ Church, Oxford
April 9, 1880

Dear Mr. Frost,

Let me first offer my sincere sympathy in all the trouble and anxiety you have gone through since last you wrote, and also in the relief it must be to find that matters are looking brighter and more hopeful. Pray do not scruple to lay aside my work whenever you feel it *necessary* so to do in order to do "pot-boilers." However, with the hope of making that necessity less urgent, I am directing my banker to pay, per Coutts and Co., to your credit with Messrs. Morris Walrond, and Co., £50, which you can set down as paid "on account" of drawings hereafter to be sent. I have this day sent off by rail a parcel, which I hope will reach you safely, containing 14 proofs of the blocks that have been cut (the vignette of a head and shoulders, "a shadow growing on his face," is not cut yet), also 10 proofs sent me by Dalziel to forward to you, of your drawings for *American Notes* (or some such name), also 6 photographs which I did of a child, recommended by Sir F. Leighton, to whom she has been sitting as a model. *He* thinks her well made: *I* don't much admire such massive wrists and ankles: and her face is lamentably ugly. A lady-artist, who had employed her as model, brought her to Oxford for the day, and helped to arrange the attitudes. The results are not very satisfactory, a chemical fault having caused "pin-holes" in the films, which makes her look rather like a small-pox patient: still I hope they may interest you as transcript of living anatomy.[1]

The more I look at "The Three Voices" pictures, the better I like them: in fact, there is but one fault that my friends and I can find, and that is but a trifling matter. It is that you have not preserved much likeness in the various portraits of the hero: *she* keeps to one face, but *he* changes so much that it almost suggests her having had various companions for her walk. I fancy you would find it a good plan (e.g. with the hero of "Phantasmagoria") to get some one to sit for 3 or 4 photos or sketches of different views of his face: and this would give you a foundation to work on, so as to preserve a likeness.

I don't think the "half-lighted room" would be favourable to comic effect; better make it a bright lamplight. I *think* the ghost should be transparent, but *you* will be the best judge of that.

I am glad you like the little acrobat.[2] I have a list of photos promised to you, which I hope to send before long. Believe me

Very truly yours,
C. L. Dodgson

1. On July 4, 1879, Dodgson wrote: "Called, by appointment, on Sir F. Leighton, whom I had never seen before and whom I was much taken with. He showed me some lovely unfinished paintings, a sort of 'Hero' on the shore (nude figure seated: back view), a standing figure in green drapery, with a child leaning over and kissing her, painted from two sisters (he recommends the child for Miss Thomson, who wants a model), and a female figure which looks very queer at present, as the (unfinished) drapery only reaches to the waist" (*Diaries*, p. 381). Sir Frederic Leighton (1830–96), president of the Royal Academy, later Lord Leighton, arranged for Dodgson to photograph the child model. "As previously planned," Dodgson wrote on July 17, 1879, "Miss E. G. Thomson arrived from London about 11, bringing little Ada Smith, aged 11. . . . I did an ordinary portrait of her, and six 'studies,' in arranging which Miss Thomson was of great use. She has very plain features, but is well formed" (DIARIES, 7:190). For more about Miss Thomson, see chapter 5.

2. The "little acrobat" was probably a photograph Dodgson took of Lily Gray in 1876. For more about Lily Gray, see *Letters*, p. 259, n. 1.

Christ Church, Oxford
December 9, 1880

Dear Mr. Frost,

Your first letter, and 4 sketches, reached me November 24. Having let a week or so go by without writing, I thought I might as well wait for the next, which has just arrived. I will go through both *seriatim*, but first let me assure you how sincerely I feel with you in your domestic troubles. As you say nothing of health in this morning's letter, I trust it means that things have gone on better. Work, in the midst of anxiety and sick-nursing, must be very difficult, and comic work next to impossible. The account you give of your own health, in your first letter, was indeed alarming: I hope your next may announce that you are really well again, I should say, for you did say you were "almost entirely recovered."[1] Now first, as to the £50 advanced. You are not doing in the least what I meant you to do with it, in keeping it scrupulously untouched in the bank. *I* meant it to be spent, just as need arose, so as to save your having to say "I must do a 'pot-boiler' for some magazine" and having to drop "Phantasmagoria" in consequence. You seem to fear spending it, lest you might not be able to do the work for it after- wards. But I don't mind *that* risk, a bit. If you spent it all, and then (which I trust for your sake may never happen) had to write and say "I am obliged to give up the pictures altogether, and cannot repay the money," I should not give another thought to it—the money, I mean: not the question of *your* health. So please spend it all freely, as a loan, if life, and health, and circum- stances, enable you to repay it in pictures: if not, as a gift.

Before I go to the sketches, I will answer your question about the *num- ber* of pictures to be done for the book. I think 50 in all, counting both big and little, will be as much as the book will bear. "The Three Voices" is over- pictured, I now think. It was my fault, in commissioning you to do so many for it: but now they are drawn, they are so brilliantly good, I cannot possibly omit one of them. I have written a few more verses to it, and I think that tail-piece (which you will remember I did not like) had better *not* be drawn again: the large picture of the man lying on his face will do very well to end with. That leaves the poem with 14 pictures.[2] Mr. Sambourne is to draw 5 pictures for the "Lang Coortin'." That leaves 31, or so, for the rest of the book. "Phantasmagoria" will perhaps take 20, "Hiawatha" 4, and the others about one apiece.

In this calculation I have not allowed for that extra poem (of which I think you have the MS) beginning with "Five little girls, etc." It has 7 verses, of 2 lines each: and, if the thing is worth illustrating *at all* (which admits of doubt) each verse ought to have a picture. Then the question would be "Half a page, or a whole page, for picture and couplet?" As there must be 5 figures in each picture, I doubt if they could be effectively treated in less than a page. I should like your opinion about it. It would be a fearful thing to draw. You would have to represent *every* age from 1 to 35! If that poem is illustrated as well, it would bring the total to nearly 60, of which 19 may be reckoned as drawn.

Now for the half-dozen delicious little sketches, which I herewith return to you.

(1) *First meeting of old gentleman and ghost.* The former is *not* my idea. I think the "stoutish city man" would vulgarise the poem. I don't like his stoutness (when so displayed), nor his tail-coat, nor his course features, nor his bald head. I want him to be a thorough *gentleman,* of the old school. My idea of his face is a rather long face, grave, benevolent, a little weak: abundance of gray hair (*my* idea of "turnip-top" was a *bunch* of hair on the top of his head, something like this).

However, if you think you can make him more effective with a bald head, so let it be. But please make him a *gentleman.* Another idea occurred to me about him, that, considering he is the *narrator,* there would be an appropriate modesty in his *never* showing his face. What do you think of it? All depends on whether you can make effective pictures with the uniform trick that either he shall turn his back on the spectator or that some accidental object shall hide his face. The ghost's *expression* I like in this picture, but for *figure* I prefer No. 1, the one with the big head and thin legs.[3]

(2) Little Ghost No. 1. This is very charming. His head might be even bigger, and his body more like a gooseberry. I don't like the legs striped *different* ways. I know they used to do it in the olden time: but it is a sort of monstrosity. I think I like *horizontal* stripes best, for both legs. I suppose you will make him partly transparent?[4]

(3) Little Ghost No. 2. Comic, but too human. I like No. 1. best.[5]

(4) "Drenched to the skin, etc." This is a *great* success, I think. One can almost hear him howl![6]

(5) Ghost in cavern frightening small boy. The sheet is rather too hackneyed, perhaps. I prefer[7]

(6) Ghost frightening excursionists. I have some dread about the Ramsgate excursionists getting into, and vulgarising, the book. However, if you can't think of any other victims who would be equally funny, and more refined, keep them, by all means. It is a *very* comic picture, as it is, and the two gigantic feet in the air are first rate.[8]

As to what you say of getting the book done by February, I have one thing to say, and that very strongly. *Please don't hurry.* Any delay will be better than hurried work, and it does not the *least* matter to me at what time of the year the book appears. I am so far from thinking Easter, or Christmas, the only 2 times for it, that I would almost prefer its appearing in what booksellers talk of as "the dead time," when London is out of town. With such pictures, the book will be famous at once, whenever it appears.[9] Believe me

Very sincerely yours,
C. L. Dodgson

1. We do not know what illness plagued the Frost family, but Frost reports his own ailment in his letter to Dodgson of May 5, 1881.

2. See January 30, 1879, n. 1, and May 1, 1881.

3. This illustration does not appear in *Rhyme? and Reason?*

4. *Rhyme? and Reason?*, p. 2. The stripes on both legs have disappeared, and the ghost is partly transparent.

5. Ibid., p. 9.

6. Ibid., p. 49.

7. This illustration does not appear in *Rhyme? and Reason?*

8. *Rhyme? and Reason?*, p. 7.

9. The book took another three years to complete.

MS: Rosenbach

Christ Church, Oxford
February 5, 1881

Dear Mr. Frost,

I have 2 letters of yours to answer, but I will take the last (as being the most important) first. And I must again begin by offering my sincere sympathy on the continued illness of your mother and sister, and hopes that you will be able to give a better report next time you write. You yourself are really, I hope, out of the doctor's hands.

As to the money matter, although you say you understand me, it is clear to me that you do *not*, and I must explain myself once more. The evil I wished to remedy was that you seemed to find it necessary, for want of *ready* money, to lay aside *my* work every now and then, and undertake work for others who paid more rapidly. I thought *prepaying* would remove all that hindrance to your going on *exclusively* with my work, and it has been a great disappointment to me to have failed so entirely, and to hear that you, first, scruple to use my money till you have earned it, and, secondly, find yourself *still* under the necessity of undertaking other work while mine is kept waiting. I know nothing about Mr. Harper, so I have no idea which has the prior claim on your time and labour, but I am quite sure that this *alternating* plan will not do justice to either of us. If Mr. Harper had entered into engagements with you before I did, then let me earnestly beg that you will lay aside my book *entirely*, and devote yourself entirely to *his* work till you have fulfilled your engagements with him: and then confer the same favour on *me*. If *I* have the first claim, I am not Quixotic enough to offer to surrender it. Life is uncertain, and I like to get things *finished*. Of course all this is a *request* merely: I made no stipulation that you should work exclusively on my book, and undertake no other work till it was done: but I do hope you will see your way to doing one thing or the other, and devote yourself either to Mr. Harper's work, or else to mine, *exclusively and till it is done*.[1]

If £50 in hand is not enough to relieve you from the *necessity* of undertaking other work, only let me know and you shall have another £50. And pray put aside altogether the idea of only spending it as you earn it: to do that simply defeats the whole object I have in advancing it.

If you feel *obliged* to give March, as you say, to Mr. Harper, please give him what remains of February also, and April, and as much more time as will enable you to get clear of all further claims from him.

And now I turn to your letter dated December 8, 1880. You say Tibbets gives little chance for fun. That is quite my idea. I *don't* want him to be ridiculous, or to be drawn in any way to put the reader out of sympathy with him. If you know by sight any "Professor" at one of your Universities, who is a gentle and genial old man, draw *him*.[2]

You say it won't be necessary to stick to one costume for the ghost. I think in all pictures where he is in the room with the host he should be in *one* dress: what opportunity has he of changing it? Where he is in a cave, or on a battlement, etc., dress him as you like: *that* is another part of his history.

As to the enclosed sketches, I like the ghost sitting on the table (only his *face* should be made more like the one I selected of the experimental ghosts sent last time), but I *don't* like the man's face. However you know now the sort of hero I want: I think the ghost should have a little more room on the table, for his knife and fork, etc.[3]

The other picture is much the best of the two, I think. The ghost is charming, and I like very much that long tail of ghostly drapery. And the night-light is an excellent idea.[4]

I will save the weight of another half-sheet, and stop. (N.B. The ghost drawing the curtain is not necessarily the hero-ghost, so you can keep the face (a new one) which you have given him).[5]

Sincerely yours,
C. L. Dodgson

1. Frost was hired by Harper's in New York soon after his success with *Out of the Hurly-Burly* in 1874. He took a leave of absence to travel to England in 1877. On his return, he continued to work for Harper's, then one of the largest publishers in America producing not only books but also weekly and monthly magazines. The nature of Frost's work allowed him to take other commissions that came his way.

2. Tibbets is the man whose house the little ghost attempts to haunt in "Phantasmagoria."

3. *Rhyme? and Reason?*, p. 17, or possibly p. 9, although Dodgson describes the latter in his previous letter.

4. Ibid., possibly p. 13 or p. 19.

5. Ibid., p. 11.

To Messrs. Dalziel Brothers
MS: *Harvard*

Christ Church, Oxford
February 12, 1881

Mr. Dodgson hopes to receive more blocks soon from Mr. Frost, which he will send to Messrs. Dalziel to be cut.

He will thank them to send those already done to Messrs. Clay, Son, and Taylor, 6. Bread Street Hill, Upper Thames Street.

To Messrs. Dalziel Brothers
Facsimile MS: Huntington

Christ Church, Oxford
March 31, 1881

Mr. C. L. Dodgson has sent off this day, by Passenger Train, carriage *not* prepaid, a box containing 20 blocks, drawn by Mr. Frost, which he wishes to have cut in the best possible style. He encloses the key of the box, and has for security sealed a piece of paper over the key-hole, with 4 seals. In returning the box, it will of course be enough simply to lock it and send the key by post.

He thinks Messrs. Dalziel will like to see what Mr. Frost says about the 14 blocks, cut by Messrs. Dalziel at the beginning of 1879. He says they "were *splendidly* engraved. I don't ask better treatment than they received, and, knowing that these would be equally well done, I have not been sparing of difficult work. It hampers an artist very much to have to feel that anything like free execution will be cut all to pieces, and it is a correspondingly great relief to feel that when you want to throw a little dash and go into a thing it will come out as you have drawn it." Mr. Frost is now drawing some pictures on paper, with pen and ink, which are to be transferred to woodblocks by photography, but he does not say whether he will have them photographed in America or in England. If he sends them to be done in England, would Messrs. Dalziel be able to get them photographed on the blocks? Or if not, to whom had Mr. Dodgson best entrust them?[1]

The blocks had better be sent as soon as they are cut, to Messrs. Clay, to whom the former lot were sent.

---

1. The Dalziels' reply to Dodgson is missing, but they agreed to photograph Frost's drawings directly onto the woodblocks.

Facsimile MS: Rosenbach

Christ Church, Oxford
April 5, 1881

Dear Mr. Frost,

It is difficult to find words which will express, as strongly as I wish, how *thoroughly* I admire your pictures to the ghost-poem. They really are *wonderful*. I sent on all the blocks the same day to Messrs. Dalziel, that they may put the cutting of them in hand at once. Those on paper I will send on very soon (with the exception of the one which I am returning to you), but there is no hurry, as he will have his hands quite full for some time to come. The plan, of drawing on paper, and photographing that on to wood, will do perfectly well. I have consulted Mr. Dalziel about it, and also Mr. G. du Maurier, the *Punch* artist, and both are quite in favour of that method.

The enclosed picture is the solitary exception to the collection you have sent: and I candidly admit I do *not* like the man in it. I will try to put my reasons into an intelligible form. He is to my mind too *real* in his anger to be funny. If you were illustrating *Oliver Twist*, such a man would be quite in character for "Bill Sykes murdering Nancy." And the warming-pan (taken in connection with his savage expression) is too really murderous a weapon. The little ghost begging for mercy is perfectly charming, but the man has "murder" written in his face, and would terrify young readers more than amuse them. Also I don't think his night-shirt (though of course quite proper) is at all an artistic costume. I think a flowery dressing-gown would do much better. I think he ought to be a gentle man who has been terrified and worried into unusual violence, which should be preposterous and burlesque: also I think a pillow or bolster would be more hopelessly useless for exterminating ghosts, and therefore more comic than a warming-pan, which would really be a very deadly weapon. I can't draw, myself (a remark which the enclosed sketch makes quite superfluous), but this will perhaps give you a better idea, than words alone would, of what I have in my head. I hope you will be able to patch the drawing with a bit of paper, so as to save the trouble of drawing a new ghost.[1]

The naturalists I think are a great improvement on the Margate swells.[2] The Inn Spectre is first-rate:[3] but really it will not do to begin specifying all that has delighted me in the drawings. I should never get it all said.

You have not yet told me whether you think you can make anything of the "Five little girls." I may as well name the poems I think of *omitting*: "A Valentine," "A Double Acrostic" (which, even if I include it, does not seem to give material for a picture) and "The Elections to the Hebdomadal Council," a political poem of by-gone interest. I will look over my MS and see if I have anything, not yet printed, worth including.

What do you think we had better have as frontispiece to the book (if it has one at all)?

Don't trouble any more about those books of Meigs. I fancy it was some other writer I had seen quoted. I can't find any references to such books by Meigs.[4]

As to the money, never scruple to mention it, whenever you would like more. I have ordered £100 to be paid to your credit with Morris, Walrond, & Co. So I shall be ahead of you again. But please spend it as you like. Don't

FIG. 11
*Dodgson's sketch for
"Phantasmagoria" in letter
dated April 5, 1881.*

again be so particular about not drawing the money till you have done work to correspond.[5] Believe me

Very sincerely yours,
C. L. Dodgson

1. *Rhyme? and Reason?*, p. 55. Frost adopted Dodgson's suggestions: the man wears a dressing gown, his expression is unthreatening, and the warming pan has been replaced by a cushion.
2. *Rhyme? and Reason?*, p. 7.
3. Ibid., possibly p. 21.
4. See January 30, 1879, n. 7.
5. For Frost's reply, see his letter dated May 5, 1881.

To Messrs. Dalziel Brothers
MS: *Harvard*

Christ Church, Oxford
April 11, 1881

Mr. C. L. Dodgson encloses 4 pen-and-ink drawings by Mr. Frost which he will thank Messrs. Dalziel to have transferred to wood by photography, and cut. He would like one of these to be put in hand for cutting, so soon as one of the blocks, now in hand, is finished, as he is anxious to see the exact effect of the new process.

Some of the pictures are meant to go round portions of the printed text. Mr. Dodgson would like to know how this will be managed. Will a piece of the block be cut entirely out, leaving a piece of this shape?

And is this done before the picture is cut, or after?[1]

1. We do not have the Dalziels' reply. Three illustrations, all for "Phantasmagoria," are shaped as Dodgson wanted them. See *Rhyme? and Reason?*, pp. 11, 26, and 45.

Facsimile MS: *Rosenbach*

Christ Church, Oxford
April 25, 1881

Dear Mr. Frost,

Though I am beginning to expect another set of drawings from you, yet I will not wait for them before writing, as I have several things to say which had better be said at once.

(1) I enclose a poem, hitherto unpublished, which I think will furnish a good subject for the frontispiece. I think it better that it should illustrate a *new* poem, and I propose to end the volume with this ("Fame's Penny Trumpet") as being the only thing in the volume that has anything like a *serious* purpose in it. I propose that the frontispiece should have under it, as motto, the lines

"And oil each other's little heads
With mutual Flattery's golden slime,"

and that it should represent a *conversazione* of conceited young *soi-disant* Philosophers, complimenting and being complimented. I have too much reverence for *real* Science to wish to make any fun of its votaries: but there is a class of upstarts who, without brains of their own, trade on extracts from the brains of wiser men, and who think it the height of cleverness to throw doubts on truths held by their forefathers—specially religious truths—they themselves probably never having understood the arguments either for them or against them. So, intellectual *weakness* ought to be written in their faces, as well as arrogance and conceit. As a *frontispiece*, of course the picture ought to be full and elaborate: still, it ought not to be a mere *mob*, but should have one or two chief figures, the newest stars of pseudo-Science, with their worshippers round them. And if you light the group from *above*, and give some of them large heads of shiny hair (the *heads* themselves should be small), it would carry out the idea of "oil." Also please put some of the most boyish looking of them into *spectacles*. Of course all would be in evening-dress. I shall be glad if you can make a good frontispiece of this: but if you think you can find a better subject, I shall be quite disposed to defer to your judgement.[1]

(2) If this comic volume has a good sale, I shall be very much disposed to follow it up with the *serious* poems in a companion volume. It would be a very thin book, and would not furnish subjects for more than a dozen pictures (or 20 at the outside). How would you like to try your hand at *serious* pictures? If you feel it would be working "against the grain" I will not press the matter: but if you feel at all up to it, it would give you an opportunity for showing versatility of talent in Art. No form of Beauty would be out of place, Beauty of face, Beauty of form (I fear they would have to be *draped* forms only, though), and, if you can do it, Beauty of scenery. What do you think of the idea? Next year would be time enough for it.[2]

(3) I have a grand scheme in my head, that I want you to hold yourself engaged for, as you are *the* man, of all the artists I know of (now that Tenniel is past hoping for) whose help I should wish to have. It is to write another child's book. I have a good deal of material for it already, and I think I can manage *one* more without repeating myself and making people say "It is only a repetition of *Alice*." The pictures would require the same *sort* of skill that Tenniel showed in *Alice*, and would include beautiful children and comic monsters. I feel sure you would illustrate it superbly, and I think it would be more worthy of your skill than this volume of poems, of which I have a very low opinion. I think fairy-tale is more in my line of work than poetry.[3] Dalziel has all your pictures in his hands now: he seems very much pleased with them, but I have seen no results.

Sincerely yours,
C. L. Dodgson

1. "Fame's Penny Trumpet" was rejected by the *Pall Mall Gazette, Punch*, and the *World*, and Dodgson had it privately printed in 1876 (*Diaries*, p. 355). The poem is an attack on young scholars who use research as a means of seeking fame and making money. It is the concluding item in *Rhyme? and Reason?*, but Frost's illustration, which follows closely the ideas Dodgson put forth, did not become the frontispiece; it appears instead at p. 213 with a different caption: "Go, throng each other's drawing-rooms."

2. On the same day Dodgson wrote, "Took the critical step of writing to A. B. Frost to propose illustrating the *serious* poems in *Phantasmagoria*, and to engage him as illustrator for a fairy-tale for 1882" (*Diaries*, p. 396). The serious poems appeared posthumously in February 1898, but Frost did not illustrate them.

3. The "fairy-tale" was probably to become *Sylvie and Bruno*.

Facsimile MS: *Rosenbach*

Christ Church, Oxford
May 1, 1881

Dear Mr. Frost,

I enclose the prints of your drawings for "The Three Voices" (except the vignette of a face, which is not yet cut), and will be much obliged if you will kindly mark on them which of the outlines we may *thin*, and let me have them again. I am glad to find that they have not yet been electrotyped. I think I told you before that I shall not use the little vignette of the man lying on his face, with the ghostly umbrella hovering above, which I thought too like a ballet-dancer. The large picture of the same attitude will do perfectly well to end with.

I don't quite like the plan of your doing *finished* pen-and-ink drawings for the other poems, before we have come to *any* agreement as to the style of treatment. And I feel specially nervous about "Hiawatha," as to which I am still quite uncertain whether the figures should be North American Indians, or English. I really think it would be a safer plan if you were to let me have rough sketches (mere outlines, not nearly so finished as those you sent for the ghost-poem) to see before you go to the trouble of making elaborate drawings. It would be so very vexatious to have to reject an entire set of pictures, owing to your conception of a poem being wholly different from mine.

If *sketches* would be too troublesome to do, *descriptions* of the way you propose to treat a poem, the dresses you design to introduce, etc., etc., would do almost as well, and would avoid the risk of an *entire* difference of views.

One chief point I wish to secure is that *none* of the pictures shall represent commonplace, everyday life, but that all shall have something out-of-the-way in dress and treatment.

Sincerely yours,
C. L. Dodgson

MS: Berol

1338 Chestnut Street,
Philadelphia
May 5, 1881[1]

Dear Mr. Dodgson,

I am very glad indeed that you are so well satisfied with the ghost drawings and appreciate your kind letter thoroughly. I had certainly not looked for so very little alteration in them and am delighted that you like the ones *I* do. I agree with you that the warming-pan man *is* a savage looking individual and I will draw him again as you suggest. He will come very well in a dressing gown; and I can put a lounge in in place of the bed as though he had been taking a nap.

I have not yet done the little tail-piece for "Melancholetta" because I have had to hurry some work for Harper Brothers and have not had a girl sitting for me since I sent your drawings but I know there is no rush for it and will get a lady friend who visits my studio sometimes to sit when she comes in.

I received the money on Saturday last and am very much obliged indeed for your kindness in send[ing] the other in advance. I am still in your debt.

The money was here nearly a week before I received it, but it was my fault. Messrs. Morris, Walrond & Co. sent twice to my studio but I was away and then they wrote me to call. I know the young men in the firm very well.

As soon as I hear from you in relation to the remaining poems I will go right on with them and can soon finish them.

I am going to start a very nice piece of work this month. A hundred illustrations for the *Reveries of a Bachelor*, by Ike Marvel.[2] It is full of nice bits for serious illustration and character and I will enjoy doing it I know.

I can not tell you how glad I feel that you are pleased with my illustrations for your book. I can honestly say I never tried as hard in my life as I have on this book and I feel well repaid by your kind letter. I feel sure that the book will add more to my reputation than anything I have done yet.

I wish I saw any prospect of seeing you soon but I'm afraid it will be a long time before I will be in England again. I would not dare to go into so damp a climate till my lungs are all right again. I feel perfectly well and strong again now but am very susceptible to colds.

I will write again soon and enclose a business-like receipt for the money. Again thanking you for your letter I am

Yours very sincerely,
Arthur Burdett Frost

1. This letter clearly replies to Dodgson's dated April 5, 1881. Letters took about a month to cross the Atlantic.

2. Ike Marvel, pseudonym of Donald Grant Mitchell (1822–1908), first published *Reveries of a Bachelor* in 1850. The book was frequently reprinted.

Facsimile MS: Rosenbach

Christ Church, Oxford
May 5, 1881

Dear Mr. Frost,

Your delightful packet of drawings arrived yesterday. I read the letter first, and was much alarmed for the result. That you should have finished all the pictures without any further consultation as to treatment seemed to me to involve *great* risk that I should have to reject many. As to "Hiawatha" in particular, I felt a sad presentiment that I should have to send you back the whole set! It has been a most pleasant surprise to find that I can not only accept all (with the exception of the 2 enclosed) but that I am really charmed with them as a whole, and most of all with the "Hiawatha" ones.

Your *great* success this time is, I think, the "Stunning Cantab":[1] and it is worth all the fatigue you have inflicted on your unfortunate model to have produced so perfect a picture. An artistic friend, to whom I showed the pictures, gives the palm to the sulky boy.[2] I don't think there is much to choose between them: both are first-rate.

Now as to the two I am sending back for alteration:

"The wild man" does not seem to me to have enough interest in it for a full-page—his whole face I think should be shown. Also that *eye,* with all the effort I can make to realise it as *his,* does not seem to me to belong to him. The pump is excellent, and the man would do very well, if you could stick a bit of paper over his head and shoulders and draw them again so as to give a better view of his face. Once more I venture to enclose one of my own hopeless scrawls, to give you a notion of what the words suggest to *me.* I doubt if your man suggests the idea, at all forcibly, of "weary."[3]

The precocious infant on the old man's knee (the old man himself is capital) is to my mind too suggestive of water on the brain to be comic. The man being of normal proportions makes the child look a sort of monster. I confess I should like that head reduced. Give him a wise old face if you like, but *not* a head so suggestive of disease.[4]

As to the various points raised in your letter:

(1) "Atalanta in Camden-Town" I'm afraid has rather a vulgar tone— still I hope you will keep clear of commonplace "gents" and their "young women." Why should they not be in classical costume? But there is little use

in suggesting this, as I suppose you will have drawn it long before this reaches you.[5]

(2) As to "A Game of Fives," I think your idea excellent, to draw a head-piece for the first verse, and a tail-piece for the last, and a full-page picture for the vain effort to hook young men.[6]

I cannot easily say how heartily I appreciate the great trouble you have taken with this book, and the glorious pictures you have made for it. I sincerely hope it may have sale enough to make your talent more known to the world than it has yet been. If I ever get another fairy-tale finished, that will, I hope, be a real help to your reputation, as both book and pictures will be new, and it will have a much larger sale than this reprint has any chance of.

Our account is very near a balance again, I suppose. I will have another £50 paid to your credit.

I have got through the winter all right, thank you, and I am very glad to hear you can give such a cheerful report of your health.

Always sincerely yours,
C. L. Dodgson

1. *Rhyme? and Reason?*, p. 71.
2. Ibid., p. 75.
3. Ibid., p. 127, "Poeta Fit, Non Nascitur." Dodgson's drawing is missing, but Frost apparently adopted his suggestions.
4. Ibid., p. 123, "Poeta Fit, Non Nascitur."
5. Frost's eventual drawing is by no means "vulgar and commonplace"; see ibid., p. 187.
6. The headpiece and full-page illustrations appear, but the tailpiece did not make it to the book; see ibid., pp. 120 and 121.

Facsimile MS: *Rosenbach*

Christ Church, Oxford
May 20, 1882

Dear Mr. Frost,

Many thanks for your letter dated May 2. Most of it will best be answered when the pictures have come, but there is one sentence I must notice at once, as I have evidently given you (though quite unintentionally) offence: and I cannot allow this to happen with any friend—and specially one who has done me such signal service as *you* have—without doing my best to set the matter right. The sentence I refer to is this: "possibly it might be as well to wait till I had offered illness as an excuse before you doubt its genuineness."

It is clear to me that you think I meant to imply that you either *had* made, or were likely to make, dishonest excuses for delay in work, by pleading illness when you were well. Let me say, as plainly as possible, that such an idea had never even crossed my mind. Your previous letters, relating particulars of illness, I received, and do receive, without a shadow of a doubt. Nor have I the faintest suspicion that you would ever plead illness as an excuse, without full cause for doing so. All I *meant* to say was "I am glad to know you are well."

Your sentence, *literally* interpreted, would say that my belief in your good health would have been *less* offensive, if I had expressed it *after* receiving your plea of being ill. Of course, it would really be *more* offensive. But I quite see your meaning, viz., "I have not pleaded illness: why then charge me with making false excuses?"

I earnestly hope this explanation will remove all the offence I have unfortunately given.[1]

Sincerely yours,
C. L. Dodgson

1. Evidently some correspondence between Dodgson and Frost is missing.

Facsimile MS: Rosenbach

Christ Church, Oxford
June 27, 1882

Dear Mr. Frost,

The 11 drawings, with the 2 superseded ones, have just arrived, and I need not say how indebted to you I feel for all the great pains you have taken with them. As a whole, I think they are admirable: and the 3 altered ones (Tibbs and ghost, wild man, and "Poeta Fit") are a great improvement.[1]

There is one which I hope you won't mind my not using, the tail-piece to "Atalanta." The figure of a man walking away is hardly interesting enough to be worth having in the book: and it is too much like the tail-piece of

"Hiawatha."[2] I will send you back the drawing if you like. "Atalanta" will do very well with *one* picture.

Also "Fame's Penny Trumpet" does not seem to me to have enough detail in it for a frontispiece: but it will do very well in the poem. For the frontispiece, I think we had better take the most elaborate of the ghost-pictures: and this, in my opinion, is the ghost gliding across the window on a butter-slide.[3]

You say nothing about the pictures that were to be altered on the blocks, by thinning lines, etc. You may have forgotten the matter, it is so long ago. I wrote about them in No. 36516, and again in 36547,[4] with which I sent 12 prints of "The Three Voices," that you might mark the lines to be thinned: and in your letter dated May 23, 1881, you say "I am very glad you sent the proofs, for there are a good many places that will stand correction very well, and I will be very glad to avail myself of the chance of having it done. I will send them all marked up in a few days." I hope this does not mean that I have missed a letter of yours altogether. If so, I had better send you another set of proofs.

Sincerely hoping that your health is now restored, I am

Very sincerely yours,
C. L. Dodgson

1. *Rhyme? and Reason?*, pp. 55, 127, and 123.

2. Ibid., p. 77.

3. Dodgson's proposed frontispiece appears in *Rhyme? and Reason?* at p. 13. Instead, for his frontispiece he chose the ghost "upon a battlement," described in the poem on p. 30.

4. Dodgson kept a register of letters received and sent from January 1861 (see *Letters*, pp. 1162–63), each item numbered. The letter numbered 36516 has not come to light. Letter 36547 is the one dated May 1, 1881.

MS: *Rosenbach*
Christ Church, Oxford

April 20, 1883

Dear Mr. Frost,

I write once more, "hoping against hope," to ask if you will ever send me any picture for "A Game of Fives." All the other pictures are now cut and electrotyped, and we are fast getting the book arranged in pages. It is nearly 10 months since you said you would send it by the next mail. If you cannot do it, kindly let me know as soon as you can, as I think in that case I shall

FIG. 12

Dodgson's sketches for "A Game of Fives" in letter dated April 20, 1883, with Frost's final drawings.

ask another artist to draw it. But I will wait till this day month, before doing so, on the chance of hearing from you. If, when you get this, you have still the picture to draw; the enclosed sketch of my idea of it may be of some use. In the foreground the father is saying "Tell me what you *mean.*" The lower part of the picture should gradually fade into clouds, in which is a vision of the 5 children of the first stanza.[1]

Sincerely yours,
C. L. Dodgson

P.S. The drawing with corrections arrived January 12 (3 months ago) and the corrections have been duly made.[2]

---

1. Work on the book came to a virtual standstill in the summer of 1881, and all of 1882 passed with little progress apart from what is described in Dodgson's letter of June 27, 1882. In April 1883 he tried to find another artist to do a drawing for "A Game of Fives" and other poems, but it seems he did not succeed. "I have now arranged in pages the whole of the volume of poems (which I think of calling *Rhyme? and Reason?*)," Dodgson writes on May 19, 1883 (*Diaries*, p. 416), probably the first time he recorded what would become the title of the new book. Frost eventually supplied pictures for "A Game of Fives" (see *Rhyme? and Reason?*, pp. 120–21); he did not, however, use Dodgson's sketch that accompanied this letter.

2. We do not know which drawing Dodgson refers to.

MS: *Rosenbach*

Christ Church, Oxford
July 31, 1883

Dear Mr. Frost,

At last we seem to be nearing the end of the long correspondence about *Phantasmagoria.* I really think the book will be out in another 2 or 3 weeks, and of course you shall have a presentation copy as soon as I can get one.[1]

First, you will be glad to know that, after all, I have used the head-piece for "A Game of Fives": in my last I told you the children were not pretty enough. My chief objections were to the mouths of the two full-faces, which were heavy and shapeless, and sadly turned down at the corners, and to the right eye (*her* right, the left in the picture) of the one partly hidden by the baby, which was too far from the other, and too high up in the forehead. But, on second thoughts, I ventured on doctoring the drawing a little: I erased the turned-down corners, and made the upper lip of the kneeling child more shapely: and as to the wandering *eye*, I ventured to cover it up altogether and draw it again lower down. I hope you will forgive my having taken such liberties with your drawing.[2]

Now as to the contents of this packet. I return you 4 drawings which I am not using (you will of course charge me whatever you think reasonable for the time and trouble you have given to them), *viz.*, "Tibbs with warming-pan," the first "Wild man," the tail-piece for "Atalanta" (too much like the one in "Hiawatha"), and the tail-piece for "A Game of Fives," which seems to me too sad and dreary for a comic poem.

I also enclose 2 extra proofs received from Dalziel: *viz.*, the head-piece, and large cut, for "A Game of Fives." I have no idea what other proofs you have had. If you like, I will tell Dalziel to send you a complete set, rubbed off, as these two are, from the wood-blocks, *not* the electrotypes.

Next, as to the £. *s. d.*, which we may as well wind up, now that all is done. There are 65 pictures to pay for altogether (besides the 4 not used), *viz.*, 30 full-page pictures:

(1) Ghost on battlement (frontispiece)
(2) Ditto in cavern
(3) Ditto gliding across window
(4) Ditto drinking Port
(5) Ditto Nightmare
(6) Ditto arguing with hot man
(7) Ditto kneeling before Tibbs
(8) Scene on beach
(9) Carpet-Knight
(10) Father being photographed
(11) Son   ditto
(12) Daughter   ditto
(13) Boy   ditto
(14) Melancholetta and brother
(15) Three Voices, "she" pins down hat
(16) Ditto "he" stands behind hat
(17) Ditto both walking towards spectator
(18) Ditto both walking to right
(19) Ditto "he" has his hand on forehead
(20) Ditto "he" sits and watches tide

(21) Ditto "he" crouches, full-face
(22) Three Voices, "he" sits and hangs head down
(23) Ditto "he" lies face-down
(24) Game of Fives
(25) Wild man and pump
(26) Fat and thin man, and young lady
(27) Lang Coortin', bird laughing
(28) Ditto bird angry
(29) Ditto dog following boy
(30) Fame's Penny-Trumpet.

4 portions of full-page pictures:

(1) Ghost waking sleeper ⌐
(2) Three little ghosteses ⌐
(3) Ghosts coming down stairs ⎵
(4) Man climbing mountain ⌐.

And 31 head- and tail-pieces:

(1) Ghost's first appearance
(2) Ditto holding plate for gravy
(3) Ditto beating man with plate
(4) Ditto with glass of beer
(5) Ditto skeleton in sky
(6) Ditto trying on robes
(7) Ditto boring holes in wainscot
(8) Ditto Mayor running
(9) Ditto full-face, lamp behind head
(10) Ditto walking in rain
(11) Ditto having knuckles rapped
(12) Man seated at table
(13) Ghost's farewell
(14) Children on beach
(15) Man slipping into pool
(16) Hiawatha behind camera
(17) Ditto going away (I have ventured to erase the porter and barrow)
(18) Melancholetta and skull
(19) Three Voices, hat flying off

(20) Ditto head of man
(21) Ditto both walking away
(22) Ditto "he" seated, legs straight
(23) Ditto "he" ditto weeping
(24) Five little girls
(25) Old man, with boy on his knee
(26) Ditto head only, smoking
(27) Fat man on beach, thin man distant
(28) Ditto   ditto   ditto   near
(29) Atalanta
(30) Popinjay
(31) Lover going away.

Your rule for charging for these various sizes I have not succeeded in making out. I have 3 "accounts" from you. In the first you charge 50 guineas for "nine full-page and six small." In the second, you charge £45 for "nine full-page drawings," and £20 for "10 head and tail-pieces" (the rule here seems clear enough, only it is inconsistent with the first paper). In the third, you charge £78 for "24 drawings" (sizes not specified).

I think the simplest plan would be for you to make out a new account for the whole thing now you have the facts before you.

As to what I have already paid you: your first paper says "received on account £10.10.0: but *my* record of it is only "£10," so I had rather assume that to be right.

I have paid as follows:

May 1878— £10
Feb. 1879— £42
Ap. 1880— £50
Mar. 1881—£100
May 1881— £50
Total—   £252

So now you have all the data for making out a complete account.

You may be sure I read with much sympathy the history of all your domestic troubles and anxieties: when next you write, I trust you will be able to send a good report of them, as well as of your own health.

I have not forgotten that I promised you, years ago, some more of my photographs of children: and I have somewhere the list of those you said you would like to have. But it is one of those matters that constantly get postponed to more pressing business, and I still have to make out which of them the respective parents will allow me to give away, and then (perhaps) to look out the negatives and get the prints done. I trust to do it all *some* day.

I expect you will have to return *me* some money, instead of my having to pay more to *you*. In that case, would you kindly get your banker to pay it to my credit with Messrs. Parsons, Old Bank, Oxford. Their London bankers are Coutts and Co., 57 Strand, London. Believe me

> Very truly yours,
> C. L. Dodgson

1. "*Rhyme? and Reason?* is about off my hands," Dodgson wrote on July 13 (*Diaries*, p. 418), and on October 18, "Sent off last sheet of *Rhyme? and Reason?* marked 'Press,'" and then added, "Ordered first picture on February 7, 1878, more than five and a half years ago" (ibid., p. 420). It took almost another full year for Frost's presentation copy to be sent.

2. Dodgson's altered illustration for the headpiece in "A Game of Fives" appears on p. 120 in *Rhyme? and Reason?*

Facsimile MS: *Rosenbach*

> Christ Church, Oxford
> October 26, 1883

Dear Mr. Frost,

At the risk of crossing a letter from you, I sit down to answer your two letters dated August 3, and—I find the other is *not* dated, but I received it on October 12. I will take topics as I find them named in your letters.

First, I lament the difficulty you complain of in getting child-models, and that you can not draw them without. For I should *much* like you to illustrate a fairy-tale for me: but a pretty child would be *essential*. Won't advertising and liberal pay produce a model?[1]

Next, let me congratulate you on the marriage which when you wrote was yet to come, but has I trust now taken place with all accompaniments that could add to the happiness of your bride and yourself. And I am *very* glad to hear of your improved circumstances, and the many things that have occurred to brighten life for you.[2]

It is indeed joyful news for me that you find your powers of caricature returned, and that you would like to illustrate another book for me. You shall begin as soon as ever you like: I can send you plenty of material. As to the main current of the story, *that* includes the pretty child, and it *may* be necessary to entrust it to another artist. But there is no sort of reason why you should not illustrate all the *incidental* poems, which (like "The Walrus and the Carpenter") contain none of the characters of the story. To have the book illustrated by two artists in that way will only give variety, and do it no harm at all.

Thank you very much for the promise of a copy of the book of caricatures you are now engaged on.[3] If you like to undertake the *incidental* poems in the book I have on hand (leaving the question, as to who is to illustrate the story itself, for future settlement), please let me know when you will be ready to begin, and I will copy for you a long poem, which will require 4 or 5 full-page pictures of the size of *Alice*, and which will I hope give plenty of scope for your talent in comic drawing. In that case you may as well *not* remit me the balance due on the last transaction, but let it run on into our new account.[4]

Hoping to hear very soon that you are settled, and happy, and at leisure for caricatury, I remain

Always most sincerely yours,
C. L. Dodgson

P.S. My book will be out about the middle of November.[5]

1. Dodgson had had Frost in mind as the illustrator for his new book *Sylvie and Bruno* as far back as November 1881 (see *Diaries*, pp. 401–2).

2. Frost married Emily Louise Phillips, a part-time staff member at Harper's, on October 19, 1883.

3. Frost was working on a book of comic caricatures with a Carrollian title, *Stuff and Nonsense*, published by Charles Scribner's Sons in 1884.

4. Dodgson had some doubt about Frost's ability to draw pretty pictures of children; his experience with the headpiece to "A Game of Fives" probably added to his concern. Clearly, he needed an artist who could draw "Sylvie," the heroine of his new book, to his exacting specifications. He could have had in mind here one of the humorous poems from *Sylvie and Bruno*, probably "Peter and Paul."

5. *Rhyme? and Reason?* was published in December 1883, and on the sixth of that month Dodgson was able to send off presentation copies to friends.

Christ Church, Oxford
June 16, 1884

Dear Mr. Frost,

Your welcome letter reached me on the 9th of June. Before I answer it, let me remind you of my request, made July 31, 1883, that you would make out a new account for the pictures, for which purpose I sent all necessary details. I want to know exactly how we stand, though there is no need for you to *pay* anything: it can go to my credit in our next account.

I am very glad indeed to know that you will be able to begin work for me after August 1: before which date I hope to send you one or two of the incidental poems, which can be illustrated quite independently of the story, and as grotesquely as you like. The story itself I will get to work at as soon as I can: there is a lot of material ready, but it needs arranging: and it may easily happen that I may not be able to keep you fully and continuously supplied; so that I am very glad to know you have other commissions you can at any time take up.

As to the "children" difficulty: I only want *two* for this book, a girl of 12, and a boy of 6. They ought to be pretty, certainly, and *not* so ancient-looking as (for instance) the crying children at p. 59.[1] Could you choose a suitable nephew and niece, and send me a little study of each, and I would tell you if they suited my ideas. If all fails, there is still the possibility of leaving blanks for the children, and I would get Miss E. G. Thomson (who draws lovely children) to put them in. While on the subject, I hope you won't mind my criticising the lady-likeness of the young lady at p. 183.[2] She looks a little too much like a barmaid. Should any lady occur in the story, I should desire a little more refinement. Du Maurier's ladies, in *Punch*, will give an idea of my meaning, though of course I don't want you to imitate any other artist.

I sent off a presentation-copy of *Rhyme? and Reason?* for you, by book-post, on June the 11th.[3] I *hope* it may reach you safely, but I fear there are many risks of robbery on the way, and there have been many complaints lately of things disappearing when sent by post to other parts of the world. The book on *Folk-Lore*, which you said you would send, has not yet appeared.[4]

It will give me great pleasure to make the acquaintance of Mrs. Frost when you bring her over the water. Believe me

Very sincerely yours,
C. L. Dodgson

1. The "girl of 12" was to be the model for Sylvie, and "the boy of 6," Bruno. The aged "crying children" illustrate "A Sea Dirge" in *Rhyme? and Reason?*, p. 59.
2. Dodgson is criticizing the illustration for "Size and Tears."
3. We do not understand why it took Dodgson so long to send Frost a presentation copy of *Rhyme? and Reason?*
4. Probably *Folk-Lore* by Michael Aislabie Denham, published in 1858.

Facsimile MS: Rosenbach

7 Lushington Road, Eastbourne
July 17, 1884

Dear Mr. Frost,

My address will be as above till the end of September.[1]

I am beginning to fear that books have small chance of finding their way safely from you to me, or from me to you: the copy of *Folk-Lore* which you told me (in a letter received June 9) you were sending me, has never arrived; and I have heard nothing yet of the arrival of *Rhyme? and Reason?*, which I sent you June 11.

I have been writing, in the *Monthly Packet*, a story which I want to reprint, with a full-page picture (*Alice* size) to each chapter. There will be 10 chapters, of which 9 are already in print. I send you reprints of 3, to see if you would like to undertake it. (The old lady in Chapter 2 is sister to the old gentleman in Chapter 1).[2]

Sincerely yours,
C. L. Dodgson

1. Eastbourne, from 1877 until his death, was Dodgson's summer residence by the sea. He lodged with Mr. and Mrs. Benjamin Dyer. Mr. Dyer worked for the local post office. Dodgson's accommodation consisted of a first-floor sitting room with a balcony and an adjoining bedroom. He was able to entertain visitors, but he devoted much of his time at Eastbourne to his many literary projects.
2. Dodgson's contributions to the *Monthly Packet*, which began in April 1880 and continued

through to May 1885, became *A Tangled Tale*. The ten chapters, or knots (stories built around mathematical problems to be unraveled by the reader), were to have illustrations drawn by Frost to accompany them. Frost drew the ten, but Dodgson used only six. Lot 245 in the sale of Dodgson's personal effects in May 1898 is described as "original unused drawings in pen and ink for *A Tangled Tale*, by Frost." The *Monthly Packet*, edited by Charlotte Mary Yonge (1823–1901), was a magazine for young ladies. The first three reprinted "knots" that Dodgson sent Frost were titled "Excelsior," "Mad Mathesis," and "The Dead Reckoning"; they appeared in the April, July, and October 1880 numbers of the *Monthly Packet* and became Knots I, III, and IV of *A Tangled Tale*. Although each chapter contains an independent story, Dodgson created a family tree for the characters, thus linking the ten.

Facsimile MS: *Rosenbach*

Christ Church, Oxford
August 5, 1884

Dear Mr. Frost,

I received your letter, dated July 8, on the 21st, 4 days after my letter, enclosing 3 chapters of *A Tangled Tale*, had gone.

I am very glad *Rhyme? and Reason?* reached you safely. It encourages me to enclose 5 more chapters of the story I want you to illustrate. While I think of it, let me mention the *ages* I meant the young people to be, Norman, 20; Clara, 18; Lambert, 16; Hugh, 14. Anything near these ages would do very well. Please tell me if you think any Knot has matter enough for *two* pictures, one of which we might use as a frontispiece.

As to our account: I am quite willing to agree to pay 229 guineas, i.e. £240.9s. for the 65 pictures in *Rhyme? and Reason?*. The money actually paid is £252. So that leaves you exactly £11.11s. in my debt. This can run on into the next account.

I shall be quite content to pay, for the *Tangled Tale*, and for the new book, six guineas for a full page or broken page, and three guineas for a small picture.[1]

It is of course very welcome news that you think you can do even better than in the last book, with which I am very much pleased ("which" refers to "book"): and I am specially glad you think you can improve on the *women*. Certainly *Clara* (in this *Tangled Tale*) ought to be as *ladylike* as you can make her.

As to children (I am taking the subjects of your letter in the order in which they come) I had best wait to see, what I hope you will send me soon, some studies of your nephews and nieces. As I said in a former letter, I shall want pictures of a girl of 12 and a boy of 6. To this I may now add that through part of the book they will have to be dressed as in ordinary life: but they go through a phase of fairy-life, for which I suppose they ought to have the conventional semi-transparent dress, and wings. But for neither purpose would you need (what you tell me is so hard to find in America) child-models who would sit for nude studies. We shall not need such extreme accuracy in anatomical drawing as such studies would imply.

Many thanks for the photo, which gives me a very definite idea of your *house*, but scarcely so definite of your good lady.

August 15. I am glad to have been so long delayed in finishing this letter, that it has given time for another letter to arrive from you, so that I can answer both at once. *Folk-Lore* has also arrived safely: many thanks for it. You are probably quite right as to the *Tangled Tale* not suggesting *funny* pictures: and I don't the least want you to *strain* after comic effect: serious pictures will do very well. I will however just jot down the sort of illustrations that the chapters suggest to *me*; and you can use the ideas, or not, as you please.

Knot I. Travellers descending a nearly perpendicular mountain. (I enclose a rough sketch.) The old man looking much exhausted.[2]

Knot II. "I never smoke cigars." Clara earnestly explaining, with one hand on the boy's shoulder. Boy open-mouthed with astonishment. Old Lady inspecting him with eye-glass, rather scandalised at Clara's friendly behaviour.[3]

Knot III. "These are My passengers." Captain drawn up to full height: chin in air: the embodiment of conceit. Wild savages behind, executing war-dance.[4]

Knot IV. "The sisters exchanged looks of alarm." They should be *very* fat (see p. 30), and much terrified.[5]

Knot V. "Balbus was assisting his mother-in-law to convince the dragon." Surely *this* might be comically treated? The mother-in-law seated, with a reading-lamp, referring to law-books: Balbus fetching more books: both with eyes fixed on the unconvinced dragon.[6]

Knot VI. "Just look at the peacocks!" The travellers should be approaching you, full-face; peacocks on each side: the old man the picture of misery.[7]

Knot VII. "I tell you the cab-door isn't half wide enough!"[8]

These are merely suggested subjects. I shall be quite content if you reject them, and choose other passages to illustrate.

I had forgotten two Knots.

Knot VIII. "I must think it over again." Balbus (with *very* long legs) asleep on sofa.[9]

Knot IX. Commander-in-chief, with pig under each arm.[10]

Believe me to be

Yours very sincerely,
C. L. Dodgson

1. "Heard from Mr. Frost that last letter was a mistake," Dodgson recorded on September 8, 1884; "he abides by prices of six guineas for a large, and three guineas for a small picture" (*Diaries*, p. 428).

2. This drawing became the frontispiece for *A Tangled Tale*. Dodgson's sketch is missing.

3. This drawing, intended for Knot III, "Mad Mathesis," does not appear in the book. The quotation is from *A Tangled Tale*, p. 16.

4. Ibid., p. 24, "A Dead Reckoning," Knot IV. Frost used all of Dodgson's ideas here.

5. This drawing, intended for Knot V, "Oughts and Crosses," does not appear in the book. The quotation is from p. 32, which must have been p. 30 in the version Dodgson sent to Frost.

6. Knot V became Knot II in *A Tangled Tale*. The illustration appears at p. 5; again Frost used Dodgson's suggestions.

7. Ibid., p. 35, Knot VI, "Her Radiancy." Dodgson changed the caption to "Why do they say 'Bamboo!' so often?"; it appears on p. 34. The quotation Dodgson sends Frost appears on p. 36.

8. Ibid., p. 46, Knot VII, "Petty Cash."

9. The passage that Dodgson quotes here ended up in Knot IX. Frost chose to illustrate another passage instead, "He remains steadfast and unmoved," which appears on p. 65 of the book.

10. Dodgson intended this illustration for "De Omnibus Rebus," which became Knot VIII. The passage he quotes appears on p. 53 of the book, but, alas, he does not use an illustration for it.

MS: *Dodgson Family*

Huntington, Long Island, N.Y.
November 13, 1884

My dear Mr. Dodgson,

I send you with this a copy of the little book I wrote to you about last Summer: it is as you see nothing but the mildest nonsense and makes no pretensions to being anything else. The form of verse is not new, having been in use here for a long time. I hope you will like the Kangaroo and the man killing the moth. They are my favorites.[1]

The red back to the book is *not* my own. I utterly disclaim any share in it and will have it replaced by something harmonious in the next edition.

There are several bad errors in printing too, as the figure of the man seated on the floor, in the Power of the Human Eye: he should be flat, not running up hill.

I am again behind time with your drawings. I had seven out of the ten *done*, finished, when my eyes gave out and I had to drop pen work for a while. I had been doing too much of it during the Summer on my own book, and other work, and my eyes have felt badly for some time. I am glad I did not send you what I had done. I was not satisfied with them and will redraw four out of the seven. I find I can get a good deal of fun out of them. I feel sure you will like the Commander-in-chief with the pigs[2] and the men running down the steep hill.[3]

I am working on them again for a part of a day at a time and painting the rest of the time. I will send them before this month is out, with the rejected ones, maybe.

Will you kindly tell me what you think of my first effort in book-making: frankly, you know. I would value your criticism above any one else's.

Yours very sincerely,
Arthur Burdett Frost

1. Frost's book of comic drawings and doggerel verse, *Stuff and Nonsense*, had just been published by Charles Scribner's Sons. Frost's favorite illustrations show a kangaroo escaping from the zoo, leap-frogging over a zookeeper while horrified spectators look on. The moth incident is illustrated in two pictures showing a man striking another around the face in order to kill the moth, accompanied by this verse:

In its zigzag mysterious flight,
A moth is not easy to smite,
This gent thought he could bring
One down on the wing,
But his views were erroneous. Quite.

2. *A Tangled Tale*, intended for Knot VIII, "De Omnibus Rebus," but the illustration does not appear.

3. Ibid., frontispiece.

Christic Church, Oxford

January 21, 1885

Dear Mr. Frost,

Excuse my long silence. I have been waiting for time to write: but none occurs, I am so busy. I have much to say, but it must wait.[1]

August 15. I received *Folk-Lore*.

August 16. I wrote, agreeing to your new terms, and giving ideas of pictures for *A Tangled Tale*; and sending to end of Knot IX.

September 5. I got your letter, to same effect as previous one, except that you asked 7 guineas instead of 6.

September 8. I got another letter, returning to first terms.[2]

November 27. I got your letter about *Stuff and Nonsense*, and saying 3 pictures were done.[3]

Same day. I got the book (many thanks for it).

December 19. I got your letter saying you would send drawings.

December 29. I got the drawings (again many thanks).

I hope to write again very soon.

Sincerely yours always,

C. L. Dodgson

1. On the following day Dodgson wrote, "I have been so busy with Logic that I have not finished above paper [on Proportional Representation], nor even the review of answers to Knot X for *Monthly Packet*" (*Diaries*, p. 431).

2. See August 5, 1884, n. 1.

3. See November 13, 1884.

Christ Church, Oxford
February 24, 1885

Dear Mr. Frost,

My long delay, in writing about your drawings for *A Tangled Tale*, has been partly due to want of time, but chiefly to want of courage to enter on the subject: I fear it is inevitable that much of what I have to say *must* be displeasing to you. Let me beg pardon beforehand for this, and plead the necessity of saying what I have to say, *somehow*, though perhaps I may fail of saying it so inoffensively as it might be said by others.

I had better make the general remark to begin with, and get it over, that I fear I cannot use *any* of them in their present state. In neatness, and finish, and clearness of drawings, these seem to me to fall as far short of the average of what you drew on paper for the former book, as those in their turn fell short of what you drew on wood. To make my meaning clear, I had better begin by asking you to put before you either *Alice* or the *Looking-Glass*, and to examine the details of any one of the pictures with a magnifying-glass: and then to do the same thing with one of the best that you drew for me on wood (say the one at p. 42).[1] You will then understand what I mean (whether you agree with it or not) when I say that yours is a little, but not very far, behind Tenniel in delicate finish. He seems to me to use much fewer lines than you, but to produce a neater result. Next I would ask you to compare your drawing on wood at p. 42 with your drawing on paper at (say) p. 73, which seems to me to be another step downwards.[2] And lastly, if you will compare this again with the new drawing (say the one for Knot VI) you will see what seems to me the longest step down of all.[3] In the face of the man in the turban, for instance, there is hardly any detail made out at all. It seems to me that pen and ink drawing cannot possibly be equal to such work as Tenniel's: the ink lines run into each other, and the roughness of the paper makes it impossible to get such clear true lines as can be drawn with a pencil on wood.

I will now take the drawings one by one.

Knot I (The tourists coming down the mountain).[4] This seems clever and comic, except in one detail, *viz.*, that they are going *off* the mountain into space, which I think destroys the fun. I would not mind a very absurd degree

Frost's final drawing for A Tangled
Tale, *Knot I.*

of steepness, so long as they were really on the mountain-side: but the idea
of falling 1000 feet and being dashed to pieces is the reverse of funny. Then
the outstretched hand, a very prominent object, is surely needlessly out of
drawing? The faces are good, I think: why are they totally changed in subsequent pictures (e.g. in Knot VI)?

Knot II (Clara and ragged boy).[5] This is quite the best of Clara: but I
fear we must give up the idea of having her in any picture. She is a fairly
pretty woman of 25 or so, with abnormally long legs, and more stiff than
graceful: she is *not* like an English girl of 15. The aunt has similar long legs,
but too ugly and unpleasant altogether. The boy has no resemblance to a
London Arab, who is usually very bright and knowing: this boy is an idiot,
apparently.

Knot III. (On board).[6] The captain is (with the exception of his right
hand, which is destitute of fingers, and his right foot, which is *not* a foot)
very good indeed in general effect, and *would* be excellent if drawn on wood
in pencil: as it is, it won't bear minute examination, as all Tenniel's will: it
is full of blots, almost as if drawn on blotting-paper. The sailors' faces
are very poor, and their legs are too long. (Long legs seem to be quite a

distinguishing feature of this set of pictures.) The savages are hideous, but also fairly comic, and might do, all but the inverted one, whose neck is double the right length.

Knot IV. (Picture Gallery).[7] Perhaps the less said the better. I fear I could not consent to have Clara represented as a *very* tall and stiff woman of over 30, and evidently in a towering passion: her left arm alone, in its utter rigidity, would be fatal. I don't know what American girls may be like, but we have nothing the least like this in England. The two old ladies are unnecessarily ugly, also. But I think (as I said before) that we must give up the idea of having Clara at all.

Knot V. (Dragon).[8] The expression of the dragon's face is excellent. But his arms and legs are beyond my comprehension. He has got a good *left* arm, and a right arm about 2/3 the right length. Then he has what looks like a *right* hind-leg, clothed in scaly knicker bockers: but as these seem to develop into *another* leg, I suppose the one planted on the ground is meant for a *left* leg: but the anatomy is quite incomprehensible. The mother-in-law is a good deal too hideous. I think it *is* possible to have such an excess of ugliness as to destroy the comic element. Also I think there are too many books. Exaggeration, beyond a certain limit, ceases to be comic.

Knot VI. (Peacocks, etc.).[9] The face under the turban is fatal to this picture, being a mere collection of blots, only effective at a great distance from the eye. Also his feet are impossible in their length and shape. (So also is the elder traveller's right foot.) The general idea of the picture I like: but none of the details (e.g. the feathers in a peacock's tail are *not* parallel, as here drawn: they radiate from a centre).

Knot VII. (Railway-station).[10] Clara is *awful*: the old ladies are better, but too ugly, and too drunk. The cab-driver is good, I think.

Knot VIII. (Philosopher wading).[11] This is clever, and would do well if drawn on wood. As it is, it is too blotty.

Knot VIII. (Balbus on sofa).[12] I must simply reject this *in toto*. It is not only ugly and ungraceful, but it offends against good taste. No gentleman would place himself so as to present such a view of himself to any spectator: and, that being so, it is not suitable for a picture.

Knot IX. (Commander and pigs).[13] The figure of the Commander is good: but his head and neck spoil him. The face is *meant*, I suppose, to be in profile: but the moustache prevents this being seen, and the effect is of a nearly *full* face, one round white eye near the ear-ring, a mouth almost under the chin, and a crooked nose! The black pig is in too painful a position: there is no fun in witnessing pain. The travellers surely need not have such short hair? They look like convicts. The general effect is good.

Now to consider what can be done with all these pictures, which have cost you, I am sure, a great deal of trouble. In the first place, whether any of them are used, or not, *you* must be duly compensated. That is essential. But, unless you are willing to draw on wood again, I fear the only plan will be to return all the drawings and pay you whatever we may settle as reasonable.

If, however, you *are* willing to repeat a few on wood, using much fewer lines, but *drawing* always exactly what the engraver is to *cut* (not leaving him to invent lines for himself), then I think we may utilise several of the drawings.

FIG. 14

Frost's preliminary drawing for "The Dead Reckoning" (Knot IV, formerly Knot III) in A Tangled Tale. *By permission of the Houghton Library, Harvard University, bMS Eng 718.9(2).*

Knot I, omitting distant valley and continuing the mountain-side: and drawing hand more anatomically.

Knot III, made into an upright picture by omitting sailors, and cutting off most of umbrella, and bringing savages a little nearer.

Knot V, modified as suggested.

Knot VI,   ditto   ditto

Knot VIII (Wader),   ditto

Knot IX,   ditto

These 6 pictures (with perhaps one for Knot X, which I will send you) would be sufficient.[14] In that case I would propose to pay you full price for the 7 accepted ones, and half-price for the 4 rejected ones. If you would rather *not* draw again on wood, I propose to pay half-price for these 10, and to use none of them. But I am quite open to other proposals, if you don't think this a reasonable one.

I hope you will some day forgive me this unwelcome letter.

Yours very sincerely,
C. L. Dodgson

P.S. I think I would rather *not* criticise *Stuff and Nonsense*. The fun turns too exclusively on depicting brutal violence, terror, and physical pain, and even death, none of which are funny to me.

P.P.S. I enclose a leaf of a child's picture-book, which though a mere rough sketch, yet gives a very fair idea what a graceful English girl *does* look like. We must, I fear, abandon idea of illustrating a Fairy-Tale.[15]

---

1. The illustration in *Rhyme? and Reason?* of ghost seated in reverse position on chair, with lamp behind, for "Phantasmagoria."

2. The illustration of "eldest daughter" in "Hiawatha's Photographing."

3. *A Tangled Tale*, Knot VI, p. 35, "Her Radiancy."

4. Ibid., frontispiece. Frost did not comply with Dodgson's suggestions; the tourists remain in mid-air. In fact Frost made no changes and did no further work for Dodgson. Instead, Dodgson used six of Frost's original drawings as best he could.

5. No illustration appears for this chapter, which became Knot III, "Mad Mathesis."

6. *A Tangled Tale*, p. 24. The chapter became Knot IV, "The Dead Reckoning." Dodgson made the changes he wanted to this illustration, probably without Frost's knowledge or agreement.

7. No illustration appears for this chapter, which became Knot V, "Oughts and Crosses."

8. *A Tangled Tale*, p. 6.

9. Ibid., p. 35.

10. Ibid., p. 46. Dodgson apparently eliminated the figure of Clara, probably by enlarging and cropping the original drawing.

11. Ibid., p. 65.

12. This illustration, also intended for Knot IX, "A Serpent with Corners," does not appear.

13. This illustration, intended for Knot VIII, "De Omnibus Rebus," does not appear.

14. The illustration for Knot X did not materialize.

15. We cannot identify the child's picture book. This letter caused a complete breakdown in the working relationship between Dodgson and Frost. On March 29, when listing his literary projects on hand, Dodgson mentions "*A Tangled Tale*, with . . . perhaps illustrations by Mr. Frost" (*Diaries*, pp. 433–34).

Facsimile MS: Rosenbach

Christ Church, Oxford
July 1, 1885

Dear Sir,

(I feel I cannot, in common courtesy, persist in a form of address which *you* have discarded.) I deeply regret (as I said, by anticipation, in my last) that any remarks of mine should displease you: but I think no good would be done by discussing your letter in detail, or by mooting the question whether the change has been (as *you* think) in my views of your style of drawing, or (as *I* think) in the drawing itself.

In one point you have misunderstood my letter. I had *no* intention of haggling about *money*.

Our account stands thus:

I owe you, for 65 drawings *Rhyme? and Reason?* £240.9s., for 10 ditto *A Tangled Tale* £63. To this I add 6s.6d. to cover whatever you prepaid on parcel just received. The total of this is £303.15.6.

You owe me, cash May 1878, £10., Feb 1879, £42., Ap 1880, £50., Mar 1881, £100., May 1881, £50., Feb 1885 parcel (which you begged I would debit to you) 15s.6d. Total £303.15.6.[1]

The difference, £51, I am paying to your credit with Morris, Walrond, and Co.

Truly yours,
C. L. Dodgson

1. Dodgson errs here; the total should be £252.15.6. The difference he agrees to pay to Frost is correct.

Facsimile MS: Rosenbach

Christ Church, Oxford

July 3, 1885[1]

As it appears that Messrs. Morris, Walrond, and Co., of Philadelphia (through whom the previous remittances were made), have retired from business, the £51 will be paid, by Messrs. Coutts, of 59 Strand, London, to your credit with Messrs. Lawrence, Johnson, and Co., also of Philadelphia.

C. L. Dodgson

1. The entry in Dodgson's *Diaries* for this day reads (p. 437): "Wrote to Macmillan, and Swain, about *A Tangled Tale*, which I hope to get out as a Christmas book this year." On July 10 he added, "As Mr. Frost declines to re-draw the pictures for *A Tangled Tale*, I am going to use six of them" (*Diaries*, p. 437). This third-person reply by Dodgson ended a partnership that had lasted at least seven years. As far as we can tell, no further correspondence took place between the two. On November 3, 1885, Dodgson wrote to Macmillan: "I send a copy of *A Tangled Tale*, a little incomplete, but there will be enough to enable you to say what the price ought to be. The blocks have gone to Messrs. Clay to be electrotyped: and I hope to pass the whole for 'Press' very soon" (*Macmillan Letters*, pp. 193–94). *A Tangled Tale* was published in December 1885.

FIG. 15
*Harry Furniss.
Courtesy of the
National Portrait
Gallery, London.*

4. Harry Furniss (1854–1925)

"SENT OFF ... [a letter] to Mr. Harry Furniss, a very clever illustrator in *Punch*, asking if he is open to proposals to draw pictures for me," Dodgson wrote in his diaries on March 1, 1885. Eight days later, he "heard from Mr. Furniss, naming terms, etc., and wrote accepting them, and proposing to send him a poem to begin on. I named Xmas '86 as a *possible* date, and Xmas '87 as a more *probable* date" for completing *Sylvie and Bruno*. "Mr. Furniss has sent me," Dodgson added, "some drawings to see of children and girls, which I think charming."[1]

Thus began what would be for Dodgson a collaboration that passed through stages of cordiality, misunderstanding, disagreement, recriminations, threats, counter-threats, and near-disaster. It was for Dodgson the most difficult collaboration of his career, far more so than the one with Tenniel.

Harry Furniss was a gifted young artist who, in 1880, joined the staff of *Punch*, where Tenniel reigned supreme.[2] But the two worked different furrows, Tenniel producing his full-page political caricatures, Furniss covering Parliament. Furniss had other strings to his bow: his comic streak as cartoonist came to the fore in his writing as well, and he published numerous small volumes, with his own illustrations, some as children's books, others containing social commentary for adults. Later, he also took to the stage as what today would be called a stand-up comedian, performing one-man shows.

Before Dodgson approached Furniss, he had for years been compiling notes, verses, episodes, and at least one full chapter for what he hoped would

1. *Diaries*, p. 432.
2. No major study of Furniss's life and work has appeared. For his own autobiography and other writings, and a magazine article by his daughter that includes material on the artist's relationship with Dodgson, see his *Confessions of a Caricaturist*, 2 vols., 1901, esp. 1:101–12, 2:179–80, and *Some Victorian Men*, 1924, esp. pp. 74–80; Dorothy Furniss, ed., "New Lewis Carroll Letters," *Pearson's Magazine* (December 1930); Alison Opyrchal, *Harry Furniss, 1854–1925: Confessions of a Caricaturist*, 1983.

be a different sort of book from his *Alices*. It was to have much in common with the earlier books, for it dealt with children, fairies, and, in part, realms other than what we know as the real world. And yet it was to be a serious book, full of philosophical, scientific, and religious implications, quite different in that respect from the *Alices*.

But Dodgson had no overall plan for completing the book when he engaged Furniss to supply some occasional pictures; indeed he did not even know what direction the book would take once he assembled the pieces he had on hand and tried to construct an architectural whole. Nor, for two reasons, did he want to share his fragile thoughts with his illustrator. In the main, he preferred to let the story grow and come together slowly, asking the artist involved to draw pictures to suit specific episodes, which in turn sometimes gave him fresh ideas for going on. Furthermore, given Furniss's reputation for casualness and unreliability, Dodgson feared that he would let the cat out of the bag to the press, always eager to get word of what Lewis Carroll was up to.

At the outset, Dodgson wanted Furniss to illustrate the poems he planned to include in the book. Furniss reasonably wanted to know what the overall plot was to be, but Dodgson either could not or would not comply. Even when Dodgson ultimately sent Furniss the manuscript of the story, the artist sometimes did not pay enough attention to make the drawings fit the plot or the description of character or place. Dodgson, for his part, as the letters show, would sometimes go so far as to change the wording of his story to make it conform with the drawings that Furniss had supplied.

Furniss frequently took Dodgson's intention amiss and attributed a hidden agenda to him. In his later recital of Dodgson's misgivings, Furniss concocts an absurd fantasy of a mad Dodgson sitting up by gaslight in the middle of the night intentionally creating difficulties for the artist:

> He was determined no one should read his MS but he and I; so in the dead of night (he sometimes wrote to 4 a.m.) he cut his MS into horizontal strips of four or five lines, then placed the whole of it in a sack and shook it up; taking out piece by piece, he pasted the strips down as they happened to come. The result, in such an MS, dealing with nonsense on one page and theology on another, was audacious in the extreme, if not absolutely profane.
>
> These incongruous strips were elaborately and mysteriously marked with number and letters and various hieroglyphics, to

decipher which would really have turned my assumed eccentricity into positive madness. I therefore sent the whole MS back to him, and again threatened to strike![3]

Furniss's desire to work with Dodgson is understandable. He knew the *Alice* books and must have considered it an honor to be asked to follow in Tenniel's footsteps. And, if one can believe him, he saw the commission as another kind of challenge. In his autobiography Furniss wrote that "Tenniel had point-blank refused to illustrate another story" for Dodgson and said that the don was impossible. He went on to claim that "Tenniel and other artists declared I would not work with Carroll for seven weeks! I accepted the challenge," Furniss wrote.[4] Indeed he lasted not merely for seven weeks but, while frequently resentful or fuming, for seven years.

Furniss as artist is not to be undervalued. The cleverness that Dodgson saw in his work is almost always present. He showed a brash, often extravagant humor and a knack for capturing a close likeness to a figure while exaggerating it mercilessly. He worked rapidly, was "incomparably the quickest of his colleagues—who could produce anything from a thumbnail sketch to a full-page drawing, portraits and all, in an hour or so."[5] His work was "marked by an exuberant and irresponsible ingenuity," and his "boisterous sense of humour compensated to some extent for its lack of design and hurried drawing."[6] His haste imbues the drawings with liveliness, but it also makes for a lack of refinement that another artist, working carefully and subtly, would give to his work. Perhaps it is this hasty, almost slapdash quality of Furniss's work that has kept art historians shy of giving him his due. Surely he deserves a place in the history of journalistic art and a full study and assessment of his contribution to that medium.

One problem of dealing with Furniss may rest in the quality of the man rather than of his art. The great success of his work in *Punch* came from the way he depicted members of Parliament, achieving as he did a "*vie intime* of the House of Commons, not to be found elsewhere."[7] But we learn that to

3. Furniss, *Confessions*, 1:105.
4. Ibid., 1:103.
5. M. H. Spielman, *The History of Punch*, 1895, p. 553.
6. James Thorpe, *English Illustration: The Nineties*, 1975, p. 20.
7. Ibid., p. 551.

obtain his portraits Mr. Furniss would stalk his quarries unawares. . . .
A favourite ruse was for him to tell Mr. A. that he wanted to sketch
Mr. B., and that his work would be greatly facilitated if the hon.
member would keep the other in conversation. Mr. A. would enter
gleefully into the joke, and then Harry Furniss would sketch *Mr. A!* If
need be, he would make his sketch, unseen and unseeing, upon a piece
of cardboard or in a sketch-book, in the side-pocket of his overcoat. In
this way detail, mannerism, gesture, pose—character, in fact, would be
secured, and next week's *Punch* would contain the portrait—sometimes
severe, generally humorous, and always well-observed.[8]

Furniss was evidently hot-tempered, brash, and untruthful. "He was
notoriously argumentative and egotistical," according to one art historian.[9]
Another reports that after having "ascribed words to Tenniel and to Carroll
which neither man would have dreamed of uttering—in 1914, three months
after Tenniel's death, he wrote a four-part series for *Tit Bits* in which he
maligned the other *Punch* artists and could not say enough against Tenniel."[10]
When, in 1894, a disagreement arose between Furniss and the editor of *Punch*,
he threw over the fourteen-year connection, struck out on his own, and started
his own weekly, *Lika Joko*, to compete with *Punch*—but in a few months it
failed.

Once Furniss became acquainted with Dodgson's particular way of working with an artist, he began to seethe, and, as the letters that follow reveal, he
occasionally exploded. Dodgson throughout makes gentlemanly requests, and
although they are excruciatingly frequent and painstakingly finicky, he is always,
in the end, conciliatory. For his part, Furniss stored up all his animosity, and three
years after Dodgson's death—not before—let loose a barrage of exaggerated
complaints and outrageous falsehoods to get even with the Oxford don. But Furniss himself, ever ready to turn a phrase and shock his reader, lets the cat out of
the bag: "To Carroll I was not Hy. F., but someone else, as *he* was someone else.
I was wilful and erratic, bordering on insanity. We therefore got on splendidly."[11]
But the letters prove that they did not get on "splendidly" at all.

8. Ibid., pp. 552–53.
9. Simon Houfe, *The Dictionary of British Book Illustrators and Caricaturists*, 1978, p. 311.
10. Frankie Morris, review of *The Tenniel Illustrations to the "Alice" Books* by Michael Hancher,
Jabberwocky (Summer–Autumn 1986), p. 48.
11. Furniss, *Confessions*, 1:103–4.

Even with Dodgson gone, Furniss struggled with the paradox he himself created about the author: "Carroll," for him at one point, "was a wit, a gentleman, a bore and an egotist—and, like Hans Anderson, a spoilt child. . . . Carroll was not selfish, but a liberal-minded, liberal-handed philanthropist, but his egotism was all but second childhood." And he goes on to attribute to Dodgson attitudes that he spins out of whole cloth, berating him on the one hand, but confessing to lying to him and making promises he never intended to keep on the other. Here is only one of the ridiculous tales he relates in his autobiography:

> Lewis Carroll came from Oxford one evening . . . to dine, and afterwards to see a batch of work.
>
> [After dinner,] "Now," he said, "for the studio!" I rose and led the way. My wife sat in astonishment. She knew I had nothing to show. Through the drawing-room, down the steps of the conservatory to the door of my studio. My hand is on the handle. Through excitement Lewis Carroll stammers worse then ever. Now to see the work for his great book! I pause, turn my back to the closed door, and thus address the astonished Don: "Mr. Dodgson, I am *very* eccentric—I cannot help it! Let me explain to you clearly before you enter my studio, that my eccentricity sometimes takes a violent form. If I, in showing my work, discover in your face the slightest sign that you are not *absolutely* satisfied with any particle of this work in progress, the *whole* of it goes into the fire! It is a risk: will you accept it, or will you wait till I have the drawings *quite* finished and send them to Oxford?"
>
> "I-I-I ap-appreciate your feelings—I-I-should feel the same myself. I am off to Oxford!" and he went.
>
> . . . To meet him and to work for him was to me a great treat. I put up with his eccentricities—real ones, not sham like mine. . . . He remunerated me liberally for my work; still, he actually proposed that in addition I should partake of the profits; his gratitude was overwhelming.[12]

Not content even then, seven years later Furniss let loose with another skewed reminiscence. In this later outburst, he judges Tenniel's drawings of Alice "not successful" and accuses "poor, dear Lewis Carroll" of telling him more than once that "with the exception of Humpty Dumpty, he did not like

12. Ibid., pp. 1:104–12.

Tenniel's drawings!" Time is the sternest judge of all, and Tenniel's drawings of Alice, say what an artist or art critic might say of them, achieve more praise and popularity as the years pass. Even Furniss confesses that "*Alice* has been invaluable to the political caricaturist. . . . I have been guilty of appropriating [it] . . . for political parody." Nor does Dodgson, furthermore, record any displeasure with any of Tenniel's finished drawings.[13] Why, if he did not approve of Tenniel's work, did he repeatedly return, almost on his knees, to procure additional work from him?

The letters that follow provide a window into the ups and downs of the Dodgson-Furniss collaboration; but copious as they are, the record is somewhat incomplete. Not all the letters that passed between the two men survive, and Furniss's habit of cutting from Dodgson's letters a piece that contains the author's precise request or instruction about a given drawing and then, after working on the drawing with that piece of letter before him, probably throwing it into the wastebasket leaves some of the letters we do have incomplete.

Furniss fulfilled the challenges he set himself, and the collaboration survived to produce the two *Sylvie and Bruno* volumes. While these tales contain elements reminiscent of the *Alice* books, they veer from their predecessors sharply. Although Dodgson intended them originally for children, they turn out to be far more complex than any child's book has a right to be. And whereas the *Alice* books are all fun and nonsense (at least on the surface), the *Sylvie and Bruno* books are deeply serious and contain discourses on science, art, religion, and other heady subjects. And these are tales that teach morality — something Dodgson forswore in his earlier work.

The overall structure embraces two plots and three separate planes of existence. The episodes of one of the plots occur in the real world; those of the second in Outland, an imaginary spiritual kingdom with medieval trappings; and the third set takes place in Elfdom, the most rarified of the three and accessible to only a few sensitive souls. The first volume, *Sylvie and Bruno*, appeared in time for Christmas 1889. It contains precisely four hundred pages, a thirteen-page preface, a table of contents, forty-six illustrations by Furniss, and a five-page index. *Sylvie and Bruno Concluded* appeared four years later; it follows the same arrangement as the first volume, and again has forty-six illustrations by Furniss.

13. "Recollections of 'Lewis Carroll,'" *Strand Magazine* (January 1908).

The best one can say about the press notices is that they contained little praise. Some were respectful because the work was by Lewis Carroll, but most, like the review in *Academy*, put the case bluntly: "Ah, the pity of it! . . . [The reader] will become weary and puzzled long before he reaches the end." The book did not sell well, either, in spite of the magic of Lewis Carroll's name, and, as Dodgson's hair grew gray, a clear and unpleasant failure confronted him.

LETTERS TO HARRY FURNISS
ILLUSTRATOR OF *Sylvie and Bruno* (1889)
AND *Sylvie and Bruno Concluded* (1893)

Incomplete MS: Morgan

Christ Church, Oxford
March 9, 1885

Dear Mr. Furniss,

Your letter was a most welcome sight, and I hasten to reply to it.

First, as to the £.*s.d.*, I accept your terms.[1]

Secondly, as to pencil drawings *versus* photographing on wood, my belief is that it needn't be "versus" at all: we may combine the advantages of *both*. Pencil drawings photograph beautifully (I have often done them myself): so, if you will draw on cardboard (or whatever surface you find to be best adapted for delicate work) in pencil, I will get Messrs. Dalziel (who have always been my wood-cutters) to have them photographed on wood, and cut.

Assuming that this meets your approval, the next matter to discuss is, the actual work to be done.

I have a considerable mass of chaotic materials for a story,[2] but have never had the heart to go to work and construct the story as a whole, owing to its seeming so hopeless that I should ever find a suitable artist. Now that *you* are found. . . .

1. For details of Dodgson's financial arrangement with Furniss, see letter of November 21, 1887.

2. The nucleus of the story was "Bruno's Revenge," which appeared in *Aunt Judy's Magazine* in 1867. During the next twenty years Dodgson composed a series of episodes which he gradually shaped into a unified story that became *Sylvie and Bruno* and *Sylvie and Bruno Concluded.*

Christ Church, Oxford
[April 1?] 1885[1]

. . . climax, to draw the last picture first, and work backwards (as Poe tells us he wrote "The Raven").

I have run the risk of telling you my ideas, just for once. And you can now tell me whether you find the process tolerable or intolerable. If the latter, I will not so offend again: but patiently wait to see, in each picture, whether you have caught my meaning or not.

As to *costume*, I feel very uncertain, except that I want the costume *of the day* avoided if possible, the time of Charles I occurs to me: but maybe you will have a still better idea.

One word as to material. Is it impossible, do you think, to find any kind of cardboard which would give as good a surface as wood? If you *could* find such a thing, you would save me many pounds in box-wood blocks: but if you can't, never mind. The one important thing is, to turn out as good an article as we can.[2]

Very sincerely yours,
C. L. Dodgson.

P.S. My address, till about April 10, is "The Chestnuts, Guildford."

1. The numeral 5 (indicating the page number) and Dodgson's correspondence number 49874 (from his register of mail sent and received) appear at the top of this three-line fragment. Dodgson's letter of March 22, 1885, bears the number 49761, and his letter of April 20, 1885, the number 50092. In his reply (see note 3), Furniss alludes to Dodgson's letter dated April 1, which perhaps this is. The last three paragraphs and the postscript appear on a different sheet, but may be the end of this letter.

2. Two days earlier, Dodgson wrote (*Diaries*, pp. 433–34): "Never before have I had so many literary projects on hand at once. For curiosity I will here make a list of them." The last item on the list, number 15, is "the new child's book, which Mr. Furniss is to illustrate: he now has 'Peter and Paul' to begin on. I have settled on no name yet, but it will perhaps be *Sylvie and Bruno*." Furniss replied (ms: Berol) on April 8: "I think your suggestions for the illustrations for your poem ['Peter and Paul,' chap. 11 in *Sylvie and Bruno*] admirable, but I should like to see you before I do anything. The fact is, you have so misunderstood my letter it is quite evident I will come to grief in giving my ideas in writing. Kindly read my letter again and see if I do not particularly state that I would not attempt to illustrate your work without consultation. That so far as doing anything in the dark and you 'writing up' to anything I like to do I assure you (in your own words) 'I never dreamed in my wildest flights of fancy' of such a thing. On the contrary I will not sit

down to work until I feel we understand each other about treatment of the subjects. All I intended to ask you was not to go through your system (I apologize for using this word if it offends you) with each drawing separately, but instead to discuss the subjects for a poem (such as you did in your letter to me on the 1st) together, or say a chapter at a time. As [Lionel] Brough [1836–1909, newspaper entrepreneur and comic actor] would say 'not too much discussion but just enough.' I feel with me, too much delay in writing and the rest when I get to work is likely to take the spirit out of the first idea, *after* we have arranged what is to be done. I understand it was Mr. Tenniel who kindly mentioned my name to you, so it is not likely *he* would speak disparagingly about you. Mr. Frost and Mr. Holiday are unknown to me, but I do know three artists you tried and could not get on with. It struck me, wrongly I trust, you might not get on with me either so I thought it better to do my best to put matters on a plain business footing at starting. This I have done clumsily and you have misunderstood my letter. I think when we meet we will understand one another better. Kindly let me know a *day or two before* you intend doing us the pleasure of a visit, so that I may reply and avoid disappointment." Dodgson went up to London from Guildford to visit Furniss for the first time on April 13, but he does not give details of their conversation (*Diaries*, p. 434).

MS: *Morgan*

Christ Church, Oxford
April 20, 1885

Dear Mr. Furniss,

This is really *most* kind of you: I had no idea I was to have the privilege of seeing your sketches and being allowed to suggest alterations. The only one that occurs to me is (as I have expressed on your paper) the desirability of showing all the *faces*. I trust you won't think me *very* impertinent, for venturing to send a couple of scrawls to show my own ideas. If you approve the idea of seating Peter in a chair in Plate I, his sitting on the ground in Plate II might be desirable as a change.[1]

The accompanying book will serve two purposes: it will avert the danger of your little boy being jealous of his sister; and it will enable you to study *all* the designs Mr. Tenniel has made for me. These I think are as a whole better than those in *Alice*.[2] The one at p. 118 is a favourite of mine.[3] Believe me

Very truly yours,
C. L. Dodgson

1. "Received from Mr. H. Furniss rough sketches of the four pictures for 'Peter and Paul.' So the new book is really 'under weigh' at last!" Dodgson wrote on April 20 (*Diaries*, p. 434). "Peter

FIG. 16

Dodgson's preliminary sketch for "How cheerfully the bond he signed" from Sylvie and Bruno *and Furniss's final drawing.*

and Paul" eventually became chapter 11 of *Sylvie and Bruno* (pp. 143–55). The four sketches that Furniss sent to Dodgson for his comments survive (Berol). On the back of each sketch, Furniss adds notes for Dodgson and then indicates where Dodgson might add his own reaction. He appears to be establishing a system for an author-artist dialogue, but he abandons that good intention almost immediately. In this case Dodgson added a note to each illustration before returning the sketches to Furniss:

Plate 1. "How cheerfully the bond he signed":
Paul is splendid! Peter's attitude I do *not* like, I confess. It is an ungraceful view of him: and I think it a pity to hide his face in the only picture where he is *cheerful.* Surely a *smile* here would furnish a good contrast to the increasing woe and despair of the later pictures? Would you mind making him sit *behind* the table, and look up at Paul with a beaming smile?

Plate 2. "The legal friend was standing by":
Here again I venture to suggest that Peter's face should be seen. The series of 4 *faces*, for each hero, should make a most interesting climax. The end of the piano might be shown (Peter having just risen from singing "Begone, dull Care!"), but the pig had better *not* appear as there is a comic pig (weeping, too!) coming in another poem. The lawyer in modern dress would make a capital contrast with the others.

Plate 3. "I'm getting stout, as you may see":
I have nothing but praise for this.

Plate 4. "But there's a heart within this breast":
Is that a *coin* Paul has in his hand? If so, I think it had better be omitted: it is contrary to his character to take money *out* of his pocket! His fat hand should just spread out over where his heart might be, if he had one. Peter's face suggests horror, or despair, which is too strong for the gentle creature. We only need deep misery, and "his cheeks all wet with grateful tears."

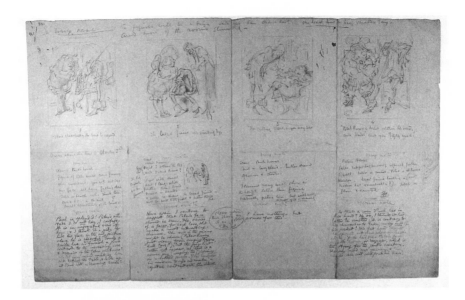

FIG. 17

Furniss's preliminary sketches for "Peter and Paul" with notes and Dodgson's manuscript comments (by permission of the Alfred C. Berol Collection, Fales Library, New York University), and two final drawings by Furniss.

Dodgson's preliminary sketch of "Peter shuddered in despair" from
Sylvie and Bruno *and Furniss's final drawing.*

Furniss altered each drawing according to Dodgson's wishes. Dodgson's "couple of scrawls" are at the Lilly Library, Indiana University.

2. The two children were probably Dorothy and Frank, aged five and six, respectively. Having given Dorothy a copy of *Alice's Adventures in Wonderland,* he was now sending a copy of *Through the Looking-Glass* to Frank. Furniss now had all ninety-two of Tenniel's illustrations for the *Alice* books at hand.

3. Humpty Dumpty meets Alice.

MS *fragment: Morgan*

Christ Church, Oxford
[April 24?] 1885[1]

. . . to commit the work to whoever you think will do it better.

I fear your words ("I had no idea you were an artist") were, to a certain extent, "rote sarkastic," which is a shame! I never made any profession of being able to draw, and have only had, as yet, 4 hours' teaching (from a young friend,[2] who is herself an artist, and who insisted on making me try, in black chalk, a foot of the Laocoön! The result was truly ghastly): but I have just sufficient of correct eye to see that every drawing I make, even from life, is altogether wrong anatomically: so that nearly all my attempts go into the fire as soon as they are finished. Believe me

Very truly yours,
C. L. Dodgson

1. This fragment is the second and last page of a letter bearing Dodgson's correspondence number 50146, which suggests this date. A letter with the correspondence number 50143 has this date.
2. Probably E. G. Thomson. For more about Miss Thomson, see chapter 5.

———

MS: *Morgan*

Christ Church, Oxford
May 6, 1885

Dear Mr. Furniss,

I rejoice to hear that a drawing is being engraved, and I entirely agree with you that it will be well to do no more till this one is worked off. *Never* hurry yourself in the least over my work, I beg. But for the uncertainty of life, I would not ask for any continuity of work at all. Still, as neither of us is secure that his life will endure for a thousand long years, it will no doubt be advisable, when this picture is done and approved, to go on with the others whenever you have time and inclination.

For the same reason I intend to devote my three months by the sea, this summer, to writing out the whole book, in consecutive form. Then, if I were to die, the book could still be brought out, and the children could read it:

that *I* should not see it would be quite a minor matter. I shall feel much more at my ease when once this is done.[1]

Very truly yours,
C. L. Dodgson

1. On August 3, Dodgson "spent the morning in classifying and transcribing fragments of the *Sylvie and Bruno* book, thus at last making a beginning of the special work I designed for this vacation" (*Diaries*, p. 438); on August 10 he added (Diaries): "I have done a good deal more on the *Sylvie and Bruno* work."

MS: *Morgan*

7 Lushington Road, Eastbourne
September 25, 1885[1]

Dear Mr. Furniss,

It occurs to me that the reason his soul was so "sad for the spider" was that he saw that the strictly honorable intentions of that well-meaning insect had been misunderstood by Miss Muffet.[2] Don't you think that would be an original view of the transaction? If you approve of it, I will alter the "and" of the last line into "yet."[3] I have made an attempt at sketching my idea of the romantic old bean, with one hand on his heart, and the other holding his handkerchief. The result is miserable—but I send it, as being possibly better than nothing: at any rate nothing could possibly be worse than it.[4]

Yours sincerely,
C. L. Dodgson

1. On May 30, Dodgson took Charlotte Rix (1867–1952) to Furniss's studio. "Spent day in town. I called on 'Lottie' Rix, at her school in St. James's Terrace; I took her with me to Mr. Furniss', where we had luncheon and a business talk," Dodgson wrote (*Diaries*, p. 436). Charlotte recorded the outing in a letter to her mother (*Letters*, pp. 578–80): "He told me that he had business with an artist who would give us some dinner. So we started. And on the way he told me that the artist was that Harry Furniss who draws those splendid parliamentary pictures in *Punch*, and that his business with him was that he was illustrating another book he was writing, which he hoped would be out by next Xmas twelve-month.... Mr. and Mrs. Furniss were *very* kind and after dinner I went down with Mr. Dodgson and Mr. Furniss to his studio. I saw the first drawing for the book; it is most absurd and will come in with a piece of poetry like the Walrus and the Carpenter. Mr. Furniss showed me some drawings he had done for a new children's

FIG. 19

Dodgson's preliminary sketch of "The romantic old bean" from
Sylvie and Bruno Concluded.

book that is coming out called *Romps*. They were splendid; and while Mr. Dodgson was talking to a Mr. Barber (who had come to show him some photographs and who has a good picture in the Academy this year) I had quite a talk with him. He is very short and has red hair and he had on his working jacket, and I liked him very much. He has three children but I only saw two: a boy and a girl, both rather pretty (about 4 or 5 I should think) and lots of the children in the book are taken from them. We were in the Studio about an hour, and I couldn't help thinking, how six months ago I little thought I should ever find myself in Mr. Furniss's studio, with an-other artist and Lewis Carroll, talking to them just as if they were anybody else, and hearing Lewis Carroll and Mr. Furniss discuss his new book!"

2. *s&bc*, chap. 17, the verses that begin, "In stature the Manlet was dwarfish." The sixth verse concerns Miss Muffet and the "misunderstood" spider. Furniss's illustration appears on p. 268.

3. Dodgson did not, in the end, alter the text.

4. Dodgson's sketch is at the Lilly Library, Indiana University. Furniss added a pencil note to this letter: "These outlines cannot be considered *portraits*; they are merely *suggestions*, and it is very very difficult (sometimes I have to draw a face three or four times)."

7 Lushington Road, Eastbourne
[September 30? 1885][1]

. . . is of goblin-fishes, winged, and transparent. (Mine won't do: they are too like the mythological dolphin.)[2]

In No. 3., I have utterly failed to get anything the least like a spider![3] Some writer says that the full-face of a spider, as seen under a magnifying-glass, is very striking. Could you find one in some book of entomology, or look at a live one?

Lest you should feel at all hampered by all these suggestions, I hasten to add that I am quite willing to welcome a total change, by your either choosing other lines to illustrate, or treating these in a different manner. Believe me

Always sincerely yours,
C. L. Dodgson

P.S. Can you find a really *pretty* boy of 5 or 6, to make studies of his face in different positions?[4] If so, we might *begin* on a little of the story itself.

FIG. 20
Dodgson's preliminary sketch of "Like a teetotum seeming to spin him" from Sylvie and Bruno Concluded *and Furniss's final drawing.*

FIG. 21
Dodgson's preliminary sketch of "That so tenderly sat down beside her"
from Sylvie and Bruno Concluded.

1. This fragment bears Dodgson's correspondence number 51782, which suggests this date.

2. Dodgson here refers to the second illustration for his lullaby "The little man that had a little gun" (s&bc, pp. 265–69), which depicts the hunter with his gun in search of a duck for supper. He is suddenly surrounded by transparent water goblins crying, "Avengement." Dodgson's drawing is at the Lilly Library, Indiana University. Furniss overcame the difficulty that Dodgson encountered, and the illustration appears on p. 267.

3. Dodgson's sketch of the spider is at the Lilly Library, Indiana University. Furniss's third illustration of the poem appears on p. 268.

4. As a model for Bruno.

---

ms: *Morgan*

Christ Church, Oxford
March 7, 1886

Dear Mr. Furniss,

I think I told you of a photograph I had seen at Eastbourne (an enlargement on porcelain) of a girl and boy, whose faces I thought would do for the children in my (very future, alas!) story. At last I have succeeded in getting a carte from the original negative, and enclose it for you to keep by you and meditate on.[1] The *girl* I am quite disappointed in: the porcelain enlargement was quite different: this one I don't admire, nor is it at all my ideal heroine. But the boy's face has come out much the same as on the porcelain, and it *does* somehow realise, to me, the roguish, and yet earnest, child I have imagined "Bruno" to be.

By the way, the enclosed little story, written years ago for Mrs. Gatty's *Aunt Judy's Magazine,*[2] will be embodied, most of it, in the future book: so you can be considering how to illustrate it. One thing I may say: I *don't* like Gilbert's illustration:[3] they both look grown-up—and something like a blacksmith and a ballet-dancer. Also another thing should be remembered: the *narrator* (the whole book will be autobiographical) must *not* appear in *any* of the illustrations.

I think I had better explain part of the plot, as to these two. They are not fairies right through the book, but *children*, though not in the real English life of the narrator, but in a sort of dreamland, of the events of which he is conscious. In their own home they are royal, or at least of high rank. They run away, and become fairies for a while, in which state the narrator meets them, and is even enabled to take them into his real life, where his friends suppose them to be ordinary children. (Of course they *grow* for this purpose: in the enclosed story they must be only a few inches high). All these conditions make their *dress* rather a puzzle. They mustn't have *wings*: that is clear. And it mustn't be *quite* the common dress of London life. It should be as fanciful as possible, so as *just* to be presentable in society. The friends might be able to say "What oddly-dressed children!" but they oughtn't to say "They are not human!"

Now I think you'll say you have "got your work cut out for you," to invent a suitable dress!

Sincerely yours,
C. L. Dodgson

1. Missing.
2. "Bruno's Revenge"; see March 9, 1885, n. 2.
3. The one illustration for "Bruno's Revenge" in *Aunt Judy's Magazine* is by Frederick Gilbert (fl. 1862–77), painter, watercolorist, and illustrator. He was the brother of Sir John Gilbert (1817–97) and lived with him at Blackheath. He specialized in genre and historical subjects and illustrations from Tennyson's works. Apart from contributing to *Aunt Judy's Magazine* in 1866, he also drew for *Cassell's Magazine* (1866) and *London Society* (1870).

MS: *Morgan*

Christ Church, Oxford
April 21, 1886

Dear Mr. Furniss,

Thanks for your note. I go tomorrow to "The Chestnuts, Guildford," intending to return here on Wednesday the 28th, and could come round by London, and call that day, if you think it desirable to have an interview.[1]

Very truly yours,
C. L. Dodgson

I enclose 5 cartes of a young friend, done at ages varying from 8 to 13, to see how you think her face would suit for "Sylvie."[2] It expresses *my* idea of the child fairly well, except that it is a *little* too sleepy: I mean Sylvie to be a child capable of being "put out" a little now and then, whereas these photographs suggest a child too languid to be "put out" by anything. The girl, in your seaside sketch in *Romps*, where 2 boys are bathing a dog in the foreground, and the girl is just behind, gathering her skirts round her to come into the sea, would also do fairly well. Of course, if you could chance on two *living* children, suitable for Sylvie and Bruno, it would be better than any amount of photographs.

1. On April 28, Dodgson went from Guildford directly back to Oxford without stopping to see Furniss (Diaries).
2. We do not know which photographs Dodgson sent.

MS: *Morgan*

7 Lushington Road, Eastbourne
July 23, 1886

Dear Mr. Furniss,

Now that I am settled down here, for (I hope) about 3 months of steady work at two subjects only,[1] one of them being the fairy-tale, I shall be glad to know that you also will be able to devote some time to my book. I think I can keep you well supplied with material for a good while to come, even before the substance of the main story is ready for you. Besides the "little man" poem, now in your hands (which I think we agreed was to have 3 pictures),[2] and "Bruno's Revenge" (which would bear 3, if not 4), I have an incidental story (of which Bruno is the hero) which would not be overdone with 6 pictures, and poems enough for I should think 15 pictures more. That's more than 25 pictures altogether.

I cannot ask you, as yet, to forbear from accepting any of the many offers of work which no doubt crowd in upon you: but if I fulfil my hopes, and get the whole book into sufficient form for illustration by the end of this year, I hope you won't think it an unreasonable suggestion that you should decline any new work for next year, and give to this book whatever time you can spare from *Punch*. This would not be so much with a view to *expedition*, as to getting the work done when eye and hand are *at their best*. I shall, for my part, do *my* best to make the text worthy of your skill as artist.

I am looking forward, anxiously, to see what you make of Bruno, with the help of the photograph, and still more to see your idea of Sylvie.[3] These will be quite the most important characters in the book: and all will depend on *their* being a success: so I hope you will forgive me if I prove hard to please in their case.

Very truly yours,
C. L. Dodgson

1. On July 21, Dodgson noted, "I have . . . begun work on the *Sylvie and Bruno* MS." The other subject was a logic book on which Dodgson had been working for some time.

2. See [September 30?, 1885], n. 2, and S&BC, pp. 265–69.

3. On November 15, 1886, Dodgson wrote (*Diaries*, p. 444): "Got the consent of Mrs. Van der Gucht to Marie sitting to Mr. Furniss for face of 'Sylvie,' and wrote to tell him about it. I sent him, some while ago a photo from Lavis, Eastbourne, of a boy, for 'Bruno': so we are now ready to do *all* the pictures for *Sylvie and Bruno*." In the end, Furniss used his own daughter Dorothy as a model for Sylvie and his son Frank for Bruno (see his *Confessions of a Caricaturist*, 1901, 1:109). For more about Dodgson's relationship with the Van der Guchts, see *Letters*, esp. pp. 639–40.

Facsimile: Collingwood, pp. 262–63

Clensick, Walmer, Kent
August 23, 1886

Dear Mr. Dodgson,

The spider in the Miss Muffet picture has been a great trouble to me. I tried to follow your idea of having the spider sitting cross-legged like a tailor. But after getting spiders and watching them, I find in the words of the latest Cockney song "it ain't built that way." The legs are too high up, and no contortion will allow of my getting the spider into that position.

So I've hit upon, what I venture to think is an original and funny view of the spider, back view. The *face* of the spider is not one to make anything out of, so there is nothing lost in leaving it out.

If you think this arrangement will do, I will finish the picture up, keeping the rest of the design as suggested in the sketch you saw, but once drawn I cannot alter the spider. I like it myself.

Very sincerely yours,
Harry Furniss

MS: *Morgan*

7 Lushington Road, Eastbourne
August 25, 1886

Dear Mr. Furniss,

It is no form of words to say that I am *most* grateful for all the thought and trouble you expend on my book. Generally speaking, I would be willing to accept any treatment of a picture that you deliberately think best. Still, as you *have* paid me the compliment of asking my opinion, I will venture to give it. My idea is that there is no necessity for being so entomologically accurate as you aspire to be, and that a creature, mostly human, but *suggestive* of a spidery nature, would be quite accurate enough.

Secondly, that by giving only a *back*-view, you lose all chance of the "Little Man" *sympathising* with the spider, and so you lose the gist of "his soul shall be sad," etc.

My idea of the ground of sympathy is that the "Little Man" sees that the spider is deeply love-striken, and is in the midst of a "declaration," quite unaware that the young lady is out of hearing! Would not *that* be a subject for pity?

I think that the 6 legs (which I have tried to represent by that tangle in front) and a globular outline to the figure, would be spidery enough. I *meant* him to be laying his hand on his heart: but his chin got in the way.[1] Haste.

Very sincerely yours,
C. L. Dodgson

1. Furniss had another go, and the published version shows the spider face-front and the "Little Man" sympathizing with him (see s&bc, p. 268).

Incomplete MS: Morgan

Christ Church, Oxford
November 11, 1886

Dear Mr. Furniss,

I have a very important request to make of you—in view of the following considerations:

(1) It is now just a year and 8 months since you undertook the illustrating of my new book, and only 4 pictures are as yet delivered: at which rate it would take more than 30 years to finish the book![1]

(2) It is most desirable to get the pictures drawn and the book published. Life is uncertain.

(3) I can undertake to keep you continuously employed from this time onwards, till it is done, even if you do as much as a picture a week.

(4) This job may fairly claim your special attention, being a tolerably big order!

(5) I notice that you are at present drawing for the *Illustrated London News*, as well as *Punch*. This must not only use up all your time, but also all your brain and hand powers.

My request is, then, that. . . .

1. More than a year before he wrote this letter, Dodgson received proofs of Furniss's four drawings for "Peter and Paul" (see April 20, 1885, n. 1).

MS: *Morgan*

Christ Church, Oxford
November 20, 1886

Dear Mr. Furniss,

Many thanks. The pictures are delicious, and *very* funny: what I like *best*, I think, is the bored Dolphin:[1] only it makes me yawn so to look at it! I will send you some more verses at once.

Very truly yours,
C. L. Dodgson

1. *S&BC*, p. 266. Dodgson's original sketch, now at the Lilly Library, Indiana University, was probably sent with the letter dated [September 30? 1885].

FIG. 23
*Dodgson's preliminary sketch of "Pays long ceremonious calls"
from* Sylvie and Bruno Concluded *with Furniss's final
drawing.*

MS: *Morgan*

Christ Church, Oxford
November 24, 1886

Dear Mr. Furniss,

I defer to another day the "3 Badgers," finding my artistic powers pretty nearly pumped out by the effort of making these 4 sketches for the "Pig-Tale," which I send for your consideration.[1]

As to your sketches, I would say that, though very graphic and suggestive, they don't seem to me quite on the most hopeful tack for realising a comic result: my reasons for thinking so are

(1) I think animals, treated as animals *only*, are *very* hard to depict comically. If animals could draw, and had a sense of humour, no doubt *they* could do it: but I think we humans need to get the human form, or dress, or something human, introduced to appeal to *our* sense of the ludicrous. So I would suggest dressing the pig as a fat farmer, and the camel as a tourist (he *might* have a knapsack on his back, which would be suggestive of a hump.) The frog perhaps would do without costume, but his form, and attitudes, might be *slightly* human.

(2) I think the *dramatis personae* should be pretty nearly of a size, for grouping's sake. Also you lose all chance of expression if you make any thing very small.

(3) I don't like *death* to be introduced into a comic poem. I didn't mean to *kill* the Pig. He was probably crippled, and learned never to do it again: but he ought to be able to take in the Camel's condolences.

(4) I think 3 pictures 3 1/2 wide by 2 1/2 high, and a little vignette tail-piece, would suit well.[2]

Please remember these are only my *ideas*, suggested for you to consider. I shall be *quite* ready to throw them overboard, if you can hit off a more funny treatment of the poem.

7 p.m. Your letter, re charges for work, is just come. I must answer it on another sheet.

Yours very truly,
C. L. Dodgson

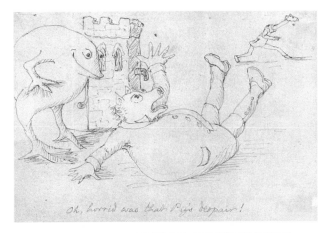

FIG. 24

Dodgson's preliminary sketch of "Oh, horrid was that Pig's despair" from Sylvie and Bruno Concluded *with Furniss's final drawing.*

1. Dodgson's four sketches for the "Pig-Tale" are at the Lilly Library, Indiana University. He returned to the question of the "3 Badgers" in a letter to Furniss two days later.

2. Furniss produced the three pictures and the vignette as suggested here, and they illustrate chap. 23, "The Pig-Tale," in S&BC, pp. 367–73.

Dodgson's preliminary sketch of "Uprose that Pig, and rushed, full whack" from
Sylvie and Bruno Concluded *with Furniss's final drawing.*

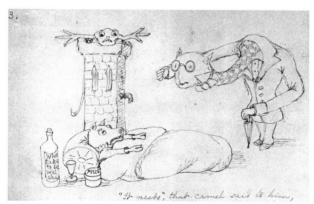

Dodgson's preliminary sketch of " 'It needs,' that camel said to him" from
Sylvie and Bruno Concluded *with Furniss's final drawing.*

FIG. 27
Dodgson's preliminary sketch of "And still he sits, in miserie" from
Sylvie and Bruno Concluded *with Furniss's final drawing.*

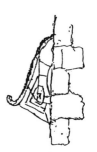

MS: *Morgan*

Christ Church, Oxford
November 26, 1886

Dear Mr. Furniss,

I enclose your pig and camel sketches,[1] and entirely agree to all you propose. I should like the pump made much more of a *ruin* than I made it—also the handle might be like *this*

(N.B. it is *meant* for a spider's web!) to show that it hadn't been used for some time.

Will write about badgers, and Bruno, by another post.

Very truly yours,
C. L. Dodgson

1. *S&BC*, p. 367.

MS: *Morgan*

Christ Church, Oxford
November 26, 1886

Dear Mr. Furniss,

I return your sketches for the "3 Badgers."

As to No. 1, my idea was that the truant Herrings had *left* the water, and gave their undesired serenade some way *inland*. Don't you think they might be made suggestive of lady-singers at a Concert? Then, would it not be more effective to make them of 3 quite different sizes? And ditto for the Badgers, who will thus make a more artistic group. My notion of the "mossy stone" is that it should not be larger than needed to make the *eldest* Badger comfortable, and the other two should be slipping off, and held up by their chins, nearly choked, and in much discomfort. This I think gives a funny turn to the fact that the Herrings were "longing to share that mossy seat"!

Your No. 2 is charming. I don't think I can suggest any improvement *there*.

Your No. 3 would have a very *pretty* effect, no doubt: but don't you think you lose some chance of funny treatment by putting the spectator where he can only see the backs of the badgers, and a distant view of the delighted old folk? Would it not be more effective to give a *side*-view of the meeting?

And I think you may get another funny effect by making the largest badger carry the smallest Herring, and vice versa?

You will not need to be told that *I can't draw badgers!*

Now, having put my ideas before you, I leave you free to draw the pictures as seems to you best and funniest.

Would you let me have my sketches again, when done with? And the "Pig" ones too. I would like to keep them as curios.

Very truly yours,
C. L. Dodgson

P.S. If you approve of my No. 3, it might be made a full-page picture and put sideways in the book.[1]

---

1. The "Three Badgers" illustrations appear on pp. 247, 249, and 252 of S&B. Furniss evidently adopted all of Dodgson's suggestions for the third picture, which appears sideways on a full page. Dodgson's own sketches are at the Lilly Library, Indiana University (see also *Lewis Carroll Observed*, 1976, pp. 152–53).

Each Herring tries to sing what she has found

FIG. 28

Dodgson's preliminary sketch of "Each Herring tries to sing what she has found" from Sylvie and Bruno *with Furniss's final drawing.*

Christ Church, Oxford
November 27, 1886

Dear Mr. Furniss,

I have picked out what seem to me 4 subjects, suitable for pictures, in "Bruno's Revenge": but I won't attempt to sketch them myself: my attempts at children are melancholy failures, and, as to the *grouping*, you will be a much better judge than I. So I will simply *describe* my idea of each:

(1) at p. 66, "Sylvie and Beetle."[1] As I said in mine of November 23, the *narrator* is never to appear: so it will only be a little picture (2 1/4 or 2 1/2 high). It should be a large beetle, so as to be a fair job for Sylvie to roll it over: *her* I imagine 6 or 8 inches high, so that most flowers (buttercups, etc.) would overtop her. Her *dress* I will discuss further on. This is a question of *great* importance, as Sylvie and Bruno are the chief characters in the book.

(2) at p. 69, "Bruno tearing up heartsease."[2] He must look in a passion, of course: but not enough to spoil his beauty, please. And the scene should be the *spoiled* portion of Sylvie's garden: his spade should be lying by him.

(3) at p. 75, "Bruno's song."[3] This I think ought to make a quaint and pretty picture, with the dead mouse and the blue-bells.

These three might be about 2 1/4 or 2 1/2 inches high. The fourth picture I think would deserve to be larger, say 4 inches high.

(4) at p. 77, "Sylvie and Bruno kissing."[4] May be made as *pretty* a group as you like.

If there is room in the pictures, it might give a little life, and interest, to introduce an insect or two, or a little frog, or lizard. A lizard, coming out of its hole (do they make holes?) to listen to Bruno's song, would be pretty.

Now as to the dresses of these children in their *fairy* state (we shall sometimes have them mixing in society, and supposed to be real children: and for *that* they must I suppose be dressed as in ordinary life, but *eccentrically*, so as to make a little distinction). I *wish* I dared dispense with *all* costume: naked children are so perfectly pure and lovely (the 3 photographs Mr. Barber[5] gave me of his children are prettier than any that could be made of them dressed): but Mrs. Grundy would be furious: it would never do.[6] Then the question is, how little dress will content her? Bare legs and feet we *must* have, at any rate.

The enclosed 11 pictures in light blue I cut out of a book called *A Tale of a Nursery Rhyme* in July 1883. They are by a Mr. Edwin Ellis.[7] He has boldly solved the question by putting the 2 children (both *girls*, according to the book) into chemises, and those nearly transparent. We must have more than *this*, I think, though the result is, to my mind, very pretty and graceful: and his elder child is something very near my idea of "Sylvie" (the other is too small for "Bruno"). They may perhaps suggest some way of treating the subject. Do not be in any hurry to return them.

Very truly yours,
C. L. Dodgson

1. *S&B*, p. 193.

2. The episode occurs in *S&B*, p. 200, but is not illustrated.

3. *S&B*, p. 213.

4. The episode occurs in *S&B*, p. 219, but again no illustration appears.

5. Charles Burton Barber (1845–94), who specialized in sport, animals, and children, painted Queen Victoria and her dogs. He exhibited *The New Whip* in the Royal Academy in 1885. Dodgson met Barber at Furniss's studio on May 30, 1885 (*Letters*, pp. 579–80). Furniss later wrote an appreciation of Barber: "Charles Burton Barber," in *The Works of Charles Burton Barber*, 1896, pp. 9–14.

6. The fictional character Mrs. Grundy, upholder of social morals, is first mentioned in *Speed the Plough* a drama by Thomas Morton (1764?–1838), but she never appears in the play. She became synonymous with conventional propriety and, as such, Dodgson often refers to her.

7. Edwin John Ellis (1842–95) also illustrated *Original Nursery Rhymes* in 1865.

MS: *Morgan*

Christ Church, Oxford
November 29, 1886

Dear Mr. Furniss,

It is really *most* kind of you, to be so ready to accept other ideas for the pictures than what you had already devised. Of course the Herrings must *not* have shark's heads, and the Badgers must *not* be the dogs I have made of them. But as to the disproportion in size, I fear you have been too much to the Zoo, and have got ideas too accurate for our present purpose. Surely it is better to get the pictures as funny as we can, than to be zoölogically correct? If you really feel that you *must* draw them in right proportion, of course I give in: but, if you *can* so far strain your standard of zoölogical propriety, I *think* we shall gain in drollery. Remember, the Badgers were very young: and surely very young Badgers are also very small? However, I leave it to you to do as you judge best.[1]

Later. As to Sylvie, I am charmed with your idea of dressing her in *white*: it exactly fits my own idea of her: I want her to be a sort of embodiment of Purity. So I think that, in Society, she should be *wholly* in white—white frock ("clinging," certainly: I *hate* the crinoline fashion): white stockings (or wouldn't socks be prettier? When children have, what is not always the case, well-shaped calves to their legs, stockings seem a pity): and I think white satin shoes would do better than black. Also I *think* we might venture on making her *fairy*-dress transparent. Don't you think we might face Mrs. Grundy to *that* extent? In fact I think Mrs. G. would be fairly content at finding her *dressed*, and would not mind whether the material was silk, or muslin, or even gauze.

If Sylvie is in white, oughtn't Bruno to be so also? But the *style* of his dress I find I can make nothing of: invention fails me.[2]

One thing more. *Please* don't give Sylvie high heels! They are an abomination to me.

> Very truly yours,
> C. L. Dodgson

---

1. *S&B*, p. 252.

2. Both Sylvie and Bruno appear in white in Furniss's illustrations. Sylvie's costume is "clinging" but not transparent. She wears full-length stockings but no high heels, just slippers. Bruno's costume is a white furry animal skin, cut short at the arms and legs. He wears white boots and a pixie cap, making him look Puckish.

MS: *Morgan*

Christ Church, Oxford
December 13, 1886

Dear Mr. Furniss,

I wonder if my letter of Dec. 8 missed reaching you. I asked therein if you would kindly return me the MS poems you have finished with, as my copies here are all one mass of corrections. Also if you would like me to send you a list of the characters in the new book, with descriptions, that you might be able to form ideas as to the sort of face to aim at for each, and (I hope) to secure a real live *sitter* for each, since one thing I am *specially* anxious about, that we may avoid the "family-likeness" effect into which the best artists are liable to glide, if they draw faces without actual life to go by. They fall as naturally into one fixed type of *face*, as we all do into one fixed type of *signature*.

I see *More Romps* is noticed in the *Observer*, and have ordered it, if it's a new one: I have 3 already (*Seaside*, *Town*, and *Holiday*). I see the *Observer* charges them with a suspicion of "vulgarity," a charge I am not at all prepared to believe in![1]

Very truly yours,
C. L. Dodgson

1. Furniss had published *Romps in Town* and *Romps at the Seaside* in 1885, *Holiday Romps* and *Romps All the Year Round* in 1886. "In *More Romps*," wrote the *Observer* ("Christmas Books," December 12, 1886, p. 6), "there is plenty of healthy spirit, but just a suspicion of vulgarity, against which Mr. Harry Furniss will do well to guard in his future illustration of childish revelry. . . . But, for all that, *More Romps* will be a great favourite in the nursery, where its frank fun will carry all before it."

Christ Church, Oxford
[?December 17, 1886][1]

... future, to feel secure that you and I are the only two living beings who know anything about the contents of the book, till it appears.)

For my own part, I have shown *none* of the MS to anybody: and, though I have let some special friends see the pictures, I have uniformly declined to *explain* them. "May I ask so-and-so?" they enquire. "Certainly!" I reply. "You may *ask* as many questions as you like!" That is all they get out of me.[2]

Now I will wait to hear your views on these matters. Then I will draw up our agreements in formal shape. And then we shall be in no risk of difficulties arising hereafter.

I am getting on well with the book, and am looking hopefully to Xmas 1887, as the time for its appearance.

Very sincerely yours,
C. L. Dodgson

1. The date is a guess. The fragment is the sixth page of the letter and bears the correspondence number 56028. The letter dated November 27, 1886, bears the number 55800, and the next to follow with a number is March 6, 1887, with the number 57243.

2. Clearly Dodgson did not approve of anyone seeing his work before it was published, and he may have thought that Furniss was showing his manuscript to others.

The Chestnuts, Guildford
January 4, 1887

Dear Mr. Furniss,

Many thanks. My mind is about 2 1/2 pounds lighter. Dreadful pictures were over-shadowing me of having to bring out my book *without pictures*. For really I know of no one else to go to, *if you* should fail me.[1]

There were other points I wanted to be sure we understood each other about: but I haven't got the copy here of the letter I wrote you. One was about copyright. Do we quite understand that the copyright is *mine?* Haste.

Sincerely yours,
C. L. Dodgson

1. Furniss evidently withdrew his threat to strike in response to Dodgson's earlier letter.

MS postcard: Morgan

Christ Church, Oxford
January 18, 1887

Four drawings, and MS, have reached me safely. Many hearty thanks for all the loving care you have bestowed on them: the result is excellent, I think. Will write very soon.

C. L. D.

MS: Morgan

Christ Church, Oxford
January 26, 1887

Dear Mr. Furniss,

I have been daily hoping to write, but can't find time.[1] Your reply about "copyright" is wholly satisfactory: and now, if you can only manage to forget, and forgive, my having once *seemed* to imply a doubt as to your perfect integrity and honourableness of dealing, we shall be all right.

Those 4 drawings for the "Pig-Tale" are simply *delicious*. But *one* of them would be the better, I think, if 2 little alterations could be introduced into the woodcut. Would it be possible to cover two small portions of it, without spoiling it for your after-possession, with little bits of white paper, so as to redraw a few lines?

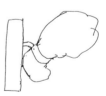

The 2 points I would like amended are (the picture is of the "fatal jump"):

(1) the spout of the pump unfortunately ends exactly behind the pig's collar, giving the effect of the pig being *fastened* to it. What is needed is to move it a *little* higher up, so that the pig may be plainly *falling* and *not* held in suspense.

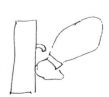

(2) In the frog's face the furthest eye is hardly distinct enough. I took it for a *nose*, and for days regarded it as a *profile* face, like this: reading the right-hand eye into a *nostril*. I expect others would be apt to make the same mistake.[2]

Will write again soon.

Sincerely yours,
C. L. Dodgson

1. The facsimile of *Alice's Adventures Under Ground* had just been published, and *The Game of Logic* was due to appear in February. These consumed much of Dodgson's time.
2. s&bc, p. 369. Furniss made both changes.

---

ms: *Morgan*

Christ Church, Oxford
February 16, 1887

Dear Mr. Furniss,

The exordium of your letter frightened me out of my wits. I thought that it was all u.p. and that I must find another artist. When I got to the end I was immensely relieved. "2 months' grace"? Why, of course! 4 months, if you prefer it! Let me mention, while I think of it, how much pleased I was at your afterthought as to the camel walking away. The dandified air, with which he is lighting his cigar, is simply perfect.[1]

Wishing you all success in your new enterprise,[2] I am

Very truly yours,
C. L. Dodgson

p.s. Would you kindly return me (1) my own sketches for illustrations (I have *some*, I think, but not all), (2) those pictures done in very faint blue ink, that I had cut out of a book.[3]

1. s&bc, p. 367.
2. Furniss was mounting an exhibition of parodies of former Royal Academy pictures, eighty-seven in all, which he called an "Artistic Joke." On the following June 4, Dodgson, in London, went to see the exhibition at the Gainsborough Gallery in Bond Street. "It is very good, and a wonderful amount of work for one man," he wrote (*Diaries*, p. 451).
3. For details of the pictures in blue ink, see letter of November 27, 1886.

MS: *Morgan*

7 Lushington Road, Eastbourne
August 21, 1887

Dear Mr. Furniss,

Thanks for letters, and for returning my "Pig" sketches and MS.[1]

Your 3 "Badger" pictures are *delicious*! The 2 little Badgers, slipping off their perches, you have made *very* funny, also the mother Herring, sitting by the sea. But indeed they are funny throughout.[2]

I will be very happy to come over on Friday: but my "little friend" will be then no longer available as companion.[3]

I had better arrive at Arundel at 2.25, and 7.08 is the last train to return by, unless (which you have not told me) Ford is accessible without the aid of the railway.

On the whole, I had rather return by the 7.08. If that is too early for your dinner, please never mind. I can dine at Brighton.

I enclose the slips, as far as they are printed. You have had most of it already.

Very truly yours,
C. L. Dodgson

1. See letter of November 24, 1886.

2. S&B, pp. 247, 249, and 252.

3. Irene Barnes had been Dodgson's guest at Eastbourne since August 17. She returned to London on August 23.

MS: *Morgan*

7 Lushington Road, Eastbourne
August 23, 1887

Dear Mr. Furniss,

Thanks for your note, but there are physical obstacles to the 3 p.m. meal you suggest. If *you* like to feed then, I shall be happy to "assist," as the French say, by my *presence*: but I can't eat at that time myself. I take no real meals but breakfast and dinner: for luncheon a couple of biscuits, or a bit of bread and cheese, will suffice. Let me dine at Brighton, on my return: that seems the best plan. Then we shall have plenty of time to talk.

I can *describe* to you, and you can take such notes as you need, the subject of any number of pictures you may like to have on hand, even though the actual text belonging to them is not finished: for I have the *backbone* of the book complete, and all the incidents and scenes arranged.

I think our first care should be to give you a clear and full idea of the *dramatis personae*, that you may form your own conception of each, and perhaps make a rough study of each, as a sort of standard to keep to. We *must* begin on the real story now: the incidental poetry is nearly exhausted.

I think we won't try to go through the whole book in one afternoon. If we can settle the subjects for (say) 20 pictures, it will occupy you for a good while to come: and I'll come over again when more matter is needed.[1]

Yours very truly,
C. L. Dodgson

1. On August 26, Dodgson went "over to Arundel, and had a long talk with Mr. Furniss, and left him a list of sixty-four subjects for pictures" (*Diaries*, p. 454).

MS: *Morgan*

7 Lushington Road, Eastbourne
August 29, 1887

Dear Mr. Furniss,

It would be best not to attempt any "Little Birds" bordering, till I send you the verses set up in pages. Then you can rule lines round, 5 1/4 long, and 3 3/8 wide, either putting the stanzas close to left margin, as in (1), or centrally, as in (2), as you think best: and then you will see the exact *shape* of the space to be filled with bordering design. Of course you will draw it larger.[1]

Very truly yours,
C. L. Dodgson

1. On August 25, Dodgson sent Furniss the complete transcript of the "Little Birds" poem, on a sheet (MS: Morgan) with the heading: "for Artist's use, verses to come before, after, and in middle of 'Pig-Tale' (the order of verses is not settled)." Only ten of the eleven stanzas that Dodgson sent appear in S&BC (pp. 364–65, 371, 377). The omitted verse reads:

Little Birds are seeking
Hecatombs of haws,
Dressed in snowy gauze:
Dressed, I say, in fringes
Half-alive with hinges—
Thus they break the laws.

On another sheet which Dodgson sent to Furniss on the same day appear five stanzas for the "Gardener's Song" (s&b, pp. 65, 90, 116, 164; s&bc, p. 319).

———————

MS: *Morgan*

7 Lushington Road, Eastbourne
August 30, 1887

Dear Mr. Furniss,

I made a mistake, in drawing the supposed pages of stanzas of "Little Birds," by leaving margins above and below. I was treating the outline (which ought to be 5 1/8 × 3 3/8) as if it were the outline of the *leaf*, instead of being the size of the *text*. Consequently you may put the top and bottom stanza *touching* the lines, and the middle stanza might be midway between them, or higher or lower than that, according to the border you think of putting, which might have portions running in *between* the stanzas.

My present idea is to omit the weakest two of the 11 stanzas, and arrange the other 9 on 3 pages, one to go *before* the "Pig-Tale," one somewhere in the middle of it, and one at the end. The two I think of omitting are

"Little Birds are seeking
Hecatombs of haws"

and

"Little Birds are feeding
Justices with Jam."

The other 9 can be arranged in any order that best suits the artist, except that the stanzas ending "I've a Tale to tell" and "So the Tale begins" must come at first and third stanzas on p. 1, and the one ending "And the Tale is told" must end p. 3.

Would you kindly arrange the other 6 stanzas in order of merit (i.e. suitability for effective pictures)? They may be indicated by the leading words

"Crocodiles"
"Tigresses"
"Bagpipes"
"Interesting books"
"Baronets"
"Crimes."[1]

Very truly yours,
C. L. Dodgson

P.S. Please say on *which* of the 3 pages you would place each of the above 6.

1. The ten stanzas appear in the following order: "Warily and well," p. 364; "Justices," "Tigresses," and "All among the pins" (Dodgson notes that these are either ninepins or skittles) all on p. 365; "Interesting books," "Bagpipes," and "Crocodiles" all on p. 371; and "Baronets," "Crimes," and "Gratitude and gold" all on p. 377.

MS: *Morgan*

7 Lushington Road, Eastbourne
August 31, 1887

Dear Mr. Furniss,

After posting to you the MS of "Tottles," I tried to decide what part of it seemed to *me* to lend itself best to illustration. I fixed on the last line, and enclose my feeble attempt at representing the picture it suggests to me.[1] You have not returned me my "Badger" sketches. Would you send them along with *your* pictures of the same, when you have drawn lines round them.

Very truly yours,
C. L. Dodgson

1. Dodgson's own sketch is at the Lilly Library, Indiana University.

ᴍꜱ: *Morgan*

7 Lushington Road, Eastbourne
September 1, 1887

Dear Mr. Furniss,

I enclose a proof of "Little Birds."

If you approve of my idea for illustrating "Tottles," I will alter line 5 of last stanza to

"Yet pleads one wish, on bended knee."

You might perhaps produce a good burlesque effect by extending her skirt along the floor, in zigzags, like a serpent.[1]

Very truly yours,
C. L. Dodgson

ᴘ.ꜱ. Parcel just come to hand. No time to discuss it for this post. Some of the sketches are *delicious*!!!

1. The changed line for the last stanza eventually became "Yet begs one boon on bended knee," and the illustration fits Dodgson's suggestion; see ꜱ&ʙᴄ, p. 248.

ᴍꜱ: *Morgan*

7 Lushington Road, Eastbourne
September 1, 1887

Dear Mr. Furniss,

I am going to give you my views as to your quite admirable series of sketches: and I do hope that if by any awkwardness of expression I wound your *amour-propre*, you will forgive it, and attribute it to clumsiness rather than to malice prepense.

First, I want to mention a type of face I am most anxious to *avoid* for "Sylvie." Is it *Judy*, or *Fun* (*Judy*, I *think*) that so often has, on the first page, a very pretty girl, very scantily dressed, sometimes in ballet-dress, sometimes in bathing-dress? She has bold black eyes and sharp-cut features, and looks too "fast" to be a real lady: one sees such girls in refreshment-rooms, but chiefly on the stage, either as a ballet-dancer, or as "principal boy" in trunks and fleshings. There is a girl, who occurs again and again in your books of

"NEVER!" yelled Tottles. And he meant it.

31/8/87.

FIG. 29
Dodgson's preliminary sketch of " '**NEVER!**' *yelled Tottles. And he meant it*"
from Sylvie and Bruno Concluded *with Furniss's final drawing.*

Romps, who is quite of this type: and, seeing that your pencil, when left to itself and with no live model to guide it, has rather a tendency to reproduce this type (you generally give her, as I was mentioning *viva voce*, sharp-cut nose and chin, the chin being unusually prominent), I mention it as a type I want specially *avoided*, both for "Sylvie" and "Lady Muriel." I want both to be perfect *ladies*. (That is one thing I like Marie[1] for: her face is, to my mind, thoroughly *refined*, without an atom of boldness about it. And there is a lovely girl, an old friend of mine, just turned 20, who would do splendidly for Lady Muriel. She lives at Weybridge.[2] Would you mind going over to see her when you are back in London? I am sure she will sit if I ask her.)

Now for your sketches:

(1) *Sylvie helping beetle*: a quite charming composition.[3]

(2) *Sylvie and hare*: Sylvie I like very much: but I don't at all like the hare on its back, nor under *her*. Will you kindly place it on its side, with its back towards her, and its head in the foreground (i.e. it should lie on its *right* side): and let her have only her head and arms *on* the hare. I *think* her face should not be seen. I believe a child, in deep grief, would naturally hide her face in her hands.[4]

(3) *"The Doctor"* and *"Eric"*: No! The Doctor won't do *at all*! He is a smug London man, a great "ladies' man," who would hardly talk anything but medical "shop." He is 40 at least, and can have had no love affair for the last 15 years. I want him to be about 25, powerful in frame, poetical in face: capable of intelligent interest in any subject, and of being a passionate lover. How would you draw King Arthur, when he first met Guinevere? Try *that* type.

Eric's attitude is capital: but his face is a little too near to the ordinary "masher." Please avoid *that* inane creature: and please don't cut his hair short. That fashion will be "out" directly.[5]

(4) *"Lady Muriel"* (head), ditto (*full length*), *"Earl"*: I don't like *either* face of Lady Muriel. I don't think I could talk to her: and I'm quite sure I couldn't fall in love with her. Her dress ("evening," of course?) is very pretty, I think.

I don't like the Earl's face, either. He is proud of his title, very formal, and one who would keep one "at arm's length" always. And he is too prodigiously tall. I want a gentle, genial old man: with whom [one] would feel at one's ease in a moment. This man would do admirably as Dickens' "Sir Leicester Dedlock," whereas I want him to be much more like Agnes' father in *David Copperfield*.[6]

(5) "*Warden of Noland*," ditto (head), ditto (as beggar): In the first I think the attitude a little too like the military "attention!" The "head" is *just* my conception of it. The beggar I like *very* much.[7]

(6) "*My Lady*," "*Uggug*", "*Warden's younger brother*" (His Excellency): The upper half of "My Lady" is admirable. But please avoid all risk of suggesting, in her figure, that she is "as ladies long to be who love their lords."[8]

"Uggug" is very good, except that his face is too *old*. To me it looks as if he might easily be 40.

"His Excellency" is *splendid*: it couldn't be improved on![9]

(7) "*Lover, and girl becoming umbrella*": This I think will do well: but you had better wait to see text.

(8) "*Uggug becoming Porcupine*" is *exactly* my conception of it. I expect this will be one of the most effective pictures in the book. The faces of the people should express intense *terror*.[10]

(9) "*The Professor*" is altogether *delightful*. When you get the text, you will see that you have hit the very centre of the bull's-eye.[11]

(9) [*sic*] "*His Excellency takes Uggug for nail*": Couldn't be bettered.[12]

(10) "*The Gardener*" is delicious. But wouldn't it be better to have his hands as big as his feet?[13]

Now comes the most anxious matter of all!

(11) 7 of "*Sylvie*," 7 of "Bruno":

(1) pretty: a little too old (looks about 15): eyes too far down.

(2) very near indeed to my ideal: poetical, pathetic, the right age, and *sweetly* pretty.

(3) very pretty, but a *little* too old.

(4) ditto but older still: looks 17.

(5) very pretty attitude.

(6) even more so: but the features are too sharp.

(7) looks a little too stiff and defiant; you have this very child in *Romps*—too much of a tomboy.

(8) too cross.

(9) ditto

(10) best of the lot, but not enough *expression*: can you hit off the *photograph* I sent?[14]

(11) and (12) I don't care for.

(13) good attitude: body a little too fat.

(14) No, no! Please don't give us the (to my mind) very ugly, quite modern costume, which shows with such cruel distinctness a podgy, pot-bellied (excuse the vulgarism) boy, who couldn't run a mile to save his life. I want Bruno to be *strong*, but at the same time light and active, with the figure of one of the little acrobats one sees in a circus, not "Master Tommy," who habitually gorges himself with pudding.[15] Also that dress I dislike very much. Please give him a short tunic, and *real* knickerbockers, not the tight knee-breeches they are rapidly shrinking to.

Hoping I have not *very* much "rubbed you the wrong way," I remain

Very truly yours,
C. L. Dodgson

[words missing] . . . me a graceful and acceptable present, you will let me have one or two of the rough drawings. I don't care how rough they are. Being drawn for *my* book would give them, to me, a historical interest, over and above their artistic value.[16]

1. Marie Van der Gucht; see July 23, 1886, n. 3.
2. Nora Mary Woodhouse, later McFarlane (1867–1936) was the daughter of Henry Melville Woodhouse and his wife, Mary Lakemore Woodhouse, formerly Berkeley. Mr. Woodhouse was in the cotton trade. Dodgson met the Woodhouse sisters on the Parade at Eastbourne on September 4, 1879, and later visited the Woodhouse family at Weybridge. Nora was the elder of the two sisters, the one Dodgson alludes to here (*Diaries*, pp. 383, 386, 391).
3. S&B, p. 193.
4. S&B, p. 321.
5. "The Doctor" and "Eric" must have been canceled; illustrations of them do not appear in either book.
6. S&B, pp. 240, 296. Sir Leicester Dedlock is in *Bleak House*.
7. Dodgson later changed "Noland" to "Outland." The Warden is the father of Sylvie and Bruno. He appears in S&B in the frontispiece and on p. 11. Later in the story he assumes the role of a beggar (illustration S&B, p. 53, and S&BC, 382). No Warden or head pictures appear in either book.
8. "As women wish to be who love their lords": John Home, *Douglas* 1.1.
9. S&B, p. 53. "His Excellency" is the Warden, here disguised as a beggar.
10. S&BC, p. 388.
11. The Professor appears in a number of illustrations, and this preliminary sketch may have been the basis for any one of them (S&B, pp. 11, 15, 24, 134, 268; S&BC, pp. 103 and 163, both as Mein Herr, 265, 326, 345, 352, 398).
12. S&B, p. 115.
13. S&B, p. 66.
14. Missing.
15. Bruno appears in a number of illustrations. This preliminary sketch may have been the

basis for any one of them (s&b, frontis. and pp. ii, 24, 108, 134, 172, 176, 213, 226, 268, 285, 307, 341, 373; and s&bc, frontis. and pp. 8, 62, 64, 83, 88, 163, 230, 236, 242, 265, 326, 352, 382, 398, 411). "Master Tommy" is probably the nursery rhyme character Tommy Tucker, although Dodgson may be confusing him with Jack Horner.

16. The first line or two of this postscript, which appeared at the bottom of the page bearing Dodgson's close and signature, has been cut away, leaving this fragment on the following page.

MS: *Morgan*

7 Lushington Road, Eastbourne
September 3, 1887

Dear Mr. Furniss,

I ought to have expressed in my last long letter, what I feel very strongly, that any want of harmony, between *my* ideas of the "Doctor," the "Earl," and Lady Muriel, and *your* pictures of the same, is wholly *my* doing. I had given you quite incomplete descriptions of their characters, and it would have been miraculous if you had put upon paper ideas that were in *my* mind but not in *yours*. Very soon I hope you will have text enough in your hands to realise my conception of all three. I keep sending bits of MS to the printer, now from one part of the story, now from another: I *can't* write it straight off, but am obliged to do such bits as I feel in the humour for.

I hope you've got safe, what I ask for periodically, my "Badger" sketches.

As to the "Doctor," I ought to have told you that I am putting into *his* mouth some of the maddest nonsense in the book. He ought to be thoroughly up to *fun*, and to have a laughter-loving face.

As to the "Earl," I ought to have said that I am putting into *his* mouth a good deal of gentle, dreamy talk, quite destitute of formality and aristocratic reserve.

But you shall have some of the dialogues, as soon as I can get them into type, and then you will see my meaning.

As to Lady Muriel, would you mind *not* giving her an aquiline nose? I don't admire it in young ladies, but much prefer a "tip-tilted" one. Though perhaps *straight* is best.

Very truly yours,
C. L. Dodgson

7 Lushington Road, Eastbourne
September 9, 1887

Dear Mr. Furniss,

I enclose 5 photographs of Nora Woodhouse,[1] which I distinguish thus:

(1) cabinet, riding-habit, parasol
(2) ditto, ditto, stick
(3) ditto, leaning on chair
(4) carte, 3/4 face
(5) ditto, full-face.

It seems to be my fate, when I mention to you a peculiarity in faces, that I want avoided, to send you a photograph, from life, which contains it! That boy, whose photo I sent, certainly had the far-apart *eyes* I dislike:[2] and now I must confess that Nora has a deeper and a more prominent *chin* than I like. I *don't* want my heroine to have the small, receding chin which is said to show a weak character: but I certainly would like Nora's chin a *little* reduced. If you take No. 3, and cover the chin up to 1/3 of the way from its point to the mouth, you will see the face I admire most.

She is a very sweet-natured girl, with plenty of life and good abilities, I should think. All that would do well for "Lady Muriel." But I am not intimate with her, and do not know if she has all the depth of thought (specially of religious thought) that I imagine Lady Muriel to have. But No. 4 looks to me quite the expression I should expect Lady Muriel to have while discussing some serious subject. And No. 1 would do capitally for her face when enjoying a joke, or talking nonsense, as I mean her to do in some parts of the book.

On the whole, I doubt if you could have a better guide for the head of Lady Muriel than No. 4. It is, to my mind, sweet, and thoughtful, and poetical, and *thoroughly* refined. I like the hair very much too, specially the fringe, which is neither too much nor too little. A greater wealth of back-hair would be an advantage. Do not ladies, who have plenty of *back*-hair, wear it done up in a great loop?

Mrs. Woodhouse says "Should Mr. Furniss care to copy either for your book, I should esteem it an honour." So, if *you*, as an artist, approve of any of these heads, I am sure she will let you keep them by you, for reference, for some months at any rate. And if you think it worth while to go over to Weybridge for a day, and make studies of her head in different positions, I will arrange for her to give you a sitting.

Lots of MS has gone to the printer: and I am daily expecting proofs, which I will forward to you. Believe me

Very truly yours,
C. L. Dodgson

1. Dodgson photographed Mr. and Mrs. Woodhouse on May 15, 1880, while they were visiting Oxford (Diaries), but the photographs of Nora were probably by another hand. In any case, they are missing.
2. See July 23, 1886.

———

MS fragment: Morgan

7 Lushington Road, Eastbourne
[September 23?, 1887][1]

As to (3), it might be well to make the Professor a comic caricature of "Mein Herr," or rather, since we have now settled what the Professor is to be like, to make Mein Herr the sort of face and figure of which the Professor would be a caricature. The details of description, in this text, can easily be altered to suit this picture.[2]

My idea is, that the narrator, while talking with Mein Herr, gradually passes into the trance-state, in which Mein Herr becomes the Professor: but, if you draw a picture, I would suggest the point where I have put a double line ||, before the change takes place.

The party contains the Earl, Lady Muriel, the 2 children (in evening dress, of course), the Doctor, Mein Herr, a French Count (who will sing a song in a stentorian voice), and other guests. It will be for you to say how many figures you will introduce. My idea of the picture is Mein Herr seated in the foreground, looking right at the spectator (i.e. at the narrator), having just turned round after looking at the children. Some way behind might be (if there is room) a group consisting of the 2 children turning over music, and behind them Lady Muriel and the French Count. I doubt if it would be well to put in any more figures: perhaps even these would crowd it too much.

(I forgot to say that Eric Linden is *not* present at this party.)

What I have said will, I hope, be some help to you in imagining the "Earl." I hope you will not find I have added to your difficulties!

Very truly yours,
C. L. Dodgson

1. This fragment, consisting of pages 2 and 3 of a letter, bears the correspondence number 59209. Dodgson's letter to Furniss of September 9 bears the number 59059, and the one dated November 20 the number 59820.

2. Dodgson may have intended this illustration for either chapter 9 ("The Farewell-Party") or chapter 16 ("Beyond These Voices") in s&bc, but no such drawing appears in either book.

MS: *Morgan*

Christ Church, Oxford
November 20, 1887[1]

Dear Mr. Furniss,

I will now make my few remarks on the last 4 drawings, trusting that you do not find my criticisms *very* worrying.

"Uggug treated as a nail" is very charming: but somehow Uggug looks *older* than 12: I don't understand why. In the large picture (where the map is being shown) he looks older still, more like a grown-up man. Is it something in the size of the head, or the length of limbs, that makes the real difference between 12 years old and 24 years old? Anyhow, I don't want to trouble you to cover up and re-draw, unless (what occurs as possible) you could do something with his *face* to make him look more of a child. Would larger eyes do it, I wonder? I fear there is no such thing in *life*, as so bloated a child of 12; so that you *must* [be] drawing without a model.[2]

The "map" picture still seems to me to have too many lines in it. I regret that you should do so much *more* work than necessary. I hope the lines will *not* be all cut on the wood, as I fear that, if they are, we shall get something of that *soft* effect that the American Magazines give us so much of. It is an effect *I* don't like. One seems to lose the boldness and crispness of a wood-cut, and get nearer to a *lithograph*. There is one addition I hope you won't object to making, and that is to put a little shadow to the feet of Uggug and the Vice-Warden, so as to give them the effect of standing on *ground*. At present their feet have blank white all round them, and one *cannot* imagine them to be resting on the ground. They seem to be floating in the air. The expressions of the faces of the Vice-Warden, etc., leave nothing to be desired. You are certainly *very* successful in hitting off expressions.[3]

The "Porcupine" is delicious, but the man in the crowd who has his *back* to the monster is confusing. Is it meant for the top of his head? And could he have a bald head, and *yet* such a mop of hair hanging over his face? I fancy a *face* would improve him. But perhaps it is not now possible.[4]

In "Tottles" you seem to have paid me the compliment of adopting my sketch entirely, merely putting bad drawing into good. But the lady's face is an instance of liability (which we *must* face, of course, as you do not feel at home in pencil-drawing) of the *minutiae* not coming as intended, owing to *ink* being less tractable than *lead*, and having a tendency to *blot*, which lead cannot do. The lady can scarcely be said to have a *mouth*: and the outline of her profile suggests (to *my* eye at least) a very old face, where all the teeth have gone, and the lips have fallen in. With a fine hard pencil, on wood, I have no doubt you would have made that face twice as good. I rather tremble to think what may happen with pictures of Sylvie, when ever so little running of the ink may make all the difference between beauty and ugliness. Do you think you could add any touches to this face? And could you give the silhouette a more definite *chin?*[5]

. . . As to the pictures, it may be hoped that you will soon "beat the record," for our average pace hitherto has been 6 a year, which would put the date for publishing on to 1894 or 1895. But even when the pictures are done, I shall be in no hurry about the text.

Thanks for promise of my sketches. I have not yet given up all hope: but they are a little like the jam offered to Alice by the White Queen, "jam yesterday, and jam tomorrow, but never jam today."[6] (Excuse my quoting myself: but it is the only illustration that occurs to me).

Yours very truly,
C. L. Dodgson

1. On October 25, Dodgson, in London, went "to Mr. Furniss for a talk about pictures" (*Diaries*, p. 456).

2. s&b, p. 115.

3. Although the drawing retains a good quantity of lines, a shadow appears beneath the Vice-Warden's feet. Uggug's feet are, however, still planted in a blank white space (s&b, p. 96).

4. The figure still has flowing hair and no face (s&bc, p. 388).

5. s&bc, p. 248. The next leaf, the fourth page of the letter, is missing.

6. *Through the Looking-Glass*, chap. 5.

Incomplete ms: Lilly

Christ Church, Oxford
November 21, 1887

Dear Mr. Furniss,

Thanks for your letter just received. Though I have been so many years a Mathematical Lecturer, I must confess that Arithmetic is *not* my strong point! I shall be very happy to tack on the £28.13s. to our account, if you will kindly point out the mistake I have made: I can't find it at present.

The discovery does *not*, however, quite destroy my peace of mind, for I feel sure you will not have thought me capable of trying to stretch in my own favour, our original bargain.

That bargain we have (as is always the most satisfactory . . . [1]

On March 7, 1885, you wrote as follows: "Taking *Alice's Adventures in Wonderland* for exact sample my charges for similar drawings are as follows:

Frontispiece	£15.15.0
size p.188	£12. 2.0
size p. 18	£10.10.0
size pp. 29, 35, 63, etc.	£8. 8.0
smaller ones	£5. 5.0

Should I draw them a little larger for reduction on to wood by photography, the price is the same."

And on March 9, 1885,[2] I wrote to you "as to the £.s.d., I accept your terms."

These terms were (as I think I admitted to you) heavy for me to *give* (but at the same time they were, I know, light for *you* to *receive*). Still, heavy as they were for me, I have accepted them, and do not wish to recede, by even a penny, from them.

The mode of calculation, which I proposed, was, as I will proceed to show, to *your* advantage, as it allows for increase of size *between* the 5 definite sizes: which cannot be done with 5 prices only.

Its application, to your scale, is as follows:

(1) "Frontispiece": this is 5 1/4 high and so gives £3.0.0 per inch.

(2) "size p. 188": this is 4 1/2 high, and so gives £2.16.0 per inch.

(3) "p. 18": this is 3 7/8 high and gives £2.16.1 per inch.

(4) "pp. 29, 35, 63, etc.": these are 2 5/8, 3 5/8, 2 5/8. The lesser size would give £3.4.0 per inch, the larger would give £2.6.4, the *average* being £2.15.2.

(5) "smaller ones": the one at p. 103 is one of the smallest. This would give £2.11.9 per inch.

However, as you do not like this method, by all means let us abandon it, and change, for each picture, according to the 5 fixed prices in your scale.

On this principle, our account for the 14 pictures named in the account I sent you November 1, would be as follows:

	£	s	d
4 "Peter and Paul" (well under No. 2, so must reckon as No. 3)	42.	0.	0
3 "Little Man" (not up to No. 4, so are, strictly speaking "smaller ones," but call them No. 4)	25.	4.	0
3 "Pig and Camel" (well under No. 3, so must reckon as No. 4)	25.	4.	0
1 ditto vignette (a "smaller one")	5.	5.	0
1 "Badgers" (large, i.e. No. 1)	15.	15.	0
1 ditto (smaller, size of smallest kind named in No. 4)	8.	8.	0
1 ditto (smaller still)	5.	5.	0
	£127.	1.	0
paid September 23, 1885	£50.	0.	0
	£77.	1.	0

This is little enough, I feel fully conscious, for *you* to receive for such admirable work: and I *much* hope that future profits may enable me to do more: but of this I cannot, prudently, give any formal *promise*.

Very truly yours,
C. L. Dodgson

1. At this point in the letter a piece has been torn away, and only the right-hand strip remains. The words that remain make no sense and we consequently omit them.

2. Dodgson actually writes 1855.

MS: *Morgan*

Christ Church, Oxford
March 29, 1888

Dear Mr. Furniss,

Many thanks for the 3 pictures: I had seen them when last at your house.[1] Also for the rough sketches, etc. Your parcel found me in all the distraction of going off to Guildford for a little holiday, and the best thing I could think of was to send you my own set of slips, which are complete and properly arranged, and to return the summary, as I should not have time at Guildford for copying it.

Now, however, my plans are changed, owing to an inflamed knee, for which my doctor orders bandages, and a week of perfect rest:[2] so, as I shall have a good deal of leisure time, I would like to have the summary back again, to copy some of it: my own one is not nearly so complete.

I congratulate you on the success you have had as a Lecturer,[3] a rôle which I tried for 26 years, without ever attaining such world-wide celebrity as you have done!

I would gladly send you more text, if I could, but it is *very* difficult to do any of the book here—my days are too much broken up with all sorts of business-worries, etc.[4]—and it isn't a kind of work that I can do in *scraps* of time: it needs several hours of silence and solitude at a time. But I hope the text you have will last you a good while yet. Please *don't*, if you can possibly help it, do pictures on summary only, without having the actual text.

Yours very sincerely,
C. L. Dodgson

1. On January 16 (*Diaries*, p. 457).
2. "While packing my bag to go to Guildford for Easter, I found something wrong with my right knee," Dodgson writes on March 29 (*Diaries*, p. 459), "so went to consult Mr. Doyne, who pronounced it to be 'synovitis,' and sentenced me to a week of sofa. He came and bandaged the knee (from foot upwards), after painting the knee with iodine." Dodgson remained housebound for many days, and not until he acquired an elastic knee-cap support in May was he able to get about more easily.
3. In the late 1880s and through the 1890s, Furniss took to the stage as a lecturer-entertainer. He devised parodies and skits which he illustrated on a large screen with his own drawings. So popular were these performances that he took them all over the British Isles and to Canada and the United States. He parodied British politics in a performance titled "The Manners and Men of the House of Commons" and other established institutions in other programs.

4. Dodgson, as head of household, dealt with all financial matters relating to his family, including the running of the family home, "The Chestnuts." Also, in accepting the position of curator of the Common Room at Christ Church, he assumed the role of business manager. "All this term past I have been so busy, in Common Room work, etc., that I have only done *one* new sentence of my story-book," Dodgson wrote on December 10, 1887 (*Diaries*, p. 456). "But today I wrote three MS pages, the substance of which I have had in my head for some time." On February 22–23, 1888, he records that he completed the scene of "disguises" for chapter 9 of S&B (*Diaries*, p. 458).

MS: *Morgan*

7 Lushington Road, Eastbourne
August 13, 1889[1]

Dear Mr. Furniss,

Many thanks for letting me see these 7 studies.

I add my ideas about them, not that I *insist* on your adopting any of them. Now that you have the text before you, I consider you a better judge than myself on the suitability of the pictures, and am prepared to defer in all points to your judgement.

(1) The Chancellor (or "Chamberlain," whichever *you* prefer) is excellent. Only please don't let him clasp his hands *under* his coat-tails. It is the regular *low*-comedy "business," in which the actor always manages to show a little more, of the least beautiful part of his figure, than is quite seemly. I *don't* want to have an atom of "playing for the Gallery"! They can be under his *gown*, by all means, which may float about as wildly as you like. As to his face, remember he is as bad a scoundrel as the Sub-Warden. Don't make him too *benevolent*: he is crafty and deceitful. The arrangement of this picture seems excellent.[2]

(2) Excellent, but do you think Bruno would be *dancing* with a stranger so near? I *think*, when the Prof. appeared, he would leave off dancing, and be a little shy and demure. However, *you* have children of your own, and should know best.[3]

(3) Bravissimo!

(4) Looks all right, I think

(5) Best omit—the idea is too much like (6)

(6) All right, I think. The autobiographer couldn't *see* it that way: but really that doesn't matter. It'll do very well.

(7) All right. *Don't* put in the autobiographer. *He* is never to appear, you know.[4]

Haste.

Yours very sincerely,
C. L. D.

Drawings not come yet.

1. It is inconceivable that no letters passed from Dodgson to Furniss between March 29, 1888, and August 13, 1889, but none for that period have come to light. Dodgson's *Diaries* chronicle his labors on the books: "I spent a good deal of yesterday in mounting 'slip' of *Sylvie and Bruno* on sheets of paper," he recorded on July 29, 1888 (*Diaries*, p. 463), and on August 4: "I have finished mounting the slips of *Sylvie and Bruno*, both for myself and Mr. Furniss and am now making daily progress in writing" (ibid.). On November 30 (p. 466): "The idea occurred to me of making parts I, II, of my new book into one book for Christmas '89, and III, IV, into another, for Christmas '90. Each would be a volume as big as *Alice*. I think of calling them *Sylvie and Bruno*, and *More about Sylvie and Bruno*: and then, if ever I publish the two in one cheap volume, it might be called *All about Sylvie and Bruno*."

2. Probably s&b, p. 3.

3. Probably s&b, p. 268.

4. We cannot identify (3), (4), (5), (6), or (7).

Incomplete ms: *Lilly*

7 Lushington Road, Eastbourne
August 26, 1889

Dear Mr. Furniss,

I echo, most sincerely, your words "I am truly sorry." It is a severe disappointment to me to find that, on account of a single square-inch of picture, as to which we disagree, you decline to carry out your engagement.[1] Well, I have far too much horror of "Law," to *insist* on your promise being carried out: moreover, I am not quite so foolish as to believe that Art-work, extorted by legal process, would be worth anything at all. So I release you from all your engagements. Before I end this letter I will enter on the question of the *comic* pictures, which do *not* include Sylvie and Bruno. But first I am going to surprise you, I think, by telling you that the *rest* of your letter is simply *delightful* to me!

For a good many years (long before I had the pleasure of knowing you) I have projected a magazine-article (or pamphlet) on the subject of "Authors' Difficulties with Illustrators": but I did not see my way to bringing it out with any *raison d'être*. This *you* have just given me: and I thank you sincerely for doing so. *You* shall have your say first: and my paper will come out, most appropriately, as an answer to yours. I not only fully authorise you to print the "5 pages" of my letter,[2] which you say would win you "the sympathy of all the Artists," but I call upon you to do so. The following conditions I think I may reasonably demand:

(1) that no name but "Lewis Carroll" shall be used for me.

(2) that you shall print *the whole* of what I wrote about the "Sylvie and Beetle" picture, verbatim.

(3) that the picture itself shall, if possible, be published along with the article. (I will pay the *whole* expense of this: and it is obvious that "the Artists" cannot possibly extend their sympathy, with justice, either to you or to me, without seeing the picture).

(4) that you make it *quite* clear that we make this appeal in a *friendly* spirit: and that our *artistic* differences have left our *human* relations untouched.

Like you, I shall await with confidence the verdict of "all the Artists," on the question at issue between us, as to whether the figure of Sylvie is, or is not, in the correct proportions of an ordinary child of 11 or 12.

I am going to prepare the article at once. I think of offering it to the *Magazine of Art* in the first instance: if they decline, I shall publish it else-where—at my own expense, if necessary.

It will be a unique, and I think rather a funny, controversy, as we shall put in the *same* evidence on both sides! For *I* also shall print the picture itself: and my own letter to you: and yours to me (which I presume you won't object to?). I shall also give careful reproductions of the faces, in *Romps*, and that of Mrs. Tottles,[3] to which my letter alludes. I shall also give, as an illustration of what *I* consider the right proportions for a child, a reproduction of a *quite* lovely picture, drawn by a friend of mine, of a child lying face-downwards, with a dead hare.[4] In connection with this, I am sure you will not object to my giving a few mathematical statistics (which my readers can easily verify for themselves), and pointing out that, by actual measurement (I have just done it, carefully) the height of Sylvie, with dead hare, is just under *six* diameters of her own head; while the height of Sylvie, with beetle, is just over *eight* of the same.[5] Also you won't mind my appealing to common Logic, and pointing out that it is impossible for *both* pictures to be in true proportion; and that the artist of the two is under a necessity, not unknown to racing-men, of choosing on *which* of his two horses he "declares to win."

Would you mind quoting, in your article, the following words from your letter dated August 23. "John Tenniel, George du Maurier, or Harry Furniss, must be accepted as they are—as the public are willing to accept them: you cannot alter them."

It had better appear in your article, to make the thing complete. For *I* also am going to quote Tenniel as an instance of the direct *contrary*! By a most curious coincidence, the very thing, which has upset all your plans, happened in *his* case! There was a *face*, and that's the face of the *heroine*, to which I objected. But instead of saying, as you would have expected, "you cannot alter John Tenniel: I cannot illustrate your book," he kindly consented to re-draw it, though this required the block to be "plugged."

Now as to the comic pictures yet to be drawn. The book must of course be now illustrated by *two* artists, the new one taking all the *Sylvie and Bruno* pictures, while most of the others are already drawn by you. Is there any reason why you should not complete the series you have so nearly completed, and with such marked . . .

---

1. On the same day, Dodgson wrote (*Diaries*, p. 474): "Yesterday I got the disastrous news that Mr. Furniss throws up the job he had undertaken, because I have told him I cannot use (but will pay for) his picture of 'Sylvie helping beetle' (in which she is *eight* heads high!). I wrote to Mrs. Morgan [Alice Havers, who drew the locket illustration on p. 77 of s&b], to get her for all the *Sylvie and Bruno* pictures. I still hope that Mr. Furniss will finish the *grotesque* ones." For more on Dodgson's relationship with Alice Havers, see *Letters*, p. 711. Dodgson also wrote to George Denman (1819–96), M.P., judge of the High Court (1881–92), for advice about the "disastrous" situation with Furniss. He had been friendly with the Denmans since 1864, and occasionally visited them in London. Dodgson's letter is missing, but Denman's reply (ms: Dodgson Family) says that the agreement being so vague, he recommends that Dodgson and Furniss "submit the matter to some one in whom both parties have confidence, and the right man to say 'what should be done.'"

2. Missing.

3. s&bc, p. 248.

4. Missing.

5. For "Sylvie and dead hare," see s&b, p. 321; for "Sylvie with beetle," p. 193.

7 Lushington Road, Eastbourne
August 30, 1889

Dear Mr. Furniss,

I assure you that I do indeed "take in good part" all you say, and rejoice to feel that we are still friends.[1]

Your words, "I in no way decline to carry out my engagement to illustrate your book," are truly welcome. The words, in your previous letter, "I cannot illustrate your book," had seemed to me to leave no room for hope: and my "haste" in seeking another artist may perhaps be excused when it is remembered how near at hand Xmas is.

Of course I won't publish the now-so-happily-ended controversy, as you think it would damage you to such a fearful extent! I had quite understood that the challenge proceeded from *you*, and that you really would like to appeal to the artistic world for sympathy.

And now what *can* I say, worthy of the occasion, in reply to your generous offer to re-draw the heads I objected to? You put me to shame by such kindness: and I will try to reply in the same spirit, by saying "let them remain as they are." I will print them, even without alteration. Every time I look at the "Sylvie and beetle" picture, it seems prettier and more child-like: and, when the picture is reduced to the necessary dimensions, I doubt if what I objected to will be noticeable at all. And Mrs. Tottles will do very well, I daresay, when reduced and cut.

So forgive, if you can, my super-fastidiousness: and let us get on with the other pictures.

And please don't trouble yourself to draw Sylvie's head, first, for approval, in each picture of her. The "dead hare" picture will do very well to show you the sort of Sylvie I want. Believe me

Gratefully and sincerely yours,
C. L. Dodgson

P.S. In writing to my other artist-friend, I have said nothing more definitive than "are you now free to undertake work?"

---

1. Furniss's reply to Dodgson's letter of August 26 is missing, but on August 29, Dodgson wrote in his *Diaries* (p. 474) that "Mr. Furniss wrote again, revoking his decision, and offering

to re-draw the faces of 'Sylvie and beetle' and 'Mrs. Tottles' (which two I had said I could not use). This is welcome news. I wrote to say I would relent on my side, and accept them unaltered."

Incomplete MS: *Morgan*

7 Lushington Road, Eastbourne
September 3, 1889

Dear Mr. Furniss,

I enclose the drawings you ask for, *viz.*, "Sylvie and beetle," "Sylvie and dead hare," "Professor and boots," "Tottles." It was only to spare you trouble that I didn't send them before: in return for your kind concession to my prejudices, I wished to concede something on *my* side, by putting aside the prejudices. Also by all means send *heads* of Sylvie, before doing rest of picture: it will perhaps be the best plan: but I'm costing you a real *appreciable* outlay in postage. When we wind-up, I'll make a rough estimate of that item (perhaps *you* can give me the exact sum) and repay it.

You have now devised 28 pictures for this volume, and have drawn (so far as I have seen them) 20, leaving 8 to be finished. But 28 isn't nearly enough! I should like 40, if you have the patience to draw so many. If necessary, I am prepared to postpone the publication till Easter 1890, or even Xmas 1890. Delay is a mere trifle, compared with the importance of giving the public as good an article as I possibly can.

I will add a few suggestions as to pictures.

(1) In the 1st meeting of Prof. and children, I've altered Bruno's speech "what a funny *waistcoat*, etc." to "coat." I mention this to save you the trouble of making the waistcoat visible. Bruno's term "coat" of course refers to the *dressing-gown*.[1]

(2) I think you've illustrated quite enough verses of the Gardener's song. I have put the illustrated verses into new places, so as to *spread* them as much as possible, as follows:
"Buffalo" just before arrival at Elveston Station
"Banker's clerk" I have kept in present place
"Kangaroo" just after watching crab on sea-shore
"Coach and four" just after Uggug and umbrella[2]

(3) What do you think of a picture (just after departure of Warden) of

Vice-Warden and Chancellor skipping round room, and my Lady waving her handkerchief? I think it would be funny.[3]

(4) The Vice-Warden, as "Fool," and his wife as "Bear," might be a good subject. Uggug entering in background, amazed. The others should be in foreground, so that their faces may be visible to reader, though unseen by Uggug.[4]

(5) As to the Dogs in Dogland: what do *you* think about dress? *Complete* dress would, I think, be too much like dancing-dogs at a fair. *Half*-dress looks disagreeable, I think, as suggesting that there ought to be *more* of it. My present view is that *head*-dresses, and *collars*, are all it would be wise to put in. The King should have a magnificent crown on, when at home: but a coronet, when escorting the children. By the way, *have* Newfoundlands long ears? I have made Bruno tie the King's ears under his chin. If they haven't, perhaps the King had better be a bloodhound; or I could erase the sentence.[5]

. . . I most *earnestly* hope that I have not so expressed myself as to cause needless annoyance to my Artist![6]

The pictures are, as a whole, quite *admirable*, and I should find it hard to express how much I enjoy their beauty — specially the graceful form of *Sylvie*, which will be quite a feature in the book.

I am going to send the other drawings to Swain,[7] and to get to work, as soon as I can manage it, at arranging and completing the text: and I will very soon send you my ideas, with rough sketches, for some 6 or 8 more pictures. Perhaps you can suggest some? Believe me always.

Sincerely yours,
C. L. Dodgson

1. *S&B*, p. 11.
2. For the verses of the "Gardener's Song," see "Buffalo," p. 79; "Banker's Clerk" (Hippopotamus), p. 91; "Kangaroo," p. 106; "Coach and Four" (A Bear without a Head), p. 117; and "Albatross," p. 165.
3. *S&B*, p. 48.
4. *S&B*, p. 123.
5. *S&B*, p. 176.
6. This fragment without date or correspondence number, which completes the letter, appears on a different size of sheet. It may possibly fit here.
7. Joseph Swain (1820 –1909), eminent engraver of his day, engraved all of Tenniel's illustrations for *Punch* and Holiday's illustrations for *Snark*. The "Piano" block is probably the illustration in *S&B*, p. 96.

7 Lushington Road, Eastbourne
September? 1889[1]

. . . Now as to that picture itself. I think it's simply *lovely*. And I can hardly leave off looking at *Sylvie*: face, figure, everything, is *the* Sylvie I want for my book. She is *perfect*. Bruno is very pretty indeed: but nothing can approach the beauty of that fairy-child. You have indeed made me noble amends for sinking my objections to the under-sized features of Sylvie in the "Beetle" picture, by drawing me 3 Sylvies, whose. . . . [section of letter missing]

. . . So it means very little, I fear, when I say I think the picture first-rate. The King dog is exceptionally beautiful. By the way, I want to put in a paragraph of description, . . .

1. The content of these fragments without date or correspondence number suggests that Dodgson wrote them about this time. They may be part of the previous incomplete letter.

––––––––

7 Lushington Road, Eastbourne
September 16, 1889[1]

Dear Mr. Furniss,

I enclose mounted text, pp. 39 to 51. I have taken memoranda of the beginnings of all pages, now in your possession, so that I can quote the actual *page*, in writing to you. Also I have put, for your convenience, running headings, to each of this batch, showing what *Chapter* you are in. You will find it convenient, I think, to put similar headings (which I don't remember doing) to the first 38 pp.

I will now go through your rough sketches, with your remarks thereon (I presume you are keeping, for reference, a duplicate of the numbered list of pictures which you sent me):

No. 5 (Chancellor and Vice-Warden skipping about): Looks first-rate, and very funny. I don't know what you mean by "width of page, i.e. across page." Do you mean a full-page *sideways* picture? (when you mean that, would you say "sideways picture"?). If you mean *that*, I venture to demur: it does not seem to me important enough to fill a page. And the fewer *sideways* pictures we have, the better. I *don't* like making my readers twist the book *round* to look at a picture: although, with *some* subjects, this is inevitable, e.g. your magnificent conception of Dogland Court must *of course* be sideways: 3 3/8 inches isn't nearly width enough to do it justice.[2]

No. 10 (Warden with his 2 children): Admirable, I think. This seems to me quite the best for *Frontispiece*. I don't want a *grotesque* picture for Frontispiece. There will be a good deal of *serious* writing in the book: and I want the *keynote*, struck in the Frontispiece, to be *serious*. As I suppose you mean me to criticise the rough sketches *freely*, I will venture to say that I think Sylvie's face too small, both for her head, and for her figure. The "mathematical statistics" (which you think so irrelevant, but which I think you will find all great figure-painters observe to a hair's-breadth) say that the eyes should come half-way between the top of the head and the point of the chin.[3] [section of letter missing]

. . . No. 37 (Dogland Court): It's quite delicious. By all means have it a full-page sideways picture. *What* a job you're undertaking, with your "dogs of all kinds"! Sylvie and Bruno are *just* what I want.[4]

There remain 2 un-numbered rough sketches.

One is Sylvie (already drawn in, in ink) seated on *something*, and surrounded with *things*. Are they *Frogs*? If so, what moment in the history does it represent? And will not *two* large pictures be too much for the Frog-entertainment? You've already sent me *one*, you know, where Bruno is turning a somersault.

On looking at this again, I see what perhaps *is* the somersault, in the background. So I suppose you have changed the former picture into this.

Sylvie is very sweet, though her face is different from the "Mastiff Sentinel" picture. However, it will do very well. What is she looking up at? And what is she doing with her hands?[5]

The other is the Nurse-maid going "in two halves." Well, no, I can't say this *does* realise my idea. First, you've made her a sort of "Tilly Slowboy,"[6] a sort of half-daft "slavey" from a cheap lodging house . . .[7]

1. "Wrote the concluding scene of the volume of *Sylvie and Bruno*, which I hope to bring out next Christmas," Dodgson wrote in his *Diaries* (p. 474) on September 9. "There are now only some portions of dialogue to write in."
2. s&b, p. 48. It appears sideways.

3. *s&b*, frontispiece.

4. *s&b*, p. 176.

5. *s&b*, p. 373.

6. In Dickens's *Cricket on the Hearth* (1845), Tilly Slowboy is "of a spare and straight shape, insomuch that her garments appeared to be in constant danger of sliding off her shoulders. Her costume was remarkable for its very partial development, and always afforded glimpses of the back of a pair of dead-green stays" (Chirp the First).

7. *s&b*, p. 285.

---

* MS fragment: Morgan*

7 Lushington Road, Eastbourne
[?September 16, 1889]

[probably part of previous incomplete letter]
. . . It is very delightful to read such a sentence as "I can easily draw the number you require well in time." But have you realised what "in time" means? We ought to begin working off the 20000 copies of the first sheet *this month*, I fancy, and then be able to supply the printer with the other 19 sheets *continuously*, to have any chance of being out by Xmas. I would like to have 40 pictures, if possible. Of these we have

finished	-	15
nearly so	-	2
in progress	-	4
sketched	-	<u>10</u>
		31 . . .

MS: Berol

7 Lushington Road, Eastbourne
September 17, 1889

Dear Mr. Furniss,
Many thanks for your very satisfactory letter.
I find we shall want a month to print, and a week to dry, before binding can *begin* even. So I shall be very glad if we can get the *first sheet* arranged by the beginning of October. And then, if you will get the pictures finished as far as you can manage, in the order they come in the book, we may be able to

keep the printers' hands full. Thus you might be drawing the *last* picture (which I should like to be a vignette of sunrise over the sea) close to the *end* of October.

I'll send you nearly all the book in a few days, noting what seem to me fit subjects for the *serious* pictures. But it will be a great help to have *your* views also, as to what you think will draw well.

"Piano" block may go straight to Swain.

> Yours very sincerely,
> C. L. Dodgson

MS: *Morgan*

7 Lushington Road, Eastbourne
September 21, 1889

Dear Mr. Furniss,

Many thanks for the pictures.

(1) "*Sylvie and dead hare*": quite charming. This I *think* will be the *chef d'oeuvre* of your pictures done for me: at least you'll find it very "hard to beat"![1]

(2) "*Tottles*": It was *most* kind of you, after I had abandoned my objections to printing this and the "Beetle" picture, still to insist on re-touching them: and I thank you sincerely. You have *much* improved the lady's face.[2]

(3) "*Prof. and boots*" will do capitally.[3]

(4) "*S. and Beetle*": As in the case of No. (2), I thank you sincerely for whatever alterations you have made.[4]

(5) "*Bruno and dead mouse*": That's *just* the kind of *face* I want for Bruno. It's *roguish*, which is what I mean him to be: and it's just the right *age*. Please keep as near this face as you can in other pictures. His body is a little too *bulky* for my taste. (I remember writing once to urge that point on you: but it's years ago, and you may have forgotten it.[5] I haven't got a copy down here, but the *effect* of what I said, and wish to repeat with regard to future pictures, was "*don't* draw a podgy boy, a great eater of pudding, like the one on the left at p. 7 of *Romps by the Seaside*, but give us a little *acrobat*: a boy that *can* run and jump.") However, I don't mention that as constituting an objection to *this* picture. But there *is* a point I do, and must, object to in all these 3

pictures of Bruno which I send you herewith. He is *not dressed enough.* From there being no sort of collar, or even an *edge* to a garment, indicated round the neck, the *effect* is one of *nakedness* to a great extent. This isn't a question of *art*, but of suitability to my book. I can't have partly naked figures. Could you not devise some fantastic kind of collar, and belt, for him? I don't suggest a "Lord Fauntleroy" sash for his *fairy*-state (though I *hope* you'll give him one when he appears as a *child*): but I think some kind of belt would be a great improvement: while some kind of collar, to indicate a *top* to the garment, is absolutely "necessary." (I use your own word. You said you didn't object to "necessary" alterations).[6] Another quite "necessary" alteration (or omission if you prefer it) is the group of flowers. You have drawn *blue*-bells (which grow singly) not *hare*-bells (which grow 5 or 6 together, along the lower side of a single stalk). The above is copied from Sowerby's *Botany.*[7] Your blue-bells are very pretty, but, if you look at the text, you'll see they don't suit it. Bruno can't run his hand along them, like a row of bells, unless he has a lot, close together, on one stalk. If, however, you'd rather not be bothered with more flower-drawing (and I am *very* loath to bother you any more) I'll simply tell Swain to leave out the flowers. It will make quite a pretty little picture without them. If you *do* alter (easily done by adding a flap of paper to cover these flowers) and think it would look better to have more than a single spray of hare-bells, I'll strike out the words about there being only *one* spray of them within reach.[8]

The mouse is charming: but his tail looks to me *in the air.* You want it to look *on the ground*, don't you? Would a few touches of grass, *beyond* the tail, make it look more flat?[9]

I *don't* want *another* picture of Bruno playing on hare-bells. One is enough.

(6) *"Warden, S., and B., visiting Professor"* will do capitally. Sylvie is just *delicious*, just the face and figure I want, and *what* a pretty pair of legs you've given her! Bruno, being back in the shadow, looks quite dressed enough.[10]

(7) *"S. and B. and mouse-lion"*: The mouse-lion is a stroke of genius! Sylvie's legs look a little "skin-and-bony," specially the left one. But I'm not sending it back for *that*, but for *Bruno.* He is *much* too naked. Excuse my using coarse language (I don't know how to put it more euphemistically), but a picture, exhibiting the naked posteriors, even of a very young boy, can not *possibly* go into the book. Bruno's *face* is charming.[11]

(8) "*S. and B. with mastiff*": I'm delighted with the way you've managed the blunderbuss. I hadn't thought of that dodge. Sylvie is charming. But Bruno is again too *puddingy*. And he looks nearly naked.[12]

Thanks for suggestion about Swain. I sent him all I could, this morning, and told him which would be wanted first.

I'll erase "Italian" in description of greyhound. Do just as you think best about crown and robes.[13]

By the way, don't forget about the *correspondences* I told you of between the fairy-world and the real world. You may give a family-likeness to

(1) Warden and Earl

(2) Sylvie and Lady Muriel

(3) Professor and "Mein Herr" (but this belongs to Vol. II).

Hoping *very* much that you won't be annoyed with this letter, I am

Very sincerely yours,

C. L. Dodgson

1. S&B, p. 321. Dodgson actually writes "bad to beat."

2. Possibly S&BC, p. 248. If not, this illustration did not materialize.

3. S&B, p. 15.

4. S&B, p. 193.

5. See letter of September 1, 1887.

6. S&B, p. 213. The "necessary" collar and some faint wispy lines to suggest a belt appear.

7. James Sowerby's monumental work *English Botany*, 1790–1814.

8. Dodgson retained the hare-bells passage (p. 213), but if he intended a separate drawing of the hare-bells, it did not materialize. In the drawing of Bruno and the mouse (ibid.), we seem to get a tuft of grass, but it may have been meant to be a tuft of hare-bells.

9. Furniss added the touches of grass to make the mouse's tail appear on the ground (p. 213).

10. S&B, p. 134.

11. S&B, p. 108.

12. S&B, p. 172.

13. Dodgson substituted "beautiful" for "Italian" greyhound in the text (S&B, p. 177), and the greyhound illustration appears on p. 176. The crown is carried by one of the dogs in the background, and the King's robes appear briefly on the ground behind its front paws.

MS: *Morgan*

7 Lushington Road, Eastbourne
September 23, 1889

Dear Mr. Furniss,

Now that I have drawn up the enclosed paper,[1] I see exactly *where we are* with regard to the pictures. The case looks *almost* hopeless, with 7 chapters still blank of pictures: still, we are lucky in having the *first* half of the book pretty nearly illustrated; and, if *you* can only manage to work, continuously, till the end of October, I *think* it's just possible to get it out by Xmas, and so not lose the Xmas selling-season. We ought to aim, I think, at getting the 25 chapters into the printers' hands not *later* than the first 25 days of October, a day for a chapter. So the question for *you* to consider is, aiming at 40 pictures (not counting the "locket"),[2] and reckoning 21 as *done*, and 8 in progress, do you think you can finish those 8, and draw 11 more, before the end of October? I fear me much you will say "No! It's impossible!" as it means *at least* 2 pictures a week. However, we'd better go ahead for the present. If you cannot manage it, we must make it an *Easter* book.

The first thing to be done, clearly, is to finish "Prof. showing portable bath"[3] for Chap. II: then to draw "Chancellor removes Uggug"[4] for Chap. III, and finish "Uggug"[5] for Chap. IV. When once *that* is done, we can work off 9 chapters, which will keep the printers at work till October 10.

Now for subjects for the other 11 pictures.

(1) For Chap. XII, I suggest "Albatross fluttering round lamp, and turning into postage-stamp"[6] I'm aware it's an almost *impossible* subject! But don't you think there is a certain zest in trying impossibilities?

(2) For Chap. XVIII, I suggest Bruno swinging on Eric Lindon's arm, Sylvie pushing, Professor in background.[7]

(3) For beginning of Chap. XIX Sylvie as invalid child, holding up her arms to be taken up. She should look *very* ill, and in a *quite* different dress from any other picture of her. I think a *black* frock, with a rather long narrow skirt and a black hood, would be a capital disguise.[8]

(4) For Chap. XX (we've not had the *Earl* yet) what do you think of the Earl, Lady M., and Arthur, at tea? In house, or garden, as you prefer.[9]

(5) For Chap. XXI, Bruno crying, Sylvie hugging him.[10]

(6) For Chap. XXII, Eric lifting up Bruno to Lady M.[11]

(7) For Chap. XXIII (all the Magic Watch incidents are commonplace), Pug-dog guarding *Daily Telegraph*.[12]

(8) For Chap. XXIV (besides "Bruno as Macbeth"), Mouse, as dentist, extracting tooth of crocodile, who should be seated in a dentist's chair.[13]

(9) For Chap. XXV, Sunrise over the sea.[14]

That would make a total of 38 pictures, which will *do*, if there's no time for more. If you found you *had* time, perhaps you could find subjects for 2 more small ones, as "forty" would be a better number to advertise.

Very sincerely yours,
C. L. Dodgson

1. Missing.
2. Alice Mary Havers drew the small illustration of the locket (s&b, p. 77).
3. s&b, p. 24.
4. s&b, p. 41.
5. s&b, p. 53.
6. s&b, p. 165. Dodgson's sketch attempts the metamorphosis from Albatross to postage stamp, an "impossibility" that Furniss must have thought beyond his means.
7. s&b, p. 268. Furniss adopted Dodgson's suggestions.
8. s&b, p. 280. Following Dodgson's instructions, Furniss successfully disguises Sylvie as an invalid child.
9. s&b, p. 296. Furniss draws the Earl, Lady Muriel, and Arthur having tea indoors.
10. s&b, p. 307.
11. s&b, p. 341. Dodgson's sketch views the scene from a high vantage point looking down onto the station platform. Furniss chooses to view the scene from the railway line looking upward to the platform.
12. s&b, p. 351.
13. s&b, p. 380.
14. s&b, p. 395.

MS: *Morgan*

7 Lushington Road, Eastbourne
September 27, 1889

Dear Mr. Furniss,

Many thanks for your hope-inspiring letter just received.

As to "Albatross": If any other trisyllable will suit you better, please let me know. It can be a "cormorant," or a "dragon-fly," etc., etc., so long as the accent falls on the *first* syllable. I made the very same offer to Mr. Tenniel, when he remonstrated against "The Walrus and the Carpenter" as a hopeless combination, and begged to have the "carpenter" abolished. I remember offering "baronet" and "butterfly" (which, by the way, might suit *you?*), but he finally chose "carpenter."

Even with your correction, of "Carriage" for "Station," I still don't understand your suggestion of a picture of Lady Muriel for p. 14. Nor your remark that "there is a long gap without illustration during the conversation." The picture "old man at Station" is already set down for p. 14, and "Uggug and jug" for p. 13: and the "conversation" comes *between* these 2 pictures.[1]

The groups of "S. and B." (I *won't* call them "B. and S.": that means "Brandy and Soda"!), which you suggest, would be very pretty, no doubt. We might have it as No. 40, when 39 are done. But the interval (between "B. on Mouse" and "Crocodile"), which you propose to occupy with it, is not longer than either of the 2 intervals next preceding, *viz.* the one between "Dogland" and "S. and Beetle," and the one between "S. and Beetle" and "B. on Mouse."[2]

"Pig-Tale" really *can't* come into Vol. I. It's to be the salient feature of the climax, *viz.* the Banquet: and the Other Prof. is to recite it to the whole assembly.[3] Besides, anything which would have the effect of connecting the book with *Alice* would be absolutely *disastrous*. The thing I wish, above all, to avoid in this new book, is the giving any pretext for critics to say "this writer can only play one tune: the book is a *réchauffé* of *Alice*." I'm trying my very best to get *out* of the old groove and to have no "connecting link" whatever.

I sent off "Dogland," by Registered Post, yesterday.

Very sincerely yours,
C. L. Dodgson

It occurs to me that "Lame child lifting her arms to be taken up" will not be picturesque if she has to hold her crutch in one hand. Could it be slung round her neck, like the Sentinel's musket?[4]

---

1. Dodgson prevailed: for "old man at Station," see s&b, p. 62; for "Uggug and jug," p. 53; for "conversation," pp. 56–60.
2. Dodgson accepted this suggestion, and the drawing appears in s&b, p. 226; it comes close to the illustration of the crocodile on p. 229.
3. The "Pig-Tale" was held over for s&bc; see pp. 366–69 and 372–73.
4. Furniss did not alter the drawing, and the disguised Sylvie continues to hold her crutch in her hand (p. 280).

[7 Lushington Road, Eastbourne]
[September? 1889]

... it from a fall, which would necessarily be *headlong*. But perhaps fairy-babies do not obey the Law of Gravity.[1]

(2) *Frontispiece*: Sylvie is too obviously *en chemise*! And how lovely she looks in it! And its a perfectly proper dress, in *itself*: only it looks insufficient for

appearing in *Society*. Would you mind making it a more obvious frock, specially just above the knee, where you've given it no definite limit at all. I fancy an edge, like the sleeve, with some indication of embroidery, would say, plainly enough, "this is a *frock*, and *not* a chemise!"

Secondly, would you mind making her *shoes* a little more distinct?

Thirdly, I confess I *don't* admire Bruno's mouth, or his eye either, but the mouth is the point I most object to. It doesn't look right: it looks as if he were *making faces*, after taking medicine. I can't tell what it needs: but it seems to need *something*.[2]

Having mentioned these little matters, I leave it in your hands, to do what seems best: and will you then forward both drawings to Swain, marking them "to be reduced to full-page size" ...

1. Dodgson may be referring to "Titania's Baby" (S&B, p. 363), but we cannot be sure. This sheet does not contain a date, but the discussion of these illustrations fits other letters he wrote at the time.

2. Furniss adopted Dodgson's suggestions for the frontispiece in S&B.

[7 Lushington Road, Eastbourne]
[September? 1889][1]

... Another objection is that so small a face makes her look *older* than I want. It makes her look, to my eyes, more like 15 than 12, the age I want her to look like.

(I've just tried covering up the heads of Sylvie and father with the lowest left-hand corner of this page, and drawn her head larger. I see I've got it *too* large. But it will serve to show how *much* younger it makes her look, to draw her features on a larger scale.)

Do you think you'll be able (having a full page to work with) to get in any of the *back-ground* details, of which I have given a rather elaborate description?[2]

No. 15 (Children and Lion): Yes, by all means! I like your idea very much. Will you excuse me for saying that the face of Sylvie in this picture is *exactly* what I want. The eye *is* half-way between chin and top of head: and the features are on a decidedly *larger* scale, relatively to the figure, than they are in No. 10. And what a pretty, childlike, and innocent face your sketch suggests![3]

No. 18 (Jester and Bear): I think this will make a capital picture.[4]

No. 19 (Professor waking Other Prof.): Sylvie looks delicious, very graceful, and very child-like. (Once more, face and head seem to me in per-fect proportion for child of 12). The Professors make a very funny group: and, if you prefer to draw it so, I'll alter the text to suit. As the text *now* stands, the other Prof. is *sound-asleep, until* his nose is shut up in the book: when he *instantly* rises and walks away. *You* have made him wake up while thumping is still going on. I can easily alter the text. Shall I?[5] . . .

1. No date appears here, but again the discussion of these illustrations fits other letters that Dodgson wrote about this time.
2. Possibly the frontispiece for s&b.
3. s&b, p. 108.
4. s&b, p. 123.
5. The text does not appear to have been changed, and Furniss may have altered the drawing. The picture appears in s&b, p. 134.

[7 Lushington Road, Eastbourne]
[September? 1889][1]

... p. 51. (Ch. XVI) Crocodile walking along its own back:

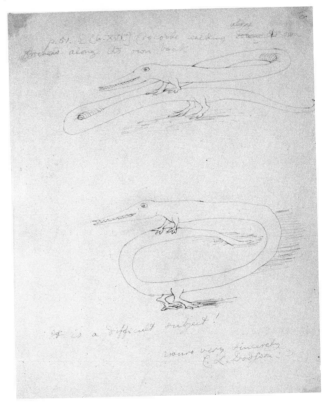

FIG. 30
*Dodgson's sketch for "Crocodile walking along its own back"
in letter dated September? 1889.*

It is a difficult subject![2]

Yours very sincerely,
C. L. Dodgson

1. This sheet does not contain a date, but it fits in with the other letters Dodgson sent Furniss at the time.

2. *S&B*, p. 229.

MS: *Morgan*

7 Lushington Road, Eastbourne
September 30, 1889

Dear Mr. Furniss,

Many, many thanks for the quite delightful set of finished drawings. I am *entirely* satisfied with them, and have not a criticism to offer. Bruno's dress is charming. And Sylvie's legs and feet are now beautiful, in the "Mouse-Lion" picture.[1] I've just succeeded in getting all 6 drawings packed off to Swain: and I now hasten to offer suggestions about the sketches. Here again I have *no* artistic criticisms to offer: and the *faces* all promise to be as good as possible. The only suggestions I have to offer concern the arrangement of details, so as to suit the text.

The railway-scene (which I return herewith) will be the better, I think, for considerable change of treatment. May I suggest, then, that I don't believe any lady, in a dress for which she had any value, would *kneel down* on a railway-platform, except under the stress of a *great* emergency: and the mere lifting up of Bruno, when the danger is past, is *not* such an emergency. Don't you think she would come more within the bounds of probability (and perhaps, even, be more graceful also) if standing?

Another remark. The Express, if visible at all, would be *quite* in the distance, at least *1/2 a mile* off, I should say. Remember it is going at 40 or 50 miles an hour: and it would be nearly a minute, *after* picking up Bruno, before Eric could have *re*-crossed the line, and be handing him up to Lady M. Where you have put the train, it looks about 100 yards off, so that it could only be 2 seconds since it passed. My idea would be, to abolish the *tunnel*, and put a bit of background landscape (the sort of bleak open country, with few small trees, that one finds near the seaside), the railway winding away in the distance, and the train seen as a little black speck, distinguishable only by its trail of smoke. Taking Eric as 6 feet high, and a R.W. carriage as 10 feet high, and your picture as 30 inches from the eye, the height of the train at 1/2 a mile, would be less than an 1/8th of an inch.

I think, to give width for Eric's run, there should be 4 lines of rails, the Express being supposed to have passed on No. 3 (counting from the platform on which Lady M. is, and from where Eric started), which would give room for his *run*, and space *beyond* the train for him to run *into*. He wouldn't have time to pick up Bruno, and *turn* with him: he would have to pick him up as he ran.

Another remark. Would not Eric be looking *up*, *at* Lady M.? Remember he is her accepted lover. Even in such a moment as that, he would think of *her*, not of *Bruno*.

I've made the rails a good deal too narrow, in this scrawl.[2]

The other drawings, with remarks, shall follow speedily.

> Very sincerely yours,
> C. L. Dodgson

Thanks for list of dogs. Is the spotted one *really* a Dingo? Or a coach-dog?

1. s&b, p. 108.
2. s&b, p. 341. Furniss adopted some of Dodgson's suggestions, but not all of them. Lady Muriel does, indeed, kneel to take Bruno in her arms; the Express has vanished from the scene, leaving just a cloud of smoke; the tunnel is gone and no background scenery appears; only one railway track is visible; but Eric does look up at Lady Muriel.

Incomplete ms: *Morgan*

> 7 Lushington Road, Eastbourne
> October 1, 1889

Dear Mr. Furniss,

I have had a good laugh over the delicious trio of pictures which reached me this morning. Nothing could be better! There is evidently no danger at all that the shortness of the time, and the sense of hurry which that might produce, will cause any falling-off in the artistic finish of your work! I've sent two of them to Swain, but the third I return, to ask you to be so kind as to put a line round it, as you offer, and to fill in the corners a little. It certainly ought to be a full page: it would lose so much by being reduced; and I think it would be a pity to put the line further off than the enclosed experiment,[1] even though that *does* cut off a bit of the arched roof. However that is a matter I leave to your judgement. But a *line* I would like it to have, as I shouldn't like the effect of a vignette on a page, and nothing else.

Sylvie, in this picture, is *most* lovable . . .

1. Dodgson's sketch is missing.

Incomplete MS: *Morgan*

> 7 Lushington Road, Eastbourne
> October 3, 1889

Dear Mr. Furniss,

You are doing nobly, and the "War-Dance" is capital.[1] I am sending it to Swain. As to the sketch (I *believe* you don't mind perfectly candid critiques on *sketches?*) I think Bruno and Eric do very well (only by the way, I observe one *great* danger ahead, of your getting Eric and Arthur too much *alike*. Remember, they are no relations at all. Please, if you can, give them distinct types of face, and give Arthur the best. I mean *him* to be a grand, noble character, Eric to be much shallower, good-natured, and with no harm in him, but not much *thought*, or anything else, though of course many degrees better than an idiotic "masher").

But Lady M.'s attitude I venture to think *clumsy*. One thing is, her feet are too far apart: a woman *cannot* look graceful when taking anything at all suggesting a man's *stride*. The other is, she is overbalancing herself. I *think* (to talk mathematically) that her "centre of gravity" is *already* beyond the "base of support": at all events, if not, she is only *just* balanced, and is *quite* incapable of taking anything of Bruno's weight into her hands, without upsetting. Possibly Eric *might* hand her a *3d. Bradshaw*[2] without overbalancing her: but I think a *6d.* one would do it!

Next, who is to be the figure behind? If you mean it to be the Stationmaster, well and good. But it mustn't be the *Earl*. *He* is supposed to be far away. *Sylvie* of course is present: you can put *her* in, if you like. I leave it to your judgement.

If you wouldn't mind the trouble, I should like another sketch of this picture.

Couldn't you get some live woman to actually *stand* on a raised place, and have something, as heavy as a child of 6, handed up to her? That would show, practically, the limits of safe balancing.[3]

As to the other 3 sketches (I must write quickly, to save the post):

(1) *5 p.m. tea*: Arthur excellent: handsome, earnest and thoughtful, capital attitude. Lady M., chin a *little* too far below mouth. Could you give a rather longer nose, and less chin? More like the girl in *Romps* who you know is a favourite of mine. Her *expression* is charming. Earl excellent.

It is such a relief to me to find that the *real* people are all coming right: I was very nervous about it.[4]

(2) Child with crutch: The steps should be *behind* her, not in front. If you were going to carry Dorothy upstairs, you would hardly *begin* by going 3 steps up, without her, and then *stooping* for her. Her face is excellent. I want her to look . . .[5]

1. s&b, p. 48.

2. *Bradshaw's Railway Guide*, a timetable of passenger trains running in Great Britain, first issued in 1839 by George Bradshaw, printer. For a description of Dodgson's juvenile skit based on the *Bradshaw* guide, see "La Guida di Bragia," *Handbook*, p. 4.

3. s&b, p. 341. Furniss drew another sketch using Dodgson's suggestions. Lady Muriel looks well balanced and the stationmaster has vanished. Sylvie does not appear.

4. s&b, p. 296.

5. s&b, p. 280. Furniss has drawn the steps behind the child; she is Sylvie in disguise.

---

ms: *Morgan*

7 Lushington Road, Eastbourne
October 5, 1889

Dear Mr. Furniss,

Mouse-Dentist and Albatross are first-rate.[1] I can't make any variety in my remarks! They're *all* first-rate, now.

I leave for Oxford on *Wednesday*, after 1st post has come in.

As to omission of steps in "Child and crutch" picture, I leave it entirely to *your* judgement. For myself, I confess I should like to have them: they seem to me to give a *raison d'être* for her attitude, and completeness to the picture. However, I am not an artist: and it is mainly an *artistic* question.[2]

Very sincerely yours,
C. L. Dodgson

My list of your pictures for Vol. I is now 42 in number. No need to invent any more, unless a happy thought strikes you. Of the 42, I have now received 31. The remaining 11 are:

(9) Shakespeare scene
(2) Other Prof. asleep
(1) Old man at Station
(11) Warden and children (under ground)
(6) Nurse bisected
(4) Eric swings B.
(8) Eric saves B.
(7) 5 p.m. tea
(5) Child and crutch
(3) Crocodile on itself
(10) Sunrise

(numbered in order they will be required).

I hope you've not given up idea of "Crocodile on itself."[3] Its omission would cause a blank of 28 pp.

There is one more picture I *suggested*, but you haven't accepted as yet, B. sitting on bank, crying, and S. comforting him (Ch. 21). It's not absolutely *necessary* (its omission would cause a gap of 20 pp. only): but I think it would be pretty.[4]

There is *one* gap of 20 pp. which would be nicely broken if you would draw a little one of "Royal Baby in Buttercup" (Ch. 24). It should be some flower that is out in *October*.[5]

1. S&B, pp. 380 and 165.
2. S&B, p. 280. Furniss redrew the steps behind the girl.
3. S&B, p. 229.
4. S&B, p. 307.
5. S&B, p. 363. On the day after he sent this letter, Dodgson wrote to his publisher: "Would it not be a good plan to print 10,000 copies of *Sylvie and Bruno* to begin with, and then, while these are drying, to work off a second 10,000? Would not that enable the binding to begin much sooner than they would if the whole 20,000 were worked off at once? . . . Mr. Joseph Swain is anxious about the pictures. They are very delicate work (and of course must not, on *any* consideration, be *hurried*), and he fears he cannot finish them by the end of October. . . . So I want to allow him, if possible, more time." Macmillan replied on October 7 advising Dodgson that not much time would be saved by printing S&B in two installments and that much time could be saved if Swain would send the exact measurements of the woodblocks that were not yet ready, and if Dodgson would advise the printer where those prints were meant to fit into the text.

"The sheets could then be prepared and the text electrotyped," Macmillan wrote (*Macmillan Letters*, p. 260).

MS: *Morgan*

7 Lushington Road, Eastbourne
October 9, 1889

Dear Mr. Furniss,

I am sincerely sorry to hear so bad an account of Mrs. Furniss's health, and must heartily sympathise with you in all the anxiety her illness must cause you. And I sincerely trust a winter at Bournemouth will be of real benefit to her.

The other subjects of your letter I will take in the order in which they come, so as to be sure not to overlook any of your remarks.

I had fancied "buttercup" wouldn't suit the time of year. Would "marsh marigold" do better? It would be well, if possible, to have one in keeping with the *frogs*.[1]

Crocodile in chair will do capitally. You've got over the difficulty *most* ingeniously.[2]

Eric lifting up Bruno: Really it's a shame to be so troublesome: but would you mind returning to the *kneeling* attitude? Somehow I don't fancy the standing one: though no doubt it is quite correctly drawn. I like the kneeling arrangement: and my only objection (that it would spoil her dress) is not worth thinking about. If you'll do that, you needn't trouble to send another sketch, but can finish it off. And, if you possibly can, please give Eric the face you gave him where he is swinging Bruno: I liked that very much.[3]

Crocodile walking on himself: capitally *drawn*: and quite unobjectionable on any score of *propriety*, *but*, it doesn't suit the text! If there *is* any fun in the text (I don't say there is) it depends *wholly* on the fact that the crocodile's march is in the direction *from tail to head*, so that its ultimate destiny is the very Irish Bull of its walking on its own *head*, and down its own nose. *Your* crocodile's prospects are simply a walk *down* his tail, and so off upon the ground, with no peculiar result except a "kink" in his back.[4]

Sylvie comforting Bruno is quite *lovely*. The attitude doesn't matter a bit. I'll alter the text to suit it. The reason I'm returning it is to ask if you would mind erasing the (accidental) extra line just above her mouth, which gives her (what I'm sure you don't mean her to have) a moustache!

By all means draw S. and B. on trunk of tree. It will be *very* pretty, I expect.[5]

I understand that you would like to make some alteration in the block for No. 3 of the "Peter and Paul" series: which of course you are most welcome to do: and I've no doubt it will be an improvement. I've written to Messrs. Clay, giving authority "to deliver, or send, to Mr. Harry Furniss or to Mr. Joseph Swain, the block of the picture representing a fat man seated in a chair, and a thin man bowing in front of him," and have told them they did quite right in applying to me for leave, before handing over the block.[6]

But to Mr. Joseph Swain, who probably acted in ignorance in sending to Messrs. Clay without first writing to me, I thought I had better explain how matters stand legally, and have told them that the *blocks* are my exclusive property, that Messrs. Clay merely hold them in trust for me, and that, were they to deliver them up, to any one whatever, without authority from me, they would exceed their rights and incur a serious responsibility. So I think all will be clear now.

I wonder what alteration you have thought of. Please *don't* make one that will entail altering the *text*! Verses are *much* harder to alter than prose. I've just had to make another alteration in text to suit your picture (you are not fairly chargeable with a *slavish* adherence to the text you illustrate!) of "pug guarding paper." I had stated them to be "on an easy-chair." *You* have (apparently) placed them on the *ground*. So I have meekly "followed suit."[7]   I've pretty nearly settled on *these* as the medallions for the cover: Sylvie from the picture where she is comforting Bruno, and Bruno from the one where he is seated on a dead mouse. Can you suggest any better ones?

Please remember that the "Picnic" is the picture we shall want *next*: after that

42. "Nurse going into halves"
43. "5 p.m. tea"
44. "Eric lifting up Bruno to Lady Muriel"
45. "Frogs' Entertainment"
46. "Sunrise"

and then you can say, with the Spirit in *Comus,* "Now my task is smoothly done, I can fly, or I can run!"[8]

Very sincerely yours,
C. L. Dodgson

Mouse-Dentist card was *torn* when I received it.

1. S&B, p. 363. Furniss drew a Michaelmas daisy, which flowers from August to December. The marsh marigold flowers only in the spring. See Furniss's letter dated October 10, 1889.

2. S&B, p. 380.

3. S&B, p. 341. For Dodgson's detailed discussion of this picture, see his letter dated September 30, 1889. Lady Muriel adopts a kneeling attitude.

4. S&B, p. 229. Furniss has succeeded in getting the crocodile to walk from tail to head along its own back.

5. S&B, p. 307. The "accidental" line above Sylvie's mouth still appears, but Furniss has obviously reduced it, and it no longer looks like a mustache. See Furniss's letter dated October 10, 1889.

6. S&B, p. 150.

7. S&B, p. 351. Dodgson altered the text so that the pug is lying in front of the easy chair rather than in it.

8. Milton's *Comus,* l. 1012.

MS: Morgan

On the R.W.
(somewhere near Croydon)
October 9, 1889

Dear Mr. Furniss,

A sudden thought: Couldn't she be kneeling on *one* knee? I think it would be both more graceful, and better adapted for receiving B., and then rising to her feet.

And, if you could make the picture of her a dreamy echo of that of S. helping the beetle, it would be a pretty "conceit," and quite in harmony with the spirit of the book.[1]

Very sincerely yours,
C. L. Dodgson

1. Throughout the two books, Dodgson intends the characters from the "fairy-state" to pair with characters from the world of "reality," but the reader has to detect the pairings; they are not

explicit. Lady Muriel is, for instance, the alter ego of Sylvie. Furniss apparently did nothing about Dodgson's "sudden thought" of making a subtle connection between Lady Muriel (p. 341) and Sylvie (p. 193). Either he did not grasp Dodgson's point or he chose to ignore it. Consequently we get no "dreamy echo" of the two characters.

MS: Berol

23 St. Edmund's Terrace, London
October 10, 1889

Dear Mr. Dodgson,

I find the flower is the "Michaelmas Daisy" (which flowers from August to the end of the year). For your purpose, it is something like this. But I have a careful study of it.

> Thy tender blush, thy simple frame,
> Unnoticed might have passed;
> But now thou com'st with softer claim,
> The loveliest and the last.[1]

I suppose the baby King is to have some sort of covering, but what?[2]
Yes, I'll draw Lady M. kneeling in Railway scene. I really think it more natural.[3]

FIG. 31
Furniss's preliminary drawing for "Crocodile walking along its own back" in letter dated October 10, 1889, and his final drawing.

Crocodile walking along its own back. I'll draw it like the above, which is a copy of your sketch, and is evidently correct.[4]

It seems I made a mistake.

I also seem to have made a slip with the Picnic pompous man. I got it into my head you intended him to be vulgar, but re-reading the text I find you having made him eccentric and a bore, so I'll alter the character.[5]

Sylvie's moustache I cannot find!

You surely didn't refer to this line, for that is usual in drawing the mouth. Take it away and it gives a long upper lip. But I'll make it more a *part of the mouth*. Without blurring it all will be well.[6]

Do you want *separate* heads for the medallions for the cover or two together?[7]

By the way you do not give size of Mouse Dentist for Swain, or Bruno crying. Do not make it too small. Give as much space as possible.[8]

I send you Sylvie and crutch, and the Other Professor asleep.[9]

I will probably send you Old Man at Railway Station tomorrow Saturday and Frontispiece early next week, then Frog page, so that the important work will be all at Swain's.[10]

I shall be delighted to get the material for Vol. II. in hand soon, as having to work long hours, as I am doing now, is rather trying, and prevents my doing anything else. I have had to refuse all sorts of work and, but for having my *Punch* work done well in advance gives all time to you, it would not have been possible to get Vol. I. out this year.

You might let me have all you can early in the year. I shall be at Bournemouth for six months, and there quietly I can do your work in peace. Summer *should be* holiday time, and Autumn is my very *busiest* time always. Therefore I feel sooner the better for your work.

Will you kindly let me have a cheque on account. My expenses are frightfully heavy and as I have been giving all my time to your book, I cannot bill on others. If you have a memorandum of what you have sent me, I can get my Secretary to make out an account for your approval which will save both your time and mine.

I am glad to say Mrs. Furniss is *much better*.

Very sincerely yours,
Harry Furniss

1. From "The Michaelmas Daisy" (*The Gazette Poetry*, 1820) by Letitia Elizabeth Landon (1802–38).

2. s&b, p. 363. The picture shows a dressed fairy baby.

3. s&b, p. 341.

4. s&b, p. 229.

5. s&b, p. 240.

6. s&b, p. 307.

7. Dodgson wanted two separate heads for the medallions.

8. s&b, pp. 380 and 307.

9. s&b, pp. 280 and 134.

10. s&b, pp. 62, frontispiece, and 373.

MS: *University of Toronto*

Christ Church, Oxford
October 12, 1889

Dear Mr. Furniss,

I'm distracted with business, so please excuse a telegram-style of letter.

"Michaelmas Daisy" by all means. I think baby should have usual long clothes. Could they be wrapped spirally round the stalk? That looks a fairly safe arrangement.[1]

Crocodile all right now.

Sylvie's lip ditto, when upper line is completed. I see it wouldn't do to erase it as I proposed.

We want two *separate* heads for medallions, as in case of *Alice* and *Looking-Glass*. One should be pretty, and one grotesque, I think: or, perhaps better, one might be Sylvie, and the other Bruno.[2]

I wrote to Swain to expect those 2 drawings from you, and told him what size to reduce to (Mouse-Dentist to be page-width, i.e. 3 3/8; S. and B. 2 1/2).

I don't know how our account stands: except that I have memoranda of having sent you £170 altogether. I enclose £100. Please understand that I abandon all attempts to calculate value of pictures by *dimensions*: so please charge what seems to you a fair interpretation of the scale of prices we originally agreed on, in which you named pictures in *Alice* as standards.

I'm *very* glad you give so good a report of Mrs. Furniss.

I write this at 1 3/4 a.m., but I'll keep letter open till first post comes in, to see if anything arrives.

By the way, you've made *another* slip, for want of reading text carefully through. "Professor and umbrella-boots": the umbrellas were meant to be *upside-down*, to guard against *upward* rain. You've put them in *ordinary* position. You will hardly guess, after all my cantankerous behaviour, how amiable I've been about it. I've *altered the text* to suit the picture![3]

9 a.m. Pictures just come, *quite* delicious! What do you think of the daisy-stalk going up one edge of the page, and across top, and text being arranged to fill in?

Very sincerely yours,
C. L. D.

1. *S&B*, p. 363. Furniss complied with Dodgson's wish.
2. Furniss chose to do Sylvie and Bruno.
3. *S&B*, p. 15. Instead of rain traveling upward, as he originally intended, Dodgson decided to have "horizontal" rain.

MS: *Morgan*

Christ Church, Oxford
October 29, 1889

Dear Mr. Furniss,

I find it difficult to express how much I admire this last picture of yours. It's the greatest success (I *think*, but it's very hard to choose!) of all your *Sylvie and Bruno* pictures. What I must marvel at is that you have realised *three* of my ideals in *one* picture. That is *exactly* my conception of Arthur, of the Earl, *and* of Lady Muriel!

As to alterations, I've only *one* to suggest, small but yet important. At present, Lady Muriel looks a *little* as if she were blind of her left eye. The reason is that there isn't the shadow under the upper eyelid which the other eye has. Consequently, it looks lighter-coloured than the other eye.

These figures are so splendidly drawn that I should like them as large as we can get them without losing artistic effect. Would you consider the possibility of sacrificing a little of the foliage at the top, and making the dimensions 9 x 5 3/4 instead of 9 3/4 x 6 1/4? If, after consideration, you think the present dimensions best, then keep to them.[1]

When you forward it to Swain, would you tell him he need *not* send me any photo-prints from the negative?

Very sincerely yours,
C. L. Dodgson

1. S&B, p. 296. Furniss made the minor alteration to Lady Muriel's left eye. Whether some of the foliage was sacrificed in order to make the figures larger is difficult to tell.

MS: Morgan

Christ Church, Oxford
October 29, 1889

Dear Mr. Furniss,

I write in haste to catch this post.

Sylvie's face, in the proof you send of "Bath" picture, looks to *me* very pretty. If *you're* satisfied, I am. The dark oval (background), between her throat and arm, would not, I presume, really come out so much blacker than all else? As it now stands, it looks just like an accidental blot of ink.[1]

5 p.m. tea is *excellent*. Yes: it must be a full page, of course. I'll send it you by a later post.[2]

Very sorry to say Swain announces it's quite impossible to get pictures done for Xmas. This upsets everything. Sale this winter will be 5,000 or 10,000 less than it might otherwise have been. I reckon we *might* get it out by middle of January: but particular dates don't matter *now*: we can take our time. One consolation is, we are now safe from all risks that attend the working, at high pressure, against time.[3]

Very sincerely yours,
C. L. Dodgson

1. S&B, p. 226. The dark oval works well in the picture.
2. S&B, p. 296.
3. "Heard from Swain (the engraver) that pictures cannot be finished in time for Christmas. Wrote to Macmillan, Clay and Mr. Furniss announcing this," Dodgson recorded that day (*Diaries*, p. 475). To Macmillan he wrote,

> I am sorry to tell you that Mr. Joseph Swain says it is quite impossible to finish the pictures for *Sylvie and Bruno* in time for Xmas. Please give me your opinion on the following points.

(1) I reckon, roughly, that we might get the book worked off by the middle of December, and the sheets dry for binding early January. My idea is that it would be worth while to advertise it, among other Xmas books, as "in the Press: will probably be ready by the middle of January." I fancy many purchasers of Xmas books would *wait* for it. But it is a point as to which you are *far* the best judge. (2) The sale will necessarily be much *less*, this year, than it would have been if we could have got it out by Xmas. I fancy the wisest course, now, would be to print 10,000 only, and store up the rest of the paper. To print 20,000, and sell (perhaps) 5,000, would bring my account for June 1890 terribly on the wrong side!" (*Macmillan Letters*, p. 266).

MS: *Morgan*

Christ Church, Oxford
October 30, 1889

This will do first-rate. Please put in hand (Swain or whoever else you like) *at once.*[1] Things are about desperate. Will write also: but this had better go.

Yours very sincerely,
C. L. Dodgson

1. "Mr. Furniss proposes to put some of the work into the hands of other wood-cutters," Dodgson wrote on this day (*Diaries*, p. 475). "Wired to him to do so; and wrote to Macmillan to see if *printing* can be similarly divided. It would be a great pity to miss the Christmas sale." Furniss responded immediately, as Dodgson notes (ibid.): "The same day a telegram from Mr. Furniss announced the thing to be impossible: so after all the publication must be deferred."

MS: *Morgan*

Christ Church, Oxford
November 1, 1889

Dear Mr. Furniss,

Let me congratulate you on having finished your 4–years' job! (It was begun, with the "Peter and Paul" drawings, in 1885.) If only we could have reached our present point a month ago! However there's no use crying over spilt milk. It was a good deal *my* doing in not keeping you better supplied with complete, and arranged, text. I haven't yet heard whether Macmillan advises to aim at middle of January, or Easter, for publication. I much prefer the former date myself, if only that life is uncertain, and I want very much to see it *out*. Besides, the sooner I can get this job off my hands, the sooner I can begin on Vol. II. So I am continuing to work at it 6 or 8 hours a day.

Now as to the concluding pictures of your series, which I got this morning—both are capitally drawn, in my humble opinion: but I hope you won't be very angry at my saying I can't make use of the *whole* of the railway-picture. It would have to be a full-page picture, and so trivial an incident is not fitted to fill a page. But I find it makes an excellent vignette, allowing of 10 lines of text (say 7 below and 3 above), by including all that is of real interest, and merely leaving out some of the tops of the houses, and a certain amount of Eric's long legs, which rather absorb too much attention in the picture looked at as a whole. I have tried (from memory, as the drawings have gone to Swain) a sketch to show how much picture I want to introduce. Of course I haven't marked the picture *itself*: but I cut an opening in a piece of paper, and told Swain to lay it on the card, and photograph what could be seen through it, and to send me a couple of prints. I'll send you one, and hope you will kindly consent to my using only that bit of your drawing, and will shade over (on the block, when it has been transferred to wood) the figures of the 2 railway-men, whom I have ruthlessly beheaded![1]

The sunrise is delicious![2]

Very sincerely yours,
C. L. Dodgson[3]

1. The picture appears as Dodgson apparently altered it, reduced at the expense of Eric's long legs and the two railwaymen, who were at first beheaded and then removed entirely. The picture then matched the proportion of its fairy equivalent, Sylvie with beetle (s&b, p. 193). The page has three lines of text above the picture, and seven lines below.

2. The last illustration in s&b, p. 395.

3. "The history of *Sylvie and Bruno* is one of perpetual oscillation!" Dodgson wrote on this date (*Diaries*, p. 475). "Today I hear from Macmillan that they think the thing [publishing before Christmas] quite *possible*. I have written to Mr. Furniss and left it in *his* hands to decide. It would never do to risk spoiling his pictures by too much haste." On November 5, Dodgson adds (ibid.): "Went to town to meet by appointment, at Messrs. Macmillans, Mr. Webb (secretary to Mr. Furniss), Mr. Swain, and Mr. Clay. Also went, with Mr. Webb, to see Mr. Cooper, to whom nine blocks have been given, to be cut. The outcome is, that we are to get it out this Christmas: it will be tough work." Two days later, Dodgson adds (ibid.): "My share of the work is no light one. To-day I worked on, with hardly a pause, from 9.30 a.m. to 8.30 p.m., and then had supper, instead of Hall." This pace continued for some days. On November 15, Dodgson reports (ibid.): "Both today and yesterday I worked from breakfast to 9.30 p.m., and at last the whole book is arranged

in pages. If only Mr. Cooper can satisfy Mr. Furniss with his nine wood-cuts, we can get *Sylvie and Bruno* out at Christmas." On November 24, Dodgson wrote to Clay instructing him to go to press, and on November 30 he received the remaining sheets (ibid., p. 476). Macmillan advertised that the book would be ready by December 13. On the twelfth, Dodgson went "to town for the day, to write in about 150 copies of *Sylvie and Bruno*, which will be published tomorrow" (ibid.). He sent a copy to Mrs. Furniss inscribed: "Presented to the Wife of Harry Furniss by Lewis Carroll in grateful recognition of the exceptional skill and the painstaking and patient labour that have made this book an artistic treasure. Christmastide, 1889" (Morgan). *Sylvie and Bruno* was reviewed in the *Academy* (December 21, 1889), which asked, "What are we to say about this new book by 'Lewis Carroll'?" It insisted that no critic who had read *Alice* wanted to speak ill of its author. "But ah, the pity of it! . . . We can assure . . . [the reader] that he will become weary and puzzled long before he reaches the end." The *Literary Churchman* (January 10, 1890) found that it fell short of the *Alice* books, although the reviewer also found much in it that was attractive and thought Sylvie and Bruno "delightful little creatures." The *Spectator* (January 18), in a long notice, said bluntly that Carroll had "failed in his attempt to produce a third work which can be put on a level" with the *Alice* books; but the *Athenaeum* (January 4), in another long notice, all jam and no vinegar, thought it "full of amusing things," the characters "delightful," and Carroll a "gay and witty writer."

Incomplete MS: *Morgan*

7 Lushington Road, Eastbourne
August 5, 1890

Dear Mr. Furniss,

Presuming that you will receive, in due time, the 58 pages of mounted text which I sent off this morning, I think I had better at once lay before you the ideas for pictures which have occurred to me.[1] Of course you will understand that these are mere *suggestions*. I am quite prepared to throw them all on one side, should you fix on other subjects, or find better ways of treating these subjects.

You have already drawn *nine* pictures for this volume:[2] and I have marked 26 more subjects, which, with the second "Locket" picture, will make 36 altogether. The first Vol. had 47 altogether; but then it had more than 380 pages. At present I only see my way to about 250 pages, for which I think these pictures would suffice.[3]

In paging the 58 sheets I have sent you, I have left large intervals in the numbers. It does not mean that *all* the omitted numbers will be filled in, but simply that more text has to be written in those intervals.

As to the places marked for pictures:

p. 2: Sylvie and Bruno, fairy size. Bruno swinging on ivy. Sylvie below, beckoning to him. This, I think, might be a *very* pretty picture.[4]

p. 4: King Fisher courting Lady Bird. We have discussed this, already: and I think we agreed that the picture should be an *interior*, with open window at the back, and King Fisher looking in (might he be serenading her, with a guitar?). Lady Bird should be doing tapestry, or some kind of work, and modestly looking down.[5]

p. 83: Thief trying to escape. I *have* ideas of this, but feel quite unable to draw them. Perhaps it would be a more effective picture if Nero wasn't . . . [strip of letter cut away]
. . . The boy should be about a head taller than Bruno. Nero should be crouching on the ground, holding thief by ankle, B. facing thief, S. behind Nero.[6]

p. 86: Bessie about to sing. She should be sitting on ground, doll (a good large one) across her lap, S. kneeling behind. Branch of apple-tree seen above.[7]

p. 88: S. and B. preventing "Willie" from entering public-house. Open windows might . . .[8]
[strip of letter cut away]
. . . *p. 89*: Willie's wife kneeling.[9]

p. 90: Lady M. seated on ground, at Arthur's feet. I haven't sent the text of this: it is mere *dialogue*. The sentence to illustrate is " 'See,' said she, suiting the action to the word, 'I am sitting at your feet, as if you were a second Gamaliel!' " Later on, she says " 'This tree, and the grass, make a very comfortable easy-chair.' "[10]

p. 141: Count asking S. the name of the song. *I* fancy the prettiest attitude for her would be *seated* at the piano, with her back to the spectator, but looking round over her shoulder. My attempts at illustrating my ideas get more fearfully bad, every time, I think![11]

p. 149: B., with Lion and Lamb, setting off for Picnic. I think B. might look well, dressed as Robinson Crusoe, or as an Esquimau.[12] He should *not* be in the usual Bruno dress. I enclose an attempted sketch.[13]

p. 150: Lion rescuing Lamb. Here again I enclose a sketch.[14] The *thing* under the table is the *Lamb*. (You would hardly guess it, but it is!) It is supposed to have seized the opportunity, of the interruption, to escape under the table.[15]

p. 152: Little Foxes' delight at finding feast awaiting them. I doubt if this is worth drawing: it would be so much of a repetition of the previous one. If you do draw, it would perhaps be best to have the feast in the background, and Bruno and the 3 foxes, hand-in-hand in a ring, dancing in front.[16]

p. 171: B. Lying on fern-leaf. S. rocking leaf. Professor seated with outlandish guitar.[17]

p. 173: Lady M. leaning her head on Arthur's breast. Might be very pretty. Daren't attempt sketch.[18]

p. 201: Lady M. prostrate weeping before marble cross. This, I think, ought to recall the attitude of Sylvie weeping over dead hare.[19]

p. 204: S. and B. coming, singing, through wood. This seems to me quite the best subject in the book for the Frontispiece. The children should be radiant (specially the faces) with magic light. And the dark shadows of the wood, all round them, will make a lovely contrast.[20]

p. 206: Open cupboard door, showing the Other Professor seated inside. We must keep to the rule of never showing his *face*. Perhaps the dish of nuts had better be on his knees, instead of a book; and he could then be bending over it, so as only to show the top of his head.[21]

p. 208: My Lady is surprised. Can't sketch it. She must look *silly* (having become semi-idiotic).[22]

p. 210: The Explosion. This, I think, might make a far funnier picture than the above poor sketch. Everything blowing up, and the Professor lecturing on, undisturbed![23]

p. 211: Lady M. kissing the old man. He should be seated in an armchair, in cottage-porch, small table by him with cup of tea, long pipe in his hand, and Lady M. leaning over him from behind, with her arms round his neck.[24]

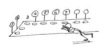

p. 212: Banquet. Other Professor, holding open book over his face, in act of falling. I think the following order of guests is right.

(1) Vice-Warden
(2) My Lady
(3) Room for Other Professor
(4) Sylvie
(5) Bruno
(6) Professor
(7) Chancellor.[25]

p. 215: There are 4 Introductory Verses *before* the Pig-Tale, and *7 after* it. You have the verses, I think? Can you find 1 or 2 of them capable of small pictures? The Little Birds should be the *shape* of half-fledged chickens, or goslings: but they should be quite as *large* as the other figures drawn with them, e.g. crocodiles, or seaside tourists.[26]

p. 216: Old beggar entering room, S. and B. clinging to his hands. Grand footmen, etc., starting back in horror.[27]

p. 222: Arthur on sofa. Lady M. kneeling by him.[28]

p. 223: Concluding vignette of Sylvie (half-length only), with clasped hands and up-turned eyes.[29]

Very sincerely yours,
C. L. Dodgson

1. Both Dodgson and Furniss evidently welcomed the chance to rest from their labors after *Sylvie and Bruno* was published. Dodgson was nevertheless intent on going through with his plans for *Sylvie and Bruno Concluded*. On March 31, 1890, he wrote to his friend Edith Blakemore (*Letters*, p. 781): "One piece of work . . . I am clear ought to be done this year, and it will take *months* of hard work: I mean the 2nd Vol. of *Sylvie and Bruno*. I fully *mean*, if I have life and health till Xmas next, to bring it out then. When one is close on 60 years old, it seems presumptuous to count on years and years of work yet to be done." He began work on *Sylvie and Bruno Concluded* on July 15, 1890, soon after his arrival at Eastbourne for the summer. On July 30 he received "from Clay some slips, of the MS lately sent, of the beginning of *Sylvie and Bruno Concluded*" (*Diaries*, p. 478). On August 2, on the train to Eastbourne from London, he told various stories including "Bruno's Picnic" to a little boy and girl he encountered. "Bruno's Picnic" became chapter 14 of *Sylvie and Bruno Concluded*.

2. Furniss prepared some of these drawings between 1885 and 1887 for poems that Dodgson wrote for *Sylvie and Bruno* but subsequently decided to use for volume 2: three for "The Little Man that had a Little Gun" (pp. 266, 267, and 268) and four for "The Pig-Tale" (pp. 367, 369, 372, and 373). Furniss drew one for "The Beggar's Return" (p. 382), another for "Uggug becoming Porcupine" (p. 388). The ninth picture, "Tottles," appears in chapter 16 (p. 248).

3. In the end, S&BC contained more pages than S&B: 411 as compared to 395.

4. S&BC, p. 8. Sylvie and Bruno are larger than the fairy size Dodgson wanted.

5. S&BC, p. 15. See August 11, 1890.

6. S&BC, p. 62. The thief is considerably taller than Dodgson suggested. Furniss complied with the other suggestions.

7. S&BC, p. 75. Furniss did as Dodgson wished, but omitted the apple-tree branch.

8. S&BC, p. 83. The open window reveals the public house clientele watching the scene with interest and mirth.

9. S&BC, p. 88.

10. S&BC, p. 119. The picture comes just before the dialogue Dodgson quotes. Furniss has made the base of the tree into a comfortable resting place for Lady Muriel. Gamaliel is, of course, the distinguished rabbi (see Acts 5:34).

11. *S&BC* p. 178. Furniss has adopted all of Dodgson's suggestions.

12. A variant spelling of "Eskimo."

13. *S&BC*, p. 230. Furniss has given Bruno the Robinson Crusoe costume.

14. Missing.

15. *S&BC*, p. 236. The Lamb has escaped under the table.

16. Appears not to have been drawn.

17. *S&BC*, p. 265. See August 15, 1890, n. 5.

18. *S&BC*, p. 277.

19. *S&BC*, p. 291. The illustration does match Sylvie with the dead hare in *S&B*, p. 321.

20. Indeed it appears as the frontispiece.

21. *S&BC*, p. 317. The Other Professor's face is not revealed. He holds the dish of nuts in his left hand, leaving room for a book on his lap.

22. *S&BC*, p. 326.

23. *S&BC*, p. 345. Furniss manages to create the explosion and yet allows the Professor to continue his lecture without disturbance.

24. *S&BC*, p. 350. Furniss has not adopted all the suggestions; the armchair is more like a garden seat, and the old man carries his cup of tea instead of its resting on a table beside him. Furniss adopted Dodgson's other recommendations.

25. *S&BC*, p. 352. Furniss adhered to Dodgson's order of guests.

26. The idea for the "Little Birds" illustrations changed and became a series of silhouette borders (pp. 365, 371, and 377).

27. *S&BC*, p. 382. Only one footman appears in the picture.

28. *S&BC*, p. 404.

29. *S&BC*, p. 411. Furniss had to make a number of changes to this illustration before Dodgson was satisfied with it.

MS: *Morgan*

7 Lushington Road, Eastbourne
August 8, 1890

Dear Mr. Furniss,

Swain may as well cut these 6 pictures at once: but I find it so difficult to settle what *size* they should be reduced to, that I think I had better tell you my ideas, and then leave it to you to tell Swain the sizes required.

(1) *Porcupine.* If we put this *upright*, and reduce it to 3 3/8 wide, I expect Swain will say, as he did about the "Uggug's Music" picture, that it is impossible to cut so many lines in that space. If made a sideways picture, it would want adding to the sides, to make it the right shape: and even then I expect such fine shading would beat the wood-cutters power. The fact is, you are *too enthusiastic* in the work you do for me! Such a quantity of lines in each square inch seems to me not only a waste of your time and trouble, but the

result is actually *less effective*, in my opinion, than a coarser style of shading would be. However, I leave the matter in your hands. My own view is that it had better be added to, and made a full-page picture.[1]

(2) *Tottles*. It seems pretty clear that this must be an *upright* picture, 3 3/8 wide. Will you kindly examine the *verticals* of this picture? It seems to me that the projecting angle of wall is not parallel to the side of the doorway, but leans to the right: at any rate the "dado" part of it does.

In the silhouette of the mother-in-law, does not the chin look rather too much like a beard?[2]

(3) The four "Pig-Tale" pictures. The two enclosed in lines must of course be 3 3/8 wide: and I presume the same may be said of the "fatal jump." But the vignette of "frog on tower" is very puzzling to fix the size for. Full width (3 3/8) would kill the other pictures. I have tried many sizes, and am inclined to think it had better be reduced to 2 1/4 wide. But *you* will be the best judge on this point.[3]

Yours very sincerely,
C. L. Dodgson

1. s&BC, p. 388. Furniss complied with Dodgson's wish and added to the composition; the picture became a full-page illustration, set sideways.

2. s&BC, p. 248. In this instance, Furniss did nothing with Dodgson's requests. The wall and doorway still do not appear to be parallel; likewise, the silhouette of the mother-in-law still has a chin resembling a beard. See November 20, 1887.

3. s&BC, pp. 367, 369, 372, and 373. The first and third of these pictures are enclosed in lines, and they in turn take up approximately half a page. The second illustration depicting the "fatal jump" has similar dimensions. The vignette of the "frog on tower" is less wide. See letter of January 26, 1887.

MS: *Morgan*

7 Lushington Road, Eastbourne
August 11, 1890

Dear Mr. Furniss,

This is really quite a first-rate plan of yours, to send rough sketches of your proposed treatment, before beginning the actual drawings. I can quite understand how vexatious it must be to an artist, after taking much trouble over a drawing, to be asked to make *any* change whatever in it: but rough sketches can be abandoned, and others tried, without any appreciable expenditure of time and trouble: and I am happy to think that you really do not mind my objecting to details in them, which do not seem to me to realise my conceptions.

p. 2: Bruno swinging. My idea was that he should hang by his hands from an ivy-twig. Don't you think that there would be a certain sameness in having him lying on an ivy-leaf in one picture, and on a fern-leaf in another? Your tone is so encouraging as to my trying my own hand at rough sketches, that I venture on one of this subject. I'm not sure if a boy *would* draw up his legs, Turk-fashion, as I have drawn them, or with the knees together. You might try your own little boy (without showing him the picture) and see how *he* does it![1]

p. 4: My idea is of a King, made to look like a bird, and a lady, made to look like an insect: and that they should be much more of a size. Here again I have ventured on a sketch. I didn't put a guitar into the King's hands as I found it would hide his beard. Suppose he has *dropped* his guitar, and she has *dropped* her work. Wouldn't that express deep emotions?[2]

p. 83: Nero catching thief. Yes, by all means put both children behind Nero. But don't make Bruno *jeer* at him. That's *not* his mental attitude, but rather *indignation.* Also I should like the thief to be *decidedly* bigger than the children. He might be dropping an apple or two in his terror.[3]

p. 86: I would prefer Bessie to sit on the *ground,* as in the text. You know it's in the *orchard.* Please make her a *pretty* little rustic. I think Sylvie had better kneel at the side *opposite* to the doll's head. Again I venture on a sketch. Bessie's legs are rather unintelligible. What I *mean* is, socks, and then bare leg. I think you'll find little rustics dressed so. And one sock or other usually needs pulling up! I've made Sylvie's skirt a good deal too long, I see.[4]

p. 88: "Willie" and children. This looks capital, in the rough. Please make Willie *quite* unconscious of presence of children. *They* ought to be semi-transparent, I think.[5]

p. 89: Do you *strongly* object to a "stage-effect"? Surely they are *meant* to imitate real life? I fear it sacrifices interest, not to show her full-face. But I would rather leave this point to *your* judgement. I will be content with it either way.[6]

As to *sizes,* I think they had better be as follows:

p. 2: (If you adopt my treatment) width of page, and leaving room for about 6 lines of text.

p. 4: Ditto, ditto, ditto.

p. 83: I don't think it important enough for a full page: but, if you like to treat it so, I've no objection. *Across* a page, it would only be about 10 lines deep, wouldn't it?

p. 86: Width of page, leaving about 10 lines below.

p. 88: I think would look best as an upright, *nearly* full-page. It might have 4 lines of text below, like the R.W. station at p. 62 of Vol. I.

p. 89: Sideways picture, full-page.

These suggestions as to sizes are merely *tentative*. If you prefer other sizes, please say so.[7]

As to the *chair*, at p. 90, by all means make it a *rustic* chair, as you suggest.[8]

Very sincerely yours,
C. L. Dodgson

P.S. By the way, you mustn't make Willie look *tipsy*. He looks a little so in the sketch. Remember he hasn't touched a drop of drink![9]

---

1. *S&BC*, pp. 8 and 265. Furniss complied. In the second, however, Bruno's feet are crossed, not drawn up. Dodgson's sketch is missing.

2. *S&BC*, p. 15. The picture is indeed an interior with King Fisher looking in through an open window. He has been serenading Lady Bird, but has momentarily dropped his guitar. Lady Bird has likewise dropped her wool knitting, not the tapestry work suggested by Dodgson, and is modestly looking down. Dodgson's sketch is missing.

3. *S&BC*, p. 62. Both children are behind Nero. Bruno appears smiling rather than jeering. The thief is not much larger than Sylvie, but he is in the act of dropping his apples in trying to get away from Nero.

4. *S&BC*, p. 75. Furniss apparently adopted Dodgson's suggestions, but again Dodgson's sketch is missing.

5. *S&BC*, p. 83. Furniss succeeded in making the children look transparent.

6. *S&BC*, p. 88. Willie's wife is shown full-face.

7. The sizes adopted are as follows: p. 8, room was made for five lines of text instead of six; p. 15, room was made for six lines of text; p. 62 became a full page; p. 75, space was made for eleven lines of text below; p. 83, size as indicated; p. 88, full page. Furniss did not make all of these adjustments.

8. *S&BC*, p. 119. Arthur's chair is rustic.

9. *S&BC*, p. 83. Willie still looks unsteady on his feet as if he is slightly tipsy, although his expression is sober.

7 Lushington Road, Eastbourne
August 15, 1890

Dear Mr. Furniss,

Many thanks for the inscribed copy of *R.A. Antics*.[1] I've not had time to do more than glance at it, but can see it treats of certain defects in the management of the R.A. I'm quite an outsider, and know very little of the matter, but no doubt your book will enlighten me.

As to our pictures, we are indeed getting on "like a house o'fire"!

By all means make it a *back*-view of "Willie's Wife," if you think that the best.[2]

As to the rough sketches herewith returned to you:

p. 141: What *you* call "Count asking S. to sing"—only he *doesn't* ask her to do so! (Please read all the *text* before drawing any picture.) However, what he is *saying* doesn't affect the picture. Yes, this is *exactly* my idea of the Count. Have any piano you like. A "grand" would have the advantage of being able to put in a background of listening guests. If you did *that*, I think it would be best as a full-page, "sideways" picture. But perhaps it's not a sufficiently important incident for a full page: and it would be *awfully* difficult to draw an audience hearing, for the first time, *supernatural* music. You would need to get into the faces some of the spirit of that wonderful picture (I wonder if you have ever seen it?) where Beethoven is playing, and a circle of *real* connoisseurs are listening. To my mind, when one "reads between the lines" and remembers what rare and heavenly music they were listening to, it is a *very* touching picture. There are photographs of it about: it was a photograph *I* saw.[3]

p. 152: Will come capitally, I expect. And I think you are quite right *not* to repeat the idea of the 3 foxes at a dinner-table.[4]

p. 171: B. on fern-leaf. I still think the Professor and Sylvie had better be (as in the text) on *opposite* sides of the leaf. However, if you think this best, I'll alter the text. My chief objection to it is that it makes him so completely turn his back on B., to whom he is supposed to be playing. A new idea occurs to me: to have the Professor seated on a *snail-shell*. I enclose a rough sketch of it. You will observe that my idea of a *snail* is, if possible, more vague than my idea of badgers and herrings! Whichever way you put it, I think it should be a full page.[5]

p. 173: Arthur and Lady M. I am *quite* charmed with the *lapsus pennae*[6] in the motto beneath. "She had never done such a thing in his presence before." As if she . . .[7]

1. Furniss's book *Royal Academy Antics*, published that year.
2. A front view of Willie's wife appears (*s&bc*, p. 88).
3. No background of listening guests is in the picture, even though we get the grand piano. We cannot find the Beethoven illustration that Dodgson describes, but he is probably conflating more than one picture. It may be Joseph Danhauser's "Liszt at the Piano," which is dominated by a larger-than-life bust of Beethoven. Albert Graefle's lithograph "Beethoven Playing for His Friends" and the anonymous "Beethoven Playing for Mozart" are also possibilities, but the Danhauser painting was widely reproduced and is the most likely candidate. See Alessandra Comini, *The Changing Image of Beethoven*, 1987, esp. following p. 16 in the color section.
4. *s&bc*, p. 236.
5. Furniss complied with all of Dodgson's ideas (*s&bc*, p. 265). The Professor sits on the shell of a snail, and he carries his outlandish guitar. Dodgson's sketch is missing.
6. The "slip of the pen" is Furniss's use of "in his [Arthur's] presence" instead of Dodgson's text, which reads "in my presence" [i.e., the narrator's]. See *s&bc*, p. 276.
7. *s&bc*, p. 277.

MS: *Morgan*

7 Lushington Road, Eastbourne
August 25, 1890

Dear Mr. Furniss,

Please return to me pp. 209, 210. They need to be cut up and pieced together again with some new matter.

By all means have Sylvie and Count only in the pianoforte picture. The piano had better be an "upright," I should think: but I leave that point to your decision.[1]

These sketches look most promising. In the "cupboard" picture, pray don't consider yourself to be strictly bound to the articles mentioned in the text. If you can think of other things, which will be yet *more* incongruous, and *less* likely to be found in a cupboard, I daresay it would improve the picture. In that case, perhaps I had better know what you propose, before you proceed to draw the actual picture.[2]

Very sincerely yours,
C. L. Dodgson

P.S. How would it do to have a spider's web in the [portion cut away] should think). It would show what a long time he must have been there.

That's rather *too much* web, I'm afraid. It should not be quite so prominent.[3]

1. The picture shows a grand piano (s&bc, p. 178).
2. s&bc, p. 316. The objects mentioned in the text include "two spiders," "the cover of a picture book," a "tortoise," and a "dish of nuts."
3. Furniss added the "dish of nuts," "a complete book," and the spider's web on p. 317.

MS: *Morgan*

7 Lushington Road, Eastbourne
September 23, 1890

Dear Mr. Furniss,

In the first place, all the drawings for the published *Sylvie and Bruno* (except the "Sylvie comforting Bruno" picture, which I told Swain to send to you) are stowed away, carefully packed, in the fireproof cellar of the Oxford Bank. How to get them safely to *you* is the next problem. The parcel is too wide for Registered Post: to insure, by Parcel Post, for £10 (the maximum allowed) a parcel which I suppose you would value at hundreds of pounds, seems ridiculously inadequate. Can you suggest any method? My idea is that it had better wait till you come over to Oxford, and then I can deliver it into your own hands.[1]

The new text that I have mounted for you requires a good deal of alteration in the paging. I enclose the necessary directions.

As to the new text:

p. 53: This *might* supply subject for picture: but it would be rather commonplace, I fear.

p. 54: Here it would be difficult to draw anything that would not recall the "Dogland" picture.

p. 122: I enclose a rough sketch.[2] I want "Mein Herr" to be the mundane counterpart of the Professor: but with a more sensible face. Could you manage this, and yet infuse a dreamy likeness of the Professor?

p. 123: I don't feel at all clear if it would be worth while to draw a little vignette like this.

It might amuse childish readers.[3]

p. 145: I enclose sketch, also my book of Oxford costumes: you could make the hunters M.A., or D.D., as you preferred. The one [who] is just catching the victim should have a perfectly *spherical* body.[4]

p. 149: This is a *very* poor picture that I have drawn. Perhaps the plough, with horses and donkeys, would be a better subject?

p. 210: I enclose sketch.

p. 211: I think a good picture might be made of the flea trampling people down.[5]

Sincerely yours,
C. L. Dodgson

1. Dodgson must have delivered these original drawings to Furniss somehow. They are, for the most part, in the Pierpont Morgan Library.

FIG. 32
Dodgson's preliminary sketch of "Mein Herr's fairy-friends"
from Sylvie and Bruno Concluded.

2. Dodgson's sketch is at the Lilly Library, Indiana University, but others (for pp. 145, 149, 210, and 211) are missing.

3. Neither this idea nor the earlier suggestions for illustrations in this letter materialized.

4. The text and two drawings of the "Scholar-Hunt" appear at pp. 188 and 189. Furniss complied with Dodgson's request for gowns worn by the Masters of Arts and Doctors of Divinity.

5. On the day he wrote this letter, Dodgson composed on the back of a sheet of axioms a list of alterations to be made in paging S&BC (MS: Morgan).

MS: *Morgan*

7 Lushington Road, Eastbourne
August 21, 1891

Dear Mr. Furniss,

As you said you were going to write, I thought I would wait to hear, before writing myself.[1] But, as no letter has come, I will delay no more to tell you what I fancy will be some relief to you to know, that I see *no* chance now of getting *Sylvie and Bruno Concluded* out before Easter. I was rather seriously ill at the beginning of the year: and it has spoiled my work very much, as a day's hard work used to give me a bad headache.[2] That liability has come almost to an end, now, I am thankful to say: but I'm not up to much work yet, and I think that it will be as much as I am likely to do, to get the book into the printer's hands, ready to begin working off the 10,000 I want done, by the beginning of the year (say the end of January) in which case we might have it out by Easter. I should be *very* glad to do that, as I don't think I have any right to reckon much on the coming years, and there is a great lot of work I want to finish before the end comes. But of course it depends on whether the pictures can be finished. It will, I hope, be quite needless, now, for you to hurry yourself *at all*: but do you think it reasonably likely that, taking it easy, and working only when "*i*' the vein,"[3] you will get them done this year?

Yours sincerely,
C. L. Dodgson

I hope Mrs. Furniss is better?

1. Certainly letters passed between Dodgson and Furniss between September 23, 1890, and August 21, 1891, but they are missing. Perhaps, too, the two visited each other, but if so, the *Diaries* do not report the meetings.

2. On February 6, 1891, Dodgson fainted during morning chapel. He struck his head and suffered a serious nosebleed. He was ill for some days and suffered frequent headaches. Although he worked on other writing projects, *Sylvie and Bruno Concluded* stood still for several months. On June 15, 1891, he wrote to a cousin (*Letters*, p. 846), "Every day I stay on here [Christ Church], is so much deducted from the time I am hoping to give, down at Eastbourne, to hard work at *Sylvie and Bruno Concluded*." On July 19 he wrote from Eastbourne to an acquaintance (p. 852): "I expect to be here for 3 months, hard at work on *Sylvie and Bruno Concluded*, for next Xmas."

3. *Richard III* 4.2 or *Troilus and Cressida* 5.3.

MS: *Lilly*

7 Lushington Road, Eastbourne
August 19, 1892[1]

Dear Mr. Furniss,

5 delightful pictures have just arrived.

The letter-register I have here only goes back to August 1890.[2] The enclosed list,[3] made from it, gives only twenty-six projected pictures:

21 sketches received,

17 drawings received.

Whatever other sketches I have seen were sent me, no doubt, before August 1890.

Would you kindly complete the list of the 36 of which you say I have seen your sketches?

What did we settle about pictures for the "Little Birds" stanzas?[4]

My idea *once* was to have *borders*, round the pages, containing mixed-up illustrations for the verses. But I think we must have given up the idea: it would be a difficult job: you would have to draw an outline, whatever size you liked, of the shape of a page, then to put in outlines of the places occupied by stanzas, which would have to be enlarged to scale from the printed stanzas. I think we must have given up the idea. I don't remember seeing *any* sketches for them, border or otherwise.

As to sending drawings to Swain, I had meant not to trouble you with any business-details not immediately connected with your own share in the matter. But, as you are anxious about it, I will explain. I do not wish to bring the book out with only 36 pictures. But I quite recognise the reasonableness of not expecting more drawings from you, this year, than you had understood *would* be expected of you. So I defer the matter till such time as you can draw some more. As we had 46 in Vol. I, and I would not like to have *less* in Vol. II, that would mean 10 more. I should, however, *like* if possible to have 50 altogether: it would be a very attractive advertisement. If there is a fair prospect of your being able to do 14 more, in time to publish at *Easter* (so that there would be some "receipts on sale" to go into my annual account with Macmillan, made up for the end of June each year) I would begin having the wood-cutting done *at once*. But if there is no reasonable prospect of publishing till Xmas 1893, I could not afford it: to pay for the 36 *drawings* would be as much as I could manage.

Very sincerely yours,
C. L. Dodgson

Is there any one of the 36 pictures that you think would make a good frontispiece?

1. We can trace Dodgson's progress with the book through his letters. On September 17, 1891, he wrote to one of his young friends (*Letters*, p. 862): "No chance of *Sylvie and Bruno Concluded* this year. I am now hoping to bring it out in the summer of 1892." Writing to a stranger in January 1892 (p. 880), he hoped to finish the book "this summer"; and on January 13 (p. 886), he wrote that "most of *Sylvie and Bruno Concluded* is in type: though in the most chaotic order, and a good many of the pictures are drawn: and, if God grants me life, and enough brain-power, it is my hope to get the book out by Christmas next." On February 28 he confides to a friend that he hopes to resign the curatorship of Christ Church Common Room. "Once free of that," he writes (p. 894), "I hope to give all the best hours of the day, all this summer, to bringing out *Sylvie and Bruno Concluded*." On July 10 he confides to his sister Mary from Eastbourne (p. 916) that his "principal occupation for 3 months to come" will be finishing the book. By the end of July, he writes to a favorite child friend (p. 922): "I'm getting on grandly with *Sylvie and Bruno Concluded*. . . . It won't be out before Easter-tide, I'm afraid"; and on July 31 he writes in his *Diaries* (p. 493): "The work I came to do, *viz.* to get *Sylvie and Bruno Concluded* through the Press, cannot be finished this year, since Mr. Furniss has reckoned on completing thirty-six pictures only, and I want to have at least forty. So I shall carry on . . . and shall . . . possibly get *Sylvie and Bruno Concluded* finished in time to publish by Easter, 1893."

2. For details of Dodgson's letter register, see chap. 3, letter of June 27, 1882, n. 4. Apart from assigning numbers to each letter sent or received he entered a précis of the contents of outgoing mail. Clearly, he took recent sections of his register with him when he went to Eastbourne for the summer.

3. Missing.

4. Dodgson discusses the pictures for the "Little Birds" stanzas in his letter dated August 5, 1890.

MS fragment: Morgan

[?late 1892][1]

... to *exist*, in your case. To the best of my recollection, one of the first things that suggested to me the wish to secure your help, was a marvellously successful picture, in *Punch*, of a House of Lords entirely composed of Harcourts, where the figures took all possible attitudes, and gave all possible views of the face; yet each was a quite unmistakable Sir William Harcourt![2]

(3) Trivial matters, where a touch or two would improve matters, and trivial omissions, easily supplied.

I am loath to worry you with business-matters, specially when on tour with your entertainment; and will wait till you are once more settled in your studio, before sending you the drawings, with full details of the points I wish to bring to your notice.

Some makers of biscuit-boxes have issued, with my sanction, a box ornamented with pictures from *Through the Looking-Glass*, and I have sent in the names of some of my friends, to have boxes. On September 2, I sent the name of your little Dorothy; and, on October 21, the name of Mrs. Furniss. Has either of them reached its destination, I wonder. Some, ordered to be sent, have failed to arrive.

Yours very sincerely,
C. L. Dodgson

1. Dodgson wrote this letter after October 21, 1892. The query about the safe delivery of the gifts to members of Mr. Furniss's family seems to indicate that the letter was written soon after the *Looking-Glass* biscuit tins (produced in mid-1892) were dispatched. For more about the biscuit tin, see *Letters*, pp. 924–38.

2. Sir William George Granville Venables Vernon Harcourt (1827–1904), the distinguished politician, was educated at Trinity, Cambridge, called to the bar in 1854, Liberal member of Parliament for Oxford in 1869, Home Secretary in 1880, and Chancellor of the Exchequer in Gladstone's cabinet. He was the uncle of Aubrey Harcourt (1852–1904), J.P., High Sheriff, who had been engaged to marry Edith Liddell at her death in 1876, and uncle also of Augustus George Vernon Harcourt (1834–1919), Lee's Reader in Chemistry at Christ Church and friend of Dodgson. Furniss's drawing "The House of Lords all Harcourts; or, 'Arcourt's 'All" appeared in *Punch* on October 25, 1884, p. 193. The picture, suggested from a design by Lord Randolph Churchill, has a caption from a speech made by Churchill in Birmingham stating, "Good gracious, Gentlemen, picture to yourself for one moment a House of Lords composed of nothing else but facsimiles of Sir William Harcourt!"

[1893?][1]

. . . (§3 continued)

78. *Churchyard*. I think it will be far better to use only *part* of this picture, so as to have it as an *upright* one, and to make the figure fill (as in "Sylvie and dead hare") most of it. My idea is, counting from the lower left-hand corner, to include 5 inches wide and 3 1/2 inches high. Do you think this will do? Or would it look better in an oval vignette, like "Sylvie and dead hare"?[2]

———

§4

Pictures *not* sent for alteration, as I think I can modify the text to suit them.

———

Spinach brought to Empress. This happens *before* they go to the banquet-hall. *You* have made it happen *at the banquet*. It will be rather a job to re-arrange the text, but I think I can do it.[3]

"*Other Professor*" *falling*. I *meant* him to *fall*, on the *floor*—not to *jump* upon the *table*! But I'll do the best I can to suit the picture . . .[4]

1. The fragment does not contain a date, but the contents match other letters written at this time.
2. S&BC, p. 291.
3. S&BC, p. 326.
4. S&BC, p. 352.

———

MS: *Morgan*

Christ Church, Oxford
May 17, 1893

Dear Mr. Furniss,

One more appeal to your good nature I will venture to make, in reference to Lady Muriel in the enclosed drawing. You have given her quite a new type of face; and one that I *cannot* say I admire. The mouth so *close* to the nose is almost suggestive of a very *old* face, where the front teeth are gone, and where, in consequence, the lips have fallen in. If you will put a little bit of paper over the lower part of her face, from the end of the nose down-wards, and repeat on it the outline of the chin, and then put in a mouth rather further down, and with an interval between it and the nose, you will see what a wonderful change it makes for the better, and how it restores to her the beauty you have given her in Vol. I.

And *could* you, at the same time, cut off those high shoulders from her sleeves? Why should we pay any deference to a hideous fashion, that will be extinct a year hence? Next to the unapproachable ugliness of "crinoline," I think these high-shouldered sleeves are the worst things invented for ladies in our time. Imagine how horrified they would be if one of their daughters were *really* shaped like that![1]

Swain is now hard at work cutting for me. I have put aside my other work, and am going to arrange the new book, and get the pictures into their places. I want to *begin* working off the earlier sheets in *August* if possible.

Sincerely yours,
C. L. Dodgson

1. Furniss quotes from this letter in *The Confessions of a Caricaturist* (1:107) to illustrate that he thought Dodgson too fastidious in his dislike of some current fashions.

MS: *Morgan*

Christ Church, Oxford
June 8, 1893

Dear Mr. Furniss,

In the hope that you have leisure-time *now*, to go to work on the rest of the pictures for *Sylvie and Bruno Concluded*, I have gone through the book, to see what appropriate subjects remain, and have found subjects for 7 pictures besides the 3 borders that I want for the enclosed stanzas[1] about "Little Birds." I shall be glad to hear how many of them commend themselves to *you* as suitable.

The Numbers, enclosed in oblongs, refer to the pages of mounted text already in your hands.

One preliminary remark. It is *most* desirable that, before you make the finished drawings, I should see sketches, however rough, of what you propose to draw. This may prevent serious mistakes. Already there are, in the drawings which I have had cut (of which I had not seen sketches) many departures from the text, which will cause me much trouble in re-writing the text so as to make it agree with the picture.

51 "Are not those *orchises* under the hedge?"

I have tried a sketch, which I enclose:[2] but really my sketches come out so wretchedly bad, that I must try to convey my meaning by *descriptions*. This picture should contain Arthur and Sylvie. I have drawn Arthur looking *sideways,* which is a mistake: he ought to be looking *at* the spectator, because the picture represents what the "I" of the book *saw,* and of course he saw Arthur looking at *him,* while addressing him. He should seem to be *pointing,* only, with his stick, and should be quite unconscious that he is really being pulled along by Sylvie. I think she should pull rather *harder* than I have made her do. And her figure should be *semi*-transparent, showing *dimly* whatever is behind her (a gate or rail would do very well), but not *quite* transparent (see my remarks on the drawing of "Nero holding thief"), as, in that case, she would seem to be *behind* the rail, instead of in *front* of it.[3]

84 "It's summat gone wrong wi' my spectacles." In one side of the picture, the farmer's wife should be standing in the doorway, looking very much surprised at seeing Bruno seated in the air. Though wearing spectacles, she must not look too old to be the mother of Bessie. In the middle of the picture is Sylvie, walking towards her, and looking up at her, and leading by the collar a *very* shadowy Nero (*nearly* transparent), with Bruno riding on its back, so drawn that his feet are well off the ground. The *tail* of Nero should be distinct and *non*-transparent.[4]

148 "The Merchant stroked his beard." The two figures should be in *Arab* dress, I think: and sitting cross-legged on the ground. The Merchant has his basket (or box?) of eggs by him. He might be fat, with a vacuous but solemn face, gazing up into the sky: the citizen might be lean, with a cunning smile, looking out of the corners of his eyes at the unconscious merchant. I suppose the merchant would have a camel, or (better) a donkey, carrying his wares: this might be placed *behind* the groups, so as not to dwarf them by occupying part of the foreground.[5]

172 Lords of the Creation. The Earl and Arthur are lying back in rocking-chairs, facing to one side, where the fire is supposed to be. Hanging lamp overhead, which would give good effects of light and shade. Lady M. leaning

over Arthur from behind, to place something (e.g. a tumbler of soda-water) on a little table standing between him and the Earl (who I think should be *behind*, so as to make Arthur and Lady M. the foreground figures.)[6]

218 "I's always *welly* sorry, etc." This, I think, might be made very comic. 2 or 3 dead mice lying in front, and behind them the cat, sitting up on its hind-legs, holding a pocket-handkerchief in its fore-paws, with a long face of utter misery, and tears running down its cheeks.[7]

224 "Good-night, Professor." The Professor propped up with cushions, on a sofa, the foot of which comes forwards. All but his head and arms covered with blankets. Bruno on one side, grasping his hand; and Sylvie on the other, kissing his cheek.[8]

226 His wife knelt down, etc., etc. I think the text sufficiently describes the scene.[9]

The 3 borders for stanzas. I enclose a drawing of the shape the border should be, in the right proportions, enlarged to the size you usually draw. I have divided the stanzas into 3 sets, A, B, and C. Each border should contain many little figures, rather mixed together. In the early vols. of *Punch*, you will find borders, by Doyle,[10] of the kind I mean. I have an idea that they would look well, if *all* done as silhouettes. I enclose a feeble attempt at it.[11] The stanzas can, of course, be re-arranged, if you think that would make them more suitable for illustrating.[12]

I enclose a list of references to Vol. I,[13] where you will find the different characters drawn with the faces that I wish preserved. Why should you not *copy* the actual faces in the new pictures? We do not expect our friends to appear with new faces every day: then surely, in an illustrated book, when a character recurs again and again, he should, however different his *surroundings*, have always the same *features* (though of course their *expression* may vary to suit the scene).

I shall be much interested to hear what you think of all these suggestions.

You have a good many of my old sketches, now done with. Would you kindly return them?

Very sincerely yours,
C. L. Dodgson

1. The manuscript stanzas for the "Little Birds" are missing. They appear in s&bc on pp. 364 – 65, 371, and 377.

2. Dodgson's sketch is missing.

3. Arthur looks "sideways," not at the spectator (s&bc, p. 50). Furniss adopted Dodgson's other suggestions. For Dodgson's remarks on "Nero holding thief," see August 5 and August 11, 1890.

4. Furniss acted on all of these suggestions (s&bc, p. 64).

5. In the final version (s&bc, p. 197), the characters are standing rather than sitting cross-legged. Two camels, instead of a donkey, appear in the background.

6. Furniss complied with most of these suggestions, but not the Earl's chair (s&bc, p. 271).

7. This picture did not materialize. The text appears in s&bc, p. 361.

8. Sylvie and Bruno appear on the same side of the Professor. Otherwise Furniss followed Dodgson's suggestions (s&bc, p. 398).

9. s&bc, p. 404.

10. Richard Doyle (1824–83), the famous early *Punch* artist. Dodgson at one point entertained the possibility of getting Doyle to illustrate *Through the Looking-Glass*. For more on Dodgson and Doyle, see *Letters*, p. 36.

11. Missing.

12. The silhouette borders occur in s&bc, pp. 365, 371, and 377, covering three sides of the page in each case, away from the book's hinge.

13. Dodgson's list of references is missing.

---

ms: *Morgan*

[Christ Church, Oxford]
June 19, 1893

Dear Mr. Furniss,

First, let me thank you most heartily for the great patience and kindness with which you have treated my many troublesome criticisms and requests.

Next, while I think of it, would you send me back, in your next packet, the old sketches of mine that are now done with?[1]

I will now go through, in their numerical order, the 11 finished drawings received on 17th:

(62) *Arthur's Farewell*: Quite satisfactory now. Am sending it to Swain.[2]

(64) *Sylvie and Count*: Sylvie's face will do very well: and her dress is charming. I enclose it, as there is a small detail I should like corrected, if you can do it without much trouble. There ought not to be any *music-book* on the piano. I certainly *meant* (and it is implied in the text) that Sylvie did *not* bring any music with her: it was *fairy*-music. If the picture needs something there, we might have the empty music-desk: but please erase the *book*, if you can. You can then send it to Swain.[3]

(65) *Scholar-Hunt*: Thanks for altering. It goes to Swain.[4]

(66) *Bruno swinging on tendril*: Ditto, ditto.[5]

(67) *Lady Bird*: Ditto, ditto.[6]

(68) *Nero holding thief*: This also I enclose. Will you please forward it to Swain, and explain to him how it will have to be cut (after I have seen photo)?[7]

(69) *Bessie singing*: The alterations are quite satisfactory. But I enclose it, because a new remark occurs to me. It is a *one-sided* picture, and seems to me to need something in the lower right-hand corner to balance Bessie's foot. Don't you think it would be an improvement to have the doll's hat and cloak, thrown down on the grass in that corner, and to put your initials elsewhere?[8]

(71) *Willie's Wife in Cottage*: This also I enclose, for you to forward to Swain with your own instructions. Also please consider if the upper edge of the woman's arm ought not to show through Bruno's face, in the same way as the table shows through his body.[9]

(78) *Churchyard*: I have put, on the back, instructions for Swain, and have of course *not* drawn the line *across* the picture, as that would injure the drawing for your own purposes when returned to you. But I enclose it for *you* to forward, because there are two or three little alterations that seem to me desirable. One is that her hands would look better *without* gloves. I presume you mean her to wear *black* gloves: but she would not be likely to put them on, merely to go into the churchyard. Another is, you will find in the text that she was "hanging a wreath of flowers" round the cross. Do you think it would be inartistic to introduce them? They would have to be *snowdrops*, considering the time of year. Another is, you have made part of her left wrist show *through* the cross. Lastly, her foot looks, to *me*, wrong. Ought not the *heel* to show a little? (The alteration in the *hands* would, I suppose, only need that you should tell Swain to omit the shading).[10]

(80) *Lion entering Fox's house*: Will do capitally. Going to Swain.[11]

(82) *Return of Warden*: The new Bruno is perfectly *charming*! I think it will be the prettiest picture of him in the whole of the 2 volumes. Going to Swain.[12]

Now for the rough sketches, returned herewith:

(81) *Sylvie and Bruno singing*: Looks just what I want. I would like Sylvie's height to be two-thirds of the picture. My suggestions for this picture were, I find by my letter-register, sent to you, August 5, 1890: but I have no copy of

them, nor even a *précis* of the letter: and possibly you have not preserved it. Still, I have no doubt I gave you reasonable cause to suppose that I wanted the figures to be *small*. And I beg you will allow me to pay the full price for that drawing.[13]

(84) *Mein Herr with S. and B.*: Looks all right. By all means put S. and B. one on each side, as here drawn. Don't forget to put Mein Herr into *evening-dress*.[14]

(86) *Farmer's wife meeting S. and B.*: Looks all right. Remember to dress S. and B. as *children*.[15]

(87) *Lords of Creation*: This does not seem to agree with the text I wanted it for, where A. kisses her hand, as she puts down something before him. There is no place for her to put it. How would it do to give A. a little table to himself, in front? Then Lady M. might be stooping over it, and not (as she now seems to be doing) over the back of his chair.[16]

(As to No. 78, I forgot to say that I have marked it so as to include *more* than the 5 inches I first named. I think it will look better so. What do *you* think?)

Now for the "Little Birds": I *meant* my silhouettes to be *black*. I see that, in the first 2 sketches, you have put the picture on the *left* side, and, in the 3rd, on the *right*? I have a notion that it should always come on the side furthest from the hinge. I have also a notion that it is possible, in photographing the drawing, to reverse it, if necessary: I'll ask Swain about it. If this *is* possible, you can draw them either way: if not, I must settle whether they are to occupy right-hand, or left-hand, pages.

I will now take the 9 stanzas, one by one:

(Verse 1) "Justices with jam": Will do capitally. Could you introduce a few oysters? The jars might rest on heaps of them.

(Verse 2) "Tigresses to smile": Could the upper one be *full*-face, so as to get "mouth a semi-circle"?

(Verse 3) "All among the pins": Could the *ball* be introduced, knocking down a skittle?

(Verse 4) "Interesting books": I don't quite understand. What are the other figures, besides the cook who is reading?

(Verse 5) "Bagpipes on the shore": Will do. But I fear you will find bagpipes hard to draw, as played by a bird! *One* might play a *hurdy-gurdy*.

(Verse 6) "Crocodiles in cream": The *cream* should be in *jugs*, I think. Streams of it, running over the black crocodiles, would be effective.

(Verse 7) "Crimes in carpet-bags": You might have 2 carpet-bags. The first, with birds putting things in with their beaks, and a stag on its hind-legs, in the act of blessing them. The second, with birds flying away, and a stag beating them off with a stick. The third need not be drawn: only a stag sitting up with a dead bird in one hand, and another in its mouth.

(Verse 8) "Gratitude and gold": Bells hung up, at *top* of page, bird-bell-ringers at *foot*, ropes going down *edge* of page. The bells would come just above the frozen salmon.[17]

Do you think you can get the pictures done in another month or so? I should like to begin working off, early in September.

Very sincerely yours,
C. L. Dodgson

1. Furniss had written to Dodgson on June 10 to say that he would be returning these drawings, but clearly he needed to be reminded. Furniss's letter also suggests that he intended to complete and send the remaining illustrations to Dodgson directly. But Dodgson had left some problems unresolved, and Furniss adds: "I cannot find page 218, even with the aid of the alteration plan (enclosed). The last page you sent me is numbered 223 and is the wind up of the story. I cannot find the dead mice and the cat. Nor 224, nor 148. You know you did not send me all the text. What am I to do?" Dodgson's reply to these queries is missing.

2. *S&BC*, p. 277.

3. *S&BC*, p. 178; the music book is gone.

4. *S&BC*, pp. 188 and 189.

5. *S&BC*, p. 8.

6. *S&BC*, p. 15.

7. *S&BC*, p. 62.

8. *S&BC*, p. 75; Furniss complied.

9. *S&BC*, p. 88; the arm of Willie's wife does not show through Bruno's face.

10. *S&BC*, p. 291; the gloves are gone, and Furniss has added the wreath (of snowdrops) to the cross.

11. *S&BC*, p. 236.

12. *S&BC*, p. 382.

13. *S&BC*, frontispiece.

14. *S&BC*, p. 163.

15. *S&BC*, p. 64.

16. *S&BC*, p. 271; Furniss made the change.

17. In the first silhouette border (*S&BC*, p. 365), Furniss added a barrel of oysters, and, as Dodgson requested, a ball is knocking down a skittle. Neither tigress, however, is full-face to reveal a semicircular mouth. In the second border (p. 371), only the figures of two cooks can be

seen reading the "interesting books," and no other figure appears except a cat under the table. Furniss introduced the bagpipes and hurdy-gurdy, and the cream flows out of jugs and streams over the backs of the crocodiles. In the final border (p. 377), Furniss complied with all of Dodgson's suggestions.

MS: *Morgan*

Christ Church, Oxford
June 27, 1893

Dear Mr. Furniss,

You are indeed kind, to take so much trouble on already-finished pictures. Please send Nos. 68, 71 to *me*. I'm sorry I gave you the trouble of writing about No. 69. It was a trifle, merely entailing the cost of a fresh negative. In future, if I send you any drawings, I'll indicate, for *each*, to whom I wish it sent.

While you are on No. 71, I may as well mention that a lady told me that the woman's dress is *not* what a cottager would wear. I think she said the *apron* was too short; and there was something wrong with the *belt.* Perhaps you could show it to some lady who knows how cottagers dress?[1]

May I once more remind you that you have a heap of old sketches of mine, that I should like to have. Also you once kindly said I might have *your* rough sketches, when done with. They would be very interesting to me.

Very sincerely yours,
C. L. Dodgson

1. S&BC, p. 88: the apron is long, suggesting that Furniss made an alteration.

MS: *Morgan*

7 Lushington Road, Eastbourne
August 1, 1893[1]

Dear Mr. Furniss,

In the hope that you are now well on your way to convalescence,[2] and that you are able to give some attention to *Sylvie and Bruno Concluded*, I write to tell you of *one* more picture, that I think will be needed, for a longish scene I am writing.

The scene is in the garden, under a tree, with 5 o'clock tea going on, and contains two figures only, Lady Muriel and "Mein Herr."

They, as you know, are parallels to, and have a mysterious resemblance to, Sylvie and the Professor. The picture will need very little *invention*, as I want it to be a repetition, with only such changes as are necessary, of the figures of Sylvie and the Professor, in the picture at p. 24 of the 1st Vol.

The 2 figures can be brought a little nearer together, as all the other figures will have to be omitted.

Lady Muriel should be in exactly Sylvie's attitude (except, of course, that she must *not* hold her ankle in her hand!) and with Sylvie's face (no need to alter *this*, at all); her elbow resting on a small table, containing tea-things. She is supposed to be hemming pocket-handkerchiefs: so she should have a few lying on her knee, and the one she is sewing might be in her right hand, which should hang down just like Sylvie's. She will have to be seated in a *chair*, of course: but its legs might be like those of the stool on which Sylvie is sitting.

"Mein Herr" should stand, in the attitude of the Professor, having risen from his easy-chair. He should have a small table by him, with a cup of tea on it. The face, and spectacles, might be the same: but of course he must have (as I have said before) a great beard. He should have his *hat* on, I think, as the scene is out of doors. A lady-friend, who has I think been in Germany, tells me the ordinary German gentleman wears a brown straw hat with a curly brim, and a lightish-coloured frock-coat double-breasted, and buttoned up.

What he is to hold in his hands is peculiar. I think you will have to get Mrs. Furniss to make it for you. It consists of 2 pocket-handkerchiefs, with the 2 upper corners joined (the upper edges being open like the mouth of a bag), and the lower edges sewn together, after one handkerchief has been twisted so as to make its *right* lower corner join the *left* lower corner of the other, and *vice versa*. It will be something like this.
The right lower corner of the front handkerchief is at "A," and its left lower corner at "B."[3]

Very sincerely yours,
C. L. Dodgson

1. On July 15, Dodgson had moved down to Eastbourne for the summer vacation. By July 19 he was fully unpacked, and on the twenty-second "wrote some additions to *Sylvie and Bruno Concluded*" (*Diaries*, p. 500).

2. We find no details of Furniss's illness.

3. *S&BC*, p. 103; Furniss has followed Dodgson's suggestion and replaced Sylvie's ankle with Lady Muriel's sewing, producing a similar attitude for both figures.

MS: *Morgan*

7 Lushington Road, Eastbourne
September 8, 1893

Dear Mr. Furniss,

I sincerely hope this will find you about again, and well on your way to complete restoration of health. A good many pictures are, as I hear from Swain, awaiting your approval of the cuts before I can have proofs of them. The sooner I can have them the better, as I'm now getting the book arranged in pages, and we shall perhaps be working off the sheets as fast as they can be passed for Press. The paging is at a standstill just now, for want of knowing whether or not there is to be a picture of the invisible (i.e. transparent) Sylvie leading Arthur by pulling his walking-stick. I have suggested such a picture to you (I think in my letter dated June 8) but you have not yet told me whether you think it worth drawing. If you do, and can tell me the proportions of length and width of the picture, I can leave a proper space for it, and can then go on with the paging.[1] I am *very* anxious to publish, if it be possible, next Christmas.

You *do* give me a lot of extra trouble by ignoring the text so much! Several passages I have re-written, in order to make the text agree with the picture: but *one* case has been a really long and difficult job. I had made the "Spinach" scene occur in the hall where the guests were received, *not* the Banqueting Hall: then, long after that, they go to the Banquet, and *there* occurs the fall of the Other Professor (I have had to make him first *rise up* into the air, and *then* fall, in order to suit the picture). You have ignored all that, and evidently meant *both* events to occur *at* the Banquet. I decided, after much thought, that it would spoil the story to adopt that view; and, as you had (luckily) adopted a different arrangement of people, at the table, in the two pictures, I at last decided to introduce a *table* into the reception-hall, and to make it a small table for the Royal party only, and to let the spinach be brought to *that* table; and then to have a different table, and a different order of people, for the Banquet. But it was a puzzling thing to arrange.[2]

Very sincerely yours,
C. L. Dodgson

1. s&bc, p. 50; the picture materialized.

2. The two pictures are in s&bc, pp. 326 and 352. The background similarity in the two suggests that the events occur in the same place even though Dodgson sought distinctly different settings. Furniss may have modified some of the drapery at the back of the room and the stool that Sylvie uses in the first picture to suggest different settings, but the appearance of the table and the pillar at the back is similar in both illustrations.

Incomplete MS: Morgan

> 7 Lushington Road, Eastbourne
> September 30, 1893[1]

Dear Mr. Furniss,

Before making any remarks on individual pictures, I must once more thank you for all you are doing for me. I feel that you are *not* working in the spirit of "so much work is paid for; I will give so much, and be done with it": but that you are giving, to this affair, thought and pains, far beyond what any *legal* contract could exact. Believe me, I am grateful: and I feel sure that, if *pictures* could sell a book, *Sylvie and Bruno Concluded* would sell like wildfire! (I think that's a new simile, isn't it, for rapidity of sale?)

I will first discuss the finished drawings, and then the rough sketches. (The numerals refer to my list):

(68) *Nero holding thief*: This looks all right, if the portions of S. and B., seen *through* Nero, are made dim. I'll send it to Swain, who no doubt has your instructions as to cutting it.[2]

(71) *Willie's Wife in Cottage*: I am sorry to seem troublesome; but really I must ask you once more to look . . .[3]

[page missing]

. . . match the frontispiece of Vol. I. I have a passion for *symmetry*. Would you mind enclosing it in an oblong, and filling in the corners? I have put with it a paper frame, to show where it seems to me the oblong might well be placed.[4]

(84) *S. and B. and Mein Herr*: Mein Herr is delicious! But I don't at all like the *curved* folds in Sylvie's frock. One of the chief beauties, in that kind of frock, is that it falls in *straight* soft folds, from what they call the "yoke." These curves are uncomfortably suggestive of a stiff material, that has taken her shape while she was sitting down, and hasn't yet recovered itself. Also it looks too long. I fancy I *did* suggest that it should come below the knee: but I now see I was wrong: it would look much prettier if the knees were shown. But all these are trifles compared with the *high heels*. I so entirely *detest* that

monstrous fashion (and in fact have planned an attack on it in this very book), that I cannot *possibly* allow my sweet little heroine to be victimised by it. So I must really ask you, if this picture is to go into the book, to give her a pair of ordinary shoes, and *not* to make her walk on tiptoe, as she is forced to do by those abominable heels.[5]

(86) *"Summat wrong wi' my spectacles"*: Charming. I suppose if I tell Swain to treat Nero in the same way as in the "apples" picture, it will be all right.[6]

(88) *Teaching tigresses to smile, etc.*: I think these silhouettes will be *delicious!*[7]

Now for the sketches:

(85) *Concluding Vignette*: It is so sweetly pretty, that I am really sorry not to be able to use it: but "illustrations" must "illustrate," and there is no text that this *could* illustrate. Worse than that, it *contradicts* the text. I want the reader to close the book with the conception of Sylvie standing, awake, and beginning to speak. This picture would quite confuse such a conception. In Vol. I. we have the concluding vignette at the *top* of the last page. Couldn't we end Vol. II. in the same fashion, with a picture something like the accompanying scrawl? This would illustrate the concluding words.[8]

(87) *Lords of Creation*: I should *like* the arrangement to be such as would make it possible for Arthur to "stoop and kiss the tender little thumb": i.e. I should like *his* table to be within reach of his mouth, if he were to stoop. Can you manage this? If not, I must alter the text, and omit the quotation.[9]

(92) *Lady M. and Mein Herr*: This looks all right, except that Lady M. should surely have a larger table? You see she has to make the tea, and pour it out for all comers.[10]

(93) *S. pulling A. along*: This looks all right, except that Arthur ought to be looking in the direction in which he is being pulled. If you look at the text, you will see that he thinks he is *pointing*, at the orchises, with his stick.[11]

I enclose drawing (65) "Scholar-Hunt" with a photo, by which you will see what an ineffective picture it makes, when put *upright* in the page. And it is not important enough, even if it were the right proportions and were enclosed in an oblong, to put *sideways* as a full-page picture. Unfortunately for me, I have foolishly had it cut, the small size. However, this must be sacrificed. A quite brilliant idea has occurred to me: to print, from the negative, on *two* blocks, each 3 inches wide, so that the right-hand block just contains

the 2 pursuers, and the left-hand one the scholar (at its left edge). Then the 2 pictures can stand at the tops of opposite pages like this:
Of course there would be *photo'd*, on each block, some portion of the *other* picture: but this could be ignored in the cutting.[12] If you approve of this plan, would you put some more ground under the scholar? There should be a complete line of foreground to go at top of text. You can make their feet touch the ground, or remain in the air, as you prefer: but, in either case, the scholar's stick must *not* touch the ground. No one, running at full speed, helps himself along with a stick! Also please give him a *string* to his hat: the idea, of his *losing* it, is a disturbing element for the spectator, who ought to think of the *Hunt* only.[13]

You ask which way the other 2 silhouettes are to go (i.e. whether 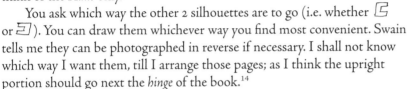 or). You can draw them whichever way you find most convenient. Swain tells me they can be photographed in reverse if necessary. I shall not know which way I want them, till I arrange those pages; as I think the upright portion should go next the *hinge* of the book.[14]

I enclose the text for "the Merchant stroked his beard."[15] The other two shall follow as soon as possible. I have ordered proofs of them to be worked off, as I have none left.

Please tell me, as soon as you can the *proportions* of the picture you are going to draw of "Arthur pointing at orchises." Then I can allow the right space for it,[16] and go on arranging sheets in pages. It is wanted for the 4th sheet.

I had better tell you the order in which the as-yet-unfinished pictures will be wanted. It is:

93. Orchises
71. Willie's Wife
92. Lady M. and Mein Herr
84. Mein Herr and S. and B
65. Scholar-Hunt
91. Merchant
87. Lords of Creation.

We had better, before attempting any concluding vignette, get *all* the other pictures done. I fear we shall be *very* short of time, and I *could*, if necessary, use the jewel (duplicate of former one, only with legend altered to "All will love Sylvie") as a concluding picture.[17]

Very sincerely yours,
C. L. Dodgson

1. "*Sylvie and Bruno Concluded* takes up (when I'm in the humour for it, which I generally am, just now) 6 or 8 hours a day," Dodgson wrote to a friend on September 13 (*Letters*, p. 972); and to his sister Mary on September 21: "*Sylvie and Bruno Concluded* goes on fairly well. I *think* it will be out by Christmas. But it won't do to 'whistle' *much*, while still as deep in 'the wood' as I am at present" (p. 978).

2. S&BC, p. 62.

3. S&BC, p. 88; this probably refers to the costume of Willie's wife, which Dodgson mentioned in his letter (June 27).

4. S&BC, frontispiece; the oblong and surrounding spaces match those in the frontispiece of S&B.

5. S&BC, p. 163: Sylvie's dress falls in straight, soft folds to about knee length, and she is not wearing high heels. Dodgson's attack on high-heeled shoes which he promises for the book did not materialize.

6. S&BC, p. 64.

7. S&BC, p. 365; Dodgson confirms his delight with these silhouette borders for the stanzas of "Little Birds" in his preface to S&BC, p. ix, where he describes them as "a triumph of artistic ingenuity."

8. S&BC, p. 411; Furniss made the changes, and the picture appears as the concluding illustration.

9. S&BC, p. 271; the quotation remains in the text, suggesting that Dodgson was satisfied with the changes Furniss made.

10. S&BC, p. 103; the table is adequate for the purpose.

11. S&BC, p. 50; Arthur now certainly looks in the direction in which he is being pulled.

12. Leo de Freitas, in his book *A Study of Sir John Tenniel's Wood-Engraved Illustrations to "Alice's Adventures in Wonderland" and "Through the Looking-Glass"* (1988), suggests that photo-transferring an image from an original onto the woodblock was fraught with technical difficulties. As this letter confirms, however, Dodgson used photographic transfers on several occasions for this book.

13. S&BC, pp. 188 and 189; Furniss adopted Dodgson's "brilliant idea."

14. S&BC, pp. 365, 371, and 377; the upright portions of the illustrations appear, in the end, away from the hinge of the book.

15. S&BC, p. 197.

16. See note 11.

17. S&BC, p. 409; Alice Havers's illustration of the "locket" appears here, but the position of the legend on the locket is as it appears in S&B, p. 77.

MS: Morgan

7 Lushington Road, Eastbourne
October 6, 1893

Dear Mr. Furniss,

The frontispiece, and the Scholar-Hunt, will do beautifully now. I am forwarding them to Swain.[1]

I return the 5 sketches:

(85) *Final vignette*: No doubt you are right in thinking that "the picture would compose better by showing the outside of the window": but surely I explained clearly, in my last letter, why such a view would be inadmissible? I have a *fancy* that this picture would look better, if Bruno were on Sylvie's *left*, so as to come into the middle of the picture. He looks, to me, rather crowded out. But I don't understand composition: so please keep to this arrangement, if you think it best. As the picture is to go at the *top* of the page, would it not be well to vignette it off into an arch, like this?  Then it would make a good match for the final picture of Vol. I.[2]

(91) *Merchant*: This will be lovely![3]

(94) *"Good-night, Professor!"*: You say "not fairy-dress, I suppose?" But they *must* be in fairy-dress. The scene is laid in *fairy-land*. The group will do capitally, I think. Wouldn't the Prof. look more comfortable, if his feet were *covered* with the blankets? But that is an artistic point, which I leave to you. One more suggestion. Wouldn't it have a pretty effect, if Sylvie were bending down, and actually *kissing* his broad forehead?[4]

(95) *"His wife knelt down"*: I have no copy of the text, just now, and can't remember whether Arthur was in bed, or on a sofa. I'll make it suit the picture. *Bed* would be best, I think, as a sofa would introduce a figure cut off at the knees. Can you manage to show her kissing the drooping hand? I fancy she does so in the text: but the picture *need* not contain it, if you prefer to draw it otherwise. I suppose you mean Arthur's eyes to be *shut*? I daresay that will look best. I leave it to you.[5]

Mice killing themselves: On further consideration, I would rather omit this. I don't think the *killing* lends itself well to comic treatment in a picture.[6]

You have now sent me sketches of all the pictures. There are 45 in all, making, with the "Locket," 46: just the same as in Vol. I.[7]

Very sincerely yours,
C. L. Dodgson

1. S&BC, pp. 188 and 189.
2. S&BC, p. 411; Furniss adopted Dodgson's suggestions.
3. S&BC, p. 197.
4. S&BC, p. 398; again Furniss complied.
5. S&BC, p. 404; a bed appears, not a sofa, and it is just possible that Lady Muriel is kissing the drooping hand. Also, Arthur's eyes are shut.
6. The picture does not appear.
7. A miscalculation. Both books have forty-seven illustrations. The symmetry, however, is preserved.

MS: *Morgan*

7 Lushington Road, Eastbourne
October 12, 1893

Dear Mr. Furniss,

I sent a card[1] to say that the parcel had come, and that we would manage the "Little Birds" stanzas by putting the lines closer together: they'll look just as well, that way.

My feelings, on looking through the 6 drawings, are of *unmixed delight*: and I *entirely* endorse your opinion that you are "in very good working order"!

(84) *Mein Herr, and S. and B*: Sylvie will do very well now. Of course, as she is leaning forwards, one *can't* have the folds in the frock quite vertical.[2]

(87) *Lords of Creation*: This makes a charming cosy domestic scene. And Arthur can easily kiss "the tender little thumb," now.[3]

(89) *Little Birds (Crocodiles, etc.)*: *What* an amount of fun you've put into it! It takes some study to realise it all. I *specially* rejoice in the Little Bird who is carrying round the hat for subscriptions![4]

(90) *Little Birds (Stags, etc.)*: The wonder, to *me*, is how you've managed to bring in so many of the things named. When the reviews appear, I quite expect the 3 "Little Birds" pictures will be picked out as some of the very cleverest in the whole book.[5]

(93) *Orchises*: This drawing is excellent, in every point but *one*. And this I *must* ask you to alter, by giving her a little more skirt floating out in *front* of her. She does look so *very* nearly naked, with the dress fitting in to the body and front of the thigh. You must remember the book has to be seen, not only by children, but by their *Mothers*: and *some* Mothers are *awfully* particular! I hope it won't give you much trouble: it seems to me that, by erasing about 1/4 inch strip of shadow, the skirt could easily be widened enough to satisfy that exorbitant "Mrs. Grundy." The sketch of this figure, *without* the drapery, must be quite lovely. I suppose you made one, from the life? You were good enough to say that I might have your "studies" for these pictures. I'm quite looking forwards to possessing *this*. By the way, how old is your model? And may I have her name and address? My friend, Miss E. G. Thomson, an artist great in "fairies," would be glad to know of her, I'm sure.[6]

(95) *"His wife knelt down"*: This makes a *beautiful* picture.[7]

We shall be in good time, now, with the book. Only 4 more pictures are due from you now.[8]

Very sincerely yours,
C. L. Dodgson

1. Missing.
2. s&bc, p. 163; altered and improved.
3. s&bc, p. 271.
4. s&bc, p. 371.
5. s&bc, p. 377.
6. s&bc, p. 50; Sylvie is now adequately dressed. We cannot tell whether Furniss sent Dodgson his "studies" for this picture.
7. s&bc, p. 404.
8. Six days after writing this letter Dodgson wrote, "Passed the first three sheets of *Sylvie and Bruno Concluded* for electro-typing," and on the following day: "Received a specimen of the paper, and passed . . . forty-eight pages for Press. Walked to Beachy Head, thence to Polegate Station, and back by rail. The walk took three and a quarter hours, and during it I composed a dedicatory sonnet for the book now printing, *Sylvie and Bruno Concluded*" (*Diaries*, p. 503). The dedication is to Enid Stevens, whose name is discovered by reading downwards the third letter in each line of the verse.

MS: *Morgan*

7 Lushington Road, Eastbourne
October 21, 1893

Dear Mr. Furniss,

On further examination, with a magnifying-glass, of this drawing, I find that Bruno *has* a waist. *Without* the glass, the effect is, distinctly, that his right side is bounded by the line of light that runs down the front of Sylvie's skirt, and thus that he is in a loose sort of shirt. Yet there is a piece of window-sill between the 2 figures, which (if it were as much illuminated as the portion to the left-hand of Bruno) would clearly show where Bruno's figure ended. But this bit, for some inexplicable reason, you have shaded. *What* is supposed to cast a shadow on it?[1]

I must really *beg* you to make *both* dresses more opaque. If you look through a magnifying-glass, you will see that the "hind-quarters" still show very plainly through: in fact, this is quite visible, even *without* a glass. The only dress, that Sylvie has, behind her, from the waist downwards, seems to consist of a few torn shreds of wet muslin!

All the upper part of the picture is so *lovely*, that I should greatly regret not being able to use it.

Do you mean that small "thing," close to Bruno's left elbow, to be cut, as you have drawn it, quite separate from the surroundings? Is it a falling leaf, or what?[2]

Very sincerely yours,
C. L. Dodgson

1. This drawing was for the final vignette, p. 411. Furniss now had the sunrise shine on the windowsill, helping to create an outline of Bruno's waist.
2. Furniss incorporated almost all of Dodgson's suggestions, although the small "thing" is distinctly still there. On November 8, Furniss wrote to Dodgson to say that he had by then "seen proof of all the pictures but one, the final vignette" (MS: Berol). On November 21, Dodgson made a check of "the working-off of *Sylvie and Bruno Concluded* (which has occupied most of my time for the last four months)." He goes on to record problems with the inferior printing of the latest issue of *Looking-Glass* (the sixtieth thousand), and because he decided to insert a flyer in *S&BC* calling back the defective *Looking-Glasses*, he stopped the production of *S&BC*: "This will very likely prevent it coming out this Christmas," he writes (*Diaries*, p. 503), "and so will be a heavy loss to me: but *anything* is better than offering the Public inferior work." The delay caused by this incident did not, however, prevent *S&BC* from appearing for Christmas. Dodgson saw the first copies of *Sylvie and Bruno Concluded* on December 24, and spent the twenty-seventh in London at

Macmillan's, signing copies. The book was published on December 29, 1893, and received many reviews. The *Athenaeum* (January 27, 1894) asked: "Where is the wit; where the 'flashes of merriment'? The story—if story 'it can be called which shape has none'—has, however, been constructed on a theory. . . . There are many good things in the book, of course, but it is much too long." The *Spectator* (March 24) exclaimed, "What a loss the world had when Lewis Carroll took to writing sense!" and continued mercilessly: "His sense is but indifferent. . . . Let us hope that Mr. Lewis Carroll's next book will be all fancy and nonsense." The *Publishers' Circular* (January 13) admitted that "it has delighted us, though in a fairy story we could dispense with discussions on ethics, on charity, on 'fate, free-will, foreknowledge absolute,' and similar topics." Overall, the notices revealed occasional respect but not general acclaim.

MS: *Lilly*

Christ Church, Oxford
May 12, 1896

Dear Mr. Furniss,

Yesterday I went to Russell's shop, and bought four 5s. tickets for your American entertainment on the 23rd, thinking that I would treat 3 young friends to it, and feeling quite confident that there could be no objectionable feature in any entertainment produced by you. An hour afterwards I chanced to notice, in the programme, the item "A Sermon in Spasms," and, in the quotations from Press-notices, a commendation of your "clever imitations of Dr. Talmage's sermons," and immediately went and returned the tickets, and explained to the people there why I could not go to the entertainment. To *them* I simply called it a piece of "outrageously bad taste." It did not seem necessary to speak of the more serious aspect of such an insult to Christianity, and such profaning of holy things. Nor need I, to you, enlarge on such considerations: you must be already aware of them.

I ask your forgiveness for writing so plainly and unpleasantly: but it seemed to me that I *ought* to say what I have done.[1]

Sincerely yours,
C. L. Dodgson

1. An advertisement appeared in the *Oxford Review* for a number of days announcing Furniss's entertainment. Thomas de Witt Talmage (1832–1902), at the time a renowned American clergyman, was a leader in the Dutch Reformed Church, editor of the *Christian Herald,* and a brilliant if sensational preacher—easily parodied. Furniss did not take criticism well, and Dodgson's accusations must have hurt him deeply. He would not forget the exchange and would have his say after Dodgson's death in his memoir *The Confessions of a Caricaturist* (2:179–80). Furniss

wrote that in his performance called "Americans in a Hurry," he "gave a wordless imitation of that eccentric American, Talmage, at the same time carefully pointing out to my audience that I imitated his gestures and voice—not Talmage in the character of a preacher, but as a showman; I was therefore surprised to receive . . . [Dodgson's letter]. I hastened to assure the reverend gentleman that Talmage was an 'entertainer,' like myself, that I used no words in imitation of him; merely his eccentric manner and showman's voice. I also hinted that I always had a number of clergymen in my audiences, and those who had heard me found nothing whatever objectionable, nor could they detect in what I did anything touching upon sacred things. This brought a lengthy rejoinder."

MS: *Lilly*

Christ Church, Oxford
May 20, 1896

Dear Mr. Furniss,

I am grateful for your letter, and for the proof it gives that my remarks did not give you mortal offence.

The points, raised in your letter, do not seem to me, I confess, to be relevant to the question.

You say "surely you do not imagine I ridicule religion?" In commenting on a letter, it is always safest, I think, to *quote*. The phrase "ridicule religion" was not used by me: my phrase was "profanation of holy things." A sermon, whoever is the preacher, has for its subject-matter "holy things": and consequently to ridicule a sermon is to treat holy things in a way that may surely be called "profanation."

The fact, that the preacher is a "humbug," "a vulgar entertainer," and "merely a showman," does not make the things, about which he preaches, less holy.

The fact, that you are careful, *in the lecture*, to explain that "it is not as a clergyman" you "take him off," is quite irrelevant to the *announcement* on the bills, the readers of which, not having the gift of prophecy, must form their judgement on that *announcement*. They cannot possibly take into account future events. And that announcement *is* that there will be comic "imitations of sermons." *That* is what deters me from going to the entertainment.

The fact, that thousands of clergymen have *not* been deterred, by that announcement, from going to the entertainment, does not surprise me. In this age of ever-increasing irreverence, it is my lot to hear many a profane anecdote told: and the *worst* offenders in this line are, I am sorry to say, *clergymen*. But, even were it not so, I cannot accept *their* judgement as a guide for *my* life. To attend an entertainment, in which it is announced that comic "imitations of sermons" will be given, is what *my* conscience condemns: and it would be no excuse, for me, to say that *other* consciences approve of it.[1]

Very sincerely yours,
C. L. Dodgson

1. "If [what Dodgson said] . . . was so—and the Rev. C. L. Dodgson could not possibly exaggerate any more than 'Lewis Carroll' could avoid exaggeration," Furniss wrote (*Confessions of a Caricaturist*, 2:180), "how much better it would have been for him to listen to my wordless and harmless imitation of a public entertainer than to sit in the Common Room and listen to profane anecdotes from the lips of his fellow ministers of religion!" Other comments by Furniss on Dodgson and their collaboration on the *Sylvie and Bruno* books abound. See, for instance, *Confessions*, 1:102–12; Harry Furniss, *Some Victorian Men*, 1924, pp. 74–80; Dorothy Furniss, ed., "New Lewis Carroll Letters," *Pearson's Magazine* (December 1930): 619–36; Beatrice and Guy Mackenzie, "Lewis Carroll Shown in New Light," *New York Times Magazine*, August 24, 1930, pp. 12–13. If Furniss thought that Dodgson would sit quietly and listen to profane anecdotes in the Common Room or anywhere else, he did not know the true nature of the man. As for Furniss's entertainment "Americans in a Hurry," the *Oxford Times* commented: "Mr. Furniss's opinions are as original as his views, and he revelled in descriptions of New York and Chicago, of the Yankees as a 'nation of blowers,' given to exaggeration and the telling of tall stories; of the 'blizzard of hospitality' that greeted him wherever he went; of the tortures suffered at the hands of pencils and endless and almost countless interviews; of the style of pulpit oratory in vogue in America, as illustrated by Dr. Talmage, and the many eccentricities of American Congressmen, Senators and Wall-street stockbrokers. On the whole Mr. Furniss seems to have had a good time in the States and to have made the most of the few weeks he spent there" (May 30, 1896, p. 8).

5. Emily Gertrude Thomson (1850-1929)

DODGSON CAME UPON some greeting cards illustrated by E. Gertrude Thomson in December 1878.[1] Impressed by her art, he wrote to the publisher Arthur Ackermann on December 22 asking for her address:

> Mr. Dodgson's reason, for asking Mr. Ackermann to send Miss Thomson's address [Dodgson writes], was his great admiration for the two sets of Christmas cards (especially the large set) which Mr. Ackermann has published. Photographing from life—and especially photographing children—has been his one amusement for the last twenty years. He has also made attempts (most unsuccessfully) at drawing them: but he has at least learned from his own failures to appreciate the difficulty of that line of Art, and to enjoy such successful pictures as those of Miss Thomson.[2]

Arthur Ackermann issued originally designed Christmas cards from 1877 to 1900 from his commercial premises at 191 Regent Street, London. Miss Thomson illustrated several sets of large cards depicting seashore, shells, fish, and nude children. Ackermann presumably replied to Dodgson's letter, and Dodgson and Miss Thomson met in London the following June. A friendship ensued.

The artist was the daughter of Alexander Thomson (1815–95), professor of Greek and Hebrew at Lancashire Independent College. She studied at the Manchester School of Art, won a number of Queen's Prizes, and became a member of the Royal Society of Miniature Painters. At various points in

---

1. For an appreciation of Thomson, see J. N. S. Davis, "E. Gertrude Thomson, Illustrator, 1850–1929," *Jabberwocky* (Autumn 1975). For a miniature portrait of Dodgson by Thomson, see *Catalogue of an Exhibition at Columbia University to Commemorate the One Hundredth Anniversary of the Birth of Lewis Carroll*, 1932, frontispiece. For her pencil drawing of Dodgson, see frontispiece.

2. MS: Harvard.

her career she painted portraits, illustrated books, and designed stained-glass windows. She exhibited in Manchester, Liverpool, Brussels, and in Canada. Her works are in the permanent collections of the Manchester Art Gallery and the Victoria and Albert Museum; her stained-glass windows can be seen at Cheltenham College and at the Church of St. John the Divine, Brooklands, Cheshire.

Before Dodgson and Thomson met, they exchanged letters and Dodgson sent her inscribed copies of the *Alice* books bound in white morocco. As Thomson tells in her reminiscence, "Lewis Carroll: A Sketch by an Artist-Friend," they met for the first time at the South Kensington Museum (now the Victoria and Albert Museum) on June 27, 1879. Dodgson recorded the meeting (*Diaries*, p. 380): "To the South Kensington Museum, to meet (by appointment) Miss E. G. Thomson, who is staying in town, and whom I had not met before. She had her sketch-book with her, and showed . . . [me] some lovely bits she had done from antiques."

They met from time to time over the following five years, and in 1885, Dodgson suggested that Thomson provide illustrations for one of his books. In *Sylvie and Bruno* he advertised a projected book, "Original Games and Puzzles" with twenty illustrations by E. Gertrude Thomson, but it never became a reality. Dodgson did, however, use some of Thomson's drawings later for his book of serious verse, *Three Sunsets and Other Poems*.

In the meantime, Dodgson commissioned Thomson to draw a design for the cover of *The Nursery "Alice."* But as with most of his other artists, Dodgson had to wait upon her convenience. "Miss Thomson writes that she hopes to send sketch for picture-cover directly," he wrote on February 26, 1889 (*Diaries*, p. 468). "We should now get the book out by Easter." On March 18, however, he recorded: "But it hasn't yet come! She has been busy, and lately unwell. Still we may get it out by Easter after all." But Thomson did not deliver the illustration, and the book did not go to press until April 18, and even then without the cover design, which was added later.

Dodgson met Thomson for the last time on November 20, 1897, when he visited her Addison Hall studio in London, where they did some sketches of her little model, Isy Watson, age thirteen. Afterwards they lunched with some of Dodgson's friends in Lowndes Square. Two months after Dodgson died Thomson published a two-part reminiscence of him, which we reproduce in full following the correspondence.

Over the last twenty years of his life, Dodgson contemplated bringing out a volume of what he considered his "serious poems," but the idea remained on a back burner. He completed it, however, just before he died, and it appeared posthumously. A slender volume, *Three Sunsets and Other Poems* contains all but two of the poems in the second "serious" part of *Phantasmagoria and Other Poems*, five new poems, and twelve "fairy fancies" by Thomson. These illustrations are antiseptic nudes that have nothing to do with the poems, simply pleasant artworks conforming to Dodgson's taste. It is the last book that Dodgson prepared for the press; it was published in February 1898, a month after his death.

MS: Harvard

Christ Church, Oxford
January 24, 1879

Dear Miss Thomson,

I too have been very busy, or I would have written long before this to thank you, first for your very interesting letter, and secondly for the tracing and the 2 photographs of drawings, whether they be loans or gifts: you do not tell me to send them back, so I shall at any rate keep them till you do so: I enjoy all 3 very much, the "frog" picture perhaps most, though I venture to think that your view as to the diameter of the knee and ankle of a child of the age of the standing girl in that picture is in excess of the truth. Still you *may* have got those dimensions from real life, but in that case I think your model must have been a country-peasant child, descended from generations of labourers: there is a marked difference between them and the upper classes—specially as to the size of the ankle. I have learned *my* scale of proportions from many years' practice in photography, my favourite subjects being children, but those have *not* been peasant-children, so that I have come to believe in slender ankles as the normal standard of beauty. Photography has also taught me, that most artists draw children's feet too small: they have some conventional ideal of beauty, which is *not* nature. I am very glad you do not fall into that error.

No doubt I have seen drawings of yours at the "Black and White," but had not remembered your name in connection with them.[1] Some day I may perhaps possess myself of some exhibited drawing of yours: but I cannot (as I said before) afford much expenditure in such luxuries. How I should enjoy photographing drawings of yours! If you ever cared to entrust me with any for that purpose, I would, after taking a few prints for myself, present you with the negative: or, if you preferred it, I would leave the negative with the photographer who prints for me, and you could order prints from him *ad libitum*.

Before I close this letter, I will look among my photographs of children for some which I am allowed to give away, and enclose them for your acceptance.

Your view of "Schools of Art" is new to me. True, I have always felt thankful, when my young-lady-friends have shown me the drawings they have done there, that *I* am not condemned to spending weary hours in copying scroll-work and cornices, but I had always believed that somehow, when the drudgery was done, one *did* learn drawing. A young lady, whom I know, in London, has devoted herself, from pure love of Art, to drawing; and has worked for a year and a half at the Slade School of Art.[2] She has now reached the blissful stage of drawing from life, and is *very* successful, I think. Still I can't understand why one shouldn't *begin* by drawing from life, and do without casts altogether.

Do you know Mr. Ruskin? I have the pleasure of numbering him among my friends, and if he returns to Oxford, as I hope he will soon be well enough to do, I promise myself the pleasure of showing him the Christmas cards and the 3 drawings: and, if you would not object, I should much like to show him your letter. I am sure it would interest him. It is possible, if you don't know the great art-critic, that it might be of use to you thus to get to know him. I don't know if you would care to be introduced to any other artists, but I will give you the names of those I know, on the chance: Sir F. Leighton, Mr. J. Sant and Mr. G. Sant, Mr. Archer, Mr. Arthur Hughes, Mr. G. Moore, Mr. H. Holiday, Mr. A. Bruce-Joy (sculptor), Mrs. Ward, Mr. and Mrs. Anderson (she paints children beautifully: they are living in Italy at present), Sir Noël Paton (his figure-drawings from life are beyond praise), Mr. Holman Hunt, Mr. Woolner (sculptor).[3] I used to know Mr. Millais, but it is many years since, and he may have almost forgotten me now.

I have now looked out a few (5) photographs of children, one of which (1369) is of Mr. Millais' second daughter, Mary, the original of Waking, and in the dress in which he painted her; (2002) is a son of a Mr. Hatch: the right foot has got magnified by being too near to the camera; (2132) is a daughter of Mr. Kitchin: she is in Danish dress; (2182) is Ethel Hatch: I call it "Guarding the barricades"; she and her sister are two of the most beautifully formed children I have ever photographed; (2536) is a daughter of Dr. Gray: she is in a Pantomime-dress—the "fleshings" come out too white:

that, and the being a little too near to the camera, makes the ankles come out thicker than they are in nature.[4]

Yours very truly,
C. L. Dodgson

P.S. As you like books of child-life, let me send for your acceptance one of two such books which I have written, whichever you prefer (if you know them; if not, I will send the first). Their names are *Alice's Adventures in Wonderland* and *Through the Looking-Glass.*

1. The "Black and White" exhibitions took place annually at London's Dudley Gallery. Dodgson visited the one for 1879 on June 17 (Diaries).

2. Dodgson's artist friend was Theodosia Heaphy (1858–1920), daughter of Thomas Frank Heaphy, portrait and narrative painter. She followed in her father's footsteps with some success and later exhibited at the Suffolk Street Exhibition (1883–85). Dodgson's friendship with Theo spanned many years; he visited her studio and occasionally took her to the theater. For more on Dodgson and the Heaphy family, see *Letters*, p. 105, n. 1.

3. James Sant (1820–1916), a portrait painter who also painted allegorical female figures, and George Sant (fl. 1856–77), his brother. Dodgson met James Sant on April 9, 1867, when he dined at his home, and encountered him again on a similar occasion on January 8, 1869 (DIARIES, 5:140, 6:75). Dodgson met the portrait painter James Archer (1822–1904) through George MacDonald, (1824–1905), cleric, novelist, and close friend. He called on Archer on April 8, 9, and 25, 1867, noting that Archer was "hearty and pleasant like his brother-artists," and that his pictures "contained a great deal of careful and delicate painting" (DIARIES, 5:214, 218, 233). Dodgson first met Arthur Hughes (1832–1915), artist and illustrator, on July 21, 1863, when he recorded that he "saw some lovely pictures, and his four little children" (DIARIES, 4:223). Dodgson visited Hughes on other occasions and took photographs of the family. By "G. Moore" Dodgson surely means John Collingham Moore (1829–80), a friend of the Holidays. Dodgson called on Moore on June 11, 1875, and "thought him very genial and pleasant: his pictures of children are quite delicious." On April 1 of the following year Moore "came over for the day to see Oxford, lunching with me, after which we visited the Bodleian, etc." (DIARIES, 6:397, 455). Albert Bruce-Joy (1842–1924), the prolific sculptor of public statues, enters the DIARIES (6:277) but once, when Dodgson encounters him at the home of a mutual acquaintance on May 17, 1873. Mrs. Henrietta Mary Ada Ward (1832–1924) was a painter of historical subjects, whom Dodgson first met on June 28, 1866 (DIARIES, 5:161). Dodgson saw the work of both Walter Anderson (fl. 1856–86) and his wife, Sophie (1823–1903), in London at the exhibition of British artists on April 7, 1864, and on the same day made their acquaintance: "I found them at home, very pleasant people, but there were no pictures in the house except some half-coloured sketches of heads, all exceedingly pretty" (DIARIES, 4:290). Joseph Noël Paton (1821–1901), painter of historical, mythical, and religious subjects, also wrote poetry. Dodgson approached Paton to illustrate *Through the Looking-Glass* when Tenniel claimed to be too busy to carry out the commission, but Paton wrote, through the MacDonalds, insisting that "Tenniel is *the* man" (DIARIES, 6:30). Dodgson visited Paton at Arran on September 15, 1871 (DIARIES, 6:181–83). William Holman Hunt (1827–1910), painter, founding member of the Pre-Raphaelite movement, was photographed by Dodgson in July 1860. On July 16, 1863, Dodgson visited his Oxford

friends the Thomas Combes and found Thomas Woolner (1825–92), the Pre-Raphaelite sculptor-poet, doing a bust of Combe. He encountered Woolner at the Combes' at least twice more (July 17 and 23) and, two years later, lunched with him in London (*DIARIES*, 4:221, 225, *DIARIES*, 5:76).

4. The numbers that appear with the photographs are from Dodgson's register of photographs (now missing). He also wrote the image numbers on the back of his photographic prints, usually in the top right-hand corner. Some of Dodgson's albums of photographs contain indexes accompanied by his image numbers. The sitters for these photographs are Mary Millais (taken 1865; Gernsheim, plate 51), Arthur Hatch (taken 1872; *Letters*, p. 252), Alexandra ("Xie") Kitchin (taken 1873; Collingwood, p. 368), Ethel Hatch (taken 1873; at Harvard), and Lily Gray (taken 1878; location unknown).

MS: Morgan

Christ Church, Oxford
February 12, 1879

Dear Miss Thomson,

After my letter had gone, a parcel arrived with some *Alice*s I had ordered, and I am now sending you *Alice* and the *Looking-Glass* as well. There is an incompleteness about giving only one, and besides the one you bought was probably in red, and would not match these. If you are at all in doubt as to what to do with the (now) superfluous copy, let me suggest your giving it to some poor sick child. I have been distributing copies to all the hospitals and convalescent homes I can hear of, where there are sick children capable of reading them, and though of course one takes some pleasure in the popularity of the books elsewhere, it is not nearly so pleasant a thought to me as that they may be a comfort and relief to children in hours of pain and weariness. Still no recipient *can* be more appropriate than one who seems to have been in fairyland herself, and to have seen, like the "weary mariners" of old,

> Between the green brink and the running foam
> White limbs unrobed in a crystal air,
> Sweet faces, rounded arms, and bosoms prest
> To little harps of gold. . . .[1]

I have more to write to you about fairies, and your un-belief (which I think a heresy) in their reality, but I must put it off to a more leisurely time. Believe me

Very truly yours,
C. L. Dodgson

1. Tennyson, "The Sea-Fairies" (1830 version), ll. 1–4.

MS: *Huntington*

[Christ Church, Oxford]
May 7 [1884]

Dear Miss Thomson,

Please be kind enough *not* to mention my real name to any persons, strangers to me, who may chance to see the signature at January 27. The fewer who know it, the happier for me.[1]

Yours very sincerely,
C. L. Dodgson

1. *Alice's Wonderland Birthday Book* had just been published with Dodgson's permission, and he received his copy on April 28. In the book, the blanks for entering the names of persons for each day of the year are accompanied by extracts from the *Alice* books selected by E. Stanley Leathes. Dodgson inscribed Miss Thomson's copy of the *Birthday Book* on the half-title page: "E.G.T. from Humpty-Dumpty. May 7. 1844," obviously making an error in writing the year. He must have written "Lewis Carroll" in the book at January 27 (Parke-Bernet catalogue, October 16, 1927, lot 54).

MS: *Huntington*

Christ Church, Oxford
July 16, 1885

Dear Miss Thomson,

I haven't yet said a word to Mr. Furniss about the "serious poems." First, it would be quite premature, as we shall probably be 2 years over our present job: secondly, because I still cherish the hope of your finding yourself well enough to undertake them.[1] Half of them, at least, ought to be landscapes, and *these* I believe you would do altogether better than he would: and even the figure-ones—the more I look at *Fairies*,[2] the more I am inclined to think you would do *them* beautifully, if only you would study a few *different* faces from real life, so as to avoid the family-likeness, which seems so entirely inevitable, when an artist draws out of his own head.

Don't you think you could draw me just a few landscapes, which I would get reduced to the *Alice* size, and cut on wood, and I would use them, even if Mr. Furniss did the other pictures?[3]

If you think favorably of this, and do not possess *Phantasmagoria*, I will lend it you (or rather a fragment of it, containing the serious poems), and you could try a sketch now and then, when you feel in the vein. It would give you some out-of-door work—ever so much healthier than indoors. You might draw as *large* as you like: the only thing to observe would be the *proportionate* height and width. We might try 3 kinds: The first would want the proportion of 2 wide to 3 high: the second 14 to 11: the third 14 to 9. You might draw the third oval, and draw up to the limit: the photographer would vignette it off, by printing it through a "vignette-glass." This kind would make a lovely tail-piece for a poem. If you don't think the proportions of No. 2 and No. 3 pretty, you can alter them: but for a *full-page* picture we have no choice.

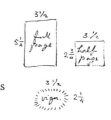

My original plan for this Long Vacation, was to go to Eastbourne as soon after July 1 as my rooms (I always go to the same) should be vacant. This, however, did not happen till July 9th, so I took them from that day, and have been paying for the empty rooms for a week now, not being able to go myself, or to find a couple of lady-friends (or even a single one) to put in as my guests. What keeps me here is a grand piece of photo-zincography which is being done (at least the photography-part) in my studio, by a man who has come, with assistant and a mass of boxes of chemicals, etc., all the way from Essex. It has taken some time and trouble to find a really good man for this: and I was resolved to have the thing done in first-rate style, or not at all. But you will be wondering, all this while, what this important work can be! The germ of *Alice's Adventures in Wonderland* was an extempore story, told in a boat to the 3 children of Dean Liddell: it was afterwards, at the request of Miss Alice Liddell, written out for her, in MS print, with pen-and-ink pictures (*such* pictures!) of my own devising: without the least idea, at the time, that it would ever be published. But friends urged me to print it, so it was re-written, and enlarged, and published. Now that we have sold some 70,000 copies, it occurred to me that there must be a good many people, to whom a facsimile of the MS book would be interesting: and that is my present task. There are 92 pages, and, though we do them 2 at a time, it is a tedious business: and I have to stay in all day for it, as I allow no hands but mine to touch the MS book. Workmen's hands would soon spoil it, and it is not my property now, so I feel a terrible responsibility in having it lent me by the owner, who (I am happy to believe) sets a certain value on it as something unique. Luckily (as it will avoid confusion) the name is different from the published book, and is *Alice's Adventures Under Ground.* In another month, or two, I hope to have the pleasure of sending to you (and also to two or three other friends!) the facsimile.[4]

The other day I had quite a new form of artistic treat. You remember those 2 little Henderson girls, whom I have so often photographed naked? (I think you have photographs of both.) It is 3 or 4 years now since I have photographed—I have been too busy: but I borrowed their little sister (aged 5 1/2) to *draw* as a nude model. (There was never time, in photographic days, to try *drawings.*) The 2 elder ones brought her, and I gave an hour to making 4 sketches, and a second hour (after dressing her up again) to showing the trio my albums, musical-boxes, etc. She *is* such a sweet little figure! If only you, or some other person who *can* draw, had been here! *Then* there would have been some result worth showing. I could have had her here again and again, but did not like to tax the patience of so young a sitter any more. Next year, they say she may come again: and then I shall venture on a rather longer sitting. Even this time she sat nearly 15 minutes, I think, for one of the drawings. The results were, I think, about 10 times as good as I ever draw out of my own head: but what good is it to multiply zero by 10? The mathematical result is zero![5]

And I have a further treat in prospect. A Mr. Paget,[6] a London artist, kindly says that, whenever I can come to his studio and he happens to have a nude model sitting, I may draw her too (of course the model's consent must first be asked). I *hope* it will be a child, if ever I do go: but I would try an adult rather than lose the chance of such splendid practice, with an artist sitting by who could correct my mistakes for me. So no more at present from

Yours very sincerely,
C. L. Dodgson

1. Dodgson contemplated a new edition of "Serious Poems" as early as November 23, 1881 (*Diaries*, p. 402), and his list of literary projects on hand dated March 29, 1885 (pp. 433–34), reaffirms his intention.

2. *The Fairies, A Child's Song* by William Allingham (1824–89), with twenty-three illustrations by E. Gertrude Thomson (1883).

3. Dodgson's notion to ask Furniss to draw illustrations for some of his serious poems soon evaporated.

4. James Noad of Hawthorn Cottage, East Ham, Essex, was engaged to photograph the ninety-two facsimile pages from the manuscript of *Alice's Adventures Under Ground*, which Dodgson had borrowed from Alice Hargreaves. "Negatives taken from p. 12 to p. 53," Dodgson noted (Diaries) on the day he wrote this letter. Noad proved to be unreliable, and Dodgson was forced, after long delays, to take legal action to procure the facsimile plates that he had paid for. The facsimile edition was eventually published in 1886.

5. For details of Dodgson's friendship with the Hendersons, see *Letters*, p. 277, n. 1. His diaries for July 2, 1885, give a longer report of the drawing session with young Lilian as model: "A new experience in Art. Little Lillian Henderson . . . was brought down by Annie and Frances, for me to try some sketches of her, naked, up in my studio. She has a charming little figure, and was a very patient sitter. I made 4 studies of her. The only previous occasion when I have had a naked child to draw from was a hasty attempt (which I quite failed) at Beatrice Hatch (I think), which would have been in 1872. To draw the figure from *life* seems to give me quite new powers." Dodgson did not draw Lilian the following year or ever again.

6. On May 23, 1885, Dodgson lent his studio to Henry P. Liddon for a sitting to the artist Henry Marriott Paget (1856–1936), who was painting Liddon's portrait. On June 5, Dodgson, in London, spent two hours or more with Paget at his studio "and saw some interesting 'studies,' and his two charming little girls" (*Diaries*, pp. 435–36). The treat of drawing in Paget's studio did not, it seems, materialize.

Printed circular letter with MS *additions: Princeton*

7 Lushington Road, Eastbourne
July 31, 1890

Dear Miss Thomson,

Would you kindly furnish me with the addresses of any Stationers (doing a good amount of business)—*one* name, in any one neighbourhood, is as much as we can afford—to whom it would be worth my while to send a specimen-copy of my new *Stamp-Case*, a copy of which I herewith enclose for your acceptance, and of the *Eight or Nine Wise Words*, written to accompany it, a copy of which I herewith enclose for your acceptance.

You will do me a further favour if you will mention it (in terms as favourable as you honestly can) to the said Stationers, and to any of your friends whom you think to be likely purchasers. Believe me

Sincerely yours,
C. L. Dodgson

P.S. We have now gone on for several years, I think, with the hope, renewed each Spring and abandoned each Autumn, that the serious poems would be illustrated during the Summer. If this year passes away like its predecessors, you will not, I hope, feel hurt if I put the thing into other hands? Life is so short.[1]

1. On February 26, 1886, Dodgson wrote: "Miss E. G. Thomson spent the day with me. We discussed drawings for serious poems" (*Diaries*, p. 440).

MS: Huntington

7 Lushington Road, Eastbourne
September 6, 1890

Dear Miss Thomson,

I've got 2 stalls for the Matinée of *Judah* at the Shaftesbury Theatre on Wednesday afternoon the 10th.

And the young friend I had designed the 2nd ticket for has seen it already. And I would much rather take some one who has not seen it than merely treat her to a second edition. Do you come under the category? And, if so, will you let me have the pleasure of treating you to it?

Please telegraph your answer if it be a negative, to give me as much time as possible for finding another companion.

If your answer be "yes," I'll come by some forenoon-train, so as to allow myself an hour or two at your studio before we go off to the play. And I would come even earlier, so as to have a couple of hours, *if* you could get a child-model that we—no, not "we"—that *you* might copy, and that I might *try* to copy. I tried "Maud Howard," [1] the other day, at the studio of my friend Mrs. Shute (an amateur-artist). I wonder if you know her? She is not far from you ("9 Hannell Terrace, Walham Green"). She has a beautiful figure, I think. And she seems nice and modest: but she is turned 14, and *I* like drawing a *child*, best. However, if you wish to get a model for Wednesday, and *cannot* find a child, Maud would be well worth having for an hour. Her mother keeps a shop, I believe: and her elder sisters are also models. But *don't* get a grown-up model, any time you are expecting *me*.

If you write "yes," please tell me how you would get from Victoria to your place—train? or cab? or bus? I can't make out which is best.[2]

Sincerely yours,
C. L. Dodgson

1. Maud Howard appears only twice in Dodgson's diaries (DIARIES, p. 478). On the previous August 2, Dodgson "had about 2 hours with Mrs. Shute, drawing her little model 'Maud Howard,' aged 14: not very pretty in face, but certainly beautiful in figure. I gave her a wire puzzle and promised her an *Alice.*" In October, Dodgson included her name in a list of new child friends. For more on Dodgson's friendship with Mrs. Edith Shute, see *Letters*, p. 689, n. 1.

2. Miss Thomson did not join Dodgson for the matinée of the Henry Arthur Jones play; instead he took Edith Lucy, who was staying with him, and who was, presumably, the young friend who had seen the play before.

MS: *Huntington*

7 Lushington Road, Eastbourne
October 5, 1890

Dear Miss Thomson,

I intend going to Oxford on Saturday the 11th, or else Monday the 13th, or Tuesday the 14th: the last-named being the most likely. Shall you be at your studio any of those days? It would not be much extra cost to come round by London: and it would be worth while, if I could get an hour or two of drawing, under your auspices from a child-model: but I rather grudge the expense of a journey from Oxford to London and back, merely for my own artistic enjoyment.[1]

Sincerely yours,
C. L. Dodgson

1. Dodgson traveled to Oxford from Eastbourne by way of London on October 11 (Diaries). If he visited Miss Thomson's studio, he makes no note of it.

MS: *Huntington*

Christ Church, Oxford
December 13, 1890

My dear Miss Thomson,

I have so many other "irons in the fire," that really I'm in no hurry about the serious poems, and you are quite welcome to do as you propose. Perhaps I may publish in the summer, if you succeed in finishing the pictures.

You do not say if you have got a workable-in studio yet. So I suppose you know nothing as yet of child-models, and have not even seen "Maud Howard" (though *she* is hardly a "child") of whom I told you.

I expect to go (more than once, very likely) next month to see *The Rose and the Ring*, which is to be played, afternoons and evenings (afternoons suit me best) at the Prince of Wales's. My motive is that 2 dear little friends of mine, Isa and Empsie Bowman, are in it. Will there be any use in offering to take *you* to it?[1]

> Always very sincerely yours,
> C. L. Dodgson

1. Dodgson went to see Henry Savile Clarke's dramatization of Thackeray's *The Rose and the Ring* (with music by Walter Slaughter) on January 5 and again on January 8, taking Miss Thomson with him on the latter occasion (*Diaries*, pp. 481–82). He reports that Isa Bowman played "Fairy Blackstick" and Empsie had two parts, a ragged child and "General Punchikoff." For more on Dodgson's friendship with the Bowmans, see *Letters*, passim, esp. p. 710, n. 2.

MS: *Huntington*

> Christ Church, Oxford
> January 18, 1892[1]

Dear Miss Thomson,

I hope you quite understood, when I asked you to do me a head of "Clara," in the style of the one you kindly gave me of "Blanche," that I meant "do it *professionally*." Your time and skill are worth so much money, and I am most glad to pay for them.

Do you think her pretty? I have heard from her: and the fancy, which you say you have taken to her, seems to be *mutual*.[2]

I'm getting my book of "Puzzles and Games" into type, and shall be able to utilise any amount of fairies you can draw for me![3]

For these, I want you to get as many different *faces* as you possibly can: for (I hope you won't be offended with me for venturing an opinion as an amateur) there does seem to me to be a considerable *family-likeness* among the faces in *Fairies*. They were drawn, I imagine, out of your head: and, in such a case, it seems to me to be as hopeless to avoid a likeness as it would be to try to sign your name differently in every letter you wrote. Cruikshank's splendid illustrations were *terribly* spoiled by his having only *one* pretty female face in them all. Leech settled down into *two* female faces. Du Maurier, I think, has only *one*, now. All the ladies, and all the little girls, in his pictures, look like twin sisters.

I should be very glad if you would use, as faces for the fairies, Clara, Isa, Nellie, and Empsie Bowman, and as many other children as you can get likenesses of. Would it not be a good thing for me to send you a lot of photographs of children's heads, and for you to try to catch the *likeness* of each? Then there would be a grand variety of faces, and you would eclipse (in that respect) Cruikshank, Leech, etc., etc., and almost every illustrator one can name![4] I write in haste.

Yours very sincerely,
C. L. Dodgson

Please give Clara my love, and thanks for her letter, and *perhaps* I'll write to her—the year after next: but oh, I have so many letters to write!

1. Letters must have passed between Dodgson and Miss Thomson during the previous twelve months, but they are missing. Dodgson and Miss Thomson did meet on July 13, 1891: "Evelyn [Hatch] and I left for Clapham at 10.24, thence to Putney, to the Bowmans, and took Isa with us. We called on Miss Thomson, who showed us a beautiful 'pastel' portrait, life-size" (DI-ARIES, p. 484).

2. Clara Maria Earle (b. 1879). Dodgson met her on September 28, 1891, when he and Isa Bowman "called in Lambeth Road, to make acquaintance with . . . Eliza Earle. We saw also her mother, Mrs. Earle, and an elder sister, Clara, aged 12 (Eliza is 7). Clara has played 'Willie Carlyle,' and other child-characters: she is very pretty, and a more attractive looking child than Eliza. There is another girl, and a boy, both of them older, I believe, than these" (Diaries). Clara Elizabeth Earle (b. 1855) lived with her parents, John and Eliza Johnstone, at 36 Lambeth Road, London. She married Robert John Earle, a mercantile clerk, with four children, Robert (b. 1876), Clara Maria, Lilian (b. 1882), and Eliza (b. 1884).

3. Dodgson's projected book, "Original Games and Puzzles," never materialized, although he prepared much of it before his death. The idea for a book of games and puzzles had long been in his mind. As early as January 1875, he contemplated the publication of "Alice's Puzzle-Book." He went as far as to have Macmillan prepare a proof title page, and he wrote to Tenniel to get him to draw a frontispiece (DIARIES, 6:381–82). On November 23, 1881, when Dodgson compiled a list of works he still hoped to publish, he included "Games and Puzzles," an original work with a frontispiece by Miss Thomson (Diaries, p. 402). He intended using Miss Thomson's fairy drawings to illustrate the book, but at a later stage he chose instead to use twelve of them for *Three Sunsets*. He kept back a few of her larger drawings, intending them for the puzzle book which never appeared.

4. On March 28, Dodgson "sent Miss Thomson 36 photographs of children, done about 1865 to 1875" (Diaries). Dodgson refers to George Cruikshank (1792–1878), John Leech (1817–64), and George du Maurier (see pp. 331–32).

MS: *Huntington*

Christ Church, Oxford
February 13, 1892

Dear Miss Thomson,

I am having the drawing sent to you.[1]

As to the ownership of the drawings for this book and for the serious *Poems* (if you do them also), I should wish it to be *yours*; and you could, after I had published them, sell them. But I should wish to retain the *copyright*, and that the purchaser should distinctly understand that he had no right to *publish* them in any way whatever.

Very sincerely yours,
C. L. Dodgson

1. Missing.

MS: *Huntington*

Christ Church, Oxford
February 16, 1892

My dear Miss Thomson,

I am so distracted with the many things I am trying to attend to, that I hardly know what to turn to first. However, this afternoon I'll try to send you these 3 drawings, with remarks which may be of service for future ones, even if they can't be altered themselves.

They are *lovely*, as a whole, and my criticisms affect quite minor details.

(1) *Boy on mushroom.* Would you mind putting your name, or initials, in some less conspicuous place, e.g. among the grass? To have it all alone, some way off the picture, catches the eye, and spoils the roundness of the outline. I want it as a tail-piece. I wish there wasn't so much mushroom: it quite dwarfs the child. Remember it's got to be reduced to about 2 *inches* wide. If you will lay, over the drawing, the enclosed piece of paper,[1] you will see how much accessory *I* should be content with. However, I suppose that must stay as it is, now. But are his wrists and ankles capable of change? They're terribly thick! Why should these fairies be so *very* plebeian?[2]

(2) *Two girls sailing in shell.* You have made their boat sail *stern-first!*

However that is a trifle. Could the little girl's wrist be thinned? It is about the same diameter as her upper arm. And could your name be more *among the waves?* The proportion, between figures and accessories, is just what I want.[3]

(3) 2 *girls in a bower.* A good deal more *bower* than I care for: but *that* I suppose is a necessity. The elder girl's ankles look rather thick: the younger is, apparently, of gentler birth![4]

But I am, I repeat, charmed with these pictures as a *whole.*

Very sincerely yours,
C. L. Dodgson

1. Missing.
2. *Three Sunsets,* p. 52. Miss Thomson's initials appear in the grass. The picture is used as a full-page illustration and has not been reduced to two inches.
3. Ibid., p. 7. The boat is sailing in the right direction as indicated by the sails, but the girls are facing toward the stern. Miss Thomson's initials appear among the waves.
4. Ibid., p. 14. Miss Thomson may have reduced the amount of bower; it does not dominate the picture.

MS: *Huntington*

Christ Church, Oxford
March 29, 1892

Dear Miss Thomson,

I enclose a print of the revised "fairy and mushroom," which *I* think comes out quite charming. If you approve, I will have it cut on wood.

Many thanks for tracing of child on shell, drawn by 2 fishes, and attended by 2 swimming fairies: but I fear the shape makes it useless: to reduce it to 3 1/2 wide would make the faces, and figures, too minute to be interesting. If it could be made into a picture *without the fishes*, it might possibly do: but I fear it needs them to give a balanced look.[1]

If you copy the "frog" picture, I think the girl standing will be quite enough to put in with the frog: to include the lying-down figure on the left would make it all too small.[2]

You don't tell me the *subject* of the big water-colour. You spoke of using "the body of Clara Earle." Does that mean that she sat as a "figure" model? And, if so, has she a pretty figure?[3]

You can do Isa's head in any style you like. But don't let it interfere with the *real* work that has been so long on hand, the serious poems, and the fairies. Believe me

Very sincerely yours,
C. L. Dodgson

1. The drawing does not appear in *Three Sunsets*.
2. *Three Sunsets*, p. 47. Miss Thomson redrew this picture without the lying-down figure, but she introduces a kneeling girl facing the frog to give the picture a balanced composition.
3. The purpose and subject of the big water-color elude us.

———————

MS: *Huntington*

Christ Church, Oxford,
March 31, 1892

My dear Miss Thomson,

Did I mention to you (I *meant* to do so) that *Fairies* is out of print? Luckily I have still a few on hand (it is a book that I often give away to young friends), but I tried to get a further supply the other day, and entirely failed: it is not to be had, anywhere. Really you should get some more done: and, if you do, let me suggest that the colour-printer should be warned that his work is falling off in quality: what I have bought lately do not seem to me so good as the early copies. I gave a copy, last November, to little Princess Alice, and got a charming little letter of thanks: but perhaps I've told you all this already?[1]

It *did* seem a little incredible that Clara should have taken to the "figure-model" line of business: I fancy it is usually children 2 or 3 steps lower in social position who do it. But have you got any child-model now? I *do* want you to do my fairy-drawings from *life*. They would be very pretty, no doubt, done out of your own head: but they will be ten times as valuable if done from life. Mr. Furniss drew the pictures of "Sylvie" from life. Mr. Tenniel is the only artist, who has drawn for me, who resolutely refused to use a model, and declared he no more needed one than I should need a multiplication-table to work a mathematical problem! I venture to think that he was mistaken, and that, for want of a model, he drew several pictures of "Alice" *entirely* out of proportion, head decidedly too large, and feet decidedly too small.

If you haven't got one, I've no doubt I could easily hear of one for you. I should like the fairies to be, mostly, about the proportions of a child of 6 or 7: so neither Ada Langley nor Maud Howard would be any good.[2]

Very sincerely yours,
C. L. Dodgson

I'll look out for *Venetian Blinds* at R. W. Stations.[3]

1. Dodgson met the Duchess of Albany and her two children, Prince Charles and Princess Alice, on a visit to Hatfield House in June 1889. He wrote: "Once at luncheon I had the Duchess as neighbour, and once at breakfast, and had several other chats with her, and found her very pleasant indeed. Princess Alice is a sweet little girl, though with rather unruly high spirits. Her brother was entirely fascinating: a perfect little Prince, and the picture of good humour" (*Diaries*, p. 471). On November 16, 1891, Dodgson records another meeting: "The Duchess of Albany is at the Deanery with her children, and sent the children to my rooms soon after ten. The little Alice is improved, I think, not being so unruly as she was two years ago: they are charming children. . . . I promised to send Alice a copy of *The Fairies*" (ibid., p. 488).

2. We cannot identify Ada Langley.

3. We cannot identify *Venetian Blinds*; it was probably a book suggested to Dodgson by Miss Thomson.

MS: *Huntington*

Christ Church, Oxford
March 31, 1892

My dear Miss Thomson,

I enclose the tracing.[1] With best wishes that you may enjoy, and be benefited by, your Scotch tour, I am

Very sincerely yours,
C. L. Dodgson

1. The tracing has survived; see figure 35.

MS: *Huntington*

Christ Church, Oxford
April 5, 1892

My dear Miss Thomson,

I've written to Mrs. E. M. Ward, Sir F. Leighton, and a Mr. Riley (an artist whose studies of the nude seem to *me*, *lovely*) enquiring for a child-model for you.[1]

What you say about not being able to get De la Rue to re-publish *Fairies* puzzles me.[2] Surely, even if he has bought the copyright, he has no legal right to keep it *out of print*, against the author's wish? I should fancy he was bound to do one of two things—either publish it himself, or else allow you to get it published elsewhere. If you like, I'll ask the question of some of my legal friends, and tell you what your legal position is. It would be a *great* pity for it to go wholly out of print. All my friends cordially admire it: I gave away a copy only last Wednesday, to one of my girl-friends here, whom I had borrowed for a walk and tea in my rooms.[3]

Mr. Edmund Evans would be delighted to have the job: and would do it well.[4]

I'll enclose, in this, a copy of the lines I wrote in the copy of *Fairies* which I gave to the little Princess. Soon I mean to write to the Duchess, and reveal to her what I fancy they have failed to discover for themselves, that there is "more than meets the eye" in the verses; and to get her leave to print

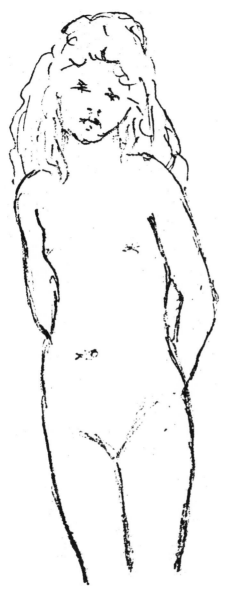

FIG. 35

Dodgson's tracing with letter dated March 31, 1892.

them in my book of "Games and Puzzles." But, *till* they so appear, please don't show them to any one outside your family circle.[5]

Yours very sincerely,
C. L. Dodgson

P.S. I can't find the verses. I've put them away safely: only I can't remember where!

1. For more on Mrs. Ward and family, see January 24, 1879, and *Letters*, p. 692. See chapter 3, August 9, 1880, n. 1 for more on Sir Frederick Leighton. Of a visit to London on July 16, 1888, Dodgson wrote: "I had a pleasant chat with . . . Mr. T. Riley, who has a beautiful 'nude' study (two nymphs) at the R.A." (Diaries). Thomas Riley (fl. 1878–90) was described as "a rising young artist who is at present engaged as assistant to Mr. E. J. Poynter, R. A." in *Art Journal* (1883): 76, when it published Riley's "Idalia," a portrait of a mature woman. Riley's etching of a mother and child, "The Firstborn," appeared in *Portfolio* (1883): 25.
2. Thomas De la Rue & Company, Bunhill Row, London, stationers, publishers, engravers, printers of postage stamps, and manufacturers of games.
3. On Wednesday, March 30, Dodgson took Winnie Stevens for "walk and tea" (Diaries). For more on Dodgson's friendship with the Stevens family, see *Letters*, passim, esp. p. 679.
4. Edmund Evans (1826–1905), renowned color printer. Dodgson met Evans on a visit to Macmillan's on January 15, 1889 (*Diaries*, p. 468). He printed *The Nursery "Alice."*
5. For more on Dodgson's acrostic verses for Princess Alice, see February 27, 1893, n. 1.

MS: Huntington

Christ Church, Oxford
May 6, 1892

Dear Miss Thomson,

Here are addresses of one "face" model, and two models (figure) aged about 6 or 7.[1]

"face" only:
Mrs. Hart,
51, Rosaville Road,
Walham Green.

Mrs. Ball (child "Edith")
75, Dawes Road,
Walham Green.

Mrs. Garnier,
11, Horder Road,
Fulham.

Always sincerely yours,
C. L. Dodgson

<hr>

1. Miss Thomson must have used Edith Ball as a model. Dodgson struck up a fleeting friendship with the child and sent her at least one looking-glass letter (*Letters*, pp. 993). The Hart and Garnier children do not enter Dodgson's diaries or any other letters in our files.

MS: *Huntington*

Christ Church, Oxford
December 2, 1892

My dear Miss Thomson,

I'm really sorry you should have had the trouble of writing at such length, in reply to what you expected I was going to say. If you will kindly wait a little, I will write: but I'm awfully busy. Much of what you have replied to by anticipation I wasn't going to say at all. Believe me

Very sincerely yours,
C. L. Dodgson

I will just reply to one sentence:

"I'm afraid I can't do anything in the manner of Stothard's vignettes." I do not in the least desire you *should*. Surely I never used the word "manner" in that connection? I've no copy of my former letters: but it does not seem possible.[1]

1. Thomas Stothard (1755–1834), book illustrator, produced vignettes for two books of poems by Samuel Rogers which were very popular for many years. He also illustrated an early edition of *Robinson Crusoe* (1820).

MS: *Princeton*

Christ Church, Oxford
December 8, 1892

Dear Miss Thomson,

I am still very busy, but hoping very soon, to write in detail about the fairy-pictures. Meanwhile, if you want to get on with work for me, why not try something for the serious poems? That book has been waiting 6 years, I think, for your pictures.

Sincerely yours,
C. L. Dodgson

———————

MS: *Huntington*

Christ Church, Oxford
December 23, 1892

My dear Miss Thomson,

I wish you a very happy Christmas: but my wishes will come a little late, as, to spare the overworked letter-carriers, I shall leave this, to be posted *after* Xmas.

There is no hurry about returning this drawing. But I want you to see it, and say what you think of it, and of the promise it gives of future excellence in Art.

The little friend who did it is such an *old* looking little thing! I have warned the mother to keep her *back*, as she is so quick, and learns every thing with such ease, that there is risk of the brain-power being too much for the bodily health.[1]

Very sincerely yours,
C. L. Dodgson

P.S. I am just off to "The Chestnuts, Guildford" for a fortnight.

1. The drawing is missing. The young artist is possibly Gladys Baly (see *Letters*, p. 866).

MS: *Huntington*

Christ Church, Oxford
February 27, 1893

My dear Miss Thomson,

Your letter was most welcome. While you are doing so much for *my* pleasure, it were churlish not to try to do something for *yours*: so, though I am writing "Logic" about 6 hours a day, I have spared the time to copy out these two little Acrostic poems[1] for you. I won't bar you from showing them to members of your own family; but please let them be seen by no one else, for the present. I'm going to apply to the Duchess for leave to print them, along with many other such things written for other children: till I get that leave, I can only show them to special friends. The allusion to "pistols" refers to my having taught the children, when they came to my rooms, how to fold paper into (so called) "pistols," which will make a *real* bang, to the great delight of children.[2]

As to your letter:

In the "bower" picture,[3] surely the elder child has the form of a *girl?* It is not an easy subject to discuss with a lady, but perhaps to a lady-*artist* I may mention, without offence, that the breasts are those of a girl, not a boy. To the best of my recollection, you have given them just the curvature which I noticed in the last child-model (Maud Howard, aged 14) whom I had the privilege of trying to copy in Mrs. Shute's studio. If you would add to the hair, and slightly refine the wrist and ankles, it would make a beautiful girl. I had much rather have *all* the fairies *girls*, if you wouldn't mind. For I confess I do *not* admire naked *boys* in pictures. They always seem to me to need *clothes*: whereas one hardly sees why the lovely forms of girls should *ever* be covered up!

If ever you fancy any of the pictures look too like real *children*, then by all means give them wings.

I shall be very grateful to be allowed to see future drawings in the "pencil" stage, when any alterations can easily be made.

One whole hour has gone since I began copying those verses! Now I must really return to my Logic.

Very sincerely yours,
C. L. Dodgson

When are you going to have a child-model that I may come and draw? And did you ever get my little friend Maud Howard? (I'm afraid she is 16 by this time.)

1. When Dodgson first saw the printed drawings for *The Nursery "Alice,"* he was appalled, and on June 23, 1889, he complained to Macmillan that they were "far too bright and gaudy." Because he had already promised copies of the book to friends, he ordered a few printed only in brown ink for his private use. Collingwood records that in 1891, when Dodgson sent a copy of *The Nursery "Alice,"* reprinted with acceptable colored illustrations, to Princess Alice, he "received a note of thanks from her, and also a letter from her mother, in which she said that the book had taught the Princess to like reading, and to do it out of lesson-time." The Dodgson family papers contain an undated letter from Princess Alice, written at Claremont, Esher, which is probably the one to which Collingwood alludes (p. 298): "Dear Mr. Dodgson, I thank you very much for the pretty book which I like very much. I like very much the painted pictures and I have read the story myself. Alice." Collingwood also reports that Dodgson gave Prince Charles a copy of *Merry Elves; or, Little Adventures in Fairyland,* illustrated by C. O. Murray and first published in 1874. In his note of thanks for the gift, the prince wrote, "Alice and I want you to love us both." Collingwood adds: "Mr. Dodgson sent Princess Alice a puzzle, promising that if she found it out, he would give her a 'golden chair from Wonderland.'" Princess Alice later recalled her early friendship with Dodgson: "[He] . . . was especially kind to Charlie and me, though when I was only five I offended him once when, at a children's party at Hatfield, he was telling a story. He was a stammerer and being unable to follow what he was saying I suddenly asked in a loud voice, 'Why does he waggle his mouth like that?' I was hastily removed by the lady-in-waiting. Afterwards he wrote that he 'liked Charlie but thought Alice would turn out badly.' He soon forgot all this and gave us books for Christmas with anagrams of our names on the fly-leaf" (Princess Alice, Countess of Athlone, *For My Grandchildren,* 1966, p. 66). Dodgson published the two acrostics that he had composed for the royal children in *Three Sunsets.* The initial letters of the verses read down spell out the prince and princess's names:

Puck Lost and Found

Puck has fled the haunts of men:
　Ridicule has made him wary:
In the woods, and down the glen,
　No one meets a Fairy!

"Cream!" the greedy Goblin cries—
　Empties the deserted dairy—
Steals the spoons, and off he flies.
　Still we seek our Fairy!

Ah! What form is entering?
　Lovelit eyes and laughter airy!
Is not this a better thing,
　Child, whose visit thus I sing,
Even than a Fairy?
　　　　　　Nov. 22, 1891.

Puck has ventured back agen:
  Ridicule no more affrights him:
In the very haunts of men
  Newer sport delights him.

Capering lightly to and fro,
  Ever frolicking and funning—
"Crack!" the mimic pistols go!
  Hark! The noise is stunning!

All too soon will Childhood gay
  Realise Life's sober sadness.
Let's be merry while we may,
  Innocent and happy Fay!
Elves were made for gladness!
                Nov. 25, 1891.

   2. Dodgson learned to fold paper pistols from Coventry Patmore's son, Francis Epiphanius, when he visited the Patmores on October 8, 1890 (*Diaries*, p. 480). He in turn taught the Albany children to make the pistols on November 16, 1891, and on at least two other occasions (January 26 and June 12, 1897) he taught the trick to other children as well (DIARIES, pp. 488, 532). For instructions on how to make a paper pistol, see *The Magic of Lewis Carroll*, ed. John Fisher, 1973, pp. 597–98.
   3. *Three Sunsets*, p. 14.

MS: *Huntington*

Christ Church, Oxford

June 2, 1893

My dear Miss Thomson,

   How I *wish* you had plucked up your courage a little sooner! I have no sort of objection to pay for the drawings, one by one, as fast as done. You said you would leave it to *me* to fix terms: but I had much rather *you* should begin, and name a scale of terms for the 3 now finished and accepted, *viz:* Boy on Mushroom, 2 Fairies in Bower, 2 ditto sailing in shell. When we have agreed on terms for those 3, we shall have a fair rule to go by to calculate for others.[1]

   The 3 above-named will do beautifully now. You call the elder fairy in the Bower a "boy": but it has quite long enough hair for a girl. I think the girls in the boat a great improvement on the girl and boy. As to the Mushroom, I accept your judgement, that the pencil-sketch, with less mushroom, is *not* so good. I would be glad to keep the pencil-sketch (and of course pay for it). Please send me a little bill for the 3 and it.

I enclose 3 drawings, *viz*:

(1) Ariel. This I am returning to you. I wrote about it, October 23, 1892.[2]

(2) Boy and Girl in boat. This also I am returning.[3]

(3) Girl on Cray-Fish. I wonder if you could alter her face a little? I do *not* admire it. It looks, to me, too old, and too large, specially the lower part. Also there is surely something wrong with her legs? Her left leg looks, to me, too short from the hip to the knee, and her right leg too broad across the thigh. You do not show the upper edge of it at all: it seems to me it ought to be visible under her left arm, some way below the point where the arm intersects the body. But I say all this "under correction."

Also, would you make the name less conspicuous? It makes a *corner* to the picture, which ought to have a curved shape, either circular or oval, so as to resemble a vignette.[4]

As all the pictures, hitherto drawn, differ from the "Rogers"[5] ones in having more accessories, we had better keep to that rule now. I've no doubt they will make a beautiful set.

You can draw Fairies, or pictures for the serious Poems, just as the fancy takes you. I'm in no hurry for either.

Yours very sincerely,
C. L. Dodgson

Don't forget to let me see preliminary pencil-sketches of future drawings.

1. The drawings appear in *Three Sunsets*, pp. 52, 14, and 7.
2. The letter of October 23, 1892, and the drawing are missing.
3. Does not appear in *Three Sunsets*.
4. *Three Sunsets*, p. 28. Miss Thomson altered the drawing, and her initials replace her signature.
5. Possibly a reference to a book of poems by Samuel Rogers (1860) illustrated by Thomas Stothard. See December 2, 1892, n. 1.

MS: *Huntington*

Christ Church, Oxford
June 5, 1893

Dear Miss Thomson,

It is *possible* that I may be able to take you, next Saturday afternoon, to *The Merchant of Venice* at the Lyceum. My plans are unsettled as yet: but I would be glad to know if you would be able to come; and, in that case, I would let you know, on Friday morning at latest, whether I can, or cannot, take you. Please tell me, also, whether you would like to meet me (say at 11 1/2) in the R.A., or in the New Gallery (121 Regent Street): I have seen neither, so that *either* would suit me. If you could not come so soon, but *could* come to the play (which begins at 2), we might meet at Charing Cross at (say) 1/2 to 1. But I would settle all this, definitely, in my Friday letter.[1]

Very sincerely yours,
C.L.D.

1. Dodgson's Friday letter has not come to light, but Miss Thomson did not accompany him to the Lyceum on Saturday, June 10.

MS: *Huntington*

Christ Church, Oxford
June 19, 1893

My dear Miss Thomson,

Your letter, received on June 16th, was most welcome, as also were the 4 lovely drawings enclosed with it.

First, to answer the rest of the letter:

By all means let us have a *few* pictures of babies: but let them all be *girls*, please.

I would much like to see the drawings in the 2 stages, as you propose.

The prices you suggest are perfectly satisfactory.

Many thanks for the little drawing: but I would much rather keep it as it is, than take up your time with altering, or adding to it. I want every *minute*, that you can spare for my work, to be spent on the 2 books, which have now been "on the stocks" so many years.

Now for the 4 new drawings, which I herewith enclose:

(1) 2 swimming girls, conducting baby on nautilus.[1] It is quite *lovely*, even in the *rough*. Then what will it be when *finished*! I'm so glad you are allowing them rather more slender ankles than in former days.

(2) 3 children visiting a squirrel.[2] The lying-down one has a lovely attitude: but is not her ankle too thick? And is not the line, from hip to instep, too straight? The middle one should have longer hair. I fear you meant it for a boy: please regard it as a girl. The outer edge of her right arm should not be so continuous with the inner edge of the further child's wrist: it makes the arm look deformed. The leg of the further child is, I venture to think, all wrong. Would you try putting a live child into that attitude? (That is, if you have yet found any child-model.)

(3) Child visited by wasp.[3] Very sweet indeed. But ought not her *further* wrist to be thinner than her *nearer* one.

(4) 3 babies on jonquil.[4] Very sweet: but oh, what thick wrists and ankles! Nos. 1, 2, have their eyes *much* too far apart, surely? No. 1 has a *very* flat top to her right knee, has she not? I think No. 3 would do well to unbend her right leg a little, so as to bring the foot into view, and to avoid having the 2 shins so parallel. To save the legs from being *quite* clear of each other, the right calf might *just* be partly behind the left knee.

I make all these suggestions with diffidence, feeling that I have *really* no right at all, as an amateur, to criticise the work of a real artist.

Please get live children, if you can, to draw from.

Yours very sincerely,
C. L. Dodgson

1. *Three Sunsets*, frontispiece.
2. Ibid., p. 33. Possibly as a result of Dodgson's comments, the third child has vanished altogether.
3. Ibid., p. 62.
4. Ibid., p. 41. Miss Thomson appears to have adopted Dodgson's comments, but the gap between the eyes of two of the fairies is still too wide.

MS: *Huntington*

Christ Church, Oxford
June 23, 1893

Dear Miss Thomson,

Please don't take it as a slight that I again offer you a *second* chance (in case of another friend failing) for a Matinée. You shall have a *first* chance soon. For next Wednesday I have an engagement to take a lady to *Charles I* at the Lyceum. But she has been ill, and *may* be unable to come. In that event, would *you* be able to come? And would you like to meet, previously, at some picture gallery?

Very sincerely yours,
C. L. Dodgson

Your letter has just come. Will answer it by another post.

MS: *Huntington*

Christ Church, Oxford
June 23, 1893
(second letter)

My dear Miss Thomson,

I have *much* pleasure in sending you this cheque: and the sooner I have to send another and the larger the amount, the better I shall be pleased! Your remarks on Art are most interesting, though I don't quite understand about fairies losing "grace," if too like human children. Of course I grant that to be like some *actual* child is to lose grace, because no living child is perfect in form: many causes have lowered the race from what God made it. But the *perfect* human form, free from these faults, is surely equally applicable to men, and fairies, and angels? Perhaps that is what you mean, that the Artist can imagine, and design, more perfect forms than we ever find in life?

Thanks for what you say of my taste for Art. I *love* the effort to draw: but I fail utterly to please even my own eye, though now and then I seem to get somewhere *near* a right line or two, when I have a live child to draw from. But I have no time left now for such things. In the next life, I do *hope* we shall not only *see* lovely forms, such as this world does not contain, but shall also be able to *draw* them. In haste

Very sincerely yours,
C. L. Dodgson

P.S. Do you think the fairies will look best at the *beginnings,* or *ends,* of chapters? i.e. at *top* of page, or as *tail*-pieces? ~~My own idea is *tail*-pieces, considering that they have nothing whatever to do with the text!~~

No. On 2nd thoughts, I think we must suit each as it happens, e.g. I think the "Sailing in Shell" should be a tail-piece, and the "Bower" at *top* of page.[1]

---

1. In fact, both drawings, though intended for "Games and Puzzles," appear as full-page illustrations in *Three Sunsets,* pp. 7 and 14. All the pictures in *Three Sunsets* are full-page, and none of Miss Thomson's illustrations appear as either head- or tail-pieces.

MS: *Huntington*

Christ Church, Oxford
June 25, 1893

My dear Miss Thomson,

I fear (or ought I to say "I hope"?) that my Oxford lady-friend will be well enough to come to town with me on the 28th, so that I shall be unable to take you to *Charles I.*[1]

But there is now a chance of *another* kind for you. I have engaged my usual lodgings at Eastbourne (a sitting-room and 2 bedrooms) for July 1. It is *possible* I may find myself unable to leave Oxford so soon, and might be able to lend them to you (or to you and some friend of yours) for a week. If so, would you be able, and willing, to go? (If you did go, I would also present you with a 2nd-class return R.W. ticket).

Very sincerely yours,
C. L. Dodgson

Thanks for "Rogers."[2]

---

1. Dodgson's companion for the outing to the Royal Academy and the Lyceum to see G. J. Wills's *Charles I* was Mrs. G. J. Burch (*Diaries,* pp. 499–500). Mrs. Burch, born Constance Emily Jeffries (1855–1937), was the wife of George James Burch (1852–1914), professor of physics, University College, Reading. Two daughters, Violet Dorothy and Irene Constance, completed the Burch family. For more of Dodgson's friendship with the Burches, see *Letters,* pp. 955–56, n. 1.

2. Probably one of the books of poems by Samuel Rogers with Stothard's illustrations: *Italy* (1830) or *Poems* (1834). See December 2, 1892, n. 1.

MS: Huntington

Christ Church, Oxford
June 27, 1893

My dear Miss Thomson,

I wanted to catch the post this morning; so had not time to say all I had to say.[1]

Please keep an account against me of *all* your travelling-expenses, i.e. cab, porter, R.W. ticket. I mean "yours" individually: your friend may pay her own.

You won't need a cab at Eastbourne, as the house is only 4 minutes' walk from the Station. There are plenty of porters, with barrows, who will wheel up your luggage, for about 3*d.* per article. I usually employ the same man; and, if you like to fill up and forward the enclosed note, he will be on the look-out for you. Any one will point him out to you.

I have written to Mrs. Dyer, and have told her that you will let her know when to expect you. You will of course also tell her what provisions to get in: you will find her an excellent cook.

I have told her to unlock my book-cupboard for you. Among the books you will find a large map of Eastbourne, another of it with environs, and also a *Guide*.

I always buy an "annual" ticket admitting to the Pier. It is "transferable," so, if you will buy one (it costs 5*s.*, I think, or perhaps more), and debit me therewith, you can use it during your stay: it will save you 2*d.*, each time you go on.

I have 2 sittings at Christ Church, at the East end of the town. You will not, I fancy, care to attend there: but, if you do, you have only to be there before service begins (services on Sunday are at 11, 3, and 6 1/2) and give my name to the pew-opener.

As to my day of coming (and yours of return to town) I will write next week.

Very sincerely yours,
C. L. Dodgson

1. No other letter of this date or the day before has come to light.

Christ Church, Oxford
July 10, 1893

My dear Miss Thomson,

I now return you the 2 drawings, with remarks: and if they seem too bold, remember you have yourself encouraged me to pose as an art-critic!

(1) *Child on cray-fish.* The *face* I will be content with, though it is still a *leetle* too old for her size. Surely the *further* arm ought not to be thicker than the *nearer* one? What I chiefly demur to is her *right thigh*, the one which supports all her weight, since she has lifted her body, and left thigh, completely off the fish. Its *diameter* seems to be too great. I *think* its upper edge is too high up, and should be visible below the point where her left elbow crosses the edge of the body. But it is the *lower* edge which seems to me all wrong. You make it go *along the fish's back.* Just imagine the left leg removed, and continue that lower edge, and see if it can *possibly* join the body. I believe that, if you take the bit of the upper edge of her left thigh, reaching from her body to the lower part of her right leg, and bisect it, you will get the *true* level for the lower edge of her right thigh. And this had better be the line of the fish's back also: and it would be all the better if the upper edge of the fish, behind the child, could be raised to the same level, so as to give her something to sit upon. Could you do this, by painting out, with white paint, the existing edge?[1]

What a lot of words it takes to explain a thing in *writing*! I could make my meaning clear, in a minute, if I could *talk* about it!

Hasn't the cray-fish got too many feet *off the ground?*

(2) *Babies on jonquil.* In No. 1, you have omitted the lower edge of her right thigh. Surely it would be quite in view, and would intersect the right calf about a stalk's diameter above the stalk? In No. 2, you have made the same omission with her *left* thigh. In all three babies, the *eyes* seem to me to be considerably too far apart.[2]

It's a *very* ungracious task, this noticing faults *only*: so let me add that, in all other respects, I think the pictures *lovely*!

I am *very* glad your trip to the sea turned out such a success, both for you and for Miss Paterson, and that the books came in usefully.[3]

When are you going to find a child-model, whom I may come and draw? Poor Maud Howard you will not see again: she has left her home, and taken to evil ways. It is very, very sad to think of.

Very sincerely yours,
C. L. Dodgson

1. *Three Sunsets*, p. 28. Dodgson's comments about the right leg appear fully justified, suggesting that Miss Thomson did not amend the drawing to comply with his wishes. In particular, the lower edge of the right leg makes the diameter appear too great. By careful shading, Miss Thomson has succeeded in making the crayfish stand on seven of its eight legs.

2. Ibid., p. 41. Miss Thomson appears to have adopted Dodgson's suggestions about the outlines of the babies' thighs and about the babies' eyes.

3. William Allingham, the author of *The Fairies*, which Miss Thomson illustrated, married (1848) Helen Paterson. Miss Thomson may have been traveling with a younger relation of Allingham's wife.

———

MS: *Princeton*

7 Lushington Road, Eastbourne
July 28, 1893

My dear Miss Thomson,

I am glad you are enjoying your tour. Shall you return to London at the end of August? I ask because I conclude that my books (you will remember that there are *two* on hand?) must wait till you are back in your studio. But there is a small matter which perhaps you can attend to even while on the move. The "child on crayfish" picture has accidentally been photographed too large: so a fresh photo must be done: and this gives the opportunity for reconsideration, now that we can see how it comes out when reduced.

The 2 enclosed prints are numbered at the back. Please look at No. 1, holding it a little way from the eye, and see if you cannot realise, as a likely interpretation of it, the impression it gives to *me* in two particulars.

The first is, that the piece of shadow, which falls between the legs, looks like a piece of the back of the fish, leaving only the white bit, above it, to represent her right thigh. This, not being broad enough, suggests that the right thigh is partly hidden by the back of the fish. And putting the thigh so far back, makes the right leg, from knee to foot, look considerably too long. Of course, when one looks at it *close*, one sees that the shadow is part of the thigh: but I can't in the least realise this fact, when holding the print at ordinary reading-distance.

The other point is, that the shadow of her left arm, falling across her right leg, is so dark and sharp-edged as to give exactly the effect of a *garter* (one of the most superfluous presents that *could* be made to that child!).

Considering how little shadow there is in the picture, my feeling is that *both* these shadows may well be dispensed with: and, in No. 2, where I have erased both of them, the effect is, to *my* eye, more satisfactory. Please compare the two, *several* times, before you come to a decision.

If you decide to omit any of the shadow-lines, it will not, I think, be necessary to alter the drawing *itself*, but simply to correct photo No. 1 (which you can easily do by painting white over the lines to be omitted), and this would be sufficient guide to the wood-cutter, as to the lines he is to omit.

I have now put the matter thoroughly before you, and will accept your decision, whatever it may be.[1]

The "Frena" Hand-Camera (I don't feel clear about the spelling. May I suggest that your hand-writing, which used to be so beautifully legible, is becoming a little puzzling?) is a name new to me. *All* "dry-plate" photography is inferior, in artistic effect, to the now-abandoned "wet-plate": but, as a means of making *memoranda* of attitudes, etc., it is invaluable. Every figure-artist ought to practise it. If *I* had a dry-plate camera, and time to work it, and could secure a child of a really *good* figure, either a professional model, or (much better) a child of the upper classes, I would put her into every pretty attitude I could think of, and could get, in a single morning, 50 or 100 such memoranda. Do try this, with the next pretty child you get as model, and let me have some of the photos.[2]

Now to return to the question of charges. Matters of business had better be clearly stated, and thoroughly understood by both parties: and you do not seem to me to have at all realised that your last bill (which I am still waiting to pay, whenever you tell me you are near a bank where you can get my cheque cashed) is virtually a setting-aside of our original agreement. In the scale of terms, proposed by you and accepted by me, only 2 prices were named, and the "utmost limit" was 4 guineas. So long as that point is clearly understood, I have no objection at all to consider the first agreement as cancelled, and a new one substituted, in which the "utmost limit" is 5 guineas, and under which you will be free to charge, for each picture, 3, or 4, or 5 guineas, as you may think proper.

And, while we are on the subject, we had better agree on a scale of charges for the "Serious Poems," for which I suppose you will *some* day be beginning to draw. I wonder if you have any idea how long my two books have been on hand? The "Serious Poems" came first: your letter, agreeing to illustrate them, came July 24, 1885: so that I have been waiting just over *8* years for the pictures, of which I have not, as yet, seen *one*. The "Games and Puzzles" you undertook in March 1886, more than 7 years ago. As the text is still very unfinished, I am in no particular hurry: even if you got a sufficient lot of pictures (say 25) done this year, I do not think I could spare the time necessary for getting it out next Christmas. But the "Serious Poems" have been ready all the time, and could have been published, any Christmas from 1885 onwards, if the pictures had been done.

Thanks for the little bookplate. It is a graceful figure: but I a little regret the evidence it affords that my payments are not *yet* frequent enough to save you from the necessity of putting aside my work in order to execute "pot-boilers" for other people. I had quite thought, from what you said in your letter received on June 2, that, if only I would pay you more frequently, you would be in a position to decline all orders from other quarters until my long-delayed work was completed. It is a little disappointment to me to find that this is not the case.

Will your address, after next Tuesday, be
    "Lary Pottage, Ballater"?
It seems such a curious name, that I thought I had better make sure about it.[3]

Very sincerely yours,
C. L. Dodgson

1. *Three Sunsets*, p. 28. Dodgson's continued criticisms of this illustration produced some changes, but Miss Thomson did not incorporate all of his suggestions. Some of the shadows that he complains about are still evident.

2. Dodgson gave up wet-plate photography in 1880 and never embraced the dry-plate process, which supplanted it at this time. Helmut Gernsheim (*Lewis Carroll, Photographer*, 1949, p. 77), writes: "The artistic inferiority of dry-plate photography complained of by Lewis Carroll in [this] letter to Gertrude Thomson was, of course, due to the vast increase in the number of

amateurs who swelled the ranks of photographers, attracted by the much simplified and cleaner darkroom manipulation which was one of the great advantages of manufactured plates and roll-films. The other advantage was their increased sensitivity, which opened up the way to instantaneous photography and brought in its wake a great number of hand cameras which made snapshooting a pastime for many enthusiasts who were devoid of artistic training and feeling. . . ."

3. Miss Thomson was on a tour of Scotland; Ballater is close to Balmoral.

———————

MS: *Huntington*

7 Lushington Road, Eastbourne
August 1, 1893

Dear Miss Thomson,

I've told Swain to send you the "crayfish" drawing. When done with, please send it to

Mr. Joseph Swain,
6 Bouverie Street,
Fleet Street,
London.

Photography does *not* need a top-light.

It's all quite clear about terms now. I'm *entirely* satisfied with the present arrangement.

Best go on with "Games and Puzzles," now, and get that done first. The "Serious Poems" may wait awhile.

I enclose cheque for £9.10.4. Haste.

Very sincerely yours,
C. L. Dodgson

MS: *Huntington*

7 Lushington Road, Eastbourne
August 11, 1893

Dear Miss Thomson,

I've received a new photograph of the "cray-fish," which will now do capitally.[1]

Didn't you tell me, a short time ago, that they had reprinted *Fairies?* I have just ordered some from my bookseller here; and his London agent reports it as "quite out of print." How I wish you had kept the copyright in your own hands! *Then* you could reprint whenever you chose; and you could also secure its being *well* printed. Recent issues have been *very* inferior.

Very sincerely yours,
C. L. Dodgson

1. *Three Sunsets*, p. 28.

MS: *Huntington*

7 Lushington Road, Eastbourne
August 12, 1893

Dear Miss Thomson,

An entirely new idea, as to the fairies you are drawing for me, has occurred to me, and, the more I consider it, the better I like it. It is that they are far better suited to the "Serious Poems" than they are to "Games and Puzzles." Those lovely vignettes of Stothard's do not, in any way, *illustrate* Rogers' *Poems*, but their poetry and their grace *harmonise* with them. And they would have looked out-of-place in a *prose* book. And that is what I fear people would say of the fairies in a book of "Games and Puzzles," "incongruous!" Also my "Serious Poems" are meant for grown-up readers, the "Games, etc.," for children and young people: now it is the *grown-ups* who will most appreciate your fairies. They are too poetical and graceful to appeal much to *children*.

So my present idea is, not to have any pictures at all in "Games, etc.";
and to have about a dozen fairy-pictures in the "Poems," with a few

landscape pieces, but *no* regular *illustrations* (which would necessarily contain *draped* figures, and so would spoil the fairies).

I should like to know what *you* think of all this. I *hope* you will approve.

Very sincerely yours,
C. L. Dodgson

MS: *Huntington*

7 Lushington Road, Eastbourne
August 19, 1893

My dear Miss Thomson,

I have no time today to write fully, but just send one line to say that I consider your view of the case to be the *right* one, and that I abandon my proposal to transfer the Fairies to the "Serious Poems."

Very sincerely yours,
C. L. Dodgson

MS: *Huntington*

7 Lushington Road, Eastbourne
August 23, 1893

My dear Miss Thomson,

The sketch is lovely. My only criticism is that I venture to think the legs of the profile figure are not in right relative proportion. The feet look the same size: but surely the further one should be smaller? And of the legs, the further one seems to me actually *larger* than the nearer, specially as to diameter of thigh. As an experiment, I have made a tracing of it, interchanging the legs, and I think it makes them look in better proportion, though the arrangement is probably less graceful.

I enclose a delicious little sketch you once made for me, to show me my *fearful* mistakes in a sketch I sent you, of a little friend in that attitude. (*My* model was on the beach, and therefore was of course draped.) Do you think a picture could be made of it? I fancy a bunch of flowers, rising from behind her, might look well. I have tried it on the enclosed tracing.

Here, again, I venture to think the right shoulder slopes too much down: and also that the upper arm is too short: and that both can be remedied by raising the shoulder a little (as I have tried in my tracing).[1]

> Very sincerely yours,
> C. L. Dodgson

1. The sketches and tracings are missing.

MS: *Huntington*

> 7 Lushington Road, Eastbourne
> September 20, 1893

My dear Miss Thomson,

I have a delightful girl-friend (aged 26!) now staying with me; and she has several artistic, etc., friends in London; and she is going to write 2 or 3 letters, enquiring for nice child-models aged about 8, for you. At my request, she is writing them all *today*, in order to lose no time. You shall hear the result.[1]

Now I have a question to ask about that "cray-fish" picture. In all the other pictures, the faces are so lovely and so *childish*, that I can't help feeling a regret about that one *old* face. (I think you agreed with me that her face is too old for her figure?) Do you think it could be remedied anyhow? *My* idea is that if a piece of paper were temporarily attached to the card, covering the head, and a new head drawn on it, it would be quite possible to photograph it so. And I would willingly pay for a 2nd wood-cut being made. I like to have all my books as *good*, in every respect, as they can be made. It *might* perhaps be possible to avoid the full cost, by what is called "plugging" (i.e. cutting a bit out of the wood-block, and letting in a new piece): but it does not much matter. I should like to know what you think about it.[2]

Do you possess *Little Thumb*, illustrated by Miss Laura Troubridge? If not, let me give you a copy. The child-figures are so lovely that I'm sure you would enjoy having it.[3]

> Very sincerely yours,
> C. L. Dodgson

If we were to "plug," you would have to draw the new face *on the wood*, as Tenniel always does.

1. Dodgson's visitor was Gertrude Chataway, who arrived at his Eastbourne lodgings on September 19 and stayed until the twenty-third. For more on Gertrude Chataway, see *Letters*, p. 230.

2. *Three Sunsets*, p. 28. Miss Thomson must have redrawn the face to make it appear young, but whether photography or plugging the woodblock was involved, we cannot tell.

3. *Little Thumb* was the English version of *Le Petit Poucet*, included in a collection of fairy stories compiled by Perrault (1697), first published in England in 1729 and much reprinted. Around this time, Dodgson borrowed a portfolio of work from the illustrator Laura Elizabeth Rachel Hope, formerly Troubridge (1858–1929), and showed it to friends: "Lily and Mabel Weddell, with their brother Chester, came to tea, and saw the drawings Mrs. Hope has lent me," he wrote (Diaries, August 31, 1893), and again, "Mr. Toms dined with me, and saw Miss Troubridge's portfolio of drawings" (ibid., September 16). For more on Laura Troubridge, see *Letters*, p. 969, n. 2.

MS: *Huntington*

7 Lushington Road, Eastbourne
September 21, 1893

My dear Miss Thomson,

I must be very brief, to catch the post. My girl-friend's sister, Mrs. Bell, 98 Portland Place, has a little girl Cynthia,[1] aged 6, who it seems would be a lovely model for you: and there is every hope that you would be allowed to draw her nude. Please call soon, and see Mrs. Bell, and settle about it. Whether she would have to be drawn at home, or could be fetched to you, can be settled hereafter. The great thing is for you and Mrs. Bell to get to know each other.

Best take this note with you, and send it up for Mrs. Bell to read. It will do as an introduction. Best call between 2 and 3.

Very sincerely yours,
C. L. Dodgson

1. See September 27, 1893, n. 2.

7 Lushington Road, Eastbourne
September 25, 1893

My dear Miss Thomson,

I'm sorry you do not think Mrs. Bell's little girl likely to be available as a Fairy. Her aunt (the girl-friend who has been with me) describes her as a lovely child. *I* have not yet seen her—nor her mother. When I have seen them, I may perhaps return to the subject. Meanwhile, my friend has got an answer, about child-models, from a lady-artist, "Miss Wren, 12 Colville Gardens, Bayswater." She does not seem to know of any *herself*: but recommends that enquiry should be made of "J. Crompton, Esq., 79 Newman Street," the present manager of what used to be "Heatherley's Studio." If you feel any difficulty in writing to him, I would be happy to write for you. I do not know him, but I could introduce myself to him, after a fashion, as a frequent visitor at the Studio under Mr. Heatherley's management.[1]

I enclose you photographs (to which you are quite welcome without payment) of the 6 drawings which are now finished: and will now discuss them a little, as I am a good deal disappointed at seeing, when one puts them together, how little they *match* each other.

On the back of each print I have put its reference-number, and its width. The word "Cut" means that it has been cut on wood: of each of these I have had 3 rubbings done: one as a guide to the printer, one for you, and one for myself. I enclose your five. But I fear at least *two* of them will have to be cut again. I will return to this point when I have discussed them separately.

The photographs are of 3 different widths: and the first thing to be settled, before any more blocks are cut, is what width we shall take as our *maximum*.

The text of the book is, as at present arranged, 3 1/2 inches. It would not look well, I think, to have vignettes the full width of the text. *My* eye demands a margin of 1/4 inch on each side, which would give 3 inches as maximum.

I think Nos. 3, 4, 8 are drawn on the same scale, and look right when reduced to the same size. Please put these side by side (using the 3 *inch* one of No. 8), and say if you think they match fairly, and also if you think they are large enough to do justice to the beauty of the drawings.

My own opinion is that they are *not* large enough, and that 3 1/2 inches wide would look much better for all of them. This would entail having the text made 4 inches wide. As there are only 25 pages in type, it would not cost much to have them re-arranged. The chief cost would be having Nos. 3, 4 cut over again (that would be 3 or 4 pounds apiece).

No. 5, as you see, does not match them at all, when photo'd to the same width. The figures become dwarfed, and insignificant. If we make 3 inches our maximum, No. 5 cannot be used at all. If we take 3 1/2 as maximum, it might *possibly* do: or it might be allowed, as a solitary exception, to be the full width of the (new) text, i.e. 4 inches.

But anyhow, please draw no more groups of 3. The trio of babies can be used: but really I don't care for babies!

The boy on mushroom, when 3 inches wide, is too big, and kills all the others at 3 inches wide. Even if we make 3 1/2 our maximum, he is too big (compare him with No. 8 at 3 1/2 wide). So anyhow he *must* be cut again. And as 2 1/2 is too small, he must be 2 3/4.

The child on crayfish is too large to match Nos. 3, 4, 8, at 3 inches. If they were made 3 1/2 inches, it would do.

All this is very confusing, I fear. It will make it all clear, if I state separately the 2 possible plans.

Plan I

Text to be 4 inches wide. Maximum width of picture to be 3 1/2; though an *exceptional* picture might be 4 inches.

No. 1. re-cut—2 3/4 wide
2. retain
3. re-cut—3 1/2 wide
4. ditto   ditto
5. cut 4 inches wide
8. re-cut—3 1/2 wide

Plan II

Text to be (as at present) 3 1/2 inches wide. Maximum width of picture to be 3 inches; though an *exceptional* picture might be 3 1/2 inches.

No. 1. re-cut—2 2/4 wide
   2. re-cut (probably 2 inches)
   3. retain
   4. ditto
   5. sacrifice (we might try photographing it 3 1/2 wide, to see if it
      could possibly be used at full width of text).
   8. retain

The first plan entails the re-cutting of 4 blocks: the second of two only. Still, I don't mind the extra expense. My *first* wish is to have the book as *good* as we can make it.

I am inclined to try Plan I. What do you advise?[2]

I enclose *Little Thumb.*

Very sincerely yours,
C. L. Dodgson

1. Thomas Heatherley (1825–1914) ran a studio for artists in Maddox Street, London, for nearly thirty years. Originally established by a group of students from the Government School of Design in 1845, Heatherley's studio maintained the tradition whereby artists could study and paint from the nude. Dodgson became acquainted with Heatherley and visited the studio to watch drawing classes and to get advice from him for some of his aspiring young artist friends.

2. Part of the text of "Games and Puzzles" has survived, set up in type, titled "Book III, Other Mental Recreations." It consists of Dodgson's rules for calculating Easter-Day for any year (MS: Stern). The galley proofs are numbered 13–17, and the text is exactly 3 1/2 inches wide. Dodgson's plan to reduce the size of Miss Thomson's illustrations was made with "Games and Puzzles" in mind. The six drawings he refers to here are among the nine he had already discussed with Miss Thomson in earlier letters, and which eventually appeared in *Three Sunsets*, as the frontispiece and at pp. 7, 14, 28, 33, 41, 47, 52, and 62. The details he provides here allow us to identify only the "Fairies and Jonquils" (p. 41), "Fairy on Mushroom" (p. 52), and "Fairy Riding on Cray-Fish" (p. 28).

7 Lushington Road, Eastbourne
September 27, 1893

My dear Miss Thomson,

The "Child and Wasp" has come, but I've no time to discuss it, or the other pictures, today. I've been working 8 hours, and I really *must* get out a bit![1]

Today I merely want to say that I've been to see the Bell children,[2] and they are *charming*: not quite *beautiful*, in face, I admit; still, I would *much* like to have the *figures* of the youngest (Cynthia), and perhaps (if she doesn't mind) the 10-year old (Iris), among the fairies. I think you haven't understood me. You needn't make regular *studies* of them; as you would with a hired model: but couldn't you put them into a few pretty attitudes, and make a few hasty *sketches* of them? These you could *finish* with the help of hired models. But hired models are plebeian and *heavy*; and they have thick ankles, which I do *not* agree with you in admiring. *Do* sketch these two upper-class children. One doesn't get such an opportunity every day!

Very sincerely yours,
C. L. Dodgson

1. *Three Sunsets*, p. 62. Dodgson was busy getting *Sylvie and Bruno Concluded* ready for publication.

2. "Went to town," Dodgson noted (DIARIES, p. 502) on September 26. "My chief object was to see, for the first time, Gertrude's sister Ethel, now Mrs. Bell, and her family. . . . I reached the Bells just before the time she had named, 1 1/2, and saw Mrs. Bell, her four daughters . . . and 2 sons. . . . The Bells seem to be a delightful family, and I spent a most enjoyable 2 1/2 hours there." Thus began for Dodgson another friendship with an eminent family well supplied with children. Mrs. Bell was Gertrude Chataway's sister (see *Letters*, p. 230, n. 1). She was married to Charles Frederic Moberly Bell (1847–1911), newspaper reporter, who became manager of *The Times*. The young Bells included Moberly (1877–1929), "somewhat a recluse," who never married, and became a barrister; Hilda (1879–98), who showed great promise as a musician, but died of typhoid before she was twenty; Enid Hester (1881–1967), a "wise and understanding woman" who later became headmistress of Lady Margaret School, Parson's Green, London, and the author of numerous historical and biographical studies, including the official biography of her father and a life of Octavia Hill; Iris Mary (1883–1968), who married (1907) Charles Ernest Pumphrey (1881–1950), a mining engineer; Clive (1885–1959), a soldier; and Cynthia (1887–1961).

MS: *Huntington*

7 Lushington Road, Eastbourne
September 30, 1893

My dear Miss Thomson,

I've decided on which plan to adopt, *viz.* II. The course to adopt with the several pictures already done is:

(1) re-photo—2 3/4 wide
(2) I *don't* want to give up. If you will give her a younger face, she'll do. I'll photo it 2 inches wide
(3) keep
(4) ditto
(5) re-photo—3 1/2 wide, and let it reach across page. (I don't like it with a figure omitted)
(8) keep to 3 inches wide

I return the 2 pencil-sketches. The girl seated on a rock is very nice, all but her right leg. Its outer margin is an almost exact quarter-ellipse. No mathematical curve has *artistic* beauty: I don't know *why*; but it *is* so. The circle is positively ugly; and I think the ellipse comes next. By a kind of fatality, you have drawn the right-hand end of the rock as a portion of the *same* ellipse! The two together suggest very plainly an elliptic arch, a horrid ugly thing.[1]

The girl-fairy flying with a lantern. You've forgotten what I said about *drapery*. Not one *scrap* of drapery will I have in the book! With the drapery removed (or even with it retained), I think the hinder part of the body is too much *en évidence*: I don't like that view of her. Seen from the *further* side, she would be lovely: all she would need would be to turn her face that way. Couldn't you use the same outline, and turn her right limbs into left? I've traced the outline, and drawn it as I mean.[2]

Now I come to the "Child and Wasp," which I enclose for your reconsideration. Her further wrist is thicker than the nearer one: but that's a trifle. It is her right leg that I wish most to call your attention to. It seems to me to rebel against all anatomical rules. Suppose her transparent, and consider where her hip-joints would be. (I daren't put dots on the picture, but have ticked their latitude and longitude on the margin). Now look at her right thigh. Why, even its upper *edge* falls below the place of the socket: and the *bone*, of course, comes a good deal lower. If you produce the upper edge, it strikes the outer edge of the left thigh at the top of the grass: if you produce the lower edge, it comes out at the indentation of the knee. In fact, this leg *can't* be joined to her! It has evidently dropped off!

Otherwise, the picture would do, though she *is* rather too plebeian, and thick-boned, for *my* taste.[3]

Would you mind making a few rules for the remaining pictures?

(1) To draw from *life* only. These figures, drawn out of your own head, only lead to endless anatomical discussions, for which neither of us can spare time.

(2) To draw faces from as many different children, or photographs, or pictures, as you can: so as to get *variety*. It is the inevitable fate of every artist, who draws faces out of his own head, to have a strong family-likeness among them, and ultimately to settle down into *one* face only. Cruikshank had only *one* female face: du Maurier has only *one*: Leech, I think had *two*: Tenniel has only *one*. Yet it would be easy to find a *hundred* pretty children, no two of whom would be taken for sisters.

(3) When composing a picture, make a rough sketch of it, making the principal figure the same size as the elder "bower" child (or the younger, if it is to be a 5-year old; or less than that, if a 3-year old). Then fix the *width* of the picture, taking care not to go *beyond* 3 inches, but as much *less* as you like. Then draw the outlines you would like to work on: and whatever ratio its width is to 3 inches, make your principal figure the same ratio to the one in the rough sketch. It doesn't the least matter *what* size you draw the picture, 12 inches wide if you like, so long as you preserve this proportion between the width of the picture and the size of the principal figure: when photographed to the width of the rough sketch, it will match the "bower" picture. Have I made myself intelligible?

I look forward with great interest to the result of your visit to the Bells'. (Oh, there is *one* more remark I had meant to make about the "Child and Wasp." Excuse my using so unconventional a word as "navel," but I know of no euphemism for it. You have drawn it too near her left hip. I think it would really come half-way between its present place and the edge of the body.)

If the children *do* come to your studio, please do some *photographs* of them for me. It would be *very* interesting to have them in the attitudes of some of these drawings. Specially you might do Cynthia as "Child and Wasp," and that would test the correctness of my remarks on it. Also I wish you would take one of Iris, standing full front, with her hands clasped behind her, like one of those little photographs I once lent you. I'm aware it would be a much *nakeder* picture than any of these fairy-attitudes, and I could not put it among ordinary nudities: it would have to go into my *honi soit* envelope. In taking any little friend, full-front, I've always asked special leave from the mother. In this case, I think the mother would allow it. She is very free from conventional proprieties.[4]

Very truly yours,
C. L. Dodgson

1. The pencil sketch of the girl seated on a rock is missing, and the drawing does not appear in *Three Sunsets*.
2. The pencil sketch of the girl fairy with a lantern is also missing. Likewise, the drawing does not appear in *Three Sunsets*.
3. *Three Sunsets*, p. 62. Miss Thomson evidently reworked the drawing.
4. For more on Dodgson's attitudes to photographing children in the nude, see Morton N. Cohen, *Lewis Carroll, Photographs of Children: Four Nude Studies*, 1979.

MS: *Huntington*

7 Lushington Road, Eastbourne
October 2, 1893

My dear Miss Thomson,

Many thanks for your interesting account of the Bells. I'm very glad your visit was such a success.

Do come over for the day. You'll be most welcome. "2 hours" isn't nearly enough! You might come by the

Victoria	9.55
Eastbourne	11.35

(I don't name an earlier train, as I'm nearly always busy with letters till 11.20) and return by

Eastbourne	4.30
Victoria	6.19

which would get you home before dark: but, if you don't mind travelling in the dark, you might stay till

Eastbourne 7.50
Victoria   10.05.

Please tell me what meals you would like, and at what hours. I'm quite indifferent as to hours.

Can you hit off *likenesses?* I've a lovely girl friend here (aged nearly 27), and would be glad to commission you to do me a small "pastel" of her head. But you'd have to catch the likeness in *one* sitting!

You misunderstood me about "Will-o'-the-Wisp." I was shy of writing plainly. I admire, very much, a back-view of a child standing: it's a lovely study of downward-rippling curves. But, when the back is bent in, as in your "Ariel" and in this figure (which is almost a repetition of "Ariel"), the *lower* part of the body becomes too prominent for beauty. In your "Ariel" it was terribly *en évidence.* In *this* it is too much so. But if you could straighten the figure a little, at the hips, so as to make it less obtrusive, I think the picture would do.[1]

Yes, I knew of Iris' scar. But still I want that photo, while it is possible to get it: in 2 or 3 years it will be impossible. The scar does not matter: the photo is only for *me,* not for exhibition.

Very sincerely yours,
C. L. Dodgson

P.S. You don't seem to know how to *fix* a restless child, for photography. I wedge her into the *corner* of a room, if standing; or into the angle of a sofa, if lying down. You might put Iris into the corner of the room, and might get a full-front-view of Cynthia, lying on one side, with her back against the back of the sofa and both legs straight.

Would you kindly do *no* sketches, or photos, for *me,* on a *Sunday?* It is, in *my* view (*of course* I don't condemn any one who differs from me) inconsistent with keeping the day holy. I do *not* hold it to be the Jewish "Sabbath": but I *do* hold it to be "the Lord's Day," and so to be made very distinct from the other days.

P.P.S. Do you remember little Frances Henderson, whom we brought to my studio? *She* had a similar scar, but it didn't show, to speak of, in the photo.[2]

1. We cannot identify the drawings that Dodgson refers to in this paragraph.

2. Miss Thomson's first visit to Oxford as Dodgson's guest took place on July 17, 1879, when she brought Leighton's model, Ada Smith. Four days later Miss Thomson returned to Oxford for another visit, and it was then that Dodgson took her to call on his friends the Hendersons: "We . . . brought Frances down with us (Annie had a cold and could not come) and took a photo of her, lying on the sofa in her favourite dress of 'nothing'" (DIARIES, pp. 380–81).

MS: *Huntington*

7 Lushington Road, Eastbourne
October 8, 1893

My dear Miss Thomson,

I have arranged to arrive at the Bells' soon after 10 1/2 next Saturday, to *try* to draw Iris and Cynthia. Could you conveniently come and draw also? The results of *my* efforts will, I expect, be "nil": but, if *you* were also to make a sketch or two, the children would not feel, quite so keenly, that their trouble in "sitting" had been wasted.[1]

Very sincerely yours,
C. L. Dodgson

1. On October 14, Dodgson went "to town by the 8.30. Reached the Bells about 10 1/2. Miss E. G. Thomson arrived soon afterwards, and, till past 12, she made, and I *tried* to make, sketches of Iris and Cynthia, who were very willing and very patient models, with lovely figures, and yet more lovely innocence. It purifies one even to see such purity" (Diaries).

MS: *Huntington*

7 Lushington Road, Eastbourne
October 15, 1893

My dear Miss Thomson,

Probably I shall hear from you tomorrow, as to your times of arrival and departure, on Tuesday, and the meals I may expect your company at. Mrs. Dyer tells me you dine early; so I am assuming *that* meal (at 1.30, or 2.00, as you may prefer) as a certainty, at any rate.[1]

Very sincerely yours,
C. L. Dodgson

1. Miss Thomson came over for the day on October 17 and drew a chalk head of May Miller "which succeeded well" (Diaries). For more on May Miller, see *Letters*, p. 443, n. 1.

MS: *Huntington*

7 Lushington Road, Eastbourne
October 18, 1893

My dear Miss Thomson,

I hope I made it quite clear that it is my distinct wish that, so far as any picture done for *me* is concerned, neither Iris nor Cynthia is ever to be drawn again, at their house, in anything but *full-dress*. The *risk*, for that poor little boy,[1] is too great to be run again.

Please tell me what you charge for chalk heads, like that of May Miller. Because, if I find such luxuries reasonably *within* my means, I would like some more. I would like you to come over again (of course at *my* expense) and do another of May, full-face: and then I would give one to Mrs. Miller. Also I should like you to come over to Oxford, and do Enid Stevens, a *very* especial child-friend of mine, and a *splendid* beauty, in *my* opinion!

I hope you got home all right?

Yours very sincerely,
C. L. Dodgson

1. No doubt the youngest son, Clive, then eight.

MS: *Huntington*

7 Lushington Road, Eastbourne
October 20, 1893

My dear Miss Thomson,

Please fix a day, not later than Thursday the 26th, to come over (at my expense) and do another head of May. And you can then touch up No. 1. Come by the earliest train you can, and bring your camera, and May shall take you to "Holywell," a sweet little bay (perhaps you know it?) where you can get some "bits" for "Serious Poems."

I am telling Macmillan to send you a *Nursery "Alice"* to give Edith Ball, from the Author.

It *may* pave the way for possible "sittings." But I'm not *wholly* selfish. She is *heartily* welcome to it, even if it leads to no such result. Haste.

Very sincerely yours,
C. L. D.

30s. will do capitally. You'll come to Oxford and do Enid?[1]

1. Miss Thomson came to Eastbourne on October 24 and did another head of May Miller (Diaries).

MS: *Huntington*

7 Lushington Road, Eastbourne
October 27, 1893

My dear Miss Thomson,
The "mushroom" is lovely. The Fairy on the left is evidently reciting

> Here, in cool grot and mossy cell,
> We rural fays and fairies dwell.[1]

Shall I call the picture "A Dress Rehearsal"?[2]
I have just promised to give the little girl, of the porter who always carries my luggage, a book: and had intended it to be *The Nursery "Alice,"* as the child is 10, and I consider children of the lower orders to be 2 or 3 years behind the upper orders. But a lady, whom I consulted, advised me to give the real *Alice*, as probably more interesting, even now, to the child (they do get very well taught now-a-days), and certainly of more *permanent* interest. So I think I'll do the same in this case: so will you kindly give *The Nursery "Alice"* to Edith's little sister (you see I'm indebted to *both*, as having sat as fairies for me), and tell Edith *she* shall have the book itself, *Alice in Wonderland*.
I enclose cheque for £8.8.0, and bill to be receipted.

Very sincerely yours,
C. L. Dodgson

May thinks it may help you to get a likeness of her to know her age. She is 25. Would you have put it at that?[3]

1. The first two lines of William Shenstone's "Inscription: On a Tablet against a Root-House."

2. The drawing of three fairies without dress appears on p. 66 of *Three Sunsets*. Dodgson named it "Fairies under Mushrooms."

3. On December 2 following, Dodgson wrote: "Received the 2 chalk-heads of May Miller last Wednesday . . . the one, done *first*, is far the best" (Diaries).

MS: Huntington

Christ Church, Oxford
November 1, 1893

My dear Miss Thomson,

I enclose the photograph of the children catching fish.

How did the photographs of Iris and Cynthia turn out?

I'm very glad Edith liked her book, and hope she will like, even better, the handing it over to her sister, and having this instead.

Very sincerely yours,
C. L. Dodgson

MS: Huntington

Christ Church, Oxford
November 6, 1893

My dear Miss Thomson,

Saturdays are the only days when I can get Enid down here by daylight. She can be brought next Saturday, if you can come over. Your train would leave Paddington at 9.50, I think, and reach Oxford at 11.10, and I would meet you. Enid would come by 11 1/2, and we could keep her till dark.

I don't think I have yet told you that I wish *no* more drawings to be made, for me, of either Iris or Cynthia, naked. I find they are being brought up in a way which I consider injudicious and dangerous for their purity of mind, and I will do *nothing* which can add to the danger. It is a *real* sacrifice of inclination. I am sure she[1] would come with me, either to you or to Mrs. Shute, and I should *much* enjoy drawing her again: but, if we are to follow the voice of conscience, we cannot always do what we should like!

Very sincerely yours,
C. L. Dodgson

1. For "she" and "her" in this sentence, Dodgson probably meant to write "they" and "them." Or was he thinking only of Cynthia?

---

ms: *Huntington*

Christ Church, Oxford
November 8, 1893

My dear Miss Thomson,

"Two Fairies on Fish" is delicious.[1] I enclose cheque for £4.4.0.

I have no record of having seen sketches of it and of "3 Fairies under Mushroom."[2] *Did* I see them? My memory is not reliable. Our present arrangement is that I am to see drawings in *two* stages, before finished picture is made, (1) rough pencil sketch, (2) pencil sketch in finished state.

Will expect you on Saturday.[3] You shall choose your room when you come. Excuse brevity.

Very sincerely yours,
C. L. Dodgson

1. *Three Sunsets*, p. 58.
2. This is the first mention of "Fairies Riding on Fish." Miss Thomson apparently sent a finished pencil sketch. Dodgson's memory is indeed faulty: he mentioned "Fairies under Mushroom" (*Three Sunsets*, p. 66) on October 27, less than a fortnight earlier. Here he is probably commenting on a finished pencil sketch.
3. On November 11, "Miss E. G. Thomson came from London for day, and I got Enid Stevens to come and sit for a chalk head. It was not finished, and she is to come again next Saturday" (DIARIES, p. 503).

---

ms: *Huntington*

Christ Church, Oxford
November 19, 1893

My dear Miss Thomson,

You have seen, now, how lovely Enid looks, when she smiles: I *hope* you'll be able to record *something* of it. An actual *smile* wouldn't look well in a picture, I suppose: but please go as near to it as you think safe.

When she and Edith were ready to go, I went out to get a cab. There was a regular snowstorm, and *all the cabs had gone*! So I told them we must walk to the tram-car. However, luckily, when we got down, a Hansom had just come on the stand: so I landed both girls, *dry*, in their homes.[1]

Would you kindly let me see *all* the prints of Iris and Cynthia? I think very likely there may be one or two I should like copies of. I hope you'll let me pay for all the prints you get done for me.[2]

What *width* should the borders of the oak frames be for the chalk-heads? And should they be flat, or beaded? I think I have seen them done with 3 beads (this is a cross-section), which looked well.

I hope you got home all right, in spite of the bad weather.

Very sincerely yours,
C. L. Dodgson

1. On November 18, "Miss Thomson came again, and finished the picture of Enid. Edith Lucy also came to luncheon, and stayed till 6 1/2. Took her and Enid home in a snowstorm. I think they both enjoyed the day thoroughly" (*Diaries*, p. 503). Miss Thomson's portrait of Enid Stevens hung in Dodgson's main sitting room at Christ Church. Dodgson dedicated *Sylvie and Bruno Concluded* to Enid.

2. Miss Thomson took photographs of Iris and Cynthia Bell either on October 14 or on one of the following three days.

MS: *Huntington*

Christ Church, Oxford
November 24, 1893

My dear Miss Thomson,

Thanks for the print, of Iris and Cynthia, which I asked for: also for sending some negatives.

Would you kindly let me see *all* that were taken of them? However bad they may be, I *might* want to have prints of some. As they were all done for *me*, I think I ought to repay you whatever they cost you, as well as for that print. I hope you will let me do so.

What you say about *frames* would have been clearer if you had drawn a bit of it in "*section*." I presume you know what the phrase means? You imagine the frame sawn *across*, right through, and draw a picture of what the *end* would look like.

However, picture-dealers keep little bits of frame, to show as specimens, and, if you would send me a bit (an inch long would do) such as you approve, it would do as guide for the framer. Your words "the mount should be, etc.," puzzle me: as you distinctly advised, when at Eastbourne, that there should be *no* mount. Have you changed your mind? I shouldn't like much *flat* gold: it would *kill* the picture, to my thinking. Perhaps you mean a *white* mount, with its inner edge beveled and gilt? If so, how *broad* a mount do you advise? I want your pictures to look their *best*. I'll dispense with the *smile*! No doubt you are *quite* right on that point.

Very sincerely yours,
C. L. Dodgson

I'm sorry you gave up the idea of *full-face* for May. I think her full-face so lovely, and *you* said it was the best view. However, perhaps your change of opinion may be right.

MS: *Huntington*

Christ Church, Oxford
December 2, 1893

My dear Miss Thomson,

I return all the negatives, and would like a print of one I have put at one end of the series, Iris lying on her side, with her knees drawn up. I have 3 prints already.

To be quite candid, I *don't* much like the London picture of May: to me it looks hard, haughty, and *slightly* offended, and has missed all 3 of the charms I read in her face, *viz.* sweetness, peacefulness, and sympathy (her eyes look to me as if just ready to fill with tears). I think of giving it to Mrs. Miller, but asking her *not* to frame it yet, in the hope of her being able, some day, to give you another sitting, when perhaps you might be able to improve it. I like the first one *much* the best, but think of keeping it, also, unframed, in the same hope: it wants more *gentleness*, I fancy.

By the way, on referring to your letter, I see that you didn't finish No. 2 from *life*, but from *memory*. That accounts for much of what I don't like in it. You have *also*, in working by memory, lost some of the likeness. No. 1 is *twice* as like as No. 2.

Please look at the enclosed "List of Works," which will appear in *Sylvie and Bruno Concluded*, and see what rash announcements I am making! I hope some day you will enable me to make good my promises.[1]

Yours very sincerely,
C. L. Dodgson

1. The advertisements that accompany *Sylvie and Bruno Concluded*, published in December 1893, list two forthcoming books: "Original Games and Puzzles," with twenty illustrations by Miss E. Gertrude Thomson, as well as "The Valley of the Shadow of Death, and Other Poems," with illustrations by Miss E. Gertrude Thomson, Dodgson's early title for *Three Sunsets*. See letter dated August 12, 1893.

MS: *Huntington*

Christ Church, Oxford
December 3, 1893

My dear Miss Thomson,

The two heads of Enid have come, and I am very much obliged to you for all the pains you have bestowed on them. I made up my mind, before I saw how to know which was the original, which of the two I liked *much* the best: and then I found they were dated, and that I had chosen the original one. It is *very* charming, and a capital likeness. The other just misses the charm, and the likeness, but is very good, as long as it's not compared with No. 1. I shall not frame either, at present, but keep them in hopes of your being able to have another sitting, and put in, from life, some final touches to No. 2: and perhaps No. 1 might also be the better for another comparison with the living child.[1]

Your note is a puzzle. You say that No. 2 "would have been still more like," "if the paper had been exactly the same shade, but I'd no more at hand of the darker colour." Had I given you the impression that I was in a *hurry*, and was willing to have No. 2 *less* good than it *might* be made, so long as I could have it *quick*? If I did, I'm very sorry: I never *meant* to say a word like it: and, if you had written "I could make it still more like, on darker paper: but I've no more at hand. How long can you wait for me to get some?," I should have replied "six weeks, or six *months*, if you prefer it!"

Very sincerely yours,
C. L. Dodgson

1. On the same day, Dodgson wrote: "Received . . . the 2 chalk-heads of Enid Stevens, done by Miss Thomson. The one done from life is charming, and *much* better than the copy made from it" (*Diaries*, p. 504).

MS: *Huntington*

Christ Church, Oxford
December 13, 1893

My dear Miss Thomson,

I have been showing to various friends your lovely picture of Enid: and the regular result seems to be that they want to have their children drawn by you. It really would be a good plan for you to come, when the days are longer (say in May), and stay 2 or 3 weeks in the place: and I think we could easily arrange to get you a fresh subject every day: and you should have my photographic studio to work in.[1]

However, what I write about *today* is to ask in what form you would like your name inscribed in *Sylvie and Bruno Concluded*, which I hope to be able to send you by the end of the year. I don't know whether to put "Miss" or not.

Very sincerely yours,
C. L. Dodgson

1. Miss Thomson did not, apparently, take up Dodgson's suggestion until the end of June.

MS: *Princeton*

Christ Church, Oxford
December 14, 1893

Dear Miss Thomson,

Thanks for your letter. It confirms a resolution I had already pretty nearly formed, *not* to try for any more "duplicates" of chalk-heads. I enclose (and have much pleasure in doing so) a cheque for £4.14.0., the amount of your last account. Believe me

Yours very sincerely,
C. L. Dodgson

MS: *Huntington*

The Chestnuts, Guildford
January 8, 1894

My dear Miss Thomson,

I'm getting frightened about the number of pictures we have planned for "Games and Puzzles," and would be glad to limit them to 12, if you don't mind. Even then, I fancy it will be published at a loss. It will be but a small book, and 12 pictures will be ample. All my mathematical books are published as a loss: and the new book, though I daresay it will pay *ultimately*, is a heavy outlay to begin with: and my worldly means won't stand much more loss. I'm off to Oxford tomorrow, and will then consider those 3 drawings.

Very sincerely yours,
C. L. Dodgson

MS: *Huntington*

Christ Church, Oxford
January 20, 1894

My dear Miss Thomson,

I'll return the 3 drawings, with remarks, very soon. You've never sent me the "crayfish" one, with a younger face: I like the rest of it.[1] Also, what became of the girl seated on a stone?[2]

I like the dragon-fly picture better than the sleeping children: but I will write fully with the drawings.[3] Friends here are wondering when you are coming. I've just heard of another mother, who wants you to draw her 3 children!

Very sincerely yours,
C. L. Dodgson

Which pictures contain Iris, or Cynthia, or both?

1. *Three Sunsets*, p. 28.
2. Not in *Three Sunsets*.
3. The drawing of the dragonfly does not appear in *Three Sunsets*; the picture of the sleeping fairies is on p. 22.

Christ Church, Oxford

January 21, 1894

My dear Miss Thomson,

As you seem anxious to get the fairy-pictures done with (though there is no sort of hurry about them: the book isn't anything *like* ready) I return the 3 drawings, with remarks. Please forgive them if they seem harshly worded in any respect. I do admire your pictures *very* much: but I *have* to say what seems to me to need alteration, and, if I fail to say it courteously, please blame my want of *style*!

You will see, by the enclosed list, that, of the 14 designs, we have abandoned *one* (No. 10): so only one remains to be abandoned, to reduce the number to 12.[1]

And this one, *I* think, had better be No. 14. For, though I like the *horizontal* figure (if only her arm were a little shorter); and the other one, down to the waist (if only *her* arms were shorter), I cannot say I like the rest of her. The curve, from the in-bend of the back to the in-bend of the knee, is almost an exact semicircle, and I *don't* admire it at all. The position of the legs is uncomfortable, suggestive of her slipping down the bank. The effect of the foreshortening is to make the upper part of her left leg look too short, as compared with the lower: and the outline of her right leg is a smooth elliptic arc, giving no hint of a *knee* anywhere. I don't see how the legs *could* be made to look graceful, except by putting them horizontal: and that would make the picture too broad for its height. So *my* advice is, omit it.[2]

Now as to No. 6 (2 fairies and squirrel). I should like them to have wings, if you can add them. The more wings we can get into the book, the better "Mrs. Grundy" will be pleased! In the lying-down child, it seems to me that the distance from her shoulder to her elbow is too *short*. Is it not? Also the upper edge of her left leg, from the ankle to the hip, is an almost true *straight* line, giving no hint of the knee-cap or of the swell of the thigh between the hip and knee. The seated child's right arm doesn't look to me like an *arm* at all: I don't see where the elbow comes, or the wrist. Surely it was not drawn from life?[3]

No. 9 (girl seated on stone) I returned to you, with remarks, and have never seen it again. As far as I remember, I liked it.[4]

No. 13 (2 Children and Dragon-Fly) had better have wings, I think. The elder girl is *lovely*, both face and figure. The younger child I don't like so well. The hair is too suggestive of a *boy*: please make it *long*. The in-bend of her left elbow seems to me too near the shoulder. Her right foot looks too much of a *lump*. Her left knee is an exact *right-angle*, which is surely a thing to avoid. And all below the left knee looks rather shapeless: ought there not to be more *calf*? Would not a rather *larger* dragon-fly look better?[5]

Some time ago I returned to you a sketch you made for me long ago, of a child crouching. We thought it might do as a fairy. What became of it?

Yours very sincerely,
C. L. Dodgson

Please return *White Swans*, if done with.[6]

1. The list is missing. We cannot identify number 10, and it does not seem to be alluded to in any other letters. It could conceivably be the Ariel picture Dodgson mentions in an earlier letter.
2. The description of the drawing seems to indicate two fairy figures on a bank, but no such picture appears in *Three Sunsets*.
3. The picture of two fairies and a squirrel appears in *Three Sunsets* on p 33. Both fairies have wings, and Miss Thomson has made other alterations in line with Dodgson's suggestions. The seated child's right arm is totally obscured from view; either the child has been redrawn in this position, or Dodgson meant the *left* arm instead.
4. Not in *Three Sunsets*.
5. Not in *Three Sunsets*.
6. *White Swans* was a Danish tale by Hans Christian Anderson (1805–75). Dodgson wrote in his diary for December 11, 1885, "Heard from Miss Alice Havers (to whom I had written about her lovely illustrations to *The White Swans*)."

MS: *Huntington*

Christ Church, Oxford
January 25, 1894

My dear Miss Thomson,

The "Squirrel" is charming. I think the line of the leg has more curves in it now than it had in the unfinished drawing.[1]

You advise against "girl on stone," on the ground that we are to have only 12 pictures. But I had counted it as one of the 12. What do you propose instead of it?[2]

The *White Swans* is of no importance. I lent it you in May 1889, and have never seen it since. I also lent you (not yet returned) 36 unmounted photos, of my own doing, in March 1892; and *Game of Logic* in February 1892. But all these you are welcome to keep.

Very sincerely yours,
C. L. Dodgson

I enclose cheque for £4.4.0.

1. *Three Sunsets*, p. 33.
2. The "girl on stone" picture is not in *Three Sunsets*.

MS: *Huntington*

Christ Church, Oxford
January 27, 1894

My dear Miss Thomson,

Of the 11 pictures agreed on, 3 are single figures, 5 double, and 3 triple. I don't want any more *triples*: they are too crowded for such small pictures: but you can make the 12th single or double as you prefer. What I should like *best* would be the "Frog" picture, with 2 figures, one standing and one lying down: the standing one I specially admire: when made a little more slim, she will be lovely. Or I should much like that *crouching* one (the one you drew to show me how my sketch, of a child on the seashore, ought to have been done). *Something* (flower or live creature) would have to be put in for her to look at, but I have already written about this.[1]

Hadn't *you* better come and do Mrs. Lucy's 2 girls *now*, leaving other children for longer days? Mrs. Lucy is evidently *expecting* you. Both girls are quite grown-up, so will be easy sitters. Then I could take you to *see* other victims, and you could arrange for a future visit.[2]

Very sincerely yours,
C. L. Dodgson

1. *Three Sunsets* contains three single figures, six double figures, and three triple figures. The final picture by Miss Thomson was a redrawing of the frog picture (double figure), which originally had three figures (*Three Sunsets*, p. 47). Instead of the figure lying down, Miss Thomson used Dodgson's suggestion of a crouching fairy.
2. The two Lucy girls were Catherine Susanna ("Katie") (aged twenty-four) and Edith Eliza-

beth (aged twenty-three). For more on the Lucy family, see *Letters*, pp. 683–84, n. 2. Miss Thomson made at least one other visit to Oxford in June 1894 to draw portraits, but she did not see Dodgson at that time.

MS: *Princeton*

Christ Church, Oxford
February 21, 1894

My dear Miss Thomson,

Very well! I'll *try* to like the Will-o'-the-Wisp: though I confess that, at present, I prefer the terrestrial ones. I'm awfully busy, so excuse any curtness in my criticisms.

Her wings don't look, to *me*, as if they were attached to her shoulders. The darkness behind is, I suppose, meant for vapour: but it looks too like a shadow of her wings: and of course the *air* will not take a shadow.

Also, under her right arm, would not the arm-pit be well marked, and the sinew in front of it, would it not stand out?[1]

In frog-group, the upright figure, would not her left hip project a little more, to match right one?

The kneeling child's figure is all out of drawing. Most certainly you never got a *live* child into that attitude. Look at her right leg, and you'll see that the socket of the hip must come just behind the *front* of her left thigh. In fact her right leg is *off*. With the legs in that position, you *couldn't* see her backbone *at all*: it would be *round the corner*, so to speak. And you would only see her *left* flank, certainly none of the *right*. If you restored her leg to its socket, the knee would show very little: it wouldn't reach as far as her left arm.

I think that would be a pity. The legs are prettier as they are. In that case the *body* must be altered accordingly, and the wings put right, as only her *left* shoulder-blade would be on *this* side of her: the other would be out of sight.

Even so, I think the right knee is too far from her. I don't think it could possibly reach further than to go *just* behind the right edge of her left arm. Please draw it from *life*, and then it will be all as it should be.[2]

Very sincerely yours,
C. L. Dodgson

1. The "Will-o'-the-Wisp" drawing does not, in the end, appear in *Three Sunsets*.
2. *Three Sunsets*, p. 47. Miss Thomson made some changes, but the crouching fairy's right leg still appears to be misplaced, with the hip socket and knee too far forward. The backbone is now hidden, as is the right shoulder blade, to which the right wing is attached.

—————

MS: *Huntington*

Christ Church, Oxford
March 2, 1894

My dear Miss Thomson,

I enclose 7 of the 9 drawings. The "Mushroom" and "Nautilus" are with the wood-cutter. There is no use in re-touching Nos. 3, 4, 8, as they are already cut, and I am by no means prepared to spend any more on that costly luxury, re-cutting, *except* for the "cray-fish," which I will gladly have re-cut, if you can give her a younger face.[1]

Very sincerely yours,
C. L. Dodgson

1. For the "Mushroom,""Nautilus," and "Cray-Fish," see *Three Sunsets*, p. 52, frontispiece, and p. 28, respectively.

—————

MS: *Huntington*

Christ Church, Oxford
April 11, 1894

Dear Miss Thomson,

Many thanks for the lovely "Frog" picture. Edith must be a sweet model to draw from! I'm very glad you like Mrs. Shute so well. This is High School vacation, now, till the end of the month: and probably many children are away: so I would not advise you to come till May.[1]

Very sincerely yours,
C. L. Dodgson

1. *Three Sunsets*, p. 47. The model for the "Frog" picture is probably Edith Ball. Dodgson first suggested to Miss Thomson a visit to Mrs. Shute's studio in his letter dated September 6, 1890.

MS: *Huntington*

Christ Church, Oxford
June 19, 1894

My dear Miss Thomson,

I find it so hard to explain, to a lady, why I cannot use this picture,[1] that I *hope* you will excuse anything that seems offensively plain-spoken, as being quite contrary to my *intention*. When this business began, I told you I could have no *clothed* fairies at all. My feeling is this. First, I object to all *partly* clothed figures, altogether, as being unpleasantly suggestive of impropriety. So I will have none but *wholly* clothed, or *wholly* nude (which, to my mind, are not improper *at all*).

This figure is partly clothed; i.e. her hair is utilised, in a way artists often do utilise it and other things, as a partial concession to propriety, and to the principle, maintained by some, that a *wholly* nude figure is improper.

The presence of this picture in my book would make all the others look improper.

I have two other objections to the picture: but, without them, what I have said is enough by itself to prevent my using it.

The other two are, first, that the head is too large for the feet: she looks *top-heavy*. Secondly, I don't like the smiling and beckoning to supposed spectators. Even in a *draped* figure, such an expression would look a *little* too "bold": in an *undraped* one, it is, to me, unpleasantly so.

I'm afraid all this is unpleasant reading: but I don't see how I can avoid that result.

Very sincerely yours,
C. L. Dodgson

1. Probably an early sketch for "Sleeping Fairies" (*Three Sunsets*, p. 22).

Christ Church, Oxford
June 28, 1894

My dear Miss Thomson,

I opened your letter expecting to find you were *very* angry with me, and was relieved to find no wrath expressed. I had no idea you were coming so soon, and only heard of your arrival after you were gone.[1] I think it's a capital likeness of Edith: except that she is looking unnaturally grave. I have never seen her look so severe as that.

Very sincerely yours,
C. L. Dodgson

P.S. Drawing just arrived. Will write again.

1. Miss Thomson came to Oxford to draw the Lucy sisters but did not meet Dodgson. She wrote him on June 18 (MS: Francis Edwards, extract from Miss Thomson's letter copied by Dodgson): "I have been wondering if Mrs. Lucy would care for me to draw her two girls soon. I am quite ready now to do them. I thought it was better to put off doing them until really light days came in; but I didn't think I should postpone it quite so late as this. I have been away from town for some time: my father had been ill and I went to stay with him for a little while, and then I went to Wales."

Christ Church, Oxford
June 28, 1894
[Second letter]

My dear Miss Thomson,

I now return the sketch of the 2 sleeping fairies. It seems a very pretty and graceful idea: I offer no other criticisms, as you say you have not attempted to *draw* it.[1]

On this point let me explain what I had *understood* our arrangement to be.

In your letter dated June 16, 1892, you say "If you like, I will let you see all the drawings in two stages before they are finally finished, 1st when they are merely roughed out, and again when they are fully drawn in pencil, before they are finally inked in. This would save me having to make corrections after they are quite finished, which is always a difficult and perilous process; and it would also, I fancy, leave you greater freedom in criticising them."

On February 18, 1894, I received a pencil sketch of "2 fairies and frog." This I returned on February 21, with some criticisms on anatomy and proportions.[2]

In your letter of February 21, you said "I am afraid that you have not quite understood that those sketches were merely the 'first thoughts' of the designs, the mere *idea* of the thing roughly jotted down, with no attempt at *drawing* whatever." So my criticisms were evidently made too *soon.*

But the *next* version of the picture that I saw was on April 11, when I received the finished drawing: so any criticisms, offered *then,* would have been too *late.*

This was *not* what I had understood our arrangement to be. I had expected to have an opportunity of making suggestions as to the anatomy, etc., while the picture was still *alterable.*

I'm glad you liked my friends the Lucys. They seem to have *much* enjoyed your visit.

Yours very sincerely,
C. L. Dodgson

1. *Three Sunsets*, p. 22.
2. Ibid., p. 47.

———————

MS: *Princeton*

Christ Church, Oxford
October 25, 1894

My dear Miss Thomson,

I'm very glad you've given me a second opportunity for making suggestions about the picture of 2 sleeping fairies.

In doing this, I hope you will not suppose I am arrogating to myself a more correct eye for proportion than you have. On the contrary, I am quite sure it is much *less* correct: but I firmly believe in the value of a *first* impression, as to disproportion, as compared with the view of one who has got *used* to the picture: and I feel quite sure that, if *you* were to see, for the first time, a drawing by Sir F. Leighton, which *he* had gone over many times, it would be quite possible, and fairly probable, that *you* would see, in one moment, some disproportion *he* had quite ceased to feel.

Now I'll venture to name what strike me, at first sight, as anatomical mistakes:

(1) The seated child has her head unsupported, and in a position quite impossible to maintain in *sleep*. To keep her asleep, and make her head take a natural position, would need redrawing the head, which would be a great pity. In my opinion, she had better *open her eyes*!

(2) Her waist is too small. I think the lower ribs would bulge more, and would nearly touch the top of Cynthia's head.

(3) The distance from her left hip to the knee-cap is *slightly* too great.

(4) Her left knee is too small.

(5) The distance, from it to the end of the toes, is decidedly too great.

(6) All below the knee looks too *thin*. This I think is due to its being too long for its thickness: the calf, which now looks too thin, would probably be thick enough for a *shorter* limb.

Cynthia seems all right, except that I should have *expected* to find her right shoulder nearer her head: but this I don't feel at all sure about.[1]

May I suggest that, though I have now paid for 11 pictures, I only possess 2? I should be glad to have the other 9.

The following are not yet cut, and are therefore capable of further touches if any occur to you.

"Child on cray-fish." (This needs a *younger* face, as we have already agreed.)

"Two fairies and squirrel."

"Child and wasp."

"3 fairies under mushroom."

"2 ditto on fish."[2]

Believe me

Very sincerely yours,
C. L. Dodgson

1. *Three Sunsets*, p. 22. In the published illustration the seated fairy, modeled on Cynthia Bell, has her eyes open, but Miss Thomson seems not to have made the other anatomical changes: Cynthia's left leg is too long and too thin compared with her right leg.

2. These five pictures appear in *Three Sunsets*, pp. 28, 33, 62, 66, and 58, respectively.

ms: *Huntington*

Christ Church, Oxford
November 1, 1894

Many thanks. It is quite charming now. No: I had *not* forgotten our arrangements as to ownership. By "possess" I did not mean to refer to *ultimate*, but *present* possession. Of course I will send all, when done with: but at present I need them *all*. Several are not yet cut: and, in more than one instance, I have had a *second* woodcut made, and perhaps may wish to do so again.[1]

1. This postcard probably refers to the picture of the sleeping fairies of the previous letter.

---

ms: *Huntington*

Christ Church, Oxford
February 24, 1895

My dear Miss Thomson,

Many thanks for the pretty little "dragon-fly" drawing, and for the correction you have made in the crouching child.[1]

In a day or two I hope to write fully on the subject of the fairy-drawings: for today it will be enough to say that I fear I cannot agree to their being made public previously to their publication by me. I will also write about the other projected pictures. Believe me

Very sincerely yours,
C. L. Dodgson

1. This picture does not appear in *Three Sunsets*.

MS: *Huntington*

Christ Church, Oxford
March 4, 1895

Dear Miss Thomson,

I have had a letter to you planned for a long time, and hope now to get it written as it is of much importance to both of us.

When I wrote, the other day, objecting to let the as yet unpublished pictures appear in a public exhibition, I had no time to give any *reasons*. And it seems hardly necessary to do so. It will very likely have occurred to you, by this time, that a good deal of the value of the copyright of illustrations consists in their *novelty*: the right of publishing pictures, with which the public is already acquainted, is of very small commercial value.

In your letter dated November 6 you say "I have redrawn the face of the Fairy in the Crayfish drawing. I think she is more childlike now." She may be *slightly* so: but she still looks 4 or 5 years too old. You once offered to draw a new picture instead of this: but this offer, as you will see further on, I do not propose to avail myself of.

Further on you speak of the reduced pictures as "lamentably small," and "insignificant in size." You add that you are "very much disappointed," and that "when I saw how small the woodcuts were to be I utterly lost heart and interest" in them.

In a later letter you ask to withdraw these remarks—thinking, perhaps, that you had expressed yourself too severely. But indeed there is no need for this. All you say is perfectly true. The size of most of the drawings does *not* suit the size of the book to be illustrated. This, however, is a different thing from saying (what *you* seem to imply) that the size of the *book* does not suit the size of the *drawings*. All depends, of course, on *which* size was fixed *first*. In this case, it was the size of *book* that was fixed first. Long before the very first drawing was done, it was settled that 3 1/4, or at the outside 3 1/2, inches was to be the width.

The fact, that most of the drawings were too large to be reduced, without losing much of their beauty, to this width, has come, to *your* consciousness too late. It was present, to *mine*, all along. I find it recorded that, as soon as the *third* drawing (the 2 children in bower) was done, I wrote to you that we were on the wrong tack, and that it would not bear the necessary reduction. Unfortunately, I failed to make you see this: and the pictures got larger and larger, reaching their maximum in the Nautilus-picture,[1] which is actually 6 1/2 inches wide, and which will scarcely bear *any* reduction without sacrificing much of its beauty.

I quite agree with you that it would be a *great* pity to bring out these lovely pictures in a form which would sacrifice most of their beauty.

Well, we must now face facts as they are: and must consider what is the best thing to be done under the circumstances.

I have gone through the 12 pictures, and I find that only 3 of them (Boy on Mushroom, Child and Wasp, 2 Children on Fish,[2] which are drawn of the widths 3 3/4, 2 3/4, 3 5/8) are really *available* for the book. One (Child on Cray-fish,[3] drawn 3 7/8 wide) is not available, owing to the face being too old. The other 8 would be simply *spoiled* by being reduced to the necessary size.

My conclusion is, *not* to have any illustrations in the book.

So the practical question is, what am I to do with the copyright, for which I have paid you a total of £50.8.0.

Far the *best* way out of the difficulty seems to me to be that *you* should take the copyright, and return me the £50. You will then be able to offer for sale the drawings *with* their copyright. They are very beautiful, and I should think you would find them very saleable. If ever published in a *book*, it ought to be a quarto, with a page about 6 inches wide.

Besides paying you that £50, I have also paid £19 to Swain, for cutting a few of them. *That* loss I shall be content to bear. Luckily he has cut very few.

Hoping that you may see your way to adopting the plan I have proposed, I am

Very sincerely yours,
C. L. Dodgson

P.S. If you cannot see your way to adopting this plan, I think I might perhaps use them for the "Serious Poems," bringing it out in quarto. In that case, I should *not* want any of the pictures which we planned, more than 10 years ago. This might perhaps bring in some of the £50: but it is doubtful, as there would be about 8 large cuts to be done, which would cost another £30 or so, making my total outlay, for illustrations, £100!

---

1. "Fairies and Nautilus," the frontispiece to *Three Sunsets*.

2. "Fairy on a Mushroom," ibid., p. 52; "Fairy and Wasp," p. 62; and "Fairies Riding on Fish," p. 58.

3. "Fairy Riding on Cray-Fish," ibid., p. 28.

---

ms: Huntington

Christ Church, Oxford
May 8, 1895

My dear Miss Thomson,

Having had no answer to my letter of March 4, I presume you do *not* see your way to re-purchasing the copyright of the 12 drawings. But I would like to know for certain, as I have decided that, in that case, I will myself publish them *un*-reduced. It would be a *great* pity that such lovely things should be unpublished, or published in a reduced size. My plan is to publish my "Serious Poems" in a small thin quarto: and they will do very well as "illustrations," though *not*, perhaps, showing any *very* distinct connection with the text!

Of course this means the final abandonment of the idea, now 10 years old, of your drawing special illustrations for those poems.

The book will not pay its expenses: but I don't mind *that*. The public *must* have the pictures, in their full beauty.

Very sincerely yours,
C. L. Dodgson

---

ms: Huntington

Christ Church, Oxford
May 18, 1895

My dear Miss Thomson,

We are sufficiently "old friends," I feel sure, for me to have no fear that I shall seem intrusive in writing about your great sorrow.[1] The greatest blow, that has ever fallen on *my* life, was the death, nearly 30 years ago, of my own dear father: so, in offering you my sincere sympathy, I write as a fellow-sufferer. And I rejoice to know that we are, not only fellow-sufferers, but also fellow-believers in the blessed hope of the resurrection from the dead, which makes such a parting holy and beautiful, instead of being merely a blank despair.

When you are again at leisure, and would like to have a little artistic occupation, I would be glad of your help in what must be done for the 12 fairy-drawings, to fit them for the book of poems. They are on so many different scales of size, that it would be a real loss to their beauty as a set, to reproduce them without so reducing those on larger scales as to make them all fairly match.

I have devised a very simple process for doing this. Very likely you may know of a better process: but, if not, I think you will find my process (if you will let me send you the pictures) a very easy one to work.

The rules of procedure would be these:

(1) Find out which of the 12 is on the *smallest* scale. Let us call this picture "X."

(2) Stand, looking down on a table, and measure the height of your eye from the surface of the table.

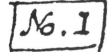

(3) Lay the 1st picture *on* the table: hold "X" a little *above* the table, so as to have both in view at once (I prefer *this* arrangement):
and move "X" up and down, putting a heap of books under it, till the two pictures look to you on the *same* scale: then measure the height of the heap of books.

I can do all the rest of the calculation, if you will merely tell me *which* picture is "X," the height of your eye from the table, and the heights of the various heaps.

You might *test* the accuracy of your results, by laying aside "X," and taking two of the pictures at random, and supplying each with its appropriate heap of books, according to your list, and then observing whether the two, when regarded from the proper height, seem to be on the *same* scale.

Of course it would be necessary to allow for the different *ages* of the children, as necessarily causing differences in *size*.[2] Believe me always

Very sincerely yours,
C. L. Dodgson

1. Miss Thomson's father had just died.
2. Dodgson noted the same day, "Wrote to ask Miss Thomson to help in reducing to uniform scale, for the 'Serious Poems,' her 12 fairy-drawings" (Diaries).

MS: *Huntington*

7 Lushington Road, Eastbourne
August 6, 1895

Dear Miss Thomson,

I know the sort of work, and worry, you have had to go through, and am very glad you have got through it. As I have had 9 of the 12 drawings photographed the exact size of the originals, I am able to avoid the risk of committing the originals to the Post: so I enclose 3 drawings and 9 prints.

Will you kindly tell me *which* of the 12 you consider to be on the *smallest* scale, and also the proportion in which each of the others needs to be reduced, to bring it to that scale?

Very sincerely yours,
C. L. Dodgson

MS: *Huntington*

7 Lushington Road, Eastbourne
August 12, 1895

Dear Miss Thomson,

Many thanks for your letter, and for marking the pictures so as to show the relative scales. Evidently, if I had tried to do the thing myself, I should have gone wrong, as several, which you have marked as on the *same* scale, seem to *me* to be on *different* scales, (e.g. the "child and wasp" looks to *me* on a decidedly *smaller* scale than the "3 under mushroom": yet *you* have marked them as the *same*).[1]

Your letter is rather bewildering, owing to your so often using the word "size" where you mean "scale." (Of course the *size* of a picture is independent of the *scale* on which it is drawn).

I enclose the "Sleeping Fairies," for the shading to be added according to your kind offer.[2]

As to putting photos of the drawings into your scrapbook (where I presume they would be visible to others than yourself), I must ask you to kindly defer doing so until I have published the book (which I hope to do this year). I don't think you have *ever* fully realised *what* it was that I bought from you, with that £50. Allow me to explain what, in *my* view, it was. I bought *two* privileges:

(1) The sole right of *selling* any *reproductions* of the pictures, at any time within the next 40 years (the originals *you* will be able to sell, after my book has appeared).

(2) The sole right of *publishing* either the pictures or any reproductions of them, at any time within the next 40 years.

What you proposed to do, a short time ago, *viz.* to send the originals to a public exhibition, would have been a distinct infringement of No. 2.

Showing them, or reproductions of them, *privately*, to strangers, would not, perhaps, be "publication" in the *legal* sense: still it would, I think, be an *actual* infringement; and as such I object to it: but, when once the book is out, I should not mind it.

Please forgive me if I seem to you to guard with superfluous jealousy the privileges which I consider I have purchased.

Very sincerely yours,
C. L. Dodgson

1. "Child and wasp," p. 62, and "Three under mushroom," p. 66, in *Three Sunsets*.
2. "Sleeping fairies," ibid., p. 22.

MS: Huntington

Christ Church, Oxford
December 5, 1895

My dear Miss Thomson,

Some while ago, I rashly gave a general order to my bookseller, to get me *Robert Louis Stevenson's Works*, and, when they came, I was dismayed to find among them a costly art-book (30s. it was) which I felt quite unable to *appreciate* as it no doubt deserves. I might of course *sell* it: but I prefer *giving* it away, if I can find any friend who would care to have it (to *keep*, I mean, not *sell*) and who would really *enjoy* looking at it. And in *you*, I think, I have such a friend. The book is a small folio; it is called *Edinburgh*, and is illustrated with etchings by A. Brunet-Debaines, from drawings by S. Bough, R.S.A. and W. E. Lockhart, R.S.A., and vignettes by Hector Chalmers and R. Kent Thomas.[1] Would you like to have it? If so, I shall have much pleasure in sending it you as a Christmas present.

Very sincerely yours,
C. L. Dodgson

I will get you a set of those photos, size of originals of your drawings. Shall they be mounted?

1. *Edinburgh: Picturesque Notes* appeared in 1879; Dodgson, in describing the illustrations, quotes from the title page.

MS: Huntington

Christ Church, Oxford
February 1, 1896

Dear Miss Thomson,

Many thanks for your letter. I have gone carefully through all the 12 pictures, in their various sizes, and propose to use them as follows:

A page of "Serious Poems" will be 4 inches wide, and 5 3/4 high, a page of "Games and Puzzles" will be 3 1/2 wide and 5 1/2 high.

(1) *Boy on mushroom*: The small size (which you approve of) I propose to use for "G.P." It would be a pity, I think, to waste the larger one, even though it is less good. Would you object to my using it in "S.P."?[1]

(2) *Cray-fish*: The large one, which you condemn, I do not propose to use at all. The small one, whose outside width is 3 inches, will do very well for "G.P." You are most kind in proposing to make a larger drawing of it for "S.P.," but I think its being in "G.P." will suffice.[2]

(3) *Shell*: This I suppose you approve of; it will do for "S.P."[3]

(4) *Bower*: The larger one, which you condemn, I do not propose to use at all. The small one, which you call "a perfect gem," I propose to use for "G.P." Its outside width is 3 inches.[4]

(5) *Nautilus*: Actually *three* sizes of this have been cut! The smallest I do not propose to use at all. The next, whose outside dimensions are 4 1/2 x 2 3/4, I propose to use, sideways, as frontispiece for "G.P.," and the largest, sideways, as frontispiece for "S.P." It is longer than a page of *text*: but there will be plenty of margin.[5]

(6) *Squirrel*: I have had no proof yet. But you approve of it: so it will do for "S.P."[6]

(7) *Wasp*: Will do for "S.P."[7]

(8) *Jonquil*: Two sizes have been cut. Smaller will do for "G.P.," larger for "S.P."[8]

(9) *3 under mushroom*: I have had no proof: but, as you approve, it will do for "S.P."[9]

(10) *Fish*: Ditto, ditto.[10]

(11) *Frog*: Ditto, ditto.[11]

(12) *Sleepers*: Ditto, ditto.[12]

I am writing to Swain for proofs of (6) and of (9) to (12).

Very sincerely yours,
C. L. Dodgson

P.S. As at present planned, "S.P." will contain *10* pictures (i.e. the set, minus the Cray-fish and the Bower), and "G.P." will contain *5* (i.e. the Cray-fish and Bower, and duplicates of Boy on Mushroom, Nautilus and Jonquil).

I propose to announce in "S.P.," "ten illustrations by E. Gertrude Thomson," and, in "G.P.," "*two* ditto, ditto" (as it will not do to take any credit for the duplicates).

What sort of *cover* shall we have for "S.P." My notion is *dark brown* cloth, and gold lettering.[13]

1. Miss Thomson did not object to using the larger "Boy on Mushroom" (*Three Sunsets*, p. 52).

2. A picture of a child on a cray-fish appears in *Three Sunsets*, p. 28. Whether it is the larger "condemned" version, or an enlargement of the smaller version, or a redrawn picture we cannot tell. The picture's charm argues in favor of one of the last two options.

3. *Three Sunsets*, p. 7.

4. The picture of "The fairies and bower" appears in *Three Sunsets*, p. 14; again, it is difficult to tell whether this is the larger, rejected picture or an enlargement of the smaller, favored one.

5. The "Nautilus" picture appears sideways as the frontispiece in *Three Sunsets*.

6. Ibid., p. 33.

7. Ibid., p. 62.

8. The larger version appears ibid., p. 41.

9. Ibid., p. 66.

10. Ibid., p. 58.

11. Ibid., p. 47.

12. Ibid., p. 22.

13. All twelve of the pictures listed in this letter eventually appeared in *Three Sunsets*.

MS: *Huntington*

Christ Church, Oxford
May 11, 1896

Dear Miss Thomson,

Thanks for your letter. For the cover of *The Lost Plum-Cake* nothing more than the *title*, in ornamental lettering, is wanted. Nothing in the nature of a *picture* is worth attempting, when it has to be printed in *gold* on a rough red paper (I enclose a specimen). The medallion-heads, on *Alice* and *Sylvie* books, done in gold on red cloth, are, in my opinion, of no *artistic* value whatever.

Please put a hyphen in *Plum-Cake*.[1]

Very sincerely yours,
C. L. Dodgson

P.S. Sir James Ramsay, an old Christ Church friend, came in to see me the other day, and mentioned that he had sat to you for his portrait, and that it was an excellent likeness.[2] I didn't know you did *men's* heads. I shall now recommend my friends not only to send their *children* to you, but to go *themselves* as well.

P.P.S. I also want an ornamental title, for the cover of the poems. It shall be the coloured linen you recommend. But no *pictures*, please: merely *Three Sunsets and Other Poems* at top, and "Lewis Carroll" (small) below. Cover will be 8 1/2 high, 7 wide.

1. *The Lost Plum-Cake* by Dodgson's cousin Elizabeth Georgina Wilcox (Mrs. Egerton Allen) was published by Macmillan in January 1898 with nine illustrations by Mrs. E. L. Shute. Dodgson wrote an introduction to the book in which he points out the optical illusion in the gilt pattern on the red cardboard cover designed by Miss Thomson. He took a particular interest in the book and wrote on May 21, 1896: "For the first (and probably only) time in my life, I have passed for 'Press,' *two* books in one day! One being Georgie Allen's *The Lost Plum-Cake*, and the other the second edition of *Symbolic Logic*" (*Diaries*, p. 526). The former was probably for a privately printed version of the book which came out in 1896. Dodgson arranged for Miss Thomson to design the cover for the book and for Macmillan to publish it. The specimen cover supplied by Dodgson in this letter is missing. For more on Dodgson and *The Lost Plum-Cake*, see *Macmillan Letters*, pp. 338–39, 360–62.

2. Sir James Henry Ramsay, Bart. (1832–1925), educated at Rugby and Christ Church, historian and Student at Christ Church (1854–61).

MS: Huntington

Christ Church, Oxford
June 9, 1896

Dear Miss Thomson,

I have much pleasure in sending you the guinea for the title of *The Lost Plum-Cake.*

The dates I sent you, of vols. of R.A. pictures which I thought I could spare, were wrong. I find that the only two I can spare are those for 1891 and 1892, and as I fancy that no friend of mine is more capable than you are of enjoying them, I am sending *both*, in a parcel by Passenger-train, unpaid. Please tell me what they charge you for carriage, and I will repay you.

Very sincerely yours,
C. L. Dodgson

MS: Huntington

Christ Church, Oxford
October 23, 1896

My dear Miss Thomson,

Whenever you have time and inclination to design the cover for *Three Sunsets and Other Poems*, I shall be glad to have it. Believe me

Very sincerely yours,
C. L. Dodgson

MS: Huntington

Christ Church, Oxford
January 27, 1897

Dear Miss Thomson,

I fear I must ask you to do without the appearance of your name on the cover. It will be on the title-page, and there is already too much on the cover.

Looking again at the first design, I do not like the *uniform* size of the lettering. If the second is like it, I must ask you to alter it, as it makes my name much too conspicuous.

"*Three Sunsets*" ought to be *much* the largest lettering: "and Other Poems" rather smaller: "Lewis Carroll" a good deal smaller: and "by" insignificant. If suitable to the general effect, I should like the first 5 words to come rather *above* the picture, and the last 3, quite separate, and *below* it.[1]

Yours very sincerely,
C. L. D.

1. All of these specifications succeeded.

MS: *Huntington*

2 Bedford Well Road,
Eastbourne[1]
August 7, 1897

My dear Miss Thomson,

Are you willing to undertake the job of drawing me a frontispiece for my book of "Original Games and Puzzles"? I want to connect it with *Alice*, somehow; and my idea is to have Alice, reading, and in the background (borrowing the idea of the old picture of "Napoleon visiting his tomb") 2 trees, the interval between them being the outline of some well-known figure from "Wonderland." I enclose a scrawl to show the sort of thing I want: but I have made the figure *much* too obvious.[2]

My sisters have the engraving of "Napoleon, etc.," which could be sent for you to see. And *I* have a puzzle-picture, I could send, that I bought years ago, of a forest: several of the openings representing animals.

On July 30 I sent you 7 specimen boards for cover of *Three Sunsets*, in various coloured linens, with your design in gold, for you to say if any of them was the kind of linen you want, and right colour.

Yours very sincerely,
C. L. D.

Picture to be 3 9/16 x 5 5/8. Draw as much *larger* as you like.

1. Dodgson's Eastbourne landlady moved from Lushington Road to this new address in 1896. Dodgson continued to rent his summer quarters from her.
2. Dodgson refers to an etching in which a veiled woman in mourning sits by Napoleon's

FIG. 36
Dodgson's puzzle sketch with letter dated August 7, 1897.

tomb, over which an eagle stands guard. Between two willow trees the emperor's ghost appears in silhouette (Anne Marie Rosset, *Un Siècle d'Histoire de France par l'Estampe* [1770–1871], Collection De Vinck, vol. 5, *La Restauration et les Cent-Jours*, 1938, p. 451).

2 Bedford Well Road,
Eastbourne[1]
August 10, 1897

My dear Miss Thomson,

It was careless of Messrs. Macmillan and their binder to forget that a specimen of the linen had been already approved by you. I have asked them, in case they kept a bit themselves, to send a part of it to me, in order to make sure it is right: in case they have *not*, I have told them you will send them the original piece in September. The thing can very well wait till then. We haven't got the book anything *like* ready yet.

Your description of the sands, and the naked children playing there, is very tempting, and I might *possibly* make an expedition there, some day (would your landlady take me in?), on the chance of getting some picturesque victims to sketch. But, alas, it is impossible *this* year. Dolly comes to me on Friday, and may perhaps stay till the end of the month;[2] and by that time the summer-*heat* will have gone, and your live fairies will have ceased to dress in "nothing."

Yet it is doubtful if I should not, after all, find I had come in vain—and that it was a hopeless quest to try to make friends with any of the little nudities. A *lady* might do it: but what would they think of a *gentleman* daring to address them! And then what an embarrassing thing it would be to *begin* an acquaintance with a naked little girl! What *could* one say to start the conversation? Perhaps a poetical quotation would be best. "And ye shall walk in silk attire."[3] How would *that* do? I'm afraid she would reply "Do I *look* like it?"[4] Or one *might* begin with Keats' charming lines "Oh where are you going, with your love-locks flowing, And what have you got in your basket?"[5] She would *have* "love-locks flowing," most likely: they wouldn't be the kind you have to hang up till you've done bathing. And, even without clothes, she might still find some use for a basket—if only a *clothes*-basket! Or a quotation from Cowper (slightly altered) might do. *His* lines are "The tear, that is wiped with a little address, May be followed perhaps by a smile."[6] But *I* should have to quote it as "The tear, that is wiped with so little a dress"!

You will think that Eastbourne air makes me talk nonsense. Perhaps it does. To return to sense. Haven't you got your little camera with you? And could you not make friends with some of these girl-fairies, and do me a photo of one, or of a group, with a background of rocks? And, if you chance to make friends with any exceptionally *nice* little nudity (no matter whether she is *beautiful* or not: only *nice* ones will do) who is willing to be victimised for my benefit, I will send you a book to give her.

Very sincerely yours,
C. L. Dodgson

P.S. The quotation to put, as a motto, *under* a photo of your little "sea-fairy," would no doubt be from Sir Noël Paton's poems:

> And there, upon the gleaming sands,
>   Between the ripples and the rocks,
> Stood, mother-naked in the sun,
>   A little maid with golden locks.[7]

1. Dodgson writes "Hastings," possibly because he had walked there several times in recent days, on July 29 and 31 and August 6 (DIARIES, p. 537); see also Dodgson to his sister Louisa in *Letters*, p. 1137.

2. For more on Dorothea Marie Caroline ("Dolly") Rivington (1883–1951), see *Letters*, p. 1120, n. 1.

3. Susanna Blamire, "The Siller Crown," quoted in Charles Dickens, *The Old Curiosity Shop*, 1840–41, chapter 66.

4. *Alice's Adventures in Wonderland*, chapter 12.

5. Actually Christina Rossetti's "Amor Mundi," l. 1.

6. "The Rose," ll. 19–20.

7. Stanza 7 of "Idyl. To D.O.H.," in *Poems by a Painter*, Edinburgh, 1861. The lines read in fact:

For there, upon the glimmering marge,
    Between the sea and sea-worn rocks,
Stood, mother-naked, in the sun,
    A little girl with golden locks.

MS: *Huntington*

2 Bedford Well Road,
Eastbourne
August 11, 1897

My dear Miss Thomson,

I'm very glad you will do me the frontispiece; and I enclose the "puzzle-picture." There are 5 animals in it, which to me, *now,* are very obvious; but I have known people, seeing it for the first time, take a long time in finding them. Possibly you might find room for *more* than *one Alice* creature: but don't reduce the figure of Alice herself to make room: she must be quite the *principal* thing in the picture.[1]

Before you *finish* the drawing, I would like to know *which* creature, or creatures, you propose to introduce, and to see a rough sketch.

Yours very sincerely,
C. L. Dodgson

1. The animal puzzle-picture which Dodgson sent to Miss Thomson is missing.

MS: *Huntington*

Christ Church, Oxford
November 12, 1897

My dear Miss Thomson,

One thing is pretty clear, that *you* have not passed many books through the Press! Printers' proofs are always done on thin cheap paper, and with no "bringing-up" of pictures, and come out *anyhow.* They are "bringing-up" the pictures (i.e. making "cushions" for them), and are to send me a set of prints, on good paper, which I will submit to you for approval.

The *small* block of the "Cray-fish" is much *too* small. Please tell me the exact *proportion* in which it ought to be reduced. (It's no good saying "make it such and such a *length,* or height" unless you indicate the exact *points* between which you measure it).[1]

I'm enquiring for Isy's address.[2]

No. I *don't* think the *pictures* will need any apology: one might, perhaps, apologise for putting such *verses* along with them!

Yours very sincerely,
C. L. Dodgson

1. The "Cray-fish" picture is on p. 28 of *Three Sunsets*.
2. Isy Watson, one of Miss Thomson's models. See the following four letters.

MS: Huntington

Christ Church, Oxford
November 15, 1897

Dear Miss Thomson,

Isy Watson's address is 194 Kingsland Road, N.E. I'll be at Addison Hall by about 11. We will lunch with friends in Lowndes Sq., for which we should start, in cab, soon after 12. We have front-stalls: so *please* bring a hat you can take off. Hats in the front-stalls are an *awful* nuisance to the 2nd and 3rd rows. After play we will (as I want to leave by the 6.50) come by Metropolitan R.W., you to W. Kensington, I to Praed St.

Very sincerely yours,
C.L.D.

MS: Huntington

Christ Church, Oxford
November 17, 1897

Dear Miss Thomson,

Could you have a *camera*, as well as a model, on Saturday? Drawing takes *time*, of which we shall have little to spare. But the lens, with which you did the Bells, is a terribly *small* one: some of the photos are very much out of proportion. Could you *hire* one, for the day, with a better lens? Charge *me* with the costs involved.[1]

Yours very sincerely,
C. L. Dodgson

1. "A delightful day," Dodgson wrote about the following Saturday, November 20 (DIARIES, p. 542). "Went to London . . . to Addison Hall, where Miss E. G. Thomson has a studio, and had about 1 1/4 hours, with her and the little model Isy Watson, a very nice and pretty child, aged 13. We tried one hasty sketch of her lying down. Then we drove to Lowndes Sq. (dropping Isy at Addison Rd. Station) and had luncheon with Mrs. Bowles, Sydney, 'Weenie,' and the governess. Then we went to the Haymarket, and saw [J. M. Barrie's] *The Little Minister*, a beautiful play, beautifully acted. . . . [We] went to Paddington, and had tea: and I returned to Oxford." For more on Dodgson's friendship with the Bowles family, see *Letters*, pp. 840–41.

MS: *Huntington*

Christ Church, Oxford
November 21, 1897

My dear Miss Thomson,

It never occurred to me—nor, I fancy, to you—that the R.W. fare to Addison Road and back would make a considerable hole in the 2s. you paid to dear little Isy. Also the 2s. was of course *my* business: I ought to have paid it you. Will you kindly repay her the R.W. fare next time you see her? And will you keep an account against me, to include those 2 items, and also the hire of that camera—and the *next* hiring of it, if you get it again (with fuller instructions!) and do some pictures of Isy? In that case, could you do one as large as the enclosed,[1] which I have just traced from a lovely photo of a girl (of about 15, I should think)? I should like her done, that way, very much. Hands behind the back is a very pretty arrangement, I think. The picture need not include the knees.

Very sincerely yours,
C. L. Dodgson

1. Missing.

MS: *Huntington*

Christ Church, Oxford
November 23, 1897

My dear Miss Thomson,

I quite agree with you that Isy is *not* a quite satisfactory subject for so exacting a process as photography, which will make no allowance for thinness. And I should much like to have some photos of Edie,[1] one in the attitude of that tracing, and others in as many attitudes as you like to take her in!

It seems incredible that Isy could have travelled 15 miles for 4*d*.! I don't quite like the idea of that small and pretty child going all that way, alone, on *my* account. If she got lost, or stolen, I should feel an awful responsibility in having caused her to run the risk. Still, it might be urged, the risk is not *greater* when travelling by railway, than when walking about the streets near her home, where she might at any time be inveigled away by some evil-disposed person. What do *you* think about it? I fear such beauty, among the very poor, is a very dangerous possession.

Here are the pictures, in the state in which Clay proposes to print them. I am woefully disappointed with them. To me they look feeble, faded, washed-out, as if done from worn-out blocks. Even if you were to declare yourself satisfied with them, I should hold to my decision that I must either have more brilliant impressions or not publish them at all. I don't lay the blame on the *printing*: I believe Messrs. Clay are excellent printers, and very painstaking. My belief is that it is the *paper* that is in fault: it does not take the ink properly. And perhaps the *ink* also is not perfectly black. That is a fault which a friend, who seems to know a good deal about artistic printing, assures me is sometimes met with. I am writing to Clay to say that he must try some other kinds of paper, and perhaps blacker ink, till the pictures come out a little more worthy of the brilliancy and beauty of the originals.

Very sincerely yours,
C. L. Dodgson

1. Edith Ball.

MS: *Huntington*

Christ Church, Oxford
December 15, 1897

My dear Miss Thomson,

If the parcel has not come to hand, please *look* at a copy of Besant's book (any bookseller could show you one) and tell me if you would object to that colour for the cover.[1]

Yours very sincerely,
C. L. Dodgson

1. *A Fountain Sealed* was Walter Besant's latest book.

MS: *Huntington*

Christ Church, Oxford
December 22, 1897

Dear Miss Thomson,

I am hoping to hear that you have either received the parcel, containing the specimen-cover and the Besant book, or, if not (in which case I had better know, that I may set enquiries on foot), that you have been to some bookseller and looked at a Besant book.

I enclose proofs, with various paper and ink, of pictures. A is said to be on "super-calendered" paper. B, C, D on "a paper with no gloss at all." 3 different inks have been used: but they omit to say *which* two are the *same* ink. Please return them to me, with comments, at "The Chestnuts, Guildford," which will be my address till about middle of January.[1]

Yours very sincerely,
C. L. D.

P.S. I'd nearly omitted to say one thing that occurred to me on reading your account of Edith Ball. That is, *please* do not draw her, nude, for my pictures, if she has any scruple *whatever*, on the score of modesty. I'm sure a child's instincts, of that kind, ought to be treated with the utmost *reverence*. And if I had the loveliest child in the world, to draw or photograph, and found she had a modest shrinking (however slight, and however easily overcome) from being taken nude, I should feel it was a solemn duty, owed to God, to drop the request *altogether*.

P.P.S. You need not return to me the little photos. I have duplicates of all that I need.

1. Miss Thomson wrote a note on this letter: "His last letter. He passed away on January 14th." *Three Sunsets and Other Poems* was published in February 1898 in green cloth with gilt lettering depicting two medallions designed by Miss Thomson; the front design shows a seated fairy, head leaning forward toward her raised knees, with stars shining in the background; the back design shows a sunset.

Stand still, true poet that you are!
I know you; let me try and draw you.[1]

In trying to sketch this outline of my beloved friend — one of the most unique and charming personalities of our time — my own shadow, so to speak, must perforce, to my regret, sometimes fall across the picture. I shall not attempt to give any of his incomparable humour, all the world knows that through his immortal books, but I want to show that little known view of him — that "other side of the moon" — visible only to those who knew him best.

It was at the end of December, 1878, that a letter, written in a singularly legible and rather boyish-looking hand, came to me from Christ Church, Oxford, and signed "C. L. Dodgson." The writer said that he had come across some fairy designs of mine, and he should like to see some more of my work. By the same post came a note from my London publisher (who had supplied my address) telling me that the "Rev. C. L. Dodgson" was "Lewis Carroll."

Alice in Wonderland had long been one of my pet books, and as one regards a favourite author as almost a personal friend, I felt less restraint than one usually feels in writing to a stranger, though I carefully concealed my knowledge of his identity as he had not chosen to reveal it.

This was the beginning of a frequent and delightful correspondence, and as I confessed to a great love of fairy lore of every description, he asked me if I would accept a child's fairy-tale book he had written called *Alice in Wonderland*, I replied that I knew it nearly all off by heart, but that I should greatly prize a copy given to me by himself. By return came *Alice* and *Through the Looking-Glass* bound most luxuriously in white calf and gold.

And this is the graceful and kindly note that came with them: "I am now sending you *Alice* and the *Looking-Glass* as well. There is an incompleteness about giving only one, and besides the one you bought was probably in red, and would not match these. If you are at all in doubt as to what to do with the (now) superfluous copy, let me suggest your giving it to some poor sick child. I have been distributing copies to all the hospitals and convalescent homes I can hear of, where there are sick children capable of reading them, and though, of course, one takes some pleasure in the popularity of the books elsewhere, it is not nearly so pleasant a thought to me as that they may be a comfort and relief to children in hours of pain and weariness. Still no recipient *can* be more appropriate than one who seems to have been in fairyland herself, and to have seen, like the 'weary mariners' of old,

> Between the green brink and the running foam
> White limbs unrobed in a crystal air,
> Sweet faces, rounded arms, and bosoms prest
> To little harps of gold."

"Do you ever come to London?" he asked in another letter; "if so, will you allow me to call upon you?"

Early in the summer I came up to study, and I sent him word that I was in town. One night coming into my room, after a long day spent at the British Museum, in the half-light I saw a card lying on the table. "Rev. C. L. Dodgson." Bitter, indeed, was my disappointment at having missed him, but just as I was laying it sadly down I spied a small T.O. in the corner. On the back I read that he couldn't get up to my rooms early or late enough to find me, so would I arrange to meet him at some museum or gallery the day but one following? I fixed on South Kensington Museum, by the "Schliemann" collection, at twelve o'clock.

A little before twelve I was at the rendezvous, and then the humour of the situation suddenly struck me, that *I* had not the ghost of an idea what *he* was like, nor would *he* have any better chance of discovering *me*! The room was fairly full of all sorts and conditions as usual, and I glanced at each masculine figure in turn, only to reject it as a possibility of the one I sought. Just as the big clock had clanged out twelve, I heard the high vivacious voices and laughter of children sounding down the corridor.

At that moment a gentleman entered, two little girls clinging to his hands, and I caught sight of the tall, slim figure, with the clean-shaven, delicate, refined face, I said to myself, "*That's* Lewis Carroll." He stood for a moment, head erect, glancing swiftly over the room, then bending down, whispered something to one of the children: she, after a moment's pause, pointed straight at me.

Dropping their hands, he came forward, and with that winning smile of his that utterly banished the oppressive sense of the Oxford don, said simply,

"I am Mr Dodgson; I was to meet you, I think?" To which I as frankly smiled and said, "How did you know me so soon?"

"My little friend found you. I told her I had come to meet a young lady who knew fairies, and she fixed on you at once. But *I* knew you before she spoke."

Thus began that close and happy friendship which gladdened and enriched my life for eighteen years, and ended only when *his* beautiful life drew to its close, scarcely a week ago.

Soon after our meeting in London he wrote from Oxford: "Are you sufficiently unconventional (I *think* you are) to defy Mrs. Grundy, and come down to spend the day with me at Oxford? Write and ask permission of your father." Needless to say the permission was given, and the visit arranged.

"What would you like to eat?" he wrote. "Choose your own lunch, and whether possible or impossible, it shall be got!" I went down by an early train, and he met me at the station with two more little girls. Always little girls! We did the lions in Oxford. Glorious, of course. Then the children were taken home, and we returned to his beautiful rooms at Christ Church.

Lewis Carroll was not only an admirable amateur photographer, but an enthusiastic sketcher of children, especially when they were "dressed in nothing," as he called it, and *apropos* of this, he once told me an amusing remark of one of Sir Noël Paton's children. They were very beautiful, and served their father as models in those two exquisite illustrations for Kingsley's *Water Babies*. In the design of the fairies floating through the water the front view figure is an absolute portrait of one little daughter. One day a friend in looking at it said to the child, "Why, that's *you*." "Yes," was the reply, "it's *me*, but I don't *often* dress like that!"

I consider that he naturally had a decided gift for drawing, but he was entirely untrained, so that his sketches, though they had a certain feeling for beauty, were, of course, very crude. He had a singularly correct eye for form, so much so that he would instantly detect slight flaws in drawing in some of the work I did for him, which had escaped my more practised eye. Complimenting him one day on his ability as art critic, he said, "I can't draw in the least myself—that's the first qualification for an Art Critic. One approaches a subject in such a delightfully open and unbiased manner if you are entirely ignorant of it!"

Writing to me once on this subject he said: "I love the effort to draw; but

I fail utterly to please even my own eye. But I have no time now left for such things. In the next life, I do hope that we shall not only *see* lovely forms, such as this world does not contain, but shall also be able to *draw* them."

He was always anxious that whatever work I did for him should be drawn from life. "I do want you to do my fairy-drawings from *life*," he wrote. "They would be very pretty, no doubt, done out of your own head, but they will be ten times more valuable if done from life. Mr. Tenniel is the only artist who has drawn for me who resolutely refused to use a model, and declared he no more needed one than *I* should need the multiplication table to work out a mathematical problem!"

Soon there followed another day at Oxford.

"Come and photograph human fairies," he wrote.

His photographic studio, on the roof of the college, was a big place filled with all sorts of properties, costumes, etc. He dressed up the children in a variety of quaint costumes, and "took" them in all sorts of attitudes; intervals for refreshment and play being very frequent. The magic cupboards were opened and there issued forth a marvellous procession. Mechanical bears and wrestlers, rabbits, monkeys, and other uncouth and delightsome beasts. We would group together on the floor, Lewis Carroll, the fairies, the beasts and myself, and gay indeed were the hours we spent. How his laugh would ring out like a child's!

And the exquisite nonsense he talked! It was like pages out of the *Alices*, only more delightful, for there was his own voice and smile to give the true charm to it all. I used to try to recall and record it. It was impossible—as impossible as to catch the gleam of colour on sunlit water, or to grasp a drifting rainbow. It was a mystic, intangible, gossamer-like thing, that, to chain it down in the words with which we should have translated it, would have been to crush out all life and grace—to destroy it altogether.

His love for children was not merely for the amusement they afforded him; it was deeper far than that. It was their purity and innocence that appealed to him; and if ever a child showed by word or look any unlovely feeling, the change in his face was startling; all the light would die out of it, and his tender reproof was inexpressibly touching.

To show his sensitiveness of conscience and dread of evil for children, I will quote a passage from one of his letters. I had a little girl model, about eight years of age, whose lovely head I had sketched and sent to him, and as I was at the time working at some fairy designs for him, in which all the little figures were to be "dressed in nothing," I wrote, "I mean to ask Edie to sit to me as a 'fairy'—that is, if she doesn't mind."

I must quote from memory, for the letter is mislaid. He wrote to say that if Edie showed the slightest shrinking from this, that he must implore me not to try to overcome it. If she had such a feeling, it would be a crime in the sight of God to persuade her to consent.

One day he came to my studio to sketch a very charming child whom I had engaged specially for him. She had travelled some little distance from the North of London to come to us, and I expressed some surprise that her mother had allowed her to come alone, but the child said she was "used to it."

On his return to Oxford he wrote to me:
"I don't quite like the idea of that small and pretty child going all that way, alone, on my account. If she got lost or stolen I should feel an awful responsibility in having caused her to run the risk. I fear such beauty, among the very poor, is a very dangerous possession."

For many years there was a delightful interchange of visits. I would go down to Oxford for the day to photograph or draw portraits of his child-friends for him. The children would return home, sometimes before, sometimes after lunch; in the afternoon Mr. Dodgson and I would each bury ourselves in a luxurious armchair and talk, or look over sketches I had brought for him to see, or go through part of his vast collection of photographs of famous people taken long years before. Many of Gabriel Rossetti and his sister Christina, Ruskin, the Millais children, the Terry family.

I remember one of Ellen Terry, taken when she was about eighteen; she happened to laugh at the moment, and she looked one of the loveliest young creatures imaginable.

Then he would make the afternoon tea himself, all in his deft and dainty fashion, and this would bring the happy visit to its close.

A lady-friend of Mr. Dodgson's—a good woman, eminently practical and steeped to the lips in conventions—once took me to task.

We had spent the morning at her house sketching her children; at least, I sketched while he talked *Alice*.

He left before lunch, and after this meal was over she sent the children away, and, taking up her sewing, sat down in front of me.

"I hear that you spent the other day in Oxford, with Mr. Dodgson?"

"Yes, it was a most delightful day."

"It's a very unconventional thing to do."

"We are both very unconventional."

"Mr. Dodgson is not at all a ladies' man."

"He wouldn't be my friend if he were."

"He is a confirmed bachelor."

"So am I; and, what is more, he is old enough to be my father."

She steadfastly regarded me for a moment, and then said, "I tell you what it is, Mr. Dodgson doesn't think of you as a 'young lady' or anything of that kind, he looks upon you as a sort of 'old child.'"

I laughed delightedly. "I don't mind if Mr. Dodgson looks upon me as a sort of old grandmother if only he will ask me down to Oxford."

But I was deeply offended. Our pure and beautiful friendship seemed hurt somehow by this coarse handling.

Sometimes he would come up to town for the day. We would meet, lunch together, and go off to a matinée, sometimes coming back to my rooms for tea. Once I had a ghastly experience.

I have an artist-friend, a rare genius, as unique in his way, perhaps, as Lewis Carroll, but as opposite as the poles. Rugged, full of angles, charming in private life, gauche in the presence of strangers. I called him Solomon Eagle, from his striking resemblance to that picturesque person, and for his holy horror of the world, the flesh, and the devil, particularly as displayed in theatrical performances.

I had spoken of this friend to Lewis Carroll, and shown him autotypes of his work which greatly impressed him.

One day Lewis Carroll had been up in town and had taken me to a matinée at Wilson Barrett's theatre. We had just returned to my rooms for tea when my artist-friend was announced. I asked permission to introduce him. "Very pleased," was the reply, and Solomon Eagle was ushered in.

Instantly my blood began to curdle, for I saw at a flash what I'd never dreamed of before, that they were denizens of different planets, so to speak.

At the sight of a "grown-up," the "Lewis Carroll" dropped from off my Oxford friend like the petals of a rudely shaken flower, leaving only the dry stalk. He stood, an aristocrat to his finger tips, the cold, serene, dignified Mr. Dodgson, the Don. Solomon Eagle, nervous, gauche, spasmodic.

The greeting passed off well enough. If only it had ended there! Feeling at a loss for the next remark my artist-friend approached the chimney-piece, against which, at either end, Mr. Dodgson and I were leaning. He caught sight of a photograph, which I had propped up against the clock, of the principal actress in the play we had seen that afternoon.

"What on earth possesses you to put a thing like that up there? It will ruin your taste!"

Before I could reply Mr. Dodgson quietly remarked: "Our friend kindly accepted that from me. It is a portrait of the chief actress in Mr. Wilson Barrett's theatre."

The fat was now fully in the fire, and I drew in my breath and braced myself for the inevitable frizzle.

"The theatre is the mouth of Hell!" shrieked Solomon Eagle, and he flashed his brilliant eyes upon me.

There was no help for it, so I meekly replied: "Yes, we've both been there this afternoon."

Like a mad bull he turned to rend another rag, and glared again at the hapless photograph.

"Photography and Ruskin have done more to destroy English art than—"

"Mr. Ruskin is one of my dearest friends, and I am proud of it. Photography is my hobby, and I am not inclined to apologise even for that!" Thus the Don.

I prayed that the earth might open and swallow me up, or that a fiery chariot would descend and whirl away Solomon Eagle on the spot; but Providence didn't see fit to interfere.

Solomon, brought to his senses by this cold douche, instantly apologised, and suddenly remembering a pressing engagement, abruptly wished me "Good-night."

The bows that were exchanged between the artist and the Don were studies in deportment. If I hadn't been so utterly wretched I should have laughed.

I took the ruffled Eagle downstairs to see him safe off the premises, and his language was more picturesque than polite.

"Bloodless fossil!" were the words he hurled into the quiet street as he left the door.

In justice to him I ought to say that he had not the faintest idea beforehand of Mr. Dodgson's views on any subject.

It was entirely my fault in bringing ice and fire together.

On re-entering the room I found that Mr. Dodgson, the don, had disappeared, and "Lewis Carroll" was standing on the hearthrug, smiling.

"I don't like your friend," he remarked airily.

"Neither do I," I groaned, dropping into a chair like a limp rag, "at present."

Oddly enough they collided on my door-step a day or two later, and after a few minutes' chat, Mr. Dodgson came up to my room.

"I met your friend," he said, "and I was mistaken—I think now that I rather do like him."

Mr. Dodgson had a great liking for the theatre, as long as the plays had a wholesome flavour, and he had a special fancy for little girl actresses. He would get to know them and load them with kindness—asking them down to Eastbourne with their mother for a few days or weeks of fresh air. But as soon as they emerged from childhood he gently detached himself. It was a strange characteristic of his, to care greatly for his little friends only so long as they were children. Their chief fascination for him passed from them as they lost their childishness. But to his tender and generous nature all appealed who were in need of sympathy.

I remember once—having offered me his rooms at Eastbourne for a week or two, as he was detained in Oxford—his writing: "If you have any overworked, tired friend who needs a holiday, take her down with you to occupy that other room, and please allow me to pay all her expenses." In small things as well as greater, his kindly courtesy and consideration were unfailing.

"While you are doing so much for my pleasure"—(I was designing some fairies for him)—he wrote once, "it were churlish not to do something for yours, so, though I am writing 'Logic' about six hours a day, I have spared time to write out these two little acrostic poems for you."

"I wish you a very Happy Christmas," began another letter, "but my wishes will come a little late, as, to spare the overworked letter carrier, I shall leave this to be posted after Christmas."

The most distinguishing features about him were his delicate reserve and dignified modesty; he shrank with painful over-sensitiveness from being "lionised" in any way. To be pointed out as the "*Alice*" man was to him abhorrent.

"I can't imagine what people saw in *Alice*," he once remarked to me. "I believe its popularity has more to do with Tenniel's lovely drawings, than with any nonsense of *mine!*"

"I never read criticisms of my work," he said to me only the other day. "If they praise one it makes one vain: if they abuse one it makes one angry, and both states of mind are bad."

I always had a mysterious feeling, when looking at him and hearing him speak, that he was not exactly an ordinary human being of flesh and blood. Rather did he seem as some delicate, ethereal spirit, enveloped for the moment in a semblance of common humanity.

His head was small, and beautifully formed; the brow rather low, broad, white, and finely modelled. Dreamy grey eyes, a sensitive mouth, slightly compressed when in repose, but softening into the most beautiful smile when he spoke. He had a slight hesitancy sometimes when speaking, that reminded one of dear Charles Lamb's immortal stammer; but though Mr. Dodgson deplored it himself, it added a certain piquancy, especially if he was uttering any whimsicality.

It is just two months today since we spent our last day together.

He had written asking me if I would go with him to the matinée of *The Little Minister*, and I suggested that he should come to my studio in the morning for an hour's sketching.

I secured a lovely little child as model, and he promptly appeared at 11 o'clock.

He was charmed with the child, and they made friends at once. In the "resting" intervals he sat with her on his knee drawing comic pictures to amuse her, and warming her little hands, for the morning was chilly.

We were to lunch with some friends of his in Lowndes Square, and being rather behindhand, we hailed a hansom. Something frightened the horse and it bolted with us.

"Well," observed Lewis Carroll serenely, "if we are alive when we reach Lowndes Square, we certainly shall not be late!"

He was exceptionally brilliant that day at lunch, full of repartee and anecdote. He looked extremely well, and as if many years of work still lay before him. As we were driving to the theatre he confessed to me that he had been working very hard lately, sitting up till 5 o'clock in the morning. When I ventured to gently remonstrate, he smiled.

"It suits me," he said; "I feel very well."

Then suddenly, turning to me, he said, while a wistful look grew in his eyes. "My time is so short. I have so much to do before I go, and the call might come any day."

Little did I dream that before two months were over the call *would* have come.

He was charmed with *The Little Minister.*

Miss Winifred Emery, by her enchanting personality, won his warmest admiration.

The part of the boy was played by a young actress with whom he had just become acquainted.

While in the theatre he scribbled a note. "May we come round and see you?" and handed it to one of the officials to send in to her.

Presently back came a note: he glanced at the superscription, and on his lips played the old whimsical smile.

"This is evidently intended for you." He said quietly. "Will you allow me to open it?"

It was addressed, "Mrs. Dodgson."

How we laughed.

"That 'we' was misleading," he remarked. "Well, we are certainly labelled *now!*"

After the play he asked, "Have you anything special to do? If not, come and have tea with me at Paddington, and see me off."

All too swiftly the last half-hour glided away, and I went with him to take his seat.

At the door of the compartment he turned to shake hands. "Good-bye, I've had such a happy day," he said simply. "I hope *you* have."

Just before Christmas he wrote, "Write to me at 'The Chestnuts,' Guildford, where I shall stay until the middle of January."

The middle of January is here.

But the hand that wrote those words has laid down the magic pen for ever; and he, who called forth the purest, gayest laughter the world has ever heard, has passed into that silent land of shadows where no voice can reach, nor footsteps follow!

A grey January day, calm, and without a sound, full of the peace of God which passeth all understanding.

A steep, stony, country road, with hedges close on either side, fast quickening with the breath of a premature spring. Between the withered leaves of the dead summer a pure white daisy here and there shone out like a little star.

A few mourners slowly climbed the hill in silence, while borne before them on a simple hand-bier was the coffin, half hid in flowers.

Under an old yew, round whose gnarled trunk the green ivy twined, in the pure white chalk earth his body was laid to rest, while the slow bell tolled the passing—

"Of the sweetest soul,
That ever looked with human eyes."[2]

1. Browning, "Popularity," ll. 1–2.
2. Tennyson, *In Memoriam* 57.11–12.

Appendix

LEWIS CARROLL AND OTHER ILLUSTRATORS

George du Maurier, Edwin Linley Sambourne, Walter Crane, and Luke Fildes

A T ONE TIME or another, and for one reason or another, Dodgson approached a number of artists other than the ones we deal with here in detail.

Casting about for an illustrator for *Looking-Glass* after Tenniel refused to do the pictures, Dodgson must have sought advice from friends. In April 1868, George MacDonald provided an introduction to Sir Joseph Noël Paton (1821–1901), illustrator of *The Water Babies*, whose paintings of scenes from fairy tales, mythology, history, and religious narratives interested Dodgson. But Noël Paton refused: "Even had it been possible for me to do so I should have felt constrained first to ask the author why anybody under the sun save only John Tenniel should be entrusted with the work."[1]

Tenniel had suggested that Dodgson consider a young artist, unknown to him, who signed himself "Bab" (W. S. Gilbert [1836–1911], famous later for his lyrics to the D'Oyly Carte operettas), whose caricatures were then appearing in *Fun*. On June 2, 1868, Dodgson wrote to Macmillan: "Have you seen the pictures in *Fun* signed 'Bab'? . . . [H]is power in grotesque is extraordinary—but I have seen no symptoms of his being able to draw anything pretty and graceful. I should be very glad if you could ascertain . . . whether he *has* such power. If so, I think he would do."[2] Macmillan wrote to Thomas Hood, editor of *Fun*, and although Hood's reply brought the assurance that Gilbert was also capable of the "pretty and graceful," nothing seems to have developed between the two.

Dodgson admired the drawings of another *Punch* artist, George du

Maurier (1834 – 96), later author of *Peter Ibbetson* and *Trilby*. He must have had an early introduction to du Maurier, or perhaps Dodgson having sent him a copy of *Alice*, the book supplied the necessary entrée. In any case, at the end of October 1867, he sent du Maurier the text of the French translation of *Alice* which Dodgson had commissioned before the book was published, eliciting his comments (du Maurier had been educated in France). He later called on du Maurier and became a friend of the family. In 1873, du Maurier agreed to supply illustrations for Dodgson's "Phantasmagoria," but nothing came of this project either.[3]

1. *Letters*, pp. 119 – 20.
2. Ibid.
3. DIARIES, 5:370, 380; *Letters*, pp. 201, 220 – 21; see also R. B. Shaberman, "Du Maurier Illustrates Carroll," in *Under the Quizzing Glass*, 1972, pp. 46 – 47.

To George du Maurier
MS: *Texas*

Christ Church, Oxford
December 17, 1873

Dear Mr. du Maurier,

You are most kind, but really you shall *not* sacrifice yourself to such an extent, nor undertake the work *at all*, unless, when the time comes, you feel quite "*i*' the vein."[1] This is partly for *your* sake, and partly (lest you should think me a model of unselfishness) for *my own*. For I feel sure that if such pictures as I want are attempted at all reluctantly and as a matter of business, in fact if they are drawn in any other way than *con amore*, they will be mere every-day-life productions, with nothing weird or ghostly about them. The artist, whoever he may be, should go at them in the spirit of the "fat boy," and say, "I want to make your flesh creep."[2] We will wait till the fatigue and nausea, consequent on your Xmas labours, have passed away, and then re-open the question.

Most truly yours,
C. L. Dodgson

1. *Richard III* 4.2 or *Troilus and Cressida* 5.3.
2. Charles Dickens, *Pickwick Papers*, 1837, chap. 8.

On May 22, 1874, Dodgson wrote to Edwin Linley Sambourne (1844–1910), another *Punch* artist and later (1885) illustrator of Charles Kingsley's *The Water Babies*, "proposing that he should illustrate 'Phantasmagoria.' He replied," Dodgson noted, "expressing willingness to draw, but would like to see the poem."[1] Over the next two years, Dodgson and Sambourne negotiated sporadically;[2] although Dodgson received at least one drawing from Sambourne, again this proposed collaboration did not succeed.

1. *DIARIES*, 6:338.
2. Ibid., pp. 385, 388, 448, and *Diaries*, p. 361.

To Edwin Linley Sambourne
MS: *Sambourne*

Christ Church, Oxford
June 10, 1874

My Dear Sir,

Your letter was very welcome, and I look forwards with much pleasure to having a series of pictures from your pencil. As to details, I don't want to hamper you with my ideas, as I think an artist should be left free as to his treatment of a theme, the writer only retaining a *veto*, in case the result should be hopelessly at variance with his meaning. I will jot down any ideas that occur to me as being desirable to introduce, and you can use the suggestions, or not, as you choose. I will try to give you a general sketch of my notion of what is wanted, but it is difficult to explain oneself in writing. It would be much more satisfactory to talk about it, and I would come over to Uxbridge for that purpose next time I am in town, if you have no objection. That *may* be next week.

I fancy we should do best by making it a thin square book (or nearly square) about the same *height* as *Alice* (7 1/2 in.) the pictures to be circular which would allow of something to fill up the corners, of the nature of gargoyles—i.e. grotesque faces, etc.; perhaps it would be better to have no ornament outside the circle. The pictures I think should be Rembrantish and weird—but, above all, wholly away from the common-place of modern life—*that* would, in my view, vulgarise the thing entirely. I hope I shan't in any way hurt your feelings as an artist by saying that I *don't* want the kind of

comic drawing which suits "Sandford and Merton" admirably—*that* style I should define as the "low comedy" of modern life, and I want to avoid that *entirely*.[1] You may say "why apply to an artist, and then ask him not to draw in his own style?" But it seems to me that you have many styles, and some of your drawings for "One-and-three" are quite of the ghostly and wild character that I want.[2] The more extraordinary, and unlike anything ever seen before, that you can make the pictures, the better I shall like them. The hero should be in some old-fashioned dress—not later than Charles I, I think. The ghost's attire I am quite uncertain about: his *face* I imagine to myself something like old Keeley when he looked frightened (did you ever see him in that condition?).[3] I presume he would have to be transparent: and it might be effective to represent him reclining gracefully, as if in an easy chair, but with no chair near him. Also ghostly things should *happen* (of which of course neither host nor ghost—by-the-way, I have never worked in the similarity of the two words—takes any notice). I mean such things as the decanter pouring out wine, and the coal-scuttle throwing on coals, of their own accord: the cat, which in one picture might be seated by the fire washing its face, in the next might be walking about the ceiling, in the next, floating in the air.

July 17.[4] At this point my letter broke off, more than a month ago. In now sending it, let me take the opportunity of expressing my *great* admiration for the drawings of Dizzy over his strawberries and cream. Really it's the cleverest thing I've seen for a long time—every corner full of suggestion, and as to the faces, I don't know which to admire most, the sleepy enjoyment (not having yet realised the horrors of the situation) of Dizzy, the cunning "now I've got him!" expression of Gladstone, or the excessively comic dismay of the footman.[5] Give me anything as good as *that* for "Phantasmagoria," and I shall be well content.

   Old as the letter is, I think you may as well have it. It may suggest some ideas to you before we meet.[6] Believe me

Very truly yours,
C. L. Dodgson

1. Sambourne had illustrated F. C. Burnand's *New History of Sandford and Merton* (1872).
2. *Punch* introduced a serialized novel titled "One-and-three" by Fictor Nogo in the issue dated April 25, 1874, with illustrations by Sambourne.

3. Robert Keeley (1793 –1869), actor much respected for his serious Shakespearean roles and also his many comic characters.

4. Dodgson adds at the head of the letter, "Observe the date! C. L. D. July 17."

5. Sambourne's illustration for "*Punch*'s Essence of Parliament" in the issue of July 18, 1874, shows Disraeli eating an enormous strawberry with a pot of Devonshire clotted cream open beside him.

6. Dodgson did not meet Sambourne until the following year. "I also called on, and made acquaintance with, Mr. Sambourne," he wrote on April 3, 1875.

To Edwin Linley Sambourne
MS: *Sambourne*

[Christ Church, Oxford]
December 29, 1875

Wishing you a happy New Year, I remain

Very truly yours,
Lewis Carroll[1]

"*He never told his love,
But sat, like patience on a monument,
Smiling at grief.*"

1. Dodgson's sketch is a quotation from *Twelfth Night*, 2.4, ll. 116 –17. See also *Letters*, p. 205, n. 1.

Dodgson sent a postcard to Sambourne dated March 29, 1878 (MS: Sambourne): "The picture has arrived in safety, and is indeed an astonishing exhibition of skill and patience. But as you say you are writing about it, I defer further remarks till I have your letter — except to beg that you will not do anything more to the others till we have discussed this." Dodgson noted on April 2, 1878 (*Diaries*, p. 370): "Yesterday I sent back to Sambourne, with approval, his first drawing on 'The Lang Coortin.'" The picture is now missing. Dodgson wrote again to Sambourne on February 19, 1885 (MS: Sambourne): "Many thanks for book, which is just come. Think no more of the £. s. d. As you consider the £25 to be your fair remuneration, you are entirely welcome to it. Consider my application unmade." The book is not identified.

"There are but few artists who seem to draw the forms of children *con amore*," Dodgson wrote to an acquaintance in 1878. "Walter Crane is perhaps the best (always excepting Sir Noël Paton); but the thick outlines, which he insists on using, seem to take off a good deal from the beauty of the result."[1]

Nevertheless, he wrote to Crane (1845–1915), who had already illustrated children's books, on November 27, 1877, asking him "if he would be willing to undertake some drawings for *Phantasmagoria* and 'Bruno's Revenge.'"[2] Although Dodgson then assumed that Crane had agreed to draw for him, nothing ever came of the plan. For his part, Crane "was a great admirer of . . . [Dodgson's] delightful invention, whimsical fun and fancy, and childlike sympathy for children." This is the artist's account of what occurred when Dodgson proposed a collaboration:

> Lewis Carroll . . . wrote to me early in 1878, saying he had been looking out for a new illustrator for a forthcoming work of his, as . . . Tenniel would do "no more." This Mr. Dodgson evidently greatly deplored, and naturally felt that it would be most difficult to find a substitute. His letters gave one the impression of a most particular person, and it is quite possible that he may have led Tenniel anything but a quiet life during the time he was engaged upon his inimitable illustrations. . . . I believe I agreed to meet his views if possible, but my hands were so full of all sorts of other work that I fear the year went by without my being able to take the matter up. The story, too, of which he sent me a portion, was of a very different character to *Alice*, a story with a religious and moral purpose, with only an occasional touch of the ingenuity and humour of *Alice*, so that it was not nearly so inspiring or amusing. . . . [Mr. Dodgson objected] to my use of a rather thick woodcut sort of line in my illustrations. . . . I can well understand that after Tenniel's hair-like pencilling, mine probably looked rough and coarse to him.[3]

1. *Letters*, p. 322.
2. Ibid.
3. Derek Hudson, *Lewis Carroll: An Illustrated Biography*, 1976, p. 24; *Diaries*, pp. 367, 370; Walter Crane, *An Artist's Reminiscences*, 1907, pp. 184–86.

To Walter Crane
Walter Crane, An Artist's Reminiscences, 1907, pp. 185 – 86

Christ Church, Oxford
January 22, 1878

My dear Sir,

I have read and re-read, with interest, your letter dated December 30, and will now make some remarks on it.

As to terms, I quite see that it is fair to charge for two or three drawings at a higher rate than for a large number. But you did not at all misunderstand me: I am *not* contemplating a book with fifty pictures *now*. No such book is at present in existence.[1] I was merely pointing out what it would come to if I *were* to write such a book and pay for the pictures at that rate. However, it is satisfactory to know that the rate in such a case would be lower, and your suggestion of "sharing profits" is well worth considering.

You are probably more learned on the subject of ancient art than I am, but my theory is that among savages there is a much earlier stage than outline drawing—*viz.*, mere reproduction (in clay, etc.) of the solid form. I *imagine* that you would find idols and other representations in solid form among nations where any kind of *drawing* is unknown. The next step I should expect to be *alto-relievo* (arising from the discovery that you can only see one side of an image at once), and this would gradually flatten down. Then the effect (with a side light) would be of a flat surface with strong black lines of shadow marking the outline of the form represented. And the next step would be to *paint* lines representing these shadows: and such lines would be broad at first, and would narrow on discovering that their breadth was not an essential feature. However, this is all rather theory than actual knowledge.

I have now made up my mind to get you to do "Bruno's Revenge" at any rate.[2] But instead of making them *all* full-page pictures, suppose you give me £60 worth of work, in any sizes and shapes you think proper, keeping the *Alice* page as your outside limit. You can take your own time for it (up to a year, let us say), and can either draw on the wood at once, or on paper and transfer to wood (at your own expense), keeping the drawings yourself. I shall be glad to hear whether this proposal is satisfactory to you. Believe me

Very truly yours,
C. L. Dodgson

1. The book Dodgson had in mind was *Sylvie and Bruno*, but he had written little of it at this time, except "Bruno's Revenge," which had appeared in the December 1867 number of *Aunt Judy's Magazine*.

2. Dodgson was under the impression that Crane would illustrate "Bruno's Revenge" for him, and recorded on April 2, 1878, that he then had three artists drawing for him, Walter Crane among them (*Diaries*, p. 370).

Sir Samuel Luke Fildes (1844–1927) painted anecdotal and melodramatic subjects and illustrated Dickens's *Mystery of Edwin Drood* (1870).

———————

To Luke Fildes
L. V. Fildes, Luke Fildes R.A.: A Victorian Painter, *1968, pp. 43–44*

Christ Church, Oxford
July 2, 1877

Dear Sir,

As I am writing this on a matter of business, and as I am unknown to you, even by name, I had better begin by stating that I am the writer of two little books (possibly unknown to you, called *Alice's Adventures in Wonderland* and *Through the Looking-Glass*) which were illustrated by Mr. Tenniel, whom I do not doubt you know well by reputation, if not personally. And my motive for addressing this to you is that I have seen (and admired more than I can easily express) your pictures in *Edwin Drood*.

My position is this: that I have some half-defined ideas, and a small amount of material, for another tale; but I have been for a long time discouraged from going on with it, by the apparent hopelessness of finding an artist worthy to succeed Mr. Tenniel, whose help is no longer to be had. May I then venture to trouble you with a few questions?

(1) Is it likely that you would be willing, at some future time, to illustrate a book of the same general character as *Alice's Adventures*? (If you do not know the book, I will send you a copy to look at.)

(2) If so, would you now undertake a small commission for me, to draw 2 or 3 pictures for a short tale? (This tale would perhaps be embodied in the book, if it is ever written.)

(3) It would be well to have some rough idea of what you would expect

to have to charge for drawings of the same amount of finish as those of Mr. Tenniel.[1]

With apologies for thus troubling you, I remain

Faithfully yours,
(Rev.) C. L. Dodgson

Such a book as I am hoping to write would require pictures of (1) children, (2) perhaps fairies, (3) Grotesques like the "Queen of Hearts" in *Alice*. It is true that neither children nor Grotesques occur in *Edwin Drood*, but I fancy I see in those pictures almost unlimited power of drawing, and wonderful variety (quite avoiding the painful family likeness that spoils so many of Cruikshank's pictures) and I am inclined to believe that the artist of those pictures can draw anything he likes!

1. The book that Dodgson wanted Fildes to illustrate was *Sylvie and Bruno*, starting with a few illustrations for "Bruno's Revenge."

To Luke Fildes
L. V. *Fildes*, Luke Fildes R.A.: A Victorian Painter, *1968, p. 45*

Christ Church, Oxford
July 14, 1877

Dear Sir,

I beg to thank you for your letter[1] and specially for a few hopeful (or at least not entirely discouraging) expressions in it, such as "I have not positively decided to do no more wood-drawing."

Twelve months hence (or whenever your present work is done) will probably find me as artistless as I am now. So, if you should then be thinking of again drawing on wood, I hope you will give me the "first refusal."

I fear you go on the theory of having only one "iron in the fire" at once. *My* theory is that you can hardly have too many. The work of my life is Mathematics, but I try light literature as well, and give a good deal of time to photography, and even trespass on *your* territory occasionally, in sketching my little friends at the sea-side, and various other "irons" as well, so that there is always *something* to turn to, in harmony with the inclination of the moment. I fancy a man with only *one* line of work must do a good deal of his work "Against the grain,"[2] and I think Ruskin is right in saying that all such work is bad work.[3] Believe me

Faithfully yours,
C. L. Dodgson

1. The reply from Luke Fildes is missing. In this biography of his father, L. V. Fildes writes: "Twelve months later my father was to take up black-and-white again for a spell, but not for Lewis Carroll. I have no knowledge of any further exchanges between him and the author of *Alice* after that delightful opening in the summer of 1877. My father may not have liked Ruskin being quoted at him!" (p. 45).

2. Dodgson may be quoting Dryden or Swift, but in this context certainly Dickens (*Edwin Drood*, chap. 20).

3. Dodgson read and admired the works of John Ruskin (1819–1900). His desire to meet the artist-critic was stimulated by long talks about him with Richard St. John Tyrwhitt (DIARIES, 3:39) and, on one occasion at least, with Tennyson (ibid., 114). Finally the meeting took place. "At Common Room [Christ Church] breakfast met, for the first time, John Ruskin," Dodgson recorded on October 27, 1857 (ibid., 122). "I had a little conversation with him, but not enough to bring out anything in him. His appearance was rather disappointing—a general feebleness of expression, with no commanding air, or any external signs of deep thought, as one would have expected to see in such a man." Dodgson went to Ruskin to seek advice about his own artistic capabilities, but, according to Collingwood (p. 102), Ruskin told him "that he had not enough talent to make it worth his while to devote much time to sketching." Dodgson took Ruskin's photograph on June 3, 1875. For more on the relationship between the two men, see *Letters*, p. 326, n. 1.

Index

Lewis Carroll Societies

UNITED KINGDOM: The Lewis Carroll Society was founded in 1969. It brings together people with an interest in Charles L. Dodgson, to promote his life and works, and to encourage research. The Society has an international membership of scholars, writers, collectors, and enthusiasts who simply enjoy reading the *Alice* books. Members receive the Society's journal *The Carrollian*, issued twice a year, a quarterly newsletter called *Bandersnatch*, and the *Lewis Carroll Review*. The Society welcomes new members; please contact the secretary, Alan White, 69 Cromwell Road, Hertford, Hertfordshire, SG13 7DP.

NORTH AMERICA: The Lewis Carroll Society of North America was formed in 1974. It is a nonprofit organization devoted to the study of the life, times, and influence of Charles L. Dodgson. The hundreds of current members include leading authorities on Carroll, students, and general enthusiasts. The Society meets twice a year at a site of an important Carroll collection and features well-known speakers and exhibitions. It maintains an active publication program and publishes a newsletter called *Knight Letter*. Further information is available from the secretary, Cindy Watter, P.O. Box 204, Napa, California 94559.

Also by MORTON N. COHEN

Rider Haggard: His Life and Works
Rudyard Kipling to Rider Haggard: The Record of a Friendship
*Russian Journal II: A Record Kept by Henry Parry Liddon of a Tour Taken with
    C. L. Dodgson*
Lewis Carroll, Photographer of Children: Four Nude Studies
Lewis Carroll and the Kitchins
The Letters of Lewis Carroll
Lewis Carroll and Alice, 1832–1982
The Selected Letters of Lewis Carroll
Lewis Carroll and the House of Macmillan
Lewis Carroll: Interviews and Recollections
Lewis Carroll: A Biography
*Reflections in a Looking-Glass: A Centennial
    Celebration of Lewis Carroll, Photographer*

Also by EDWARD WAKELING

The Cipher Alice
Lewis Carroll's Games and Puzzles
Skeffington Hume Dodgson
Lewis Carroll's Oxford Pamphlets
Rediscovered Lewis Carroll Puzzles
Alice in Wonderland Book and Deck Set
Lewis Carroll's Diaries
Lewis Carroll, Photographer